HTML
The Definitive Guide

HTML
The Definitive Guide

Chuck Musciano and Bill Kennedy

O'Reilly & Associates, Inc.

Bonn · Cambridge · Paris · Sebastopol · Tokyo

HTML: The Definitive Guide
by Chuck Musciano and Bill Kennedy

Copyright © 1996 O'Reilly & Associates, Inc. All rights reserved.
Printed in the United States of America.

Published by O'Reilly & Associates, Inc., 103 Morris Street, Suite A, Sebastopol, CA 95472.

Editor: Mike Loukides

Production Editor: Mary Anne Weeks Mayo

Printing History:

April 1996:	First Edition.
July 1996:	Minor corrections. Updated for HTML 3.2.

This book is printed on acid-free paper with 85% recycled content, 15% post-consumer waste. O'Reilly & Associates is committed to using paper with the highest recycled content available consistent with high quality.

ISBN: 1-56592-175-5   [1/97]

This book is dedicated to our wives and children,
Cindy, Courtney, and Cole, and
Jeanne, Eva, and Ethan.

Without their love and patience
we never would have had
the time or strength to write.

Table of Contents

Figures

Preface

Our Function

Learning HTML is like learning any new language, computer or human. Most students first immerse themselves in examples. Think how adept you'd become if Mom, Dad, your brothers, and sisters all spoke fluent HTML. Studying others is a natural way to learn, making learning easy and fun. Our advice to anyone wanting to learn HTML is to get out there on the World Wide Web with a suitable browser and see for yourself what looks good, what's effective, what works for you. Examine others' HTML source files and ponder the possibilities. Mimicry is how many of the current webmasters have learned the language.

Imitation can take you only so far, though. Examples can be both good and bad. Learning by example will help you talk the talk, but not walk the walk. To become truly conversant, you must learn how to use the language well and how to use the language appropriately in many different situations. You could learn that by example, if you live long enough.

Remember, too, that computer-based languages are more explicit than human languages. You've got to get the HTML syntax correct, or it won't work. Then, too, there is the problem of "standards." Committees of academics and industry experts try to define the proper syntax and usage of a computer language like HTML. The problem is that HTML browser manufacturers like Netscape and Spyglass choose what parts of the standard they will use and which parts they'll ignore. They even make up their own parts, which may eventually become standards.

To be safe, the better way to become HTML fluent is through a comprehensive language reference: a resource that covers the language syntax, semantics, and variations in detail, and helps you distinguish between good and bad usage.

There's one more step leading to fluency in a language. To become a true master of HTML, you need to develop your own style. That means knowing what's not only appropriate, but what is effective. Layout matters. A lot. So does the order of presentation within a document, between documents, and between document collections.

Our goal in writing this book is to help you become fluent in HTML, fully versed in the language's syntax, semantics, and elements of style. We take the natural learning approach with examples: good ones, of course. We cover every element of the currently accepted version (2.0)[*] of the language in detail, as well as many of the so-called "extensions" the popular HTML browsers support, explaining how each element works and how it interacts with all the other elements.

And, with all due respect to Strunk and White, throughout the book we give you suggestions for style and composition to help you decide how best to use the language and accomplish a variety of tasks, from simple online documentation to complex marketing and sales presentations. We'll show you what works and what doesn't; what makes sense to those who view your pages, and what might be confusing.

In short, this book is a complete guide to creating documents using HTML, starting with basic syntax and semantics, and finishing with broad style directions that should help you create beautiful, informative, accessible documents you'll be proud to deliver to your browsers.

Our Audience

We wrote this book for anyone interested in learning and using HTML, from the most casual user to a full-time design professional. We don't expect you to have any experience in the language before picking up this book. In fact, we don't even expect that you've ever used the World Wide Web, although we'd be surprised if you haven't at least experimented with this technology. Being connected to the Internet is not necessary to use this book, but if you're not connected, this book becomes like a travel guide for the homebound.

The only things we ask you to have are a computer, a text editor that can create simple ASCII text files, and a World Wide Web browser like Netscape, Mosaic, or Internet Explorer for your computer: the very latest version, if possible. Because HTML is stored in a universally accepted format—ASCII text—and because the language is completely independent of any specific computer, we won't even make an assumption about the kind of computer you're using. However, browsers do

---

[*] Contrary to popular misbelief, there is no HTML version 3.0. See "Is HTML 3.2 Really a Big Deal?" later in this Preface.

vary by platform and operating system, which means your HTML documents can and often do look quite different depending on the computer and version of browser. We will explain how certain language features are used by various popular browsers as we go through the book, so don't be surprised if your browser gets mentioned here or there.

If you are new to HTML, the World Wide Web, or hypertext documentation in general, you should start by reading Chapter 1, *HTML and the World Wide Web*. This chapter describes how all these technologies come together to create webs of interrelated documents.

If you are already familiar with the Web, but not HTML specifically, or if you are interested in the new features in HTML, start by reading Chapter 2, *HTML Quick Start*. This chapter is a brief overview of the most important features of the language and serves as a roadmap to how we approach the language in the remainder of the book.

Subsequent chapters deal with specific language features in a roughly top-down approach to the HTML. Read them in order for a complete tour through the language, or jump around to find the exact feature you're interested in.

Text Conventions

Throughout the book, we use the `courier` typeface to highlight any literal element of the HTML standard, and tags and attributes. We always use lowercase letters for HTML tags. (Although the language standard is case-insensitive with regard to tag and attribute names, this isn't so for other elements like source filenames, so be careful.) We use the *italic* font to indicate new concepts when they are defined and those elements you need to supply when creating your own documents, such as tag attributes or user-defined strings.

We discuss elements of the language throughout the book, but you'll find each one covered in depth (some might say nauseating detail) in a shorthand, quick-reference definition box that looks like the box on the following page.

The first line of the box contains the element name, followed by a brief description of its function. Next, we list the various attributes, if any, of the element: those things that you may or must specify as part of the element. Tags and attributes may also be parenthetically labeled if they are not included in the HTML 2.0 standard (the last official version), but are additions to the language. "Extension," as in the example, means that the nonstandard tag or attribute is supported by more than one of the popular browsers; otherwise the name of the extended browser appears—Mosaic, Netscape, or Internet Explorer—with the word "only" to identify the appropriate exception.

\<body\>

Function:
Defines the document body

Attributes:
ALINK (Netscape only)
BACKGROUND (extension)
BGCOLOR (extension)
BGPROPERTIES (Internet Explorer only)
LINK (extension)
TEXT (extension)
TOPMARGIN (Internet Explorer only)
VLINK (extension)

End Tag:
\</body\> may be omitted

Contains:
body_content

Used in:
html_tag

The description also includes the ending tag, if any, for the tag, along with a general indication if the end tag may be safely omitted in general use.

"Contains" names the rule in the HTML grammar that defines the elements to be placed within this tag. Similarly, "Used in" lists those rules that allow this tag as part of their content. These rules are defined in Appendix A, *HTML Grammar*.

Finally, HTML is a fairly "intertwined" language: Elements occasionally are used in different ways depending on context, and many elements share identical attributes. Wherever possible, we place a cross-reference in the text that leads you to a related discussion elsewhere in the book. These cross-references, like the one at the end of this paragraph, serve as a crude paper model of hypertext documentation, one that would be replaced with a true hypertext link should this book be delivered in an electronic format. [tag syntax, 3.3.1]

We encourage you to follow these references whenever possible. Often, we'll only cover an attribute briefly and expect you to jump to the cross-reference for a more detailed discussion. In other cases, following the link will take you to alternate uses of the element under discussion, or to style and usage suggestions that relate to the current element.

Is HTML 3.2 Really a Big Deal?

Depending on our mood, when people ask us about the "new" HTML 3.2 standard, we respond with a groan, a bemused smile, or uproarious laughter. Folks, HTML 3.2 doesn't shake any Web foundations. In fact, the new language standard simply confirms what most Web observers have known for some time now, that Netscape Communications is the tail wagging the HTML standards dog.

Until about mid-1995, people actually were serious about HTML standards. (Some of us still are.) Until then, standards guided the development of new browsers. After release of HTML 2.0, however, the elders of the World Wide Web Consortium (W3C) responsible for such language-standards matters lost control. The abortive HTML+ standard never got off the ground, and HTML 3.0 became so bogged down in debate that the W3C simply shelved the entire draft standard.

What mired the development of new language standards was Netscape Navigator. Most Web analysts agree that Netscape's quick success in becoming the browser of choice for an overwhelming majority of users can be attributed directly to the company's implementation of useful and exciting additions to HTML. Today, all other browser manufacturers, including the behemoth Microsoft Corp. who appreciates the meaning of "de facto standard" better than anyone in the business, have to implement Netscape's HTML extensions if they expect to have any chance of competing in the Web browser marketplace. By pushing the W3C to officially release HTML standard version 3.2, which for all intents and purposes standardizes most of Netscape's language extensions, the other browser manufacturers gain legitimacy for their products without having to acknowledge the leading competitor. Internet Explorer can now be "HTML 3.2–compliant," rather than submissively "Netscape Navigator–compliant."

The paradox is that the HTML 3.2 standard is *not* the definitive resource. There are many more features of the language in popular use than are included in this latest language standard.

This book, on the other hand, is the definitive guide to HTML. We give details for all the elements of the HTML 2.0 standard, the elements of the proposed HTML 3.2 standard, plus the variety of interesting and useful extensions to the language that popular browser manufacturers have chosen to include in their products, such as:

Frames	Inline multimedia
Dynamic documents	Java
Text font size and face controls	

And while we tell you about each and every feature of the language, standard or not, we also tell you which browsers or different versions of the same browser implement a particular extension and which don't. That's critical knowledge when you want to create Web pages that take advantage of the latest version of Netscape Navigator versus pages that are accessible to the larger number of people using Internet Explorer, Mosaic, or even Lynx, a popular text-only browser for UNIX systems.

In addition, there are a few things that are closely related but not directly part of HTML. We touch, but do not handle, for example, CGI and Java programming. CGI and Java programs work closely with HTML documents and run with or alongside browsers, but are not part of the language itself, and so we don't delve into them. Besides, they are comprehensive topics that deserve their own books, such as *Java in a Nutshell* and *CGI Programming on the World Wide Web* from O'Reilly & Associates, for instance.

In short, this book is your definitive guide to HTML as it is and should be used, including every extension we could find. Many aren't documented anywhere, even in the plethora of online guides. But, if we've missed anything, certainly let us know and we'll put it in the next edition.

Acknowledgments

We did not compose, and certainly could not have composed this book without generous contributions from many people. Our wives Jeanne and Cindy (with whom we've just become reacquainted) and our young children Eva, Ethan, Courtney, and Cole (they happened *before* we started writing) formed the front lines of support. And there are numerous neighbors, friends, and colleagues who helped by sharing ideas, testing browsers, and letting us use their equipment to explore HTML. You know who you are, and we thank you all. (Ed Bond, we'll be over soon to repair your Windows.)

We also thank our technical reviewers, Kane Scarlett, Eric Raymond, and Chris Tacy, for carefully scrutinizing our work. We took most of your keen suggestions. And we especially thank Mike Loukides, our editor, who had to bring to bear his vast experience in book publishing to keep us two mavericks corralled.

And, finally, we thank the many people at O'Reilly & Associates who poked our words into sensibility and put them onto these pages. These folks include: Mary Anne Weeks Mayo, project manager/copyeditor for the book; Len Muellner, Ellen Siever, and Erik Ray converted the book from Word for Windows to SGML and contributed their tool-tweaking prowess; Chris Reilley created the excellent figures; Edie Freedman designed the cover; Nancy Priest designed the interior layout; Hanna Dyer designed the back cover; Seth Maislin prepared the index; and Sheryl Avruch, Clairemarie Fisher O'Leary, and Kismet McDonough Chan did the final quality control on the book.

1

HTML and the World Wide Web

Though it began as a military experiment and spent its adolescence as a sandbox for academics and eccentrics, recent events have transformed the worldwide network of computer networks—aka the Internet—into a rapidly growing and wildly diversified community of computer users and information vendors. Today, you can bump into Internet users of nearly any and all nationalities, of any and all persuasions, from serious to frivolous individuals, from businesses to nonprofit organizations, and from born-again evangelists to pornographers.

In many ways, the World Wide Web—the open community of hypertext-enabled document servers and readers on the Internet—is responsible for the meteoric rise in the network's popularity. You, too, can become a valued member by contributing: writing HTML documents and making them available to Web "surfers" worldwide.

Let's climb up the Internet family tree to gain some deeper insight into its magnificence, not only as an exercise of curiosity, but to help us better understand just who and what it is we are dealing with when we go online.

1.1 The Internet

Although popular media accounts often are confused and confusing, the concept of the *Internet* really is rather simple. It's a collection of networks—a network of networks—computers sharing digital information via a common set of networking and software protocols. Nearly anyone can connect their computer to the Internet and immediately communicate with other computers and users on the Net.

What is confusing about the Internet is that it can be like an oriental bazaar: It's not well organized, there are few content guides, and it can take a lot of time and technical expertise to tap its full potential.

That's because...

1.1.1 In the Beginning

The Internet began in the late 1960s as an experiment in the design of robust computer networks. The goal was to construct a network of computers that could withstand the loss of several machines without compromising the ability of the remaining ones to communicate. Funding came from the U.S. Department of Defense, which had a vested interest in building information networks that could withstand nuclear attack.

The resulting network was a marvelous technical success, but was limited in size and scope. For the most part, only defense contractors and academic institutions could gain access to what was then known as the ARPAnet (Advanced Research Projects Agency network of the Department of Defense).

With the advent of high-speed modems for digital communication over common phone lines, some individuals and organizations not directly tied to the main digital pipelines began connecting and taking advantage of the network's advanced and global communications. Nonetheless, it wasn't until these last few years (around 1993, actually) that the Internet really took off.

Several crucial events led to the meteoric rise in popularity of the Internet. First, in the early 1990s, businesses and individuals eager to take advantage of the ease and power of global digital communications finally pressured the largest computer networks on the mostly U.S. government-funded Internet to open their systems for nearly unrestricted traffic. (Remember, the network wasn't designed to route information based on content—meaning commercial messages went through university computers that at the time forbade such activity.)

True to their academic traditions of free exchange and sharing, many of the original Internet members continued to make substantial portions of their electronic collections of documents and software available to the newcomers—free for the taking! Global communications, a wealth of free software and information: who could resist?

Well, frankly, the Internet was a tough row to hoe back then. Getting connected and using the various software tools, if they were even available for their computers, presented an insurmountable technology barrier for most people. And, too, most available information was plain-vanilla ASCII about academic subjects, not the neatly packaged fare that attracts users to the online services, such as America Online, Prodigy, or CompuServe. The Internet was just too disorganized and, outside of the government and academia, few people had the knowledge or interest to learn how to use the arcane software or had the time to spend rummaging through documents looking for ones of interest.

1.1.2 HTML and the World Wide Web

It took another spark to light the Internet rocket. At about the same time the Internet opened up for business, some physicists at CERN, the European Particle Physics Laboratory, released an authoring language and distribution system they developed for creating and sharing multimedia-enabled, integrated electronic documents over the Internet. And so was born *HyperText Markup Language* (*HTML*), browser software, and the World Wide Web. No longer did authors have to distribute their work as fragmented collections of pictures, sounds, and text. HTML unified those elements. Moreover, the World Wide Web's systems enabled *hypertext linking* wherein documents automatically reference other documents, located anywhere around the world: less rummaging, more productive time online.

Lift-off happened when some bright students and faculty at the National Center for Supercomputing Applications (NCSA) at the University of Illinois, Urbana/Champaign, wrote a Web browser called Mosaic. Although designed primarily for viewing HTML documents, the software also had built-in tools to access the much more prolific resources on the Internet, such as FTP archives of software and Gopher-organized collections of documents.

With versions based on easy-to-use graphical-user interfaces familiar to most computer owners, Mosaic became an instant success. It, like most Internet software, was available on the Net for free.* Millions of users snatched up a copy and began surfing the Internet for "cool Web pages."

1.1.3 Golden Threads

There you have the history of the Internet and the World Wide Web in a nutshell: from rags to riches in just two short years. The Internet has spawned an entirely new medium for worldwide information exchange and commerce, and its

---

* Not all browsers are free, nor are all browsers free to everyone. The various client browser and server software are commercially available, including documentation and support. Internet "bundled" software sold through mail order or retail often contains a licensed copy of one of the popular browsers like Mosaic or Netscape, possibly customized for the package. Moreover, the browsers available for download over the Internet typically contain licensing agreements which stipulate that the software is free only for use by non-profit organizations.

pioneers are profiting well. For instance, when the marketeers caught on to the fact that they could cheaply produce and deliver eye-catching, wow-and-whizbang commercials and product catalogs to those millions of Web surfers around the world, there was no stopping the stampede of blue suede shoes. Even the key developers of Mosaic and related Web server technologies sensed potential riches. They left NCSA and formed Netscape Communications to produce the Netscape Navigator browser and Web server software that is useful for Internet commercial activity.

Business users and marketing opportunities have helped invigorate the Internet and fuel its phenomenal growth, particularly on the World Wide Web. According to a recent marketing survey by *Activ*Media, Inc. (Peterborough, NH), over half of Internet enterprises become profitable within a year of launch! But do not forget that the Internet is first and foremost a place for social interaction and information sharing, not a strip mall or direct advertising medium. Internet users, particularly the old-timers, adhere to commonly held, but not formally codified, rules of *netiquette* that prohibit such things as "spamming" special-interest newsgroups with messages unrelated to the topic at hand or sending unsolicited email. And there are millions of users ready to remind you of those rules should you inadvertently or intentionally ignore them.

And, certainly, the power of HTML and network distribution of information go well beyond marketeering and monetary rewards: serious informational pursuits also benefit. Publications, complete with images and other media like executable software, can get to their intended audience in a blink of an eye, instead of the months traditionally required for printing and mail delivery. Education takes a great leap forward when students gain access to the great libraries of the world. And at times of leisure, the interactive capabilities of HTML links can reinvigorate our otherwise television-numbed minds.

1.2 Talking the Internet Talk

Every computer connected to the Internet (even a beat-up old Apple II) has a unique address: a number whose format is defined by the *Internet Protocol (IP)*, the standard that defines how messages are passed from one machine to another on the Net. An *IP address* is made up of four numbers, each less than 255, joined together by periods, such as 192.12.248.73 or 131.58.97.254.

While computers only deal in numbers, people prefer names. For this reason, each computer on the Internet also has a name bestowed upon it by its owner. There are several million machines on the Net, so it'd be very difficult to come up with that many unique names, let alone keep track of them all. Recall, though, that the

Internet is a network of networks. It is divided into groups known as *domains*, which are further divided into one or more *subdomains*. So, while you might choose a very common name for your computer, it becomes unique when you append, like surnames, all of the machine's domain names as a period-separated suffix, creating a *fully qualified* domain name.

This naming stuff is easier than it sounds. For example, the fully qualified domain name "www.ora.com" translates to a machine named "www" that's part of the domain known as "ora," which, in turn, is part of the commercial (com) branch of the Internet. Other branches of the Internet include educational (edu) institutions, nonprofit organizations (org), U.S. government (gov), and Internet service providers (net). Computers and networks outside the United States have a two-letter abbreviation at the end of their names: for example, "ca" for Canada, "jp" for Japan, and "uk" for the United Kingdom.

Special computers, known as *name servers*, keep tables of machine names and their associated unique IP numerical addresses, and translate one into the other for us and for our machines. Domain names must be registered with the nonprofit organization InterNIC. Once registered, the owner of the domain name broadcasts it and its address to other domain name servers (DNS) around the world. Each domain and subdomain has an associated name server, so ultimately every machine is known uniquely by both a name and an IP address.

1.2.1 Clients, Servers, and Browsers

The Internet connects two kinds of computers: *servers*, which serve up documents, and *clients*, which retrieve and display documents for us humans. Things that happen on the server machine are said to be on the *server side*, while activities on the client machine occur *client side*.

To access and display HTML documents, we run programs called *browsers* on our client computers. These browser clients talk to special *Web servers* over the Internet to access and retrieve electronic documents.

Several Web browsers are available—most are free—each offering a different set of features. For example, browsers like Lynx run on character-based clients and display documents only as text. Others run on clients with graphical displays and render documents using proportional fonts and color graphics on a 1024x768, 24-bit-per-pixel display. Others still—Netscape Navigator, Mosaic, Microsoft's Internet Explorer, WebCruiser from Netcom, InterCon's NetShark, and Hot Java from Sun Microsystems, to name a few—have special features that allow you to retrieve and display a variety of electronic documents over the Internet, including audio and movie multimedia.

1.2.2 The Flow of Information

All Web activity begins on the client side, when a user starts their browser. The browser begins by loading a *home page* HTML document from either local storage or from a server over some network, such as the Internet. In the latter case, the client browser first consults a domain name server to translate the home page document server's name, like *www.ora.com*, into an IP address, before sending a request to that server over the Internet. This request (and the server's reply) is formatted according to the dictates of the *HyperText Transfer Protocol (HTTP)* standard.

A server spends most of its time listening to the Internet, waiting for document requests with the server's unique address stamped on it. Upon receipt, the server verifies that the requesting browser is allowed to retrieve documents from the server and, if so, checks for the requested document. If found, the server sends (downloads) the document to the browser. The server usually logs the request, the client computer's name, document requested, and the time.

Back on the browser, the document arrives. If it's a plain-vanilla ASCII text file, most browsers display it in a common, plain-vanilla way. Document directories, too, are treated like plain documents, although most graphical browsers will display folder icons, which the user can select with the mouse to download the contents of subdirectories.

Browsers also retrieve binary files from a server. Unless assisted by a *helper* program or specially enabled by *plug-in* software or *applets*, which display an image file or play an audio file, the browser usually stores downloaded binary files directly on a local disk for later attention by the user.

For the most part, however, the browser retrieves a special document that appears to be a plain text file, but contains both text and special markup codes called *tags*. The browser processes these HTML documents, formatting the text based upon the tags and downloading special accessory files, such as images.

The user reads the document, selects a hyperlink to another document, and the entire process starts over.

1.2.3 Beneath the World Wide Web

We should point out at this juncture that browsers and HTTP servers need not be part of the Internet's World Wide Web to function. In fact, you never need to be connected to the Internet, or to any network for that matter, to write HTML documents and operate a browser. You can load up and display on your client browser locally stored HTML documents and accessory files directly. This isolation is good: it gives you the opportunity to finish, in the editorial sense of the word, a document collection for later distribution. Diligent HTML authors work locally to write and proof their documents before releasing them for general distribution, thereby sparing readers the agonies of broken image files and bogus hyperlinks.*

Organizations, too, can be connected to the Internet and the World Wide Web, but also maintain private Webs and HTML document collections for distribution to clients on their local network, or *Intranet*. In fact, private Webs are fast becoming the technology of choice for the paperless offices we've heard so much about these last few years. With HTML document collections, businesses and other enterprises can maintain personnel databases, complete with employee photographs and online handbooks, collections of blueprints, parts, and assembly manuals, and so on—all readily and easily accessed electronically by authorized users and displayed on a local computer.

1.3 *HTML: What It Is*

HTML is a document-layout and hyperlink-specification language. It defines the syntax and placement of special, embedded directions that aren't displayed by the browser, but tell it how to display the contents of the document, including text, images, and other support media. The language also tells you how to make a document interactive through special hypertext links, which connect your document with other documents in yours and others' collections, as well as with other Internet resources, like FTP and Gopher.

1.3.1 *HTML Standards and Extensions*

The basic syntax and semantics of HTML are defined in the HTML standard, currently version 2.0. HTML is a young language, barely three years old but already in its second iteration. Don't be too surprised if another version appears before you finish reading this book. Given the pace of these standards matters, one never knows when or if a new standard version will come to fruition. While the HTML 3.0 standard has faded into oblivion, the standards committee is working to collect some of the more popular browser extensions into an interim standard, known as HTML 3.2. The draft of this standard should become available in July, 1996 and defines a base set of tags that almost all current browsers support.

Browser developers rely upon the HTML standard to program the software that formats and displays common HTML documents. Authors use the standard to make

---

* Vigorous testing of the HTML collection once it is made available on the Web is, of course, also highly recommended and necessary to rid it of various linking bugs.

sure they are writing effective, correct HTML documents. Nonetheless, commercial forces have pushed developers to add into their browsers—Netscape Navigator and Internet Explorer, in particular—nonstandard extensions meant to improve the language. Many times, these extensions are implementations of future standards still under debate. Extensions can foretell future standards because so many people use them.

In this book, we explore in detail the syntax, semantics, and idioms of HTML 2.0, along with the many important extensions that are supported in the latest versions of the most popular browsers, so that any aspiring HTML author can create fabulous documents with a minimum of effort.

1.3.2 Standards Organizations

Like many popular technologies, HTML started out as an informal specification used by only a few people. As more and more authors began to use the language, it became obvious that more formal means were needed to define and manage—to standardize—HTML's features, making it easier for everyone to create and share documents.

1.3.2.1 The World Wide Web Consortium

The World Wide Web Consortium, aka W3C, was formed with the charter to define the standard versions of HTML. Members are responsible for drafting, circulating for review, and modifying the standard based on cross-Internet feedback to best meet the needs of the many.

Beyond HTML, the W3C has the broader responsibility of standardizing any technology related to the World Wide Web: they manage the HTTP standard, as well as related standards for document addressing on the Web. And they solicit draft standards for extensions to existing Web technologies, such as internationalization of the HTML standard.

If you want to track HTML's development and related technologies, contact the World Wide Web Consortium at *http://www.w3.org/*. Several Internet newsgroups are devoted to the World Wide Web, each a part of the *comp.infosystems.www* hierarchy. These include *comp.infosystems.www.authoring.html* and *comp.infosystems.www.authoring.images*.

1.3.2.2 The Internet Engineering Task Force

Even broader in reach than W3C, the Internet Engineering Task Force (IETF) is responsible for defining and managing every aspect of Internet technology. The World Wide Web is just one small part under the purview of the IETF.

The IETF defines all of the technology of the Internet via official documents known as Requests For Comment, or RFCs. Individually numbered for easy reference, each RFC addresses a specific Internet technology—everything from the syntax of domain names and the allocation of IP addresses, to the format of electronic mail messages.

To learn more about the IETF and to follow the progress of various RFCs as they are circulated for review and revision, visit the IETF home page, at *http://www.ietf.org/*.

1.4 HTML: What It Isn't

With all its multimedia-enabling features and the hot technologies that give life to HTML documents over the Internet, it is important also to understand the language's limitations: HTML is not a word processing tool, a desktop publishing solution, or even a programming language, for that matter. That's because its fundamental purpose is to define the structure and appearance of documents and document families so that they might be delivered quickly and easily to a user over a network for rendering on a variety of display devices. Jack of all trades, but master of none, so to speak.

1.4.1 Content Versus Appearance

Before you can fully appreciate the power of the language and begin creating effective HTML documents, you must yield to its one fundamental rule: HTML is designed to structure documents and make their content more accessible, not to format documents for display purposes.

HTML does provide many different ways to let you define the appearance of your documents: font specifications, line breaks, and preformatted text are all features of HTML. And, of course, appearance is important since it can have either detrimental or beneficial effects on how users access and use the information in your HTML documents.

But with HTML, content is paramount; appearance is secondary, particularly since it is less predictable given the variety of browser graphics and text-formatting capabilities. Besides, HTML contains many more ways for structuring your document content without regard to the final appearance: section headers, structured lists, paragraphs, rules, titles, and embedded images are all defined by IITML without regard for how these elements might be rendered by a browser.

If you treat HTML as a document-generation tool, you will be sorely disappointed in your ability to format your document in a specific way. There is simply not enough capability built into HTML to allow you to create the kind of documents you might whip up with tools like FrameMaker or Microsoft Word. Attempts to subvert the supplied structuring elements to achieve specific formatting tricks seldom work across all browsers. In short, don't waste your time trying to force HTML to do things it was never designed to do.

Instead, use HTML in the manner it was designed for: indicating the structure of a document so that the browser can then render its content appropriately. HTML is rife with tags that let you indicate the semantics of your document content, something that is missing from tools like Frame or Word. Create your documents using these tags and you'll be happier, your documents will look better, and your readers will benefit immensely.

1.4.2 Specific Limitations of HTML

There are limits to the kinds of formatting and document structuring HTML can provide. Extensions to the language remove some of the restrictions imposed by HTML 2.0; other limitations linger.

Specifically, the features that do not exist in the HTML 2.0 standard but are made possible by extensions implemented by the various browser manufacturers, and are generally considered part of HTML 3.2, include:

- Inline variation of font size
- Mixed font attributes like bold and italic
- Centered or right-justified text
- Justifying images
- Flowing text around figures and images
- Tables

Those niceties that just aren't available in any version of HTML are:

- Footnotes, end notes, automatic table of contents, or indices
- Headers and footers
- Tabs and other automatic character spacing
- Nested numbered lists
- Mathematical typesetting

1.4.3 Yielding to the Browser

Many novice HTML authors try to get around these limitations by taking careful note of how their browser displays the contents of certain tags and then misusing those tags to achieve formatting tricks. For example, some authors nest certain kinds of lists several levels deep, not because they are actually creating deeply nested lists, but because they want their text specially indented.

There are many different browsers running on many different computers and they all do things differently. Even two different users using the same browser version on their machines can reconfigure the software so that the same HTML document will look completely different. What looks fabulous on your personal browser can and often does look terrible on other browsers.

Yield to the browser. Let it format your document in whatever way it deems best. Recognize that the browser's job is to present your documents to the user in a consistent, usable way. Your job, in turn, is to use HTML effectively to mark up your documents so that the browser can do its job effectively. Spend less time trying to achieve format-oriented goals. Instead, focus your efforts on creating the actual document content and adding the HTML tags to structure that content effectively.

1.5 Nonstandard Extensions

You don't have to write in HTML 2.0 for long before you realize its limitations. That's why Netscape Navigator is the most popular browser used on the Web today. While others were content to implement HTML standards, the developers at Netscape were hard at work extending the language and their browser to capture the potentially lucrative and certainly exciting commercial markets on the Web. In a year after going into business, Netscape captured over 70 percent of browser users.

With a market presence like that, Netscape leads not only the market, but the standards drive, as well. Those browser features that Netscape provides and that aren't part of HTML 2.0 or the proposed version 3.2 quickly become de facto standards because so many people use them. Consequently, Netscape is the browser other developers must emulate. For instance, Internet Explorer, developed in collaboration with Spyglass and bundled with Windows 95, adopts most of Netscape's enhancements to HTML and has some embellishments of its own.

1.5.1 Extensions: Pro and Con

Every software vendor adheres to the technological standards; it's embarrassing to be incompatible and your competitors will take every opportunity to remind buyers of your product's failure to comply, no matter how arcane or useless that standard might be. At the same time, vendors seek to make their products different and better than the competition's offerings. Netscape's extensions to standard HTML are a perfect example of these market pressures at work.

Many HTML document authors feel safe using Netscape's nonstandard extensions, because of its commanding share of users. For better or worse, extensions to HTML made by the folks at Netscape instantly become part of the street version of HTML, much like English slang creeping into the vocabulary of most Frenchmen despite the best efforts of the Academie Française.

The reality, however, is that browsers are becoming less and less standard—de facto or not. The W3C isn't keeping up. And other browser developers are not about to remain quiescent for long. Netscape holds the commanding lead now, but everyone can hear the heavy footsteps of such technology powerhouses as Sun Microsystems and Microsoft heading toward the Internet and the Web. Increasingly, browser competitors are implementing many of the Netscape extensions and adding a few of their own for good measure.

1.5.2 Avoiding Extensions

In general, we urge you to resist using an HTML extension unless you have a compelling and overriding reason to do so. By using them, particularly in key portions of your documents, you run the risk of losing a substantial portion of your potential readership. Sure, the Netscape community is large enough to make this point moot now, but even so you are excluding several million people without Netscape from viewing your pages.

Of course, there are varying degrees of dependency on HTML extensions. If you use some of the horizontal rule extensions, for example, most other browsers will ignore the extended attributes and render a conventional horizontal rule. On the other hand, reliance upon a number of font size changes and text alignment extensions to control your document appearance will make your document look terrible on many alternative browsers. It might not even display at all on browsers that don't support the extensions.

We admit that it is a bit disingenuous of us to decry the use of HTML extensions while presenting complete descriptions of their use. In keeping with the general philosophy of the Internet, we'll err on the side of handing out guns and rope to all interested parties while hoping you have enough smarts to keep from hanging yourself or shooting yourself in the foot.

Our advice still holds, though: only use an extension where it is necessary or very advantageous, and do so with the understanding that you are disenfranchising a portion of your audience. To that end, you might even consider providing separate, standards-based versions of your documents to accommodate users of other browsers.

1.5.3 Beyond Extensions: Exploiting Bugs

It is one thing to take advantage of an extension to HTML, and quite another to exploit known bugs in a particular version of a browser to achieve some unusual document effect.

A good example is the multiple-body bug in version 1.1 of Netscape Navigator. The HTML standard insists that an HTML document have exactly one <body> tag, containing the body of the document. The now-obsolete browser allowed any number of <body> tags, processing and rendering each <body> in turn. By placing several <body> tags in an HTML document, an author could achieve crude animation effects when the document was first loaded into the browser. The most popular one had several <body> tags, each with a slightly different background color. This trick results in a document fade-in effect.

The party ended when version 1.2 of Netscape fixed the bug. Suddenly, thousands of documents lost their fancy fade-in effect. Although faced with some rather fierce complaints, to their credit the people at Netscape stood by their decision to adhere to the standard, placing compliance higher on their list of priorities than nifty rendering hacks.

In that light, we can unequivocally offer this advice: *never* exploit a bug in a browser to achieve a particular effect in your documents.

1.6 Tools for the HTML Designer

While you can use the barest of barebones text editors to create HTML documents, most HTML authors have a bit more elaborate toolbox of software utilities than a simple word processor. You also need, at least, a browser so you can test and refine your work. Beyond the essentials are some software tools specialized for HTML document preparation and editing, and others for developing and preparing accessory multimedia files.

1.6.1 Essentials

At the very least, you'll need an editor, a browser to check your work, and ideally, a connection to the Internet.

1.6.1.1 *Word processor or HTML editor?*

Some authors use the word-processing capabilities of their specialized HTML editing software. Others, such as ourselves, prefer to compose their work on a general word processor and later insert the HTML tags and their attributes. Still others embed HTML tags as they compose.

We think the stepwise approach—compose, then mark up—is the better way. Word processors typically have more and better writing tools, such as an outliner, spell-checker, and thesaurus, so you can craft the document's flow and content well, disregarding for the moment its look. We find that once we've defined and written the document's content, it's much easier to make a second pass to judiciously and effectively add the HTML tags to format the text. Note, too, that, unless specially trained (if they can be), spell-checkers and thesauruses typically choke on HTML markup tags and their various parameters. You can spend what seems to be a lifetime clicking the ignore button on all those otherwise valid markup tags when syntax- or spell-checking an HTML document.

When and how you embed HTML tags into your document dictate the tools you need. Some word processors, such as WordPerfect or Microsoft Word, come with automated tools, and there are third-party ones, too, that automatically translate your word-processed documents into HTML. Don't expect miracles, though. Except for boilerplate documents, you probably will need to nurse those automated HTML documents to full health.

Another word of caution about HTML editors: Not all adhere to the HTML 2.0 standard, so examine their specifications before using, and certainly before purchasing, one. Moreover, some of the WYSIWYG (what-you-see-is-what-you-get) HTML editors don't have up-to-date built-in browsers, so they may erroneously decode the HTML tags and give you misleading displays.

1.6.1.2 *Browser software*

Obviously, you should view your newly composed HTML documents and test their functionality before you release them for use by others. For serious HTML authors, particularly those looking to push their documents beyond the HTML standards, we recommend that you have several browser products, perhaps with versions running on different computers, just to be sure one's delightful display isn't another's nightmare.

The currently popular, and so most important, browsers are Netscape Navigator, Mosaic, and Internet Explorer. Sun's HotJava, although still in alpha testing state, is expected by some to have a bright future. Obtain free copies of the software via anonymous FTP from their respective servers (*ftp.netscape.com*, *ftp.ncsa.uiuc.edu*, *ftp.microsoft.com*, and *ftp.java.com*), or contact your local computer software dealer for a commercial version (about $50).

1.6.1.3 Internet connection

We think you should have bona fide access to the Internet if you are really serious about learning and honing your HTML writing skills. Okay, it's not absolutely essential since you can compose and view HTML documents locally. And for some, a connection is perhaps not even possible or practical, but make the effort; there's sometimes no better way to learn than by example. HTML examples abound on the Internet, both good and bad, whose source HTML you can download and examine.

Moreover, an Internet connection *is* essential for development and testing if you include hypertext links to Internet services in your HTML documents. But, most of all, an Internet connection gives you access to a wealth of tips and ongoing updates to the language through special-interest newsgroups, as well as much of the essential and accessory software you can use to prepare HTML document collections.

1.6.2 An Extended Toolkit

If you're serious about creating documents, you'll soon find there are all sorts of nifty tools that make life easier. The list of freeware, shareware, and commercial products grows daily, so it's not very useful to provide a list here. This is, in fact, another good reason why you should get an Internet connection; various groups keep updated lists of HTML resources on the Web. If you are really dedicated to writing in HTML, you will visit those sites, and you will visit them regularly to keep abreast of the language, tools, and trends.

Table 1-1 summarizes the most useful HTML author resources currently on the Web. Each contains dozens, sometimes hundreds, of hyperlinks to detailed descriptions of products and other important information for the HTML author. Go at it.

Table 1–1: Important Web Sites for the HTML Author

Subject	Site Address (URL)
HTML tools	*http://www.stars.com*
HTML editors	*http://www.yahoo.com/Computers/World_Wide_Web/HTML_Editors/*
HTML guides	*http://union.ncsa.uiuc.edu/HyperNews/get/www/html/guides.html*

2

HTML Quick Start

We didn't spend hours studiously pouring over some reference book before we wrote our first HTML document. You probably shouldn't either. HTML is simple to read and understand, and it's simple to write, too. So let's get started without first learning a lot of arcane rules.

To help you get that quick, satisfying start, we've included this chapter as a brief summary of the many elements of HTML. Of course, we've left out a lot of details and some tricks you should know. Read the upcoming chapters to get the essentials for becoming fluent in HTML.

Even if you are familiar with HTML, we recommend you work your way through this chapter before tackling the rest of the book. It not only gives you a working grasp of basic HTML and its jargon, you'll also be more productive later, flush with the confidence that comes from creating attractive documents in such a short time.

2.1 Writing Tools

Use any text editor to create HTML documents, as long as it can save your work on disk in ASCII text file format. That's because, even though HTML documents include elaborate text layout and pictures, they're all just plain old ASCII documents themselves. A fancier WYSIWYG editor or an HTML translator for your favorite word processor are fine, too—although they may not support the many nonstandard HTML features we discuss later in this book. You'll probably end up touching up the HTML source text they produce, as well.

While not needed to compose HTML, you should have at least one version of a popular World Wide Web browser installed on your computer to view your work, preferably Netscape Navigator, NCSA Mosaic, or Microsoft's Internet Explorer. That's because the HTML source document you compose on your text editor doesn't look anything like what gets displayed by a browser, even though it's the same document. Make sure what your readers actually see is what you intended by viewing the HTML document yourself with a browser. Besides, the popular ones are free over the Internet. If you can't retrieve a browser copy yourself, get a friend to give you a copy.

Also note that you don't need a connection to the Internet or the World Wide Web to write and view your HTML documents. You may compose and view your documents stored on a hard or floppy disk that's attached to your computer. You can even navigate among your local documents with HTML's hyperlinking capabilities without ever being connected to the Internet, or any other network for that matter. In fact, we recommend that you work locally to develop and thoroughly test your HTML documents before you share them with others.

We strongly recommend, however, that you *do* get a connection to the Internet and to the World Wide Web if you are serious about composing your own HTML documents. You may download and view others' interesting Web pages and see how they accomplished some interesting feature—good or bad. Learning by example is fun, too. (Reusing others' work, on the other hand, is often questionable, if not downright illegal.) An Internet connection is particularly essential if you include in your work hyperlinks to other documents on the Internet.

2.2 A First HTML Document

It seems every programming language book ever written starts off with a simple example on how to display the message, "Hello, World!" Well, you won't see a "Hello, World!" example in this book. After all, this is a style guide for the next millennium. Instead, ours sends greetings to the World Wide Web:

```
<html>
<head>
<title>My first HTML document</title>
</head>
<body>
<h2>My first HTML document</h2>
```

```
Hello, <i>World Wide Web!</i>
 <!-- No "Hello, World" for us -->
<p>
                    Greetings from<br>
<a href="http://www.ora.com">O'Reilly & Associates</a>
<p>
Composed with care by:
<cite>(insert your name here)</cite>
<br>&copy;2000 and beyond
</body>
</html>
```

Go ahead: Type in the example HTML source on a fresh word-processing page and save it on your local disk as *myfirst.html*. Make sure you select to save it in ASCII format; word processor-specific file formats like Microsoft Word's ".doc" files save hidden characters that can confuse the browser software and disrupt your HTML document's display.

After saving *myfirst.html* (or just *myfirst.htm* if you are using a DOS- or Windows-based computer) onto disk, start up your browser, locate, and then open the document from the program's File menu. Your screen should look like Figure 2-1.

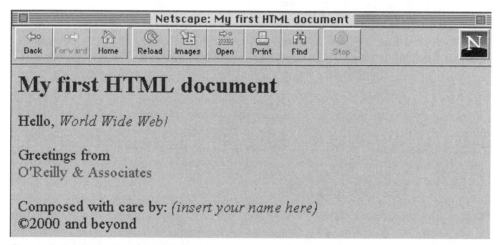

Figure 2-1: A very simple HTML document

2.3 HTML Embedded Tags

You probably have noticed right away, perhaps in surprise, that the browser displays less than half of the example source text. Closer inspection of the source reveals that what's missing is everything that's bracketed inside a pair of less-than (<) and greater-than (>) characters. [tag syntax, 3.3.1]

HTML is an embedded language: you insert the language's directions or *tags* into the same document that you and your readers load into a browser to view. The browser uses the information inside the HTML tags to decide how to display or otherwise treat the subsequent contents of your HTML document.

For instance, the `<i>` tag that precedes the word "Hello" in the simple example tells the browser to display the following text in italics.* [physical styles, 4.3.2]

The first word in a tag is its formal name, which usually is fairly descriptive of its function, too. Any additional words in a tag are special *attributes*, sometimes with an associated value after an equal sign (=), which further define or modify the tag's actions.

2.3.1 Start and End Tags

Most tags define and affect a discrete region of your HTML document. The region begins where the tag and its attributes first appear in the source document (also called the *start tag*) and continues until a corresponding *end tag*. An end tag is the start tag's name preceded by a forward slash (/). For example, the end tag that matches the "start italicizing" `<i>` tag is `</i>`.

End tags never include attributes. Most, but not all, tags have an end tag. And, to make life a bit easier for HTML authors, the browser software often infers an end tag from surrounding and obvious context, so you needn't explicitly include some end tags in your source HTML document. (We tell you which are optional and which are never omitted when we describe each tag in later chapters.) Our simple example is missing an end tag that is so commonly inferred and hence not included in the source that many veteran HTML authors don't even know that it exists. Which one?

2.4 HTML Skeleton

Notice, too, in our simple example source that precedes Figure 2-1), the HTML document starts and ends with `<html>` and `</html>` tags. Of course, these tags tell the browser that the entire document is composed in HTML. The HTML standard requires an `<html>` tag for every HTML document, but most browsers can detect and properly display HTML encoding in a text document that's missing this outermost structural tag. [`<html>`, 3.5.1]

---

* Italicized text is a very simple example and one that most browsers, except the text-only variety like Lynx, can handle. In general, the browser tries to do as it is told, but as we demonstrate in upcoming chapters, browsers vary from computer to computer and from user to user, as do the fonts that are available and selected by the user for viewing HTML document. Assume that not all are capable or willing to display your HTML documents exactly as it appears on your screen.

Inside, like our example, all HTML documents have two main structures: a *head* and a *body*,* each bounded in the source by respectively named start and end tags. You put information about the document in the head and the contents you want displayed in the browser's window inside the body. Except in rare cases, you'll spend most of your time working on your HTML document's body content. [<head>, 3.6.1] [<body>, 3.7.1]

There are several different document header tags you may use to define how a particular document fits into a document collection and into the larger scheme of the Web. Some nonstandard header tags even animate your document.

For most documents, however, the important header element is the title. Every HTML document is required by the HTML standard to have a title. Choose a meaningful one; the title should instantly tell the reader what the document is about. Enclose yours, as we do our example's title, between the <title> and </title> tags in your document's header. The popular browsers typically display the title at the top of the document's window onscreen. [<title>, 3.6.2]

2.5 The Flesh on an HTML Document

Except for the <html>, <head>, <body>, and <title> tags, the HTML standard has few other required structural elements. You're pretty free to include just about anything else in the contents of your document. (The Web surfers among you know that HTML authors have taken full advantage of that freedom, too). Perhaps surprisingly, though, there are only three main types of HTML content: tags, which we describe above; comments; and text.

2.5.1 Comments

Like computer-programming source code, a raw HTML document, with all its embedded tags, can quickly become nearly unreadable. We strongly encourage that you use HTML comments to guide your composing eye.

Although part of your document, nothing in a comment, including the body of your comment that goes between the special starting tag "<!--" and ending tag delimiters "-->" gets included in the browser display of your document. Now you see a comment in the source, like in our simple HTML example, and now you don't on the display, as evidenced by our comment's absence in Figure 2-1. Anyone can download the source text of the HTML document and read the comments, though, so be careful what you write. [comments, 3.4.3]

---

* Actually, there's an alternate, nonstandard structure: Netscape "frame" documents, which divide the browser's main display into two or more independent windows, replaces the body with special tags that describe those frames. We describe frames later in this chapter and in detail in Chapter 10, *Frames*.

2.5.2 Text

If it isn't a tag or a comment, it's text. The bulk of content in most of your HTML documents—the part readers see on their browser displays—is text. Special tags give the text structure, such as headings, lists, and tables. Others advise the browser how the content should be formatted and displayed.

2.5.3 *Multimedia*

What about images and other multimedia elements we see and hear as part of our Web browser displays? Aren't they part of the HTML document? No. The data that comprise digital images, movies, sounds, and other multimedia elements that may be included in the browser display are in documents separate from the HTML document. You include references to those multimedia elements via special tags in the HTML document. The browser uses the references to load and integrate other types of documents with your HTML text.

We didn't include any special multimedia references in the simple example above simply because they are separate, nontext documents you can't just type into a text processor. We do, however, talk about and give examples on how to integrate images and other multimedia in your HTML documents later in this chapter, as well as in greater detail in subsequent chapters.

2.6 *HTML and Text*

Text-related HTML tags comprise the richest set of all in the standard language. That's because HTML emerged as a way to enrich the structure and organization of text.

HTML came out of academia. What was and still is important to those early developers was the ability of their mostly academic, text-oriented documents to be scanned and read without sacrificing their ability to distribute documents over the Internet to a wide diversity of computer display platforms. (ASCII text is the only universal format on the global Internet.) Multimedia integration is something of an appendage to HTML, albeit an important one.

And, too, page layout is secondary to structure in HTML. We humans visually scan and decide textual relationships and structure based on how it looks; machines can only read encoded markings. Because HTML documents have encoded tags that relate meaning, they lend themselves very well to computer-automated searches and recompilation of content—features very important to researchers. It's not so much *how* something is said in HTML as *what* is being said.

Accordingly, HTML is not a page-layout language. In fact, given the diversity of user-customizable browsers as well as the diversity of computer platforms for retrieval and display of electronic documents, all HTML strives to accomplish is *advise,* not dictate, how the document might look when rendered by the browser. You cannot force the browser to display your document in any certain way. You'll hurt your brain if you insist otherwise.

2.6.1 Appearance of Text

For instance, you cannot predict what font and what absolute size—8- or 40-point Helvetica, Geneva, Subway, or whatever—will be used for a particular user's text display. Users may change their browser fonts and some browsers are text-only with no nice fonts at all.

Nonetheless, you can attach common style attributes to your text with *physical style* tags like the italics `<i>` tag in the simple example. More importantly and truer to the language's original intentions, HTML has *content-based* style tags that attach *meaning* to various text passages. All of today's graphical browsers recognize the physical and content-related text style tags and change the appearance of their related text passage to visually convey meaning or structure. You just can't predict exactly what that change will look like.

2.6.1.1 Content-based text styles

Content-based style tags indicate to the browser that a specific portion of your HTML text has a specific usage or meaning. The `<cite>` tag in our simple example, for instance, means the enclosed text is some sort of citation—the document's author, in this case. Browsers commonly, although not universally now or perhaps ever, display the citation text in italics, not as regular text. [content-based styles, 4.3.1]

While it may or may not be obvious to the current reader that the text is a citation, someday, someone might create a computer program that searches a vast collection of HTML documents for embedded `<cite>` tags and compiles a special list of citations from the enclosed text. Similar software agents already scour the Internet for HTML-embedded information to compile listings, such as the infamous Webcrawler and the Lycos Home Page databases of Web sites.

The most common content-based style used today is that of emphasis, indicated with the `<em>` tag. And if you're feeling really emphatic, you might use the `<strong>` content style. Other content-based styles include `<code>`, for snippets of programming code; `<kbd>`, to denote text entered by the user via a keyboard; `<samp>` to mark sample text; `<dfn>` for definitions; and `<var>` to delimit variable names within programming code samples. All of these tags have corresponding end tags.

2.6.1.2 Physical styles

Even the barest of barebones text processors conform to a few traditional text styles, such as italicized and bold-faced characters. While HTML is not a word-processing tool in the traditional sense, it does provide tags that tell the browser explicitly to display (if it can) a character, word, or phrase in a particular physical style.

Although you should use related content-based tags for the reasons we argue above, sometimes form is more important than function. So, to italicize text, without imposing any specific meaning, use the `<i>` tag; the `<b>` tag to display text in bold; or the `<tt>` tag so that the browser, if it can, displays the text in a teletype-writer-style monospaced typeface. [physical-based styles, 4.3.2]

It's easy to fall into the trap of using physical styles when you should really be using a content-based style instead. Discipline yourself now to use the content-based styles, because, as we argue above, they convey meaning as well as style, thereby making your documents easier to automate and manage.

2.6.1.3 Special text characters

Not all text characters available to you for display by a browser can be typed from the keyboard. And some characters have special meanings in HTML, such as the brackets around tags, which if not somehow differentiated when used for plain text—the less-than sign (<) in a math equation, for example—will confuse the browser and trash your document. HTML gives you a way to include any of the many different characters that comprise the ASCII character set anywhere in your text through a special encoding of its *character entity*.

Like the copyright symbol in our simple example, a character entity starts with an ampersand (&), followed by its name, and terminated with a semicolon. (You alternatively may also use the character's position number in the ASCII table of characters preceded by the number symbol (#) in lieu of its name in the character entity sequence.) When rendering the document, the browser displays the proper character, if it exists in the user's font. [character entities, 3.4.2]

For obvious reasons, the most commonly used character entities are the greater-than (>), less-than (<), and ampersand (&) characters. Check Appendix D, *Character Entities*, to find what symbol the character entity "¦" represents.

2.6.2 Text Structures

It's not obvious in our simple example, but the common carriage returns we use to separate paragraphs in our source document have no meaning in HTML, except in special circumstances. You could have typed the document onto a single line in your text editor and it would still appear the same in Figure 2-1!*

You'd soon discover, too, if you hadn't read it here first, that except in special cases, browsers typically ignore leading and trailing spaces, and sometimes more than a few in between. (If you look closely at the source example, the line "Greetings from" looks like it should be indented by leading spaces, but it isn't in Figure 2-1.)

2.6.2.1 Paragraphs and line breaks

A browser takes the text in the body of your document and "flows" it onto the computer screen, disregarding any common carriage-return or line-feed characters in the source. The browser fills as much of each line of the display window as possible, beginning flush against the left margin, before stopping after the rightmost word and moving on to the next line. Resize the browser window, and the text reflows to fill the new space; indicating HTML's inherent flexibility.

Of course, readers would rebel if your text just ran on and on, so HTML does provide both explicit and implicit ways to control the basic structure of your document. The most rudimentary and common ways are with the paragraph (`<p>`) and the line-break (`<br>`) tags. Both break the text flow, which consequently restarts on a new line. The only apparent difference is that with most browsers, the paragraph tag adds more vertical space after the line break. [`<p>`, 4.1.2] [`<br>`, 4.7.1]

By the way, the HTML standard includes an end tag for the paragraph tag, but not for the line break tag. Few authors ever include the paragraph end tag in their documents;† the browser usually can figure out where one paragraph ends and another begins. Give yourself a star if you knew that `</p>` even exists.

2.6.2.2 Headings

Besides breaking your text into paragraphs, you also can organize your documents into sections with headings. Just as they do on this and other pages in this printed book, HTML headings not only divide and entitle discrete passages of text, they

---

* We use a computer programming-like style of indentation so our source HTML documents are more readable. It's not obligatory, nor are there any formal style guidelines for source HTML document text formats. We do, however, highly recommend you adopt your own consistent style, so that you and others can easily follow your source documents.

† The paragraph end tag is being used more commonly now that the popular browsers support the paragraph-alignment attribute.

also convey meaning visually. With HTML, however, headings also lend themselves to machine-automated analyses.

There are six HTML heading tags, `<h1>` through `<h6>`, with corresponding end tags. Typically, the browser displays their contents in respectively very large to very small font sizes, and sometimes in boldface. The text inside the `<h4>` tag is usually the same size as the regular text. [headings, 4.2]

The heading tags also typically break the current text flow, standing alone on lines and separated from surrounding text, even though there aren't any explicit paragraph or line-break tags before or after a heading.

2.6.2.3 Horizontal rules

Besides headings, HTML also provides horizontal rule lines that help delineate and separate the sections of your document.

When the browser encounters an `<hr>` tag in your document, it breaks the flow of text and draws a line completely across the display window on a new line. The flow of text resumes immediately below the rule. [<hr>, 5.1.1]

2.6.2.4 Preformatted text

Occasionally, you'll want the browser to display a block of text as-is with, for example, indented lines and vertically aligned letters or numbers that don't change even though the browser window might get resized. The HTML `<pre>` tag rises to those occasions. All text, up to the closing `</pre>` end tag, appears in the browser window exactly as you type it, including carriage returns and line feeds, leading, trailing, and intervening spaces. Although very useful for tables and forms, `<pre>` text turns out pretty dull; the popular browsers render the block in a monospace typeface. [<pre>, 4.7.5]

2.7 Hyperlinks

While text may be the meat and bones of an HTML document, its heart is hypertext. Hypertext gives users the ability to retrieve and display a different document in your own or someone else's collection simply by a click of the mouse on an associated word or phrase (*hyperlink*) in your HTML document. Use these interactive hyperlinks to help readers easily navigate and find information in yours and in others' collections of otherwise separate documents in a variety of formats, including multimedia, HTML, and plain ASCII text. Hyperlinks literally bring the wealth of knowledge on the whole Internet to the tip of the mouse pointer.

To include a hyperlink to some other document in your own collection or on a server in Timbuktu, all you need to know is the document's unique address and how to drop an *anchor* into your HTML document. [anchors, 2.7.2]

2.7.1 URLs

While it is hard to believe given the millions, perhaps billions, of them out there, every document and resource on the Internet has a unique address known as its universal resource locator (URL; commonly pronounced "you-are-ell"). A URL is comprised of the document's name preceded by the hierarchy of directory names in which the file is stored (*pathname*), the Internet *domain name* of the server that hosts the file, and the software and manner by which the browser and the document's host server communicate to exchange the document (*protocol*):

```
protocol://server domain name/pathname
```

Here are some sample URLs:

```
http://www.kumquat.com/docs/catalog/price_list.hmtl
http:price_list.html
http://www.kumquat.com/
ftp://ftp.netcom.com/pub/
```

The first example is what's known as an *absolute* or complete URL. It includes every part of the URL format—protocol, server, and the pathname of the document.

While absolute URLs leave nothing to the imagination, they can lead to big headaches when you move documents to another directory or server. Fortunately, browsers also let you use *relative* URLs and automatically fill in any missing portions with respective parts from the current document's *base* URL. The second example is the simplest relative URL of all; it assumes that the *price_list.html* document is located on the same server and in the same directory as the current document.

Relative URLs are useful, too, if you don't know a directory or document's name. The third URL example, for instance, points to *kumquat.com*'s Web home page.

Although appearances may deceive, the last FTP example URL actually is absolute; it points directly at the contents of the */pub* directory.

2.7.2 Anchors

The anchor (<a>) tag is the HTML feature for defining both the source and the destination of a hyperlink.* You'll most often see and use the <a> tag with its href attribute to define a source hyperlink. The value of the attribute is the URL of the destination.

The contents of the source <a> tag—the words and/or images between it and its </a> end tag—is the portion of the HTML document that is specially activated in the browser display and that users select to take a hyperlink. These *anchor* contents usually look different from the surrounding content (text in a different color or underlined, images with specially colored borders) and the mouse pointer icon changes when passed over them. The <a> tag contents, therefore, should be text or an image (icons are great) that explicitly or intuitively tells users where the hyperlink will take them. [<a>, 6.3.1]

For instance, the browser will specially display and change the mouse pointer when it passes over the "Kumquat Archive" text in the following example:

```
For more information on kumquats, visit our
<a href="http://www.kumquat.com/archive.html">
Kumquat Archive</a>
```

If the user clicks the mouse button on that text, the browser automatically retrieves from the server *www.kumquat.com* a Web (*http:*) page stored there named *archive.html*, and then displays it for the user.

2.7.3 Hyperlink Names and Navigation

Pointing to another document in some collection somewhere on the other side of the world is not only cool, but it also supports your own HTML documents. Yet the hyperlinks' chief duty is to help users navigate your collection in their search for valuable information. Hence, the concept of the home page and supporting HTML documents has arisen.

None of your HTML documents should run on and on. First, there's the performance issue: the value of your work suffers, no matter how rich it is, if the document takes forever to download, and if once retrieved, users must endlessly scroll up and down through the display to find a particular section.

---

* The nomenclature here is a bit unfortunate: the "anchor" tag should mark just a destination, not the jumping off point of a hyperlink, too. You "drop anchor"; you don't jump off one. We won't even mention the atrociously confusing terminology the HTML standard uses for the various parts of a hyperlink except to say that someone got things all "bass ackwards."

Rather, design your work as a collection of several compact and succinct pages, like chapters in a book, each focused to a particular topic for quick selection and browsing by the user. Then use hyperlinks to organize that collection.

For instance, use your home page—the leading document of the collection—as a master index full of brief descriptions and respective hyperlinks to the rest of your collection. Also use the special attribute of the <a> tag called `name`.

Anchors with the `name` attribute serve as internal hyperlink targets in your HTML documents. Normally, the browser displays a freshly downloaded document at the beginning. Name anchors let you begin the display at the section of interest further down. Simply include them anywhere they make sense as a hyperlink target. They do not change the appearance of enclosed or surrounding content.

Thereafter, you may append the name, after a separating hash mark (#), as a suffix in the URL of a hyperlink that references that specific place in your document. For instance, to reference a specific topic in an archive, such as "Kumquat Stew Recipes" in our example Kumquat Archive, you mark that section with a name anchor:

```
... preceding content...
<a name="Stews">
<h3>Kumquat Stew Recipes"</h3>
</a>
```

In the same or another document, you prepare a source hyperlink that points directly to those recipes by including the section's anchor name as a suffix to the document's URL, separated by a hash mark (#):

```
For more information on kumquats, visit our
<a href="http://www.kumquat.com/archive.html">
  Kumquat Archive</a>,
and perhaps try one or two of our
<a href="http://www.kumquat.com/archive.html#Stews">
  Kumquat Stew Recipes</a>.
```

If selected by the user, the latter hyperlink causes the browser to download the *archive.html* document and start the display at our "Stew" anchor.

2.7.4 *Anchors Beyond HTML*

HTML hyperlinks are not limited to other HTML documents. Anchors let you point to nearly any type of document available over the Internet, including other Internet services.

However, "let" and "enable" are two different things. Browsers can manage the various Internet services, like FTP and Gopher, so that users can download non-HTML documents. They don't yet fully or gracefully handle multimedia.

Today, there are few standards for the many types and formats of multimedia. Computer systems connected to the Web vary wildly in their abilities to display those sound and video formats. Except for some graphics images, standard HTML gives you no specific provision for display of multimedia documents except the ability to reference one in an anchor. The browser, which retrieves the multimedia document, must activate a special *helper* application, download and execute an associated *applet*, or have a *plugin* accessory installed to decode and display it for the user.

Although HTML and most Web browsers currently avoid the confusion by sidestepping it, that doesn't mean you can't or shouldn't exploit multimedia in your HTML documents: just be aware of the limitations.

2.8 Images Are Special

Image files are multimedia elements you may reference with anchors in your HTML document for separate download and display by the browser. But, unlike other multimedia, standard HTML has a provision for image display "in line" with the text,* and images can serve as intricate maps of hyperlinks. That's because there is some consensus in the industry concerning image file formats, specifically GIF and JPEG, and the graphical browsers have built in decoders that integrate those image types into your document.

2.8.1 Inline Images

The HTML tag for inline images provides <img> whose required src attribute is the URL of the GIF or JPEG image you want to insert in the document. [<img>, 5.2.6]

The browser separately loads images and places them into the text flow as if the image were some special, albeit sometimes very large, character. Normally, that means the browser aligns the bottom of the image to the bottom of the current line of text. You can change that with the special <img> align attribute whose value you set to put the image at the top, middle, or bottom of adjacent text. Examine Figure 2-2 through Figure 2-4 for the image alignment you prefer. Of course, wide images may take up the whole line, and hence break the text flow.

---

* Browser developers are beginning to integrate other multimedia besides GIF and JPEG graphics for inline display. Internet Explorer, for instance, supports a tag that plays background audio.

Or you may place an image by itself by including preceding and following paragraph or line-break tags.

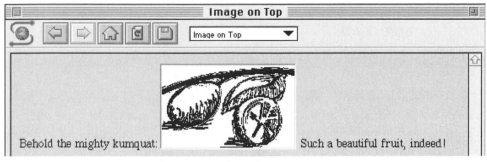

Figure 2–2: An inline image aligned with the bottom of the text (default)

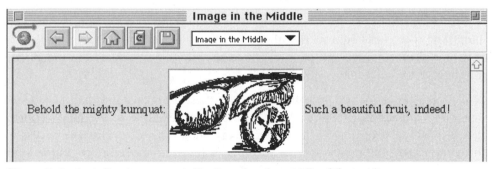

Figure 2–3: An inline image specially aligned at the middle of the text line

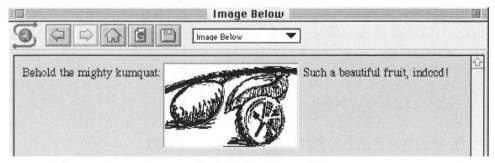

Figure 2–4: An inline image specially aligned to the top of the text

Experienced HTML authors use images not only as supporting illustrations, but also as quite small inline characters or glyphs, added to aid browsing readers' eyes and to highlight sections of the documents. Veteran HTML authors commonly add custom list bullets or more distinctive section dividers than the conventional horizontal rules. Images, too, may be included in a hyperlink, so that users may select an inline thumbnail sketch to download a full-screen image. The possibilities with inline images are endless.

2.8.2 Image Maps

Image maps are images within an anchor with a special attribute: they may contain more than one hyperlink.

The HTML standard image map is enabled by adding the `ismap` attribute to an `<img>` tag placed inside an anchor tag (`<a>`). When the user clicks somewhere in the image, the graphical browser sends the relative x,y coordinates of the mouse position to the server that is also designated in the anchor. A special server program then translates the image coordinates into some special action, such as downloading another HTML document. [`ismap`, 6.5.1]

A good example of the use of an image map might be to locate a hotel while traveling. The user clicks on a map of the region they intend to visit, for instance, and your image map's server program might return the names, addresses, and phone numbers of local accommodations.

While very powerful and visually appealing, these standard so-called *server-side* image maps mean that HTML authors must have some access to the map's coordinate-processing program on the server. Many authors don't even have access to the server. Recent innovations in browser software remove those barriers by enabling *client-side* image maps.

Rather than depending on a Web server, the special `usemap` attribute extension to the `<img>` tag and new `<map>` and `<area>` extensions let HTML authors embed all the information the browser needs to process an image map in the same document as the image. Client-side image maps are not part of standard HTML, and are not supported by most browsers. But of all the nonstandard features that emerge seemingly daily in one new browser or another, client-side image maps probably will be one of the most popular. [`usemap`, 6.5.2]

2.9 Lists, Searchable Documents, and Forms

Thought we'd exhausted HTML text elements? Headers, paragraphs, and line breaks are just the rudimentary text-organizational elements of an HTML document. The language also provides several advanced text-based structures, including three types of lists, "searchable" documents, and forms. Searchable documents and forms go beyond text formatting, too; they are a way to interact with your readers. Forms let users enter text and click checkboxes and radio buttons to select particular items and then send that information back to the server. Once received, a special server application processes the form's information and responds accordingly, e.g., filling a product order or collecting data for a user survey.[*]

The HTML syntax for these special features and their various attributes can get rather complicated; they're not quick-start grist. So we mention them here and urge you to read on for details in later chapters.

2.9.1 Unordered, Ordered, and Definition Lists

The three types of HTML lists match those we are most familiar with: unordered, ordered, and definition lists. An unordered list—one in which the order of items is not important, such as a laundry or grocery list—gets bounded by <ul> and </ul> tags. Each item in the list, usually a word or short phrase, is marked by the <li> (list-item) tag and, when rendered, appears indented from the left margin. The browser also typically precedes each item with a leading bullet symbol. [<ul>, 7.1.1] [<li>, 7.3]

Ordered lists, bounded by the <ol> and </ol> tags, are identical in format to unordered ones, including the <li> tag for marking list items. However, the order of items is important—equipment assembly steps, for instance. The browser accordingly displays each item in the list preceded by an ascending number. [<ol>, 7.2.1]

Definition lists are slightly more complicated than unordered and ordered lists. Within a definition list's enclosing <dl> and </dl> tags, each list item has two parts, each with a special tag: a short name or title, contained within a <dt> tag, followed by its corresponding value or definition, denoted by the <dd> tag. When rendered, the browser usually puts the item name on a separate line (although not indented), and the definition, which may include several paragraphs, indented below it. [<dl>, 7.7.1]

The various types of lists may contain nearly any type of content normally allowed in the body of the HTML document. So, you can organize your collection of digitized family photographs into an ordered list, for example, or put them into a definition list complete with text annotations. HTML even lets you put lists inside of lists (nesting), opening up a wealth of interesting combinations.

---

[*] The server-side programming required for processing forms is beyond the scope of this book. We give some basic guidelines in the appropriate chapters, but please consult the server documentation and your server administrator for details.

2.9.2 Searchable Documents

The simplest type of user interaction provided by HTML is the *searchable* document. You create a searchable HTML document by including an `<isindex>` tag in its header or body. The browser automatically provides some way for the user to type one or more words into a text input box, and to pass those keywords to a related processing application on the server. [`isindex`, 6.6.1]

The processing application on the server uses those keywords to do some special task, such as perform a database search or match the keywords against an authentication list to allow the user special access to some other part of your document collection.

2.9.3 Forms

Obviously, searchable documents are very limited—one per document and only one user input element. Fortunately, HTML provides better, more extensive support for collecting user input though *forms*.

You create one or more special form sections in your HTML document, bounded with the `<form>` and `</form>` tags. Inside the form, you may put predefined as well as customized text-input boxes allowing for both single and multiline input. You may also insert checkboxes and radio buttons for single- and multiple-choice selections, and special buttons that work to reset the form or send its contents to the server. Users fill out the form at their leisure, perhaps after reading the rest of the document, and then click a special send button that makes the browser send the form's data to the server. A special server-side program you provide then processes the form and responds accordingly, perhaps by requesting more information from the user, modifying subsequent HTML documents the server sends to the user, and so on. [`<form>`, 8.1.1]

HTML forms provide everything you might expect of an automated form, including input area labels, integrated contents for instructions, default input values, and so on—except automatic input verification; your server-side program has to perform that function.

2.10 Beyond the HTML Standard

We've alluded several times in this chapter to the fact that few browsers strictly adhere to the HTML 2.0 standard and stop there. The demand for innovation has many browser developers working feverishly to provide new and exciting features for HTML. Tables and frames are the two most prominent extensions to the language.

2.10.1 Tables

For a language that emerged from academia—a place steeped in data—it's surprising to find that standard HTML doesn't have any provision for data tables. Fortunately, the popular browsers support a set of language extensions for data tables that not only align your numbers, but can specially format your text, too.

Five tags enable tables, including the `<table>` tag itself and a `<caption>` tag for including a description of the table. Special tag attributes let you change the look and dimensions of the table. You create a table row-by-row, putting between the table row (`<tr>`) tag and its end tag (`</tr>`) either table header (`<th>`) or table data (`<td>`) tags and their respective contents for each cell in the table. Headers and data may contain nearly any regular HTML content, including text, images, forms, and even another table. As a result, you can also use HTML tables for advanced text formatting, such as for multicolumn text and sidebar headers (Figure 2-5). For more information, see Chapter 9, *Tables*.

Figure 2–5: HTML tables let you perform page layout tricks, too

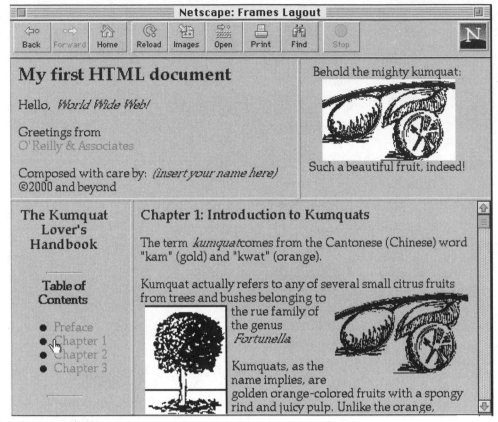

Figure 2-6: Netscape frames divide the window into many document displays

2.10.2 Frames

Anyone who has had more than one application window open on their graphical desktop at a time can immediately appreciate the special, nonstandard feature of HTML uniquely offered in the latest version 2.0 of Netscape Navigator: frames. For more information on frames, see Chapter 10.

Figure 2-6 is an example of a frame display. It shows how the Netscape document window may be divided into many individual windows separated by rule lines and scroll bars. What is not immediately apparent in the example, though, is that each frame may display an independent document, and not necessarily HTML ones, at that. A frame may contain any valid content that the browser is capable of displaying, including multimedia. If the frame's contents include a hypertext link the user selects, the new document's contents, even another frame document, may replace that same frame, another frame's content, or the entire browser window.

Frames are defined in a special HTML document in which you replace the `<body>` tag with one or more `<frameset>` tags that tell Netscape how to divide its main window into discrete frames. Special `<frame>` tags go inside the `<frameset>` tag and point to the documents that go inside the frames.

The individual documents referenced and displayed in the frame document window act independently to a degree; the frame document controls the entire window. You can, however, direct one frame's document to load new content into another frame. Selecting an item from a table of contents, for example, might cause Netscape to load and display the referenced document into an adjacent frame for viewing. That way, the table of contents always is available to the user as they browse the collection.

2.11 *Forging Ahead*

Clearly, this chapter represents the tip of the iceberg. If you've read this far, hopefully your appetite has been whetted for more. By now you've got a basic understanding of the scope and features of HTML; proceed through subsequent chapters to expand your knowledge and learn more about each feature of HTML.

3

Anatomy of an HTML Document

HTML documents are very simple and writing one shouldn't intimidate even the most timid of computer users. First, although you might use a fancy WYSIWYG editor to help you compose it, an HTML document ultimately is stored, distributed, and read by a browser as a simple ASCII text file.[*] That's why even the poorest user with a barebones text editor can compose the most elaborate of HTML pages. (Accomplished webmasters often elicit the admiration of HTML "newbies" by composing astonishingly cool pages using the crudest text editor on a cheap laptop computer and performing in odd places like on a bus or in the bathroom.) HTML writers should, however, keep several of the popular browsers on hand and alternate among them to view new documents under construction. Remember, browsers differ in how they display a page, not all browsers implement all of the HTML standards, and some have their own special extensions to the language.

3.1 *Appearances Can Deceive*

HTML documents never look alike when displayed by a text editor and when displayed by an HTML browser. Simply take a look at any source HTML document off the World Wide Web. At the very least, return characters, tabs, and leading spaces, although important for readability of the source text document, are for the most part ignored in HTML. There also is a lot of extra text in an HTML source docu-

---

[*] Informally, both the text and the markup tags in an HTML document are ASCII characters. Technically, unless you specify otherwise, text and tags are made up of eight-bit characters as defined in the standard ISO-8859-1 Latin character set. The HTML standard does support alternative character encodings, including Arabic and Cyrillic. See Appendix D, *Character Entities*, for details.

ment, mostly from the display tags and interactivity markers and their parameters that affect portions of the document, but don't themselves appear in the display.

Accordingly, new HTML authors are confronted with having to develop not only a presentation style for their HTML pages, but a different style for their HTML source text. The source document's layout should highlight the programming-like markup aspects of HTML, not its display aspects. And it should be readable not only by you, the author, but by others, as well.

Experienced HTML document writers typically adopt a programming-like style, albeit very relaxed, for their source HTML text. We do the same throughout the book, and that style will become apparent as you compare our source HTML examples with the actual display of the document by a browser.

Our formatting style is simple, but serves to create readable, easily maintained documents:

- Except for the document structural tags like `<html>`, `<head>`, and `<body>`, any HTML element we used to structure the content of a document is placed on a separate line and indented to show its nesting level within the document. Such elements include lists, forms, tables, and similar tags.

- Any HTML element used to control the appearance or style of text is inserted in the current line of text. This includes basic font style tags like `<b>` (bold text) and document linkages like `<a>` (hypertext anchor).

- Avoid, where possible, the breaking of a URL onto two lines.

- Add extraneous newline characters to set apart special sections of the HTML document, for instance around paragraphs or tables.

The task of maintaining the indentation of your source HTML ranges from trivial to onerous. Some text editors like Emacs manage the indentation automatically; others like common word processors couldn't care less about indentation and leave the task completely up to you. If your editor makes your life difficult, you might consider striking a compromise, perhaps by indenting the tags to show structure, but leaving the actual text without indentation to make modifications easier.

No matter what compromises or stands you make on source code style, however, it's important that you adopt one. You'll be very glad you did when you go back to that HTML document you wrote three months ago searching for that really cool trick you did with. ... Now, where was that?

3.2 Structure of an HTML Document

An HTML document consists of text, which defines the content of the document, and tags, which define the structure and appearance of the document. The structure of an HTML document is simple, too, consisting of an outer `<html>` tag enclosing the document header and body:

```
<html>
<head>
<title>Barebones HTML Document</title>
</head>
<body>
This illustrates, in a very <i>simp</i>le way,
the basic structure of an HTML document.
</body>
</html>
```

Each document has a *head* and a *body*, delimited by the `<head>` and `<body>` tags. The head is where you give your HTML document a title and where you indicate other parameters the browser may use when displaying the document. The body is where you put the actual contents of the HTML document. This includes the text for display and document control markers (tags) that advise the browser how to display the text. Tags also reference special-effects files like graphics and sound, and indicate the hot spots (*hyperlinks* and *anchors*) that link your document to other documents.

3.3 HTML Tags

For the most part, HTML document tags are simple to understand and use since they are made up of common words, abbreviations, and notations. For instance, the `<i>` and `</i>` tags tell the browser to respectively start and stop italicizing the text characters that come between them. Accordingly, the syllable "simp" in our barebones HTML example would appear italicized on a browser display.

The HTML standard and its various extensions define how and where you place tags within a document. Let's take a closer look at that syntactic sugar that holds together all HTML documents.

3.3.1 The Syntax of a Tag

Every HTML tag consists of a tag *name*, sometimes followed by an optional list of tag *attributes*, all placed between opening and closing brackets (< and >). The simplest tag is nothing more than a name appropriately enclosed in brackets, such as `<head>` and `<i>`. More complicated tags have attributes, which may have specific values that are defined by the document author; others modify the behavior of the tag.

Tag and attribute names are not case sensitive. There's no difference in effect between `<head>`, `<Head>`, `<HEAD>`, or even `<HeaD>`; they are all equivalent. The values that you assign to a particular attribute may be case sensitive, however, depending on your browser and server. In particular, file location and name references—universal resource locators (URLs)—are case sensitive. [URLs, 6.2]

Tag attributes, if any, belong after the tag name, each separated by one or more tab, space, or return characters. Their order of appearance is not important.

A tag attribute's value, if any, follows an equal sign (=) after the attribute name. You may include spaces around the equal sign, so that `width=6`, `width = 6`, `width =6`, and `width= 6` all mean the same. For readability, however, we prefer not to include spaces. That way, it's easier to pick out an attribute/value pair from a crowd of pairs in a lengthy tag.

If an attribute's value is a single word or number (no spaces), you may simply add it after the equal sign. All other values should be enclosed in single or double quotes, especially those values that contain several words separated by spaces. The length of the value is limited to 1024 characters.

Most browsers are tolerant of how tags are punctuated and broken across lines. Nonetheless, avoid breaking tags across lines in your source document whenever possible. This rule promotes readability and reduces potential errors in your HTML documents.

3.3.2 Sample Tags

Here are some tags with attributes:

```
<a href="http://www.ora.com/catalog.html">
<ul compact>
<input name=filename size=24 maxlength=80>
<link title="Table of Contents">
```

The first example is the `<a>` tag for a hyperlink to O'Reilly & Associates' World Wide Web-based catalog of products. It has a single attribute, `href`, followed by the catalog's address in cyberspace—its URL.

The second example shows a tag that formats text into an unordered list of items. Its single attribute—`compact`, which limits the space between list items—does not require a value.

The third example shows a tag with multiple attributes, each with a value that does not require enclosing quotes.

The last example shows proper use of enclosing quotes when the attribute value is more than one word long.

Finally, what is not immediately evident in these examples is that while attribute names are not case sensitive (`href` works the same as `HREF` and `HreF`), attribute values mostly are case sensitive. The value `filename` for the `name` attribute in the `<input>` tag example is not the same as the value `Filename`, for instance.

3.3.3 *Starting and Ending Tags*

We alluded earlier to the fact that most HTML tags have a beginning and an end and affect the portion of text in between. That enclosed text segment may be large or small, from a single text character, syllable, or word, such as the italicized "simp" syllable in our barebones example, to the `<html>` tag that bounds the entire document. The starting component of any tag is the tag name and its attributes, if any. The corresponding ending tag is the tag name alone, preceded by a forward slash (/). Ending tags have no attributes.

3.3.4 *Proper and Improper Nesting*

Tags can be put inside the affected segment of another tag (nested) for multiple tag effects on a single segment of the HTML document. For example, a portion of the following text is both emboldened and included as part of an anchor defined by the `<a>` tag:

```
<body>
This is some text in the body, with a
<a href="another_doc.html">link, a portion of which
is <b>set in bold</b></a>
</body>
```

According to the HTML standard, you must end nested tags starting with the most recent one and work your way back out. For instance in the example, we end the bold tag (`</b>`) before ending the link tag (`</a>`) since we started in the reverse order: `<a>` tag first, then `<b>` tag. It's a good idea to follow that standard, even though most browsers don't absolutely insist you do so. You may get away with violating this nesting rule for one browser, sometimes even with all current browsers. But eventually a new browser version won't allow the violation and you'll be hard pressed to straighten out your source HTML document.

3.3.5 *Tags Without Ends*

According to the HTML standard, only a few tags do not have an ending tag. For example, the `<br>` tag causes a line break; it has no effect otherwise on the subsequent portion of the document and, hence, does not need an ending tag.

The standard HTML tags that do not have corresponding ending tags are:

```
<base>
<br>
<dd>
<dt>
<hr>
<img>
<input>
<isindex>
<li>
<link>
<meta>
<nextid>
<option>
```

3.3.6 Omitting Tags

You often see documents in which the author seemingly has forgotten to include many ending tags in apparent violation of the HTML standard. But your browser doesn't complain, and the documents displays just fine. What gives? The HTML standard lets you omit certain tags or their endings for clarity and ease of preparation. The HTML standard writers didn't intend the language to be tedious.

For example, the <p> tag that defines the start of a paragraph has a corresponding end tag </p>, but the </p> ending tag rarely is used. In fact, many HTML authors don't even know it exists! [<p>, 4.1.2]

Rather, the HTML standard lets you omit a starting tag or ending tag whenever it can be unambiguously inferred by the surrounding context. Many browsers make good guesses when confronted with missing tags, leading the document author to assume that a valid omission was made. When in doubt, add the ending tag: it'll make life easier for yourself, the browser, and anyone else who might need to modify your document in the future.

3.3.7 Ignored or Redundant Tags

Browsers sometimes ignore tags. This usually happens with redundant tags whose effects merely cancel or substitute for themselves. The best example is a series of <p> tags, one after the other with no intervening text. Unlike the similar series of repeating return characters in a text-processing document, most browsers skip to a new line only once. The extra <p> tags are redundant and usually ignored by the browser.

In addition, most browsers ignore any tag that they don't understand or that was incorrectly specified by the document author. Browsers habitually forge ahead and make some sense of a document, no matter how badly formed and error-ridden it may be. This isn't just a tactic to overcome errors, it's also an important strategy for extensibility. Imagine how much harder it would be to add new features to the language if the existing base of browsers choked on them.

The thing to watch out for with nonstandard tags that aren't supported by most browsers is their enclosed contents, if any. Browsers that recognize the new tag may process those contents differently than those that don't support the new tag. For example, Internet Explorer supports a `<comment>` tag whose contents serve to document the source HTML and are not intended to be viewed by the user. However, none of the other browsers recognize the `<comment>` tag and render its contents on the user's screen, effectively defeating the tag's purpose besides ruining the document's appearance. [`<comment>`, 3.4.3]

3.4   Document Content

Nearly everything else you put into your HTML document that isn't a tag is, by definition, content, and the majority of that, in most, not all, HTML documents, is text. Like tags, document content is encoded using a specific character set, the ISO-8859-1 Latin character set, by default. This character set is a superset of conventional ASCII, adding the necessary characters to support the Western European languages. If your keyboard does not allow you to directly enter the characters you need, you can use character entities to insert the desired characters.

3.4.1   Advice Versus Control

Perhaps the hardest rule to remember when marking up an HTML document is that all the tags you insert regarding text display and formatting are only advice for the browser: they do not explicitly control how the browser will display the document. In fact, the browser can choose to ignore all of your tags and do what it pleases with the document content. What's worse, the user (of all people!) has control over text-display characteristics of his or her own browser. Imagine that.

Get used to this lack of control. The best way to use HTML markup to control the appearance of your documents is to concentrate on the content of the document, not on its final appearance. If you find yourself worrying excessively about spacing, alignment, text breaks, and character positioning, you'll surely end up with ulcers. You will have gone beyond the intent of HTML. If you focus on delivering information to users in an attractive manner, using the tags to advise the browser as to how best to display that information, you are using HTML effectively, and your documents will render well on a wide range of browsers.

3.4.2 *Character Entities*

Besides common text, HTML gives you a way to display special text characters you might not normally be able to include in your source document or which have other purposes in HTML. A good example is the less-than (<) symbol. In HTML, it normally signifies the start of a tag, so if you insert it simply as part of your text, the browser will get confused and probably misinterpret your document.

In HTML, the ampersand (&) character instructs the browser to insert a special character, formally known as a *character entity*. For example, the command "<" inserts that pesky less-than symbol into the rendered text. Similarly, ">" inserts the greater-than symbol, and "&" inserts an ampersand. There can be no spaces between the ampersand, the entity name, and the required, trailing semicolon. (Semicolons aren't special characters; you don't need to use an ampersand sequence to normally display a semicolon.)

You also may replace the entity name after the ampersand with a decimal value between 0 and 255 corresponding to the entity's position in the character set. Hence, the sequence "<" does the same thing as "<" and represents the less-than symbol. In fact, you could substitute all the normal characters within an HTML document with ampersand-special characters, such as "A" for a capital "A" or "a" for its lowercase version, but that would be silly. A complete listing of all characters, their names, and numerical equivalents can be found in Appendix D.

Keep in mind that not all special characters can be rendered by all browsers. Some browsers just ignore many of the special characters; with others, the characters aren't available in the character sets on a specific platform. Be sure to test your documents on a range of browsers before electing to use some of the more obscure character entities.

3.4.3 *Comments*

Comments are another type of textual content that appear in the source HTML document, but are not rendered by the user's browser. Comments fall between the special `<!--` and `-->` markup elements. Browsers ignore the text between the comment character sequences.

Here's a sample comment:

```
<!-- This is a comment -->
<!-- This is a
multiple line comment
that ends on this line -->
```

There must be a space after the initial <!-- and preceding the final -->, but you can put nearly anything inside the comment otherwise. The biggest exception to this rule is that the HTML standard doesn't let you nest comments.[*]

As we mentioned above, Internet Explorer also lets you place comments within a special <comment> tag. Everything between the <comment> and </comment> tag is ignored by Internet Explorer, but all other browsers will display the comment to the user. Because of this undesirable behavior, we do not recommend using the <comment> tag for comments. Instead, always use the <!-- and --> sequences to delimit comments.

Besides the obvious use of comments for HTML source documentation, many World Wide Web servers use comments to take advantage of features specific to the document server software. These servers scan the document for specific character sequences within conventional HTML comments and then perform some action based upon the commands embedded in the comments. The action might be as simple as including text from another file (known as a *server-side include*) or as complex as executing other commands on the server to dynamically generate the document contents.

3.5 HTML Document Elements

Every HTML document should conform to the HTML SGML DTD, the formal Document Type Definition that defines the HTML standard. The DTD defines the tags and syntax that are used to create an HTML document. You can inform the browser which DTD your document complies with by placing a special SGML command in the first line of the document:

```
<!DOCTYPE HTML PUBLIC "-//IETF//DTD HTML 2.0//EN">
```

This cryptic message indicates that your document is intended to be compliant with the HTML 2.0 DTD defined by the World Wide Web Organization (W3O). Other versions of the DTD define more restricted versions of the HTML standard, and not all browsers support all versions of the HTML DTD. In fact, specifying any other doctype may cause the browser to misinterpret your document when displaying it for the user. It's also unclear what doctype to use when including in the HTML document the various tags that are not standards, but are very popular features of a popular browser—the Netscape extensions, for instance, or even the deprecated HTML 3.0 standard, for which a DTD was never released.

Almost no one precedes their HTML documents with the SGML doctype command. Because of the confusion of versions and standards, we don't recommend that you

---

[*] Netscape does let you nest comments, but the practice is tricky; you cannot always predict how other browsers will react to nested comments.

include the prefix with your HTML documents either. There are other mechanisms to better define your document contents, such as the `version` attribute for the `<html>` tag.

3.5.1 The <html> Tag

As we saw earlier, the `<html>` and `</html>` tags serve to delimit the beginning and end of an HTML document. Since the typical browser can easily infer from the enclosed source that it is an HTML document, you don't really need to include the tag in your source document.

<html>

Function:
    Delimits a complete HTML document

Attributes:
    VERSION

End tag:
    </html>; may be omitted

Contains:
    head_tag, body_tag, frames

That said, it's considered good form to include this tag so that other tools, particularly more mundane text-processing ones, can recognize your document as an HTML document. At the very least, the presence of the beginning and ending `<html>` tags ensures that the beginning or the end of the document haven't been inadvertently deleted.

Inside the `<html>` tag and its end tag are the document's head and body. Within the head, you'll find tags that identify the document and define its place within a document collection. Within the body is the actual document content, defined by tags that determine the layout and appearance of the document text. As you might expect, the document head is contained within a `<head>` tag and the body is within a `<body>` tag, both of which are defined below.

The latest version of Netscape Navigator (2.0) extends the `<html>` tag so that the `<body>` tag may be replaced by a `<frameset>` tag, defining one or more display frames that, in turn, contain actual document content. See Chapter 10, *Frames*, for more information.

By far, the most common form of the `<html>` tag is simply:

```
<html>
...document head and body content
</html>
```

When the `<html>` tag appears without the `version` attribute, the HTML document server and browser assume the version of HTML used in this document is supplied to the browser by the server.

3.5.1.1 The version attribute

The `<html>` `version` attribute defines the HTML standard version used to compose the document. If included, the value of the `version` attribute should read exactly:

```
version="-//IETF//DTD HTML 2.0//EN"
```

This attribute better identifies an HTML document's origins and contents than the SGML doctype command. However, some browsers may alter their processing of the document based upon the HTML version specified by this attribute, so be careful. Again, the confusion of extensions and versions and the lack of standards guidance makes us uneasy, and we do not recommend you include version information in your document, except perhaps as part of a leading comment.

3.6 The Document Header

The HTML document header describes the various properties of the document, including its title, position within the Web, and relationship with other documents. Most of the data contained within the document header are never actually rendered as content visible to the user.

3.6.1 The <head> Tag

The `<head>` tag has no attributes and serves only to encapsulate the other header tags. Since it always occurs near the beginning of a document, just after the `<html>` tag and before the `<body>` or `<frameset>` tag, both the `<head>` tag and its corresponding ending `</head>` can be unambiguously inferred by the browser and so can be safely omitted from the document. Nonetheless, we do encourage you to include them in your documents, since it promotes readability and better supports document automation.

The `<head>` tag may contain a number of other tags that help define and manage the document's content. These include, in any order of appearance: `<base>`, `<basefont>`, `<isindex>`, `<link>`, `<meta>`, `<nextid>`, and `<title>`. For more information, see Chapter 6, *Links and Webs*.

\<head\>

Function:
   Defines the document header

Attributes:
   None

End tag:
   \</head\>; rarely omitted

Contains:
   head_content

Used in:
   html_tag

3.6.2 The \<title\> Tag

The \<title\> tag does exactly what you might expect: the words you place inside its start and end tags define the title for your document. (We told you this stuff is pretty much self-explanatory and easier than you might think at first glance.) The title is used by the browser in some special manner, most often placed in the browser window's title bar or on a status line. Usually, too, the title becomes the default name for a link to the document if the document is added to a link collection or to a user's "hot list."

\<title\>

Function:
   Defines the document title

Attributes:
   None

End tag:
   \</title\>; never omitted

Contains:
   plain_text

Used in:
   head_content

The \<title\> tag is the only thing required within the \<head\> tag. Since the \<head\> tag itself and even the \<html\> tag may be safely omitted, the \<title\> tag could be the first line within a valid HTML document. Beyond that, most browsers will even supply a generic title for documents lacking a `<title>` tag, such as the document's filename, so you don't even have to supply a title. That goes a bit too far even for our down-and-dirty tastes. No respectable author of an HTML document should serve up a document missing the `<title>` tag and a title.

Browsers do not specially format title text and ignore anything other than text inside the title start and end tags, such as images or links to other documents.

Here's an even barer barebones example of a valid HTML document to highlight the header and title tags:

```
<html>
<head>
<title>Using HTML: The Definitive Guide</title>
</head>
</html>
```

3.6.2.1 What's in a title?

Selecting the right title is crucial to defining a document and ensuring that it can be effectively used within the World Wide Web.

Keep in mind that users can access each of your documents in a collection in nearly any order and independently of one another. Each document's title should therefore define the document both within the context of your other documents as well as on its own merits.

Titles that include references to document sequencing are usually inappropriate. Simple titles, like "Chapter 2" or "Part VI" do little to help a user understand what the document might contain. More descriptive titles, such as "Chapter 2: Advanced Square Dancing" or "Part VI: Churchill's Youth and Adulthood," convey both a sense of place within a larger set of documents and specific content that invites the reader to read on.

Self-referential titles also aren't very useful. A title like "My Home Page" is completely content-free, as are titles like "Feedback Page" or "Popular Links." You want a title to convey a sense of content and purpose so that users can decide, based upon the title alone, whether to visit that page or not. "The Kumquat Lover's Home Page" is descriptive and likely to draw in lovers of the bitter fruit, as are "Kumquat Lover's Feedback Page" and "Popular Links Frequented by Kumquat Lovers."

People spend a great deal of time creating documents for the Web, often only to squander that effort with an uninviting, ineffective title. As special software that automatically collects links for users becomes more prevalent on the Web, the only descriptive phrase associated with your pages when they are inserted into some vast link database will be the title you choose for them. We can't emphasize this enough: take care to select descriptive, useful, context-independent titles for each of your HTML documents.

3.6.3 Related Header Tags

Other tags you may include within the `<head>` tag deal with specific aspects of document creation, management, linking, or automation. That's why we only mention them here, and describe them in greater detail in other, more appropriate sections and chapters of this book.

Briefly, the special header tags are:

`<link>` *and* `<base>`
> Define the current document's base location and relationship to other documents. [`<link>`, 6.7.2] [`<base>`, 6.7.1]

`<isindex>`
> Creates automatic document indexing forms, allowing users to search databases of information using the current document as a querying tool. [`<isindex>`, 6.6.1]

`<nextid>`
> Makes creation of unique document labels easier when using document automation tools. [`<nextid>`, 6.8.2]

`<meta>`
> Provides additional document data not supplied by any of the other `<head>` tags. [`<meta>`, 6.8.1]

`<basefont>`
> Defines the default font size for a font model that some advanced browsers support, but that is not part of the HTML 2.0 standard. [`<basefont>`, 4.6.2]

3.7 The Document Body

The document body is the meat of the matter; it's where you put the contents of your document. The `<body>` tag delimits the document body.

3.7.1 The <body> Tag

Within HTML 2.0, the `<body>` tag has no attributes and is little more than a placeholder in your documents. Various browsers, as we'll see, have extended the tag to give greater control over your document's appearance.

<body>

Function:
Defines the document body

Attributes:
ALINK (Netscape only)
BACKGROUND (extension)
BGCOLOR (extension)
BGPROPERTIES (Internet Explorer only)
LEFTMARGIN (Internet Explorer only)
LINK (extension)
TEXT (cxtcnsion)
TOPMARGIN (Internet Explorer only)
VLINK (extension)

End tag:
</body>; may be omitted

Contains:
body_content

Used in:
html_tag

Anything inside the `<body>` tag and its ending counterpart `</body>` is called *body content*. The simplest HTML document might have only a sequence of text paragraphs within the `<body>` tag. More complex documents will include heavily formatted text, graphical figures, tables, and a variety of special effects.

Since the position of the `<body>` and `</body>` tags can be inferred by the browser, they can safely be omitted from the document. However, like the `<html>` and `<head>` tags, we recommend that you include the `<body>` tags in your document to make them more easily readable and maintainable.

The various attributes for the `<body>` tag are explicitly nonstandard extensions to the language, supported by recent versions of Internet Explorer and Netscape, among other browsers. They give you some control over the document's appearance, such as its background, text, and hyperlink display colors. See Chapter 5, *Rules, Images, and Multimedia*, for details.

The latest version of Netscape (2.0) also implements a special type of HTML document in which you replace the `<body>` tag with one or more `<frameset>` tags. This so-called *frame* document divides Netscape's display window into one or more independent windows, each displaying a different document. We describe this innovation in Chapter 10.

4

Text Basics

In this day and age of hoopla and hype, *how* has become almost as, and in some cases more important than, *what*. Any successful presentation, even a thoughtful tome, should have its text organized into an attractive, effective document. Organizing text into attractive documents is HTML's forte. The language gives you a number of tools that help you mold your text and get your message across. HTML also helps structure your document so your target audience has easy access to your words.

Always keep in mind while designing your documents, though (here we go again!), that HTML tags, particularly in regard to text, only advise—they do not dictate—how a browser will ultimately render the document. Rendering varies from browser to browser. Don't get too entangled with trying to get just the right look and layout. Your attempts may and probably will be thwarted by the browser.

4.1 Divisions and Paragraphs

Like most text processors, a browser wraps the words it finds in the HTML text to fit the horizontal width of its viewing window. Widen the browser's window and words automatically flow up to fill the wider lines. Squeeze the window and words wrap downwards.

Unlike most text processors, however, HTML uses explicit division (`<div>`), paragraph (`<p>`), and line-break (`<br>`) tags to control the alignment and flow of text. Return characters, although quite useful for readability of the source HTML document, are ignored by the browser.

4.1.1 The <div> Tag

The `<div>` tag is actually a part of the developing HTML 3.2 standard and is not supported by any but the Netscape browser.

<div> (Netscape only)

Function:
> Defines a paragraph of text

Attributes:
> ALIGN (Netscape only)

End tag:
> </div>; usually omitted

Contains:
> *body_content*

Used in:
> *block*

As proposed in the HTML 3.2 standard, the `<div>` tag specification divides a document into separate divisions, and has a variety of formatting options that let you define a unique style for each division. You might have one for your document's abstract, another for the body, a third for the conclusion, and a fourth for the bibliography, for instance. Each division has a different default format: the abstract indented and in an italic face; the body in a left-justified Roman face; the conclusion similar to the abstract; and the bibliography automatically numbered and formatted appropriately.

Sadly, the only feature of `<div>` retained by the folks at Netscape is its ability to alter the alignment of all text within the division. Thus, in its current incarnation, Netscape's `<div>` serves just a slightly more general purpose than the `<center>` tag, which serves to center large blocks of body content.

4.1.1.1 *The align attribute*

The `align` attribute for `<div>` justifies the enclosed content to either the `left` (default), `center`, or `right` of the browser display. The `<div>` tag may be nested, and the alignment of the nested `<div>` tag takes precedence over the containing `<div>` tag. Further, other nested alignment tags, such as `<center>`, aligned paragraphs (see `<p>` below), or specially aligned table rows and cells, override the effect of `<div>`.

4.1.2 *The <p> Tag*

The `<p>` tag signals the start of a paragraph. That's not well known even by some veteran webmasters because it runs counterintuitive to what we've come to expect from experience. Most word processors we're familiar with use just one special character, typically the return character, to signal the *end* of a paragraph.

<p>

Function:
> Defines a paragraph of text

Attributes:
> ALIGN (extension)

End tag:
> </p>; usually omitted

Contains:
> *text*

Used in:
> *block*

In the recommended HTML way, each paragraph starts with `<p>` and ends with the corresponding `</p>` tag. And while a sequence of newline characters in a text processor-displayed document introduces a blank space between each one, HTML browsers typically ignore all but the first paragraph tag.

In practice, you also can ignore the starting `<p>` tag at the beginning of the first paragraph, as well as the `</p>` tag at the end of all paragraphs, since they can be implied from other tags that occur in the document and hence safely omitted. For example:

```
<body>
This is the first paragraph, at the very beginning of the
body of this document.
<p>
```

```
The tag above signals the start of this second paragraph.
When rendered by a browser, it will begin slightly below the
end of the first paragraph, with a bit of extra whitespace
between the two paragraphs.
<p>
This is the last paragraph in the example.
</body>
```

Notice that we haven't included the paragraph start tag (<p>) for the first paragraph or any end paragraph tags at all in the example; they can be unambiguously inferred by the browser and are therefore unnecessary.

In general, you'll find that human document authors tend to omit postulated tags whenever possible, while automatic document generators tend to insert them. That may be because the software designers didn't want to run the risk of having their product chided by competitors as not adhering to the HTML standard, even though we're splitting letter-of-the-law hairs here. Go ahead and be defiant: Omit that first paragraph's <p> tag and don't give a second thought to paragraph ending </p> tags, provided, of course, that your document's structure and clarity are not compromised.

4.1.2.1 Paragraph rendering

When encountering the new paragraph (<p>) tag, a browser typically inserts one character-high line plus some extra vertical space into the document before starting the new paragraph. The browser then collects all the words and, if present, inline images into the new paragraph, ignoring leading and trailing spaces (not spaces between words, of course) and return characters in the HTML text. The browser software then flows the resulting sequence of words and images into a paragraph that fits within the margins of its display window, automatically generating line breaks as needed to wrap the text within the window. For example, compare how a browser arranges the text into lines and paragraphs (Figure 4-1) to how the preceding HTML example is printed on the page. The browser may also automatically hyphenate long words, and the paragraph may be fill-justified to stretch the line of words out towards both margins.

The net result is that you do not have to worry about line length, word wrap, and line breaks when composing your HTML documents. The browser will take any arbitrary sequence of words and images and display a nicely formatted paragraph.

If you want to control line length and breaks explicitly, consider using a preformatted text block with the <pre> tag. If you need to force a line break, use the <br> tag. [<pre>, 4.7.5] [
, 4.7.1]

This is the first paragraph, at the very beginning of the body of this document.

The tag above signals the start of this second paragraph. When rendered by a browser, it will begin slightly below the end of the first paragraph, with a bit of extra white space between the two paragraphs.

This is the last paragraph in the example.

Figure 4–1: Browsers ignore common return characters in the source HTML document

4.1.2.2   *The align attribute*

The next version of HTML may standardize a way to control how the browser justifies the contents of a paragraph. The latest versions of the popular browsers already implement one way: the special `align` extension.

Justified to the left side of the display window is the default paragraph alignment for most browsers. Left-justified content is also what all browsers revert to when encountering a new `<p>` tag. Currently, Internet Explorer and some earlier Netscape versions (1.x) let you specially center-justify a paragraph with the `align` attribute and value of `center`. Netscape 2.0 supports a longer list, letting you set the paragraph to one of three possible values: `left`, `right`, or `center`.

Figure 4-2 shows you the effect of each alignment, as rendered from the following source:

```
<p align=right>
Right over here!
<br>
This is too.
<p align=left>
Slide back left.
<p align=center>
Smack in the middle.
</p>
Left's the default.
```

Notice in the example that the paragraph alignment remains in effect until the browser encounters another `<p>` tag or an ending `</p>` tag. Other body elements may also disrupt the current paragraph alignment and cause subsequent

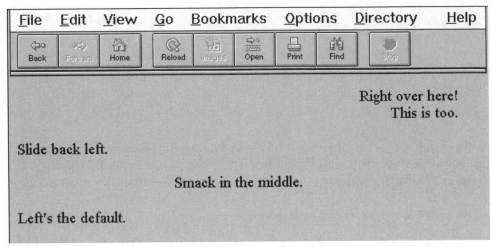

Figure 4–2: Effect of the align attribute on paragraph justification (Netscape 2.0)

paragraphs to revert to the default left alignment, including forms, headers, tables, and most other body content-related tags.

4.1.2.3 Allowed paragraph content

An HTML paragraph may contain any element allowed in a text flow, including conventional words and punctuation, links (`<a>`), images (`<img>`), line breaks (`<br>`), font changes (`<b>`, `<i>`, `<tt>`, `<u>`, `<strike>`, and `<font>`), and content-based style changes (`<cite>`, `<code>`, `<em>`, `<kbd>`, `<samp>`, `<strong>`, and `<var>`). If any other element occurs within the paragraph, it implies the paragraph has ended, and the browser assumes the closing `</p>` tag was not specified.

4.1.2.4 Allowed paragraph usage

You may specify a paragraph only within a *block*, along with other paragraphs, lists, forms, and preformatted text. In general, this means that paragraphs can appear where a flow of text is appropriate, such as in the body of a document, an element in a list, and so on. Technically, paragraphs cannot appear within a header, anchor, or other element whose content is strictly text-only. In practice, most browsers ignore this restriction and format the paragraph as a part of the containing element.

4.2 Headings

Users have a hard enough time reading what's displayed on a screen. A long flow of text, unbroken by title, subtitles, and other headers, crosses eyes and numbs the mind, not to mention the fact that it makes it nearly impossible to scan the text for a specific topic.

You should always break a flow of text into several smaller sections within one or more headings (like this book!). HTML defines six levels of headings that can be used to structure a text flow into a more readable, more manageable document. And, as we discuss in Chapter 5, *Rules, Images, and Multimedia*, there are a variety of graphical tricks that help divide your HTML document and make its contents more accessible as well as more readable to users.

4.2.1 Heading Tags

The six heading tags, written as `<h1>`, `<h2>`, `<h3>`, `<h4>`, `<h5>`, and `<h6>`, indicate the highest (`<h1>`) to the lowest (`<h6>`) precedence a heading may have in the document.

<h1>, <h2>, <h3>, <h4>, <h5>, <h6>

Function:
Define one of six levels of headers

Attributes:
ALIGN (extension)

End tag:
</h1>, </h2>, </h3>, </h4>, </h5>, </h6>; never omitted

Contains:
text

Used in:
body_content

The enclosed text within a heading typically is uniquely rendered by the browser, depending upon the display technology available to it. The browser may choose to center, embolden, enlarge, italicize, underline, or change the color of headings to make each stand out within the document. And to thwart the most tedious HTML writers, users, too, often can alter how a browser will render the different headings. Ah, well.

Fortunately, in practice most browsers use a diminishing character point size for the sequence of headers, so that `<h1>` text is quite large and `<h6>` text is quite minuscule (see Figure 4-3, for example).

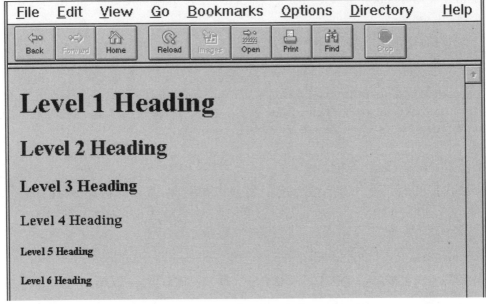

Figure 4-3: Netscape uses diminishing text sizes for rendering headings

By tradition, HTML authors have come to use `<h1>` headers for document titles, `<h2>` headers for section titles, and so on, often matching the way many of us were taught to outline our work with heads, subheads, and sub-sub-a-dub-heads.

Finally, don't forget to include the appropriate heading end tags in your document. The browser won't insert one automatically for you, and omitting the ending tag for a heading can have disastrous consequences for your document.

4.2.1.1 The align attribute

It has become *de rigueur* for browsers to let HTML authors align text inside structural tags like `<p>` and `<div>`. The headings tags are no different: The latest versions of the popular browsers, for instance, support an `align` attribute for headings.

The default alignment for most browsers is `left`. Internet Explorer lets you specially `center` a particular heading, whereas Netscape and Mosaic support all three of the common alignment attribute values: `left`, `center`, and `right`. Figure 4-4 shows these alternative alignments as rendered from the following source:

```
<h1 align=right>Right over here!</h1>
<h2 align=left>Slide back left.</h2>
<h3 align=center>Smack in the middle.</h3>
```

Figure 4-4: The headings align attribute in action

4.2.2 Appropriate Use of Headings

It's good form to repeat that title in the first heading tag, since the title you specify at the beginning of your HTML document doesn't appear in the user's main display window. It should match the title in the document header. The HTML segment:

```
<html>
<head>
<title>Kumquat Farming in North America</title>
</head>
<body>
<h3>Kumquat Farming in North America</h3>
<p>
Perhaps one of the most enticing of all fruits is the...
```

is a good example of repeating the document's title in the header and in the body of document. While the browser may place the title somewhere in the document window and may also use it to create bookmarks or hotlist entries, all of which vaguely are somewhere on the user's desktop, the level-3 title heading in the example will always appear at the very beginning of the document. It serves as a visible title to the document regardless of how the browser handles the <title> tag contents. And, unlike the <title> text, the heading title will appear at the beginning of the first page should the user elect to print the document. [<title>, 3.6.2]

In the example, we chose to use a level-3 header (<h3>) whose rendered font typically is just a bit larger than the regular document text. Levels one and two are larger still and often a bit overbearing. You should choose a level of heading that you find useful and attractive and use that level consistently throughout your documents.

Once you have established the top-level heading for your document, use additional headings at the same or lower level throughout to add structure and "scanability" to the document. If you use a level-3 heading for the document title, break your document into several sections using level-4 headings. If you have the urge to subdivide your text further, consider using a level-2 heading for the title, level-3 for the section dividers, and level-4 for the subsections.

4.2.3 Using Headings for Smaller Text

For most graphical browsers, the fonts used to display <h1>, <h2>, and <h3> headers are larger, <h4> is the same, and <h5> and <h6> are smaller than the regular text size. HTML writers typically use the latter two sizes for boilerplate text, like a disclaimer or a copyright notice. Experiment with <h5> and <h6> to get the effect you want. See how a typical browser renders the copyright reference in the following sample HTML segment (Figure 4-5):

```
resulting in years of successful kumquat production
throughout North America.
</p>
<h6>This document copyright 1995 by the Kumquat Growers of
America.
<br>
All rights reserved. </h6>
</body>
</html>
```

4.2.4 Allowed Heading Content

A heading may contain any element allowed in *text*, including conventional text, link anchors (<a>), images (<img>), line breaks (<br>), font embellishments (<b>, <i>, <tt>, <u>, <strike>, and <font>), and content-based style changes (<cite>, <code>, <em>, <kbd>, <samp>, <strong>, and <var>).

In practice, however, font or style changes may not take effect within a heading, since the heading itself prescribes a font change within the browser.

There is widespread abuse of the heading tags as a mechanism for changing the font of an entire document. Technically, paragraphs, lists, and other block elements are not allowed within a heading and may be mistaken by the browser to indicate the implied end of the heading. In practice, most browsers apply the style of the heading to all contained paragraphs. We discourage this practice since it is

Figure 4–5: HTML authors typically use header level 6 for boilerplate text

not only a violation of the HTML standard, but usually ugly to look at. Imagine if your local paper printed all the copy in headline type!

4.2.5 Allowed Heading Usage

Formally, the HTML standard allows headings only within *body_content*. In practice, most browsers recognize headings almost anywhere, formatting the rendered text to fit within the current element. In all cases, the occurrence of a heading signifies the end of any preceding paragraph or other text element. So you can't use the headings tags to change font sizes in the same line. Netscape and Internet Explorer, however, have special extensions for inline font size adjustments within a heading; see 4.6 for details.

4.2.6 Adding Images to Headings

It is possible to insert one or more images within your headings, from small bullets or icons to full-sized logos. Combining a consistent set of headings with corresponding icons across a family of documents is not only visually attractive, but an effective way of aiding users' perusal of your document collection. [<img>, 5.2.6]

Adding an image to a heading is easy. For example,

```
<h2>
<img src="info.gif">
For More Information</h2>
```

puts an "information" icon inside the "For More Information" heading as you can see in Figure 4-6.

In general, images within headings look best at the beginning of the heading, aligned with the bottom or middle of the heading text.

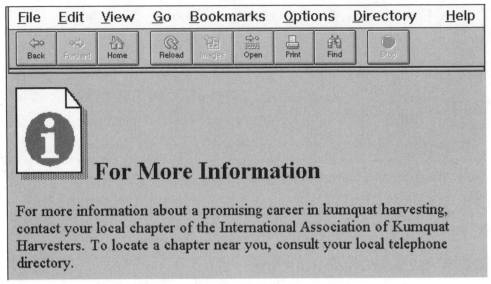

Figure 4–6: An image within a heading

4.3 Changing Text Appearance

HTML offers a number of tags that change the appearance of text. In general, these tags can be grouped into two flavors: content-based styles and physical styles.

4.3.1 Content-based Styles

Content-based style tags inform the browser that the enclosed text has a specific meaning, context, or usage. The browser then formats the text in a manner consistent with that meaning, context, or usage.

Because font style is specified via semantic clues, the browser can choose a display style that is appropriate for the user. Since such styles vary by locale, using content-based styles helps ensure that your documents will have meaning to a broader range of readers. This is particularly important when a browser is targeted at blind or handicapped readers whose display options are radically different from conventional text or are extremely limited in some way.

The HTML standard does not define a format for each of the content-based styles except that they must be rendered in a manner different from the regular text in a document. The standard doesn't even insist that the content-based styles be rendered differently from one another. In practice, you'll find that many of these tags have fairly obvious relationships with conventional print, having similar meanings and rendered styles, and are rendered in the same style and fonts by most browsers.

4.3.2 Physical Styles

We use the word "intent" a lot when we talk about content-based style tags. That's because the meaning conveyed by the tag is more important than the way a browser displays the text. In some cases, however, you might want the text to appear explicitly in italic or bold, perhaps for legal or copyright reasons. In those cases, use a physical style for the text.

While the tendency with other text-processing systems is to control style and appearance explicitly, with HTML you should avoid explicit, physical tags except on rare occasions. Rather, provide the browser with as much contextual information as possible. Use the content-based styles. Even though current browsers may do nothing more than display their text in italic or bold, future browsers and various document-generation tools may use the content-based styles in any number of creative ways.

4.4 Content-based Style Tags

It takes discipline to use the content-based styles, since it is easier to simply think of how your text should look, not necessarily what it may also mean. Once you get started using content-based styles, your documents will be more consistent and better lend themselves to automated searching and content compilation.

Content-based Style Tags

Function:
Alter the appearance of text based upon the meaning, context, or usage of the text

Attributes:
None

End tag:
Never omitted

Contains:
text

Used in:
text

4.4.1 The <cite> Tag

The <cite> tag usually indicates that the enclosed text is a bibliographic citation like a book or magazine title. By convention, the citation text is rendered in italic. For example, NCSA's Mosaic renders the source:

```
While kumquats are not mentioned in Melville's
<cite>Moby Dick</cite>, it is nonetheless apparent
that the mighty cetacean represents the bitter
"kumquat-ness" within every man. Indeed, when Ahab
spears the beast, its flesh is tough, much like the noble fruit.
```

as shown in Figure 4-7.

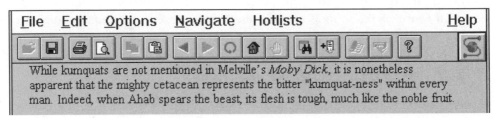

Figure 4–7: Mosaic renders <cite> in italic

Use the <cite> tag to set apart any reference to another document, especially those in the traditional media, such as books, magazines, journal articles, and the like. If an online version of the referenced work exists, you also should enclose the citation within the <a> tag and make it a hyperlink to that online version.

The <cite> tag also has a hidden feature: it enables you or someone else to automatically extract a bibliography from your documents. It is easy to envision a browser that compiles tables of citations automatically, displaying them as footnotes or as a separate document entirely. The semantics of the <cite> tag go far beyond changing the appearance of the enclosed text; they enable the browser to present the content to the user in a variety of useful ways.

4.4.2 The <code> Tag

Software code warriors have become accustomed to a special style of text presentation for their source programs. The <code> tag is for them. It renders the enclosed text in a monospaced, teletypewriter-style font like Courier familiar to most programmers and readers of O'Reilly's series of books, including this one.

This following bit of en<code>d text is rendered in monospaced font style by Netscape as shown in Figure 4-8.

```
The array reference <code>a[i]</code> is identical to
the pointer reference <code>*(a+i)</code>.
```

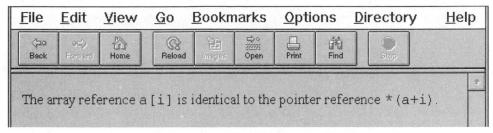

Figure 4-8: Use <code> to present computer-speak

You should use the `<code>` tag only for text that represents computer source code or other machine-readable content. While the `<code>` tag usually just makes text appear in a monospaced font, the implication is that it is source code and future browsers may add other display effects. For example, a programmer's browser might look for `<code>` segments and perform some additional text formatting like special indentation of loops and conditional clauses. If the only effect you desire is a monospaced font, use the `<tt>` tag instead.

4.4.3 The <dfn> Tag

Intended to set apart a definition, the `<dfn>` tag is only supported by Internet Explorer; it is ignored by the other browsers. Nonetheless, we recommend using the `<dfn>` tag for the reasons you use the other content-based tags: for their meaning, not how some browser formats its enclosed text formatting.

4.4.4 The <em> Tag

The `<em>` tag tells the client browser to present the enclosed text with emphasis. For nearly all browsers, this means the text is rendered in italic. For example, Mosaic will emphasize by italicizing the words "always" and "never" in the following sample:

```
Kumquat growers must <em>always</em> refer to kumquats
as "the noble fruit," <em>never</em> as just a "fruit."
```

Adding emphasis to your text is a tricky business. Too little, and the emphatic phrases may be lost. Too much, and you lose the urgency. Like any seasoning, emphasis is best used sparingly.

Although invariably displayed in italic, the `<em>` tag has broader implications as well and someday browsers may render emphasized text with a different special effect. The <i> tag explicitly italicizes text; use it if all you want are italic. Besides emphasis, also consider using <em> when presenting new terms or as a fixed style when referring to a specific type of term or concept. For instance, one of O'Reilly's book styles is to specially format file and device names. In the HTML version, <em> might be used to differentiate those terms from simple italic for emphasis.

4.4.5 The <kbd> Tag

Speaking of special style for technical concepts, there is the <kbd> tag. As you probably already suspect, it is used to indicate text that is typed on a keyboard. Its enclosed text typically is rendered by the browser in monospaced font style.

The <kbd> tag is most often used in computer-related documentation and manuals, such as in the example,

```
Type <kbd>quit</kbd> to exit the utility, or type
<kbd>menu</kbd> to return to the main menu.
```

4.4.6 The <samp> Tag

The <samp> tag indicates a sequence of literal characters that should have no other interpretation by the user. This tag is most often used when a sequence of characters is taken out of its normal context. For example,

```
The <samp>ae</samp> character sequence may be converted
to the &aelig; ligature if desired.
```

is rendered by Netscape as shown in Figure 4-9.

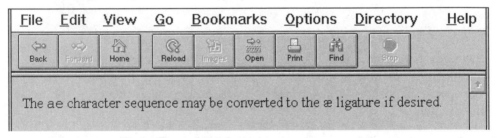

Figure 4-9: Setting off sample text using the <samp> tag

(The special HTML reference for the "ae" ligature entity is æ and is converted to its appropriate æ ligature character by most browsers.) For more information, see Appendix D, *Character Entities*.

In general, the `<samp>` tag is not used very often. It should be used in those few cases where special emphasis needs to be placed on small character sequences taken out of their normal context.

4.4.7 *The <strong> Tag*

Like the `<em>` tag, the `<strong>` tag is for emphasizing text, except with more gusto. Browsers display the `<strong>` tag differently than the `<em>` tag, usually by bolding the text versus italic, so that users can distinguish between the two. For example,

```
One should <em>never</em> make a disparaging remark
about the noble fruit. In particular, mentioning
kumquats in conjunction with vulgar phrases is
expressly <strong>forbidden</strong> by the Association
bylaws.
```

the emphasized "never" appears in italic with Mosaic, while the `<strong>` "forbidden" is rendered in bold characters (Figure 4-10).

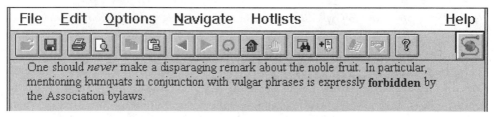

Figure 4–10: Strong and emphasized text are rendered differently by Mosaic

If common sense tells us that the `<em>` tag should be used sparingly, the `<strong>` tag should appear in documents even more infrequently. `<em>` text is like shouting. `<strong>` text is nothing short of a scream. Like a well-chosen epithet voiced by an otherwise taciturn person, restraint in the use of `<strong>` makes its use that much more noticeable and effective.

4.4.8 *The <var> Tag*

The `<var>` tag, another computer-documentation trick, indicates a variable name or a user-supplied value. The tag is most often used in conjunction with the `<code>` and `<pre>` tags for displaying particular elements of computer programming code samples and the like. `<var>` tagged text typically is rendered in monospace font, as shown in Figure 4-11 of Netscape's display of the following example:

```
The user should type
<pre>
   cp <var>source-file</var>   <var>dest-file</var>
</pre>
replacing the <var>source-file</var> with the name of
the source file, and <var>dest-file</var> with the name
of the destination file.
```

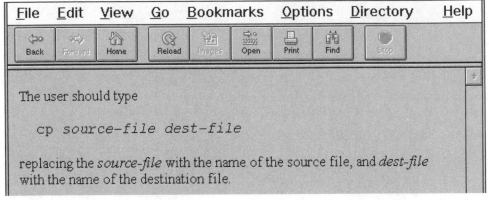

Figure 4-11: The <var> tag typically appears in preformatted (<pre>) computer code

Like the other computer programming and documentation-related tags, the <var> tag not only makes it easy for users to understand and browse your documentation, but automated systems might someday use the appropriately tagged text to extract information and useful parameters mentioned in your document. Once again, the more semantic information you provide to your browser, the better it can present that information to the user.

4.4.9 Summary of Content-based Tags

The various graphical browsers render text inside content-based tags in similar fashion; text-only browsers like Lynx have consistent styles for the tags. Table 4-1 summarizes these browser's display styles.

Table 4-1: Content-based Tags

Tag	Netscape	Mosaic	Internet Explorer	Lynx
<cite>	*italic*	*italic*	*italic*	monospace
<code>	monospace	monospace	monospace	monospace
<dfn>	n/a	n/a	*italic*	n/a
<em>	*italic*	*italic*	*italic*	monospace
<kbd>	monospace	*italic*	monospace bold	monospace

Table 4-1: Content-based Tags (continued)

Tag	Netscape	Mosaic	Internet Explorer	Lynx
`<samp>`	`monospace`	`monospace`	`monospace`	`monospace`
`<strong>`	bold	bold	bold	`monospace`
`<var>`	*italic*	*italic*	`monospace`	`monospace`

4.4.10 Allowed Content

Any content-based style tag may contain any item allowed in *text*, including conventional text, anchors, images, and line breaks. In addition, other content-based and physical style tags can be embedded within the content.

4.4.11 Allowed Usage

Any content-based style tag may be used anywhere an item allowed in *text* is used. In practice, this means you can use the `<em>`, `<code>`, or other like tags anywhere in your HTML document except inside `<title>`, `<listing>`, or `<xmp>` tagged segments. You can use text style tags in headings, too, but their effect may be overridden by the effects of the heading tag itself.

4.4.12 Combining Styles

It may have occurred to you to combine two or more of the various content-based styles to create interesting and perhaps even useful hybrids. Thus, an emphatic citation might be achieved with:

```
<cite><em>Moby Dick</em></cite>
```

In practice, Dr. Frankenstein, the browser usually ignores the monster and, as you can test by typing and viewing the example yourself, Moby Dick gets the citation without emphasis.

The HTML standard does not require the browser to support every possible combination of styles and does not define how the browser should handle such combinations. Someday, maybe. For now, it's best to choose one tag and be satisfied.

4.5 Physical Style Tags

There are five physical styles provided by the current HTML standard for bold, italic, monospaced, underlined, and strike-through text. In addition, the advanced browsers already have implemented a few other physical style tags, some of which are part of the proposed HTML 3.2 standard, including superscripting, subscripting, big, small, and blinking text. All physical style tags require an ending tag.

Physical Style Tags

Function:
    Specify a physical style for text

Attributes:
    None

End tag:
    Never omitted

Contains:
    text

Used in:
    text

4.5.1 The <b> Tag

The `<b>` tag is the physical equivalent of the `<strong>` content-based style tag, but without the latter's extended meaning. The `<b>` tag explicitly boldfaces a character or segment of text that is enclosed between it and its corresponding (`</b>`) end tag. If a boldface font is not available, the browser may use some other representation, such as reverse video or underlining.

4.5.2 The <big> Tag

The `<big>` tag is a Netscape-only HTML extension that makes it easy to increase the size of text without worrying about all of the details of virtual font sizes available with the `<font>` tag described below. It couldn't be simpler: Netscape renders the text between the `<big>` tag and its matching `</big>` ending tag one font size larger than the surrounding text. If that text is already at the largest size, `<big>` has no effect. [`<font>`, 4.6.3]

Even better, you can nest `<big>` tags to enlarge the text. Each `<big>` tag makes the text one size larger, up to a limit of size seven, as defined by the font model.

Careful with your use of the `<big>` tag, though. Because browsers are quite forgiving and try hard to understand a tag, those that don't support `<big>` often interpret it to mean bold.

4.5.3 The <blink> Tag

Text contained between the `<blink>` tag and its end tag `</blink>` does just that: blink on and off. Netscape for Macintosh, for example, simply and reiteratively reverses the background and foreground colors for the `<blink>` enclosed text.

We cannot effectively reproduce the animated effect here in these static pages, but it is easy to imagine and probably best left to the imagination, too. That's because blinking text has two primary effects: it gets your reader's attention, and then promptly annoys them to no end. Blinking text should be used sparingly in any context.

4.5.4 *The <i> Tag*

The `<i>` tag is like the `<em>` content-based style tag. It and its necessary (`</i>`) end tag tell the browser to render the enclosed text in an italic or oblique typeface. If the typeface is not available to the browser, highlighting, reverse video, or underlining might be used.

4.5.5 *The <small> Tag*

Netscape's `<small>` tag works just like its `<big>` extension (see above), except it decreases the size of text instead of increasing it. If the enclosed text is already at the smallest size supported by the font model, `<small>` has no effect.

Like `<big>`, you may also nest `<small>` tags to sequentially shrink text. Each `<small>` tag makes the text one size smaller than the containing `<small>` tag, down to a limit of size one.

4.5.6 *The <s> Tag*

The `<s>` tag is Internet Explorer's abbreviated form of the `<strike>` tag.

4.5.7 *The <strike> Tag*

Most browsers will put a line through ("strike through") text that appears inside the `<strike>` tag and its `</strike>` end tag. Presumably, it is an editing markup that tells the reader to ignore the text passage, reminiscent of the days before typewriter correction tape. You'll rarely, if ever, see the tag in use today, but expect it to become more commonplace as marketeers of consumer items hawked on the Web slash prices on their slow-moving products.

4.5.8 *The <sub> Tag*

Like its `<sup>` counterpart (see below), the `<sub>` subscripting tag is not part of the HTML 2.0 standard, but is implemented in the latest versions of Netscape Navigator and NCSA Mosaic. The text contained between the `<sub>` tag and its `</sub>` end tag gets displayed half a character lower, but in the same font and size as the current text flow. Both `<sub>` and its `<sup>` counterpart are useful for math equations and in scientific notation.

4.5.9 The <sup> Tag

Mosaic and Netscape already support this proposed HTML standard (3.2) tag.

The <sup> tag and its </sup> end tag superscripts the enclosed text; it gets displayed half a character higher, but in the same font and size as the current text flow.

4.5.10 The <tt> Tag

In a manner like the <code> and <kbd> tags, the <tt> tag and necessary </tt> end tag direct the browser to display the enclosed text in a monospaced typeface. For those browsers that already use a monospaced typeface, this tag may make no discernible change in the presentation of the text.

4.5.11 The <u> Tag

This tag, supported by Mosaic and Internet Explorer, underlines the text contained between the <u> and the corresponding </u> tag. The underlining technique is simplistic, drawing the line under spaces and punctuation as well as the text.

4.5.12 Physical Tag Examples

The following HTML source example illustrates some of the various physical tags as rendered by Netscape for Figure 4-12:

```
Explicitly <b>boldfaced</b>, <i>italicized</i>, or
<tt>teletype-style</tt> text should be used
<big><big>sparingly</big></big>.
Otherwise, drink <strike>lots</strike> 1x10<sup>6</sup>
drops of H<sub><small><small>2</small></small></sub>O.
```

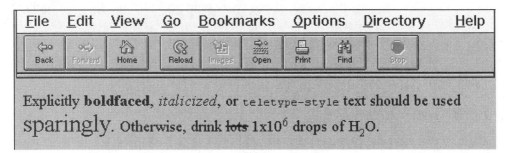

Figure 4–12: Use physical text tags with caution

4.5.13 Allowed Content

Any physical style tag may contain any item allowed in *text*, including conventional text, anchors, images, and line breaks. You also can combine physical style tags with other content-based ones.

4.5.14 Allowed Usage

Any physical style tag may used anywhere an item allowed in *text* can be used. In general, this means anywhere within a document except in the `<title>`, `<listing>`, and `<xmp>` tags. You could use a physical style tag in a heading, but the browser will probably override and ignore its effect in lieu of the heading tag.

4.5.15 Combining Styles

You probably will have better luck, Dr. Frankenstein, combining physical tags than you might have combining content-based tags to achieve multiple effects. For instance, Netscape renders the following in bold and italic typeface:

```
<b><i>Thar she blows!</i></b>
```

In practice, other browsers may elect to ignore such nesting: the HTML standard does not require the browser to support every possible combination of styles and does not define how the browser should handle such combinations. Although the extended browsers make a good attempt at doing so, do not assume that all combinations will be available to you.

Combining physical with content-based styles is not a completely bad idea, however. For instance, most browsers don't specially format definitions enclosed by the `<dfn>` tag because they don't support this as-yet-to-be-standardized content-based tag. Still, we argue you should use the `<dfn>` for its meaning more than its rendering style. To achieve the latter effect, consider adding italic physical tags to the definition segment. At worst, future browsers that support `<dfn>` will ignore the `<i>` tag. For example:

```
Kumquat: <i><dfn>A fruit some find delectable.</dfn></i>
```

4.6 Expanded Font Handling

Netscape Navigator and Internet Explorer have features beyond HTML 2.0 that give you more explicit control over the colors and sizes of the font characters that form your HTML text. Explorer even has a way for you to specify the display font itself.

Don't get overly excited, though. The font extensions and conventions don't override standard HTML. Header tags and their respective effects on font size still work. So do the various physical tags like <b> and <i>. With fonts, the extensions truly are extensions, not revisions.

4.6.1 The Extended Font Size Model

Instead of absolute point values, Netscape and Internet Explorer use a relative model for sizing fonts. Ranging in size from 1, the smallest, to 7, the largest, the default (*basefont*) font size is 3.

It is almost impossible to reliably state the actual font sizes used for the various virtual sizes. Most browsers let the user change the physical font size, and the default sizes vary from browser to browser. It may be helpful to know, however, that for the fonts-extended browsers, each virtual size is successively 20 percent larger or smaller than the default font size 3. Thus, font size 4 is 20 percent larger, font size 5 is 40 percent larger, and so on, while font size 2 is 20 percent smaller and font size 1 is 40 percent smaller than font size 3.

4.6.2 The <basefont> Tag

The <basefont> tag lets you define the basic size for the font that Netscape Navigator and Internet Explorer use to render normal document text.

<basefont> (extension)

Function:
Define basefont size for relative font size changes

Attributes:
SIZE

End Tag:
</basefont>, optionally used

Contains:
Nothing

Used in:
block, head_content

The <basefont> tag has a single required attribute, size, whose value determines the document's base font size. It may be specified as an absolute value from 1 to 7, or as a relative value by placing a plus or minus sign before the value. In the latter case, the base font size is increased or decreased by that relative amount. The default base font size is 3.

Authors typically include the `<basefont>` tag in the head of an HTML document, if at all, to set the base font size for the entire document. Nonetheless, the tag may appear nearly anywhere in the document, and it may appear several times throughout the document, each with a new size attribute. With each occurrence, the `<basefont>` tag's effects are immediate and hold for all subsequent text.

In an egregious deviation from the HTML and SGML standards, the ending `</basefont>` tag *does not* terminate the effects of the most recent `<basefont>` tag. Instead, the `</basefont>` end tag resets the base font size to the default value of 3, which is the same as writing `<basefont size=3>`.

The following example source and Figure 4-13 illustrate how Netscape responds to the `<basefont>` tag and `</basefont>` end tag, including fixed and relative attribute values:

```
Unless the base font size was reset above,
Netscape renders this part in font size 3.
<basefont size=7>
This text should be rather large (size 7).
<basefont size=-1> Oh,
<basefont size=-1> no!
<basefont size=-1> I'm
<basefont size=-1> shrinking!
</basefont>
Ah, back to normal.
```

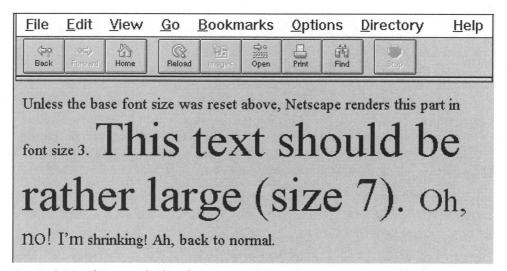

Figure 4-13: Playing with <basefont>

4.6.3 The <font> Tag

The <font> tag lets you change the size, style, and color of text. It should be used like any other physical or content-based style tag for changing the appearance of a short segment of text.

<font> (extension)

Function:
    Set the font size for text

Attributes:
    COLOR (extension)
    FACE (Internet Explorer only)
    SIZE (extension)

End Tag:
    </font>, always used

Contains:
    text

Used in:
    text

To control the color of text for the entire document, see the special extension attributes for the <body> tag described in Chapter 5.

4.6.3.1 The size attribute

The value of the size attribute must be one of the virtual font sizes (1-7) described earlier, defined as an absolute size for the enclosed text or preceded by a plus or minus sign (+ or -) to define a relative font size that Netscape Navigator or Internet Explorer adds to or subtracts from the base font size (see the <basefont> tag above). The extended browsers automatically round the size to 1 or 7 if the calculated value exceeds either boundary.

In general, use absolute size values when you want the rendered text to be an extreme size, either very large or very small, or when you want an entire paragraph of text to be a specific size.

For example, using the largest font for the first character of a paragraph makes for a crude form of illustrated manuscript (see Figure 4-14):

```
<p>
<font size=7>C</font>all me Ishmael.
```

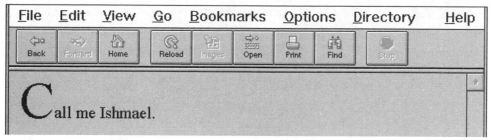

Figure 4-14: Exaggerating the first character of a sentence

Also use an absolute font when inserting a delightfully unreadable bit of "fine" print—boilerplate or legalese—at the bottom of your documents (Figure 4-15):

Figure 4-15: Use the tiniest font for boilerplate text

```
<p>
<font size=1>
All rights reserved. Unauthorized redistribution of this document is
prohibited. Opinions expressed herein are those of the authors, not the
Internet Service Provider.
```

Except for the extremes, use relative font sizes to render text in a size different than the surrounding text, to emphasize a word or phrase, for example (see Figure 4-16):

Figure 4-16: Use relative sizes for most Netscape text embellishments

```
<p>
Make sure you <font size=+1>always</font> sign and date the form!
```

If your relative size change results in a size greater than seven, Netscape uses font 7. Similarly, font sizes less than one are rendered with font 1.

Notice that, with Netscape, specifying `size=+1` or `size=-1` is identical in effect to the alternate tags, `<big>` and `<small>` respectively. However, nested relative changes to the font size are not cumulative as they are for the alternate tags. Each `<font>` tag is relative to the base font size, not the current font size. [`<big>`, 4.5.2]

For example (see Figure 4-17):

```
<p>
The ghost moaned, "oo<font size=+1>oo<font size=+2>oo<font
size=+3>oo</font>oo</font>oo</font>oo."
```

Contrast this with the `<big>` tag, which increases the size one level as you nest the tags.

Figure 4–17: Relative font sizes accumulate

4.6.3.2 The color attribute

The `color` attribute for the `<font>` tag sets the color of the enclosed text. The value of the attribute may be expressed in either of two ways: as the red, green, and blue (RGB) components of the desired color or as a standard color name. Enclosing quotes are recommended, but not required.

The RGB color value, denoted by a preceding hash mark (#), is a six-digit hexadecimal number. The first two digits are the red component, from 00 (no red) to FF (bright red). Similarly, the next two digits are the green component and the last two digits are the blue component. Black is the absence of color, #000000; white is all colors, #FFFFFF.

For example, to create basic yellow text, you might use:

```
Here comes the <font color="#FFFF00">sun</font>!
```

Alternatively, you may set the enclosed font color using any one of the many standard color names. See Appendix E, *Color Names and Values*, for a list of common ones. For instance, you could also have made the above sample's text yellow with the following source:

```
Here comes the <font color=yellow>sun</font>!
```

4.6.3.3 *The face attribute*

Internet Explorer lets you change the font style in a text passage with the `face` attribute for the `<font>` tag.[*] The quote-enclosed value of `face` is one or more display font names separated with commas.

The font face displayed by the browser depends on which fonts are available on the individual user's system. The browser parses the list of font names, one after the other, until it matches one with a font name supported by the user's system. If none match, the text display defaults to the font style set by the user in their browser's Preferences.

For example:

```
This text is in the default font. But,
<font face="Braggadocio, Machine, Zapf Dingbats">
heaven only knows</font>
what font face is this one?
```

If the Internet Explorer user has the `Braggadocio`, `Machine`, or none of the listed font typefaces installed in their system, they will be able to read the "heaven only knows" message in the respective or default font style. Otherwise, the message will be garbled because the Zapf Dingbats font contains symbols, not letters. Of course, the alternative is true, too; you may intend that the message be a symbol-encoded secret.

4.7 *Precise Spacing and Layout*

Frankly, if you find yourself overly concerned with layout, positioning, font styles, colors, and spacing of your text, you have missed the fundamental concept of HTML. It's designed for specifying document content without indicating format. The tags in HTML delineate the structure and semantics of a document, not how that document is to be presented to the user. Word wrapping, character and line spacing, and other presentation details are left to the browser. That way, the document's content—its rich information, not good looks—are what matter. Current

---

[*] For the HTML purist, for the once-powerful user, who had ultimate control over their browser, this is egregious, indeed. Form over function; look over content—what next? Embedded video commercials you can't stop?

and, in particular, future browsers will present the document in ways that best suit the needs of the user.

Unfortunately, many people consider HTML to be a primitive word-processing language whose arcane and incomplete text formatting directives poorly dictate the final appearance of a document. Using HTML in this fashion is frustrating and pointless, serving neither the author nor the reader of the document. If you find yourself using HTML in this fashion, you should seriously reconsider your approach to document creation for the World Wide Web.

That said, there are certain occasions when explicitly interrupting normal HTML text formatting makes sense. Besides, HTML currently is the *only* language of the World Wide Web. And, clearly, commercial advertising and other forms of style-over-content, short-lived HTML documents do need to have some control over format. We're adamant, not fanatic.

4.7.1 The
 Tag

The <br> tag interrupts the normal line filling and word wrapping of paragraphs within an HTML document. It has no ending tag, but simply marks the point in the flow where a new line should begin. Most browsers simply stop adding words and images to the current line, move down and over to the left margin, and resume filling and wrapping.

---

*
*

Function:
    Insert a line break into a text flow
Attributes:
    CLEAR (extension)
End tag:
    None
Contains:
    Nothing
Used in:
    text

This effect is handy when formatting conventional text with fixed line breaks, such as addresses, song lyrics, or poetry. Notice, for example, the lyrical breaks when the following source is rendered by Netscape (Figure 4-18).

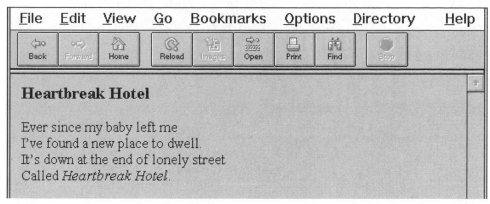

Figure 4–18: Give lyrics their breaks (<br>)

```
<h3>
Heartbreak Hotel</h3>
<p>
Ever since my baby left me<br>
I've found a new place to dwell.<br>
It's down at the end of lonely street<br>
Called <cite>Heartbreak Hotel</cite>.
</p>
```

Also notice how the `<br>` tag causes text to simply start a new line, while the browser, when encountering the `<p>` tag, typically inserts some vertical space between adjacent paragraphs. [<p>, 4.1.2]

4.7.1.1 The clear attribute

Normally, the `<br>` tag tells the browser to immediately stop the current flow of text and resume at the left margin of the next line or against the right border of a left-justified inline graphic. Sometimes you'd rather the current text flow resume below any images currently blocking the left or right margins.

Netscape and Internet Explorer provide that capability with the `clear` attribute for the `<br>` tag. It can have one of three values: `left`, `right`, or `all`, each related to one or both of the margins. When the specified margin or both margins are clear of images, the extended browser resumes the text flow.

Figure 4-19 illustrates the effects of the `clear` attribute when Netscape renders the following HTML fragment:

```
<img src="http:kumquat.gif" align=left>
This text should wrap around the image, flowing between the
image and the right margin of the document.
<br clear=left>
This text will flow as well, but will be below the image,
extending across the full width of the page. There will
```

```
be white space above this text and to the right of the
image.
```

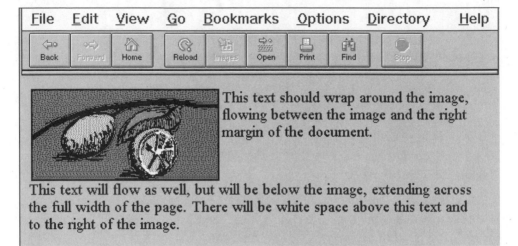

Figure 4–19: Clearing images before resuming text flow after the <br> tag

Inline HTML images are just that—normally in line with text, but usually only a single line of text. Additional lines of text flow below the image unless that image is specially aligned by right or left attribute values for the `<img>` tag. Hence, the `clear` attribute for the `<br>` tag only works in combination with a left- or right-aligned image. [image alignment, 5.2.6.4]

The following HTML code fragment illustrates how to use the `<br>` tag and its `clear` attribute as well as the extended browser's `<img>` extension attributes to place captions directly above, centered on the right, and below an image that is aligned against the left margin of the browser window (Figure 4-20):

```
Paragraph tags separate leading and following
text flow from the captions.
<p>
I'm the caption on top of the image.
<br>
<img src="kumquat.gif" align=absmiddle>
This one's centered on the right.
<br clear=left>
This caption should be directly below the image.
<p>
And the text just keeps flowing along....
```

However, it is not easy to align a text caption directly above or beneath a right-justified image because you cannot predict the exact size of the browser window.

You might also include a `<br clear=all>` tag just after an `<img>` tag that is at the very end of a section of your document. That way you ensure, at least with the

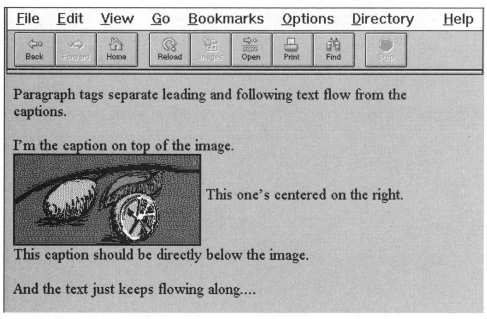

Figure 4–20: Captions placed on top, center-right, and below an image

extended browsers, that the subsequent section's text doesn't flow up and against that image and confuse the reader. [<img>, 5.2.6]

4.7.2 The <nobr> Tag

Occasionally, you may have a phrase you want to appear unbroken on a single line in the user's browser window, even if that means the text extends beyond the visible region of the window. Computer commands are good examples. Typically, one types in a computer command—even a multiword one—on a single line. Because you cannot predict exactly how many words will fit inside an individual's browser window, the HTML-based sequence of computer-command words may end up broken into two or more lines of text. Command syntax is confusing enough; it doesn't need the extra cross-eyed effect of being wrapped onto two lines.

With standard HTML, the way to make sure text phrases stay intact across the browser display is to enclose those segments in a <pre> tag and format it by hand. That's acceptable and nearly universal for all browsers. However, <pre> alters the display font from the regular text, and manual line breaks inside the <pre> tag are not always rendered correctly. [<pre>, 4.7.5]

The extended browsers offer the <nobr> tag alternative to <pre> so you can be sure enclosed text stays intact on a single line while retaining normal text style.

<nobr> (extension)

Function:

    Create a region of non-breaking text

Attributes:

    None

End Tag:

    </nobr>; always used

Contains:

    text

Used in:

    block

The effect is to make the browser treat the tag's contents as though they were a single, unbroken word. The tag contents retain the current font style, and you can change to another style within the tag.

Here's the <nobr> tag in action with our computer-command example:

```
When prompted by the computer, enter
<nobr>
<tt>find . -name \*.html -exec rm \{\}\;</tt>.
</nobr>
After a few moments, the load on your server will begin
to diminish and will eventually drop to zero.
```

Notice in the example source and its display (Figure 4-21) that we've included the special <tt> tag inside the <nobr> tag. If the <nobr>-tagged text cannot fit on a partially filled line of text, the extended browser precedes it with a line break, as shown in the figure. The <nobr> segment may then extend beyond the right window boundary.

The <nobr> tag does not suspend the browser's normal line-filling process; it still collects and inserts images and—believe it, or not—asserts forced line breaks caused by the <br> or <p> tags, for example. The <nobr> tag's only action is to suppress an automatic line break when the current line reaches the right margin.

Also, you might think this tag is needed only to suppress line breaks for phrases, not a sequence of characters without spaces that can exceed the browser window's display boundaries. Today's browsers do not hyphenate words automatically, but someday soon they probably will. It makes sense to protect any break-sensitive sequence of characters with the <nobr> tag.

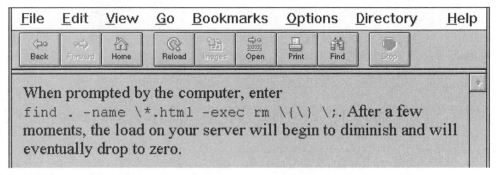

Figure 4-21: The <nobr> extension suppresses text wrapping

4.7.3 The <wbr> Tag

The <wbr> tag is the height of HTML text-layout finesse. Used with the <nobr> tag, <wbr> advises the extended browser when it may insert a line break in an otherwise nonbreakable sequence of text. Unlike the <br> tag, which always causes a line break even within a <nobr> tagged segment, the <wbr> tag works only when placed inside a <nobr>-tagged content segment and causes a line break only if the current line already had extended beyond the browser's display window margins.

<wbr> (extension)

Function:
   Define potential line break point

Attributes:
   None

End Tag:
   None

Contains:
   Nothing

Used in:
   text

Now, <wbr> may seem incredibly esoteric to you, but scowl not: there may come a time when you want to make sure portions of your document appear on a single line, but you don't want to overrun the browser window margins so far that readers will have to camp on the horizontal scroll bar just to read your fine prose. By inserting the <wbr> tag at appropriate points in the nonbreaking sequence, you let the browser gently break the text into more manageable lines:

```
<p>
<nobr>
This is a very long sequence of text that is
forced to be on a single line, even if doing so causes
<wbr>
the browser to extend the document window beyond the
size of the viewing pane and the por user must scroll right
<wbr>
to read the entire line.
</nobr>
```

You'll notice in our rendered version (Figure 4-22) that both <wbr> tags take effect. By increasing the horizontal window size or by reducing the font size, you may fit all of the segment before the first <wbr> tag within the browser window. In that case, only the second <wbr> would have an effect; all the text leading up to it would extend beyond the window's margins.

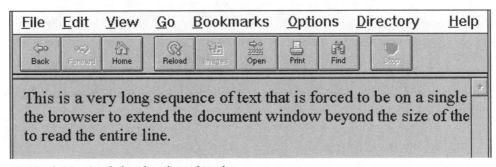

Figure 4-22: Gentle line breaks with <wbr>

4.7.4 Better Line-Breaking Rules

Unlike most browsers, and to their credit, Netscape and Internet Explorer do not consider tags to be a line-break opportunity. Consider the unfortunate consequences to your document's display if, while rendering the example segment below, the browser puts the comma adjacent to the "du" or the period adjacent to the word "df" on a separate line. Netscape and Internet Explorer will not:

```
Make sure you type <tt>du</tt>, not <tt>df</tt>.
```

4.7.5 The <pre> Tag

The <pre> tag and its required end tag (</pre>) define a segment inside which the browser renders text in exactly the character and line spacing defined in the source HTML document. Normal word wrapping and paragraph filling are disabled and extraneous leading and trailing spaces are honored. The browser displays all text between the <pre> and </pre> tags in a monospaced font.

<pre>

Function:
Render a block of text without any formatting

Attributes:
WIDTH

End tag:
</pre>; never omitted

Contains:
pre_content

Used in:
block

HTML authors most often use the <pre> formatting tag when the integrity of columns and rows of characters must be retained, for instance in tables of numbers that must line up correctly. Another application for <pre> is to set aside a blank segment—a series of blank lines—in the document display, perhaps to clearly separate one content section from another, or to temporarily hide a portion of the document when it first loads and is rendered by the user's browser.

Tab characters have their desired effect within the <pre> block, with tab stops defined at every eight character positions. We discourage their use, however, since tabs aren't consistently implemented among the various browsers. Use spaces to ensure correct horizontal positioning of text within <pre> formatted text segments.

A common use of the <pre> tag is to present computer source code, as in the following example which is displayed by Mosaic as shown in Figure 4-23:

```
<p>
The processing program is:
<pre>
main(int argc, char **argv)

{   FILE *f;
    int i;

    if (argc != 2)
      fprintf(stderr, "usage: %s &lt;file&gt;\n",
          argv[0]);
    <a href="http:process.c">
process</a>
(argv[1]);
    exit(0);
}
</pre>
```

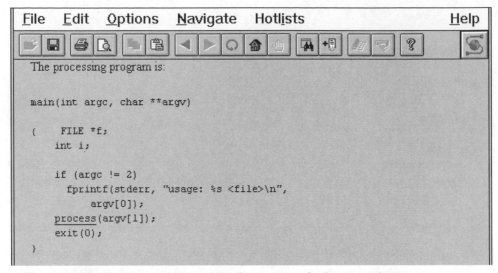

File   Edit   Options   Navigate   Hotlists   Help

The processing program is:

```
main(int argc, char **argv)

{    FILE *f;
    int i;

    if (argc != 2)
      fprintf(stderr, "usage: %s <file>\n",
          argv[0]};
    process(argv[1]);
    exit(0);
}
```

Figure 4–23: Use the <pre> tag to preserve the integrity of columns and rows

4.7.5.1 Allowable content

The text within a <pre> segment may contain physical and content-based style changes, along with anchors, images, and horizontal rules. When possible, the browser should honor style changes, within the constraint of using a monospaced font for the entire <pre> block.

Tags that cause a paragraph break (headings, <p>, and <address> tags, for example must not be used within the <pre> block. Some browsers will interpret paragraph-ending tags as simple line breaks, but this behavior is not consistent across all browsers.

Since style markup and other tags are allowed in a <pre> block, you must use entity equivalents for the literal characters: < for <, > for >, and & for the ampersand (&).

You place tags into the <pre> block as you would in any other portion of the HTML document. For instance, study the reference to the "process" function in the previous example. It contains a hyperlink (using the <a> tag) to its source file named "process.c."

4.7.5.2 The width attribute

The <pre> tag has a single optional attribute, width, that determines the number of characters to fit on a single line within the <pre> block. The browser may use this value to select a font or font size that fits the specified number of characters on each line in the `<pre>` block. It does not mean that the browser will wrap and fill text to the specified width. Rather, lines longer than the specified width simply extend beyond the visible region of the browser's window.

The `width` attribute is only advice for the user's browser; it may or may not be able to adjust the view font to the specified width.

4.7.6 The `<center>` Tag

Netscape and Internet Explorer support a special `<center>` tag that centers the text in each line, individually, after the text flow is filled and wrapped. The `<center>` alignment remains in effect until canceled with its `</center>` end tag.

`<center>`

Function:
Center a section of text

Attributes:
None

End tag:
`</center>`; never omitted

Contains:
body__content

Used in:
block

Line-by-line is a common, albeit primitive, way to center text and should be used judiciously. That's because the extended browsers do not attempt to balance a centered paragraph or other block-related elements, such as elements in a list. So, keep your centered text short and sweet. Titles make good centering candidates; a centered list usually is difficult to follow.

Beyond that, you'll rarely see conventional text centered, except for some lyrical prose, so readers may react badly to large segments of centered prose in your documents. Rather, `<center>` is more commonly used to center an image in the display window (there is no explicit center alignment option for inline images).

Because users will have varying window widths, display resolutions, and so on, you may also want to employ the `<nobr>` and `<wbr>` extension tags (see above) to keep your centered text intact and looking good. For example:

```
<center>
<nobr>
Copyright 1995 by QuatCo Enterprises.<wbr>
All rights reserved.
</nobr>
</center>
```

The <nobr> tags in the sample source help ensure that the text remains on a single line and the <wbr> tag controls where the line may be broken if it exceeds the browser's display window width.

Centering also is useful for creating distinctive section headers, although you may now achieve the same effect with an explicit `align=center` attribute in the respective heading tag. You might also center text using `align=center` in conjunction with the <div> or <p> tags.

4.7.7 The <listing> Tag

The <listing> tag is a deprecated element of HTML 2.0, meaning that its use is discouraged and that it may disappear entirely in subsequent versions of the language. We include it here for historical reasons, since it has the same effect on text formatting as the <pre> tag with a specified width of 132 characters.

<listing>

Function:
  Render a block of text without any formatting

Attributes:
  None

End tag:
  </listing>; never omitted

Contains:
  literal_text

Used in:
  block

The only difference between <pre> and <listing> is that no other markup is allowed within the <listing> tag. So you don't have to replace the literal <, >, and & characters with their entity equivalents in a <listing> block as you must inside a <pre> block.

Since the `<listing>` tag is the same as a `<pre width=132>` tag, and because it might not be supported in later version of the language, we recommend you stay away from using `<listing>`.

4.7.8 The <xmp> Tag

Like the `<listing>` tag, the `<xmp>` tag is a deprecated element of HTML 2.0 included here mostly for historical reasons.

<xmp>

Function:
  Render a block of text without any formatting
Attributes:
  None
End tag:
  </xmp>, never omitted
Contains:
  literal_text
Used in:
  block

The `<xmp>` tag formats text just like the `<pre>` tag with a specified width of 80 characters. However, unlike the `<pre>` tag, you don't have to replace the literal <, >, and & characters with their entity equivalents within an `<xmp>` block. The name `<xmp>` is short for "example"; the language's designers intended the tag be used to format examples of text originally displayed on 80-column wide displays. Because the 80-column display has mostly gone the way of green screens and teletypes, and since the effect of a `<xmp>` tag is basically the same as `<pre width=80>`, don't use `<xmp>`; it may disappear entirely in subsequent versions of HTML.

4.7.9 The <plaintext> Tag

Tired of tags? Insert a `<plaintext>` tag into your document and browsers will treat the rest of your text just as written with no markup allowed. The text will be displayed in a monospaced font with no other formatting. There is no ending tag for `<plaintext>` (of course—no markup!).

The main mission for `<plaintext>` is to make existing ASCII documents palatable to browsers. In the early days of the Web, this may have been necessary, but today's browsers, which handle exceptional documents gracefully thanks to

---

<plaintext>

Function:
    Render a block of text without any formatting

Attributes:
    None

End tag:
    None

Contains:
    literal_text

Used in:
    block

---

embedded MIME type encoding, have made this tag obsolete. It is included here for completeness, but we strongly discourage its use.

4.8 Block Quotes

A common element in conventional documents is the block quote, a lengthy copy of text from another document. Traditionally, short quotes are set off with quotation marks, while block quotes are made entirely of separate paragraphs within the main document, typically with special indentation and sometimes italicized.

4.8.1 The <blockquote> Tag

All of the text within the `<blockquote>` and `</blockquote>` tags is set off from the regular document text, usually with slightly more-indented left and right margins, and sometimes in italicized typeface. Actual rendering varies from browser to browser, of course.

The HTML standard allows any and all markup within the `<blockquote>`, although some physical and content-based styles may conflict with the font used by the browser for the block quote. Experimentation will reveal those little warts.

The `<blockquote>` tag is often used to set off long quotations from other sources:

```
We acted incorrectly in arbitrarily changing the Kumquat
Festival date. Quoting from the Kumquat Growers' Bylaws:
<blockquote>
   The date of the Kumquat Festival may only be changed by
   a two-thirds vote of the General Membership, provided
   that a <strong>60 percent quorom</strong> of the Membership
   is present.
```

\<blockquote\>

Function:
   Define a block quotation

Attributes:
   None

End tag:
   \</blockquote\>, never omitted

Contains:
   body_content

Used in:
   block

```
</blockquote>
(Emphasis mine) Since such a quorom was not present, the
vote is invalid.
```

4.9 Addresses

Addresses are a very common element in text documents and HTML provides a special tag that sets addresses apart from the rest of a document's text. While this may seem a bit extravagant—addresses have few formatting peculiarities that would require a special tag—it is an example of content, not format, that is the intent and purpose of HTML markup.

By defining text that comprises an address, the author lets the browser format that text in a different manner, as well as process that text in ways helpful to users. For instance, an online directory might include addresses the browser collects into a separate document or table, or automated tools might extract addresses from a collection of documents to build a separate database of addresses.

4.9.1 The \<address\> Tag

The \<address\> and its required end (\</address\>) tag tell a browser that the enclosed text is an address. The browser may format the text in a different manner than the rest of the document text, or use the address in some special way.

The text within the \<address\> tag may contain any element normally found in the body of an HTML document, excluding another \<address\> tag. Style changes are allowed, but may conflict with the style chosen by the browser to render the address element.

<address>

Function:
　　Define an address

Attributes:
　　None

End tag:
　　</address>, never omitted

Contains:
　　body_content

Used in:
　　address_content

We think most if not all HTML documents should have their authors' addresses included somewhere convenient to the user, usually at the end. At the very least, the address should be the author's or webmaster's email address, along with a link to their home page. Street addresses and phone numbers are optional; personal ones are usually not included for reasons of privacy.

For example, the address for the webmaster responsible for a collection of commercial Web documents often appears in source documents as follows, including the special `mailto:` URL protocol that lets users activate the browser's email tool (see Figure 4-24):

```
<address>
  <a href="mailto:webmaster@ora.com"> Webmaster</a><br>
  O'Reilly & Associates, Inc.<br>
  Cambridge, Massachusetts<br>
</address>
```

Whether it is short and sweet or long and complete, make sure every document you create has an address attached to it. If something is worth creating and putting on the Web, it is worth comment and query by your readership. Anonymous documents carry little credibility on the Web.

4.10 Special Character Encoding

For the most part, characters within HTML documents that are not part of a tag are rendered as-is by the browser. However, some characters have special meaning and are not directly rendered, while other characters can't be typed into the source document from a conventional keyboard. Special characters need either a special name or a numeric character encoding for inclusion in an HTML document.

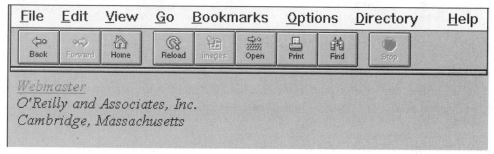

Figure 4-24: The <address> tag in action

4.10.1 Special HTML Characters

As has become obvious in the discussion and examples leading up to this section of the book, three special characters in HTML source documents have very special meaning: the less-than sign (<), greater-than sign (>), and ampersand (&). These characters delimit tags and special character references. They'll confuse a browser if left dangling alone or with improper tag syntax. So you've got to go out of your way to include their actual, literal characters in your HTML documents. The only exception to this is that these character may appear literally within the <listing> and <xmp> tags.

Similarly, you've got to use a special encoding to include double quote characters within a quoted string, or when you want to include a special character that doesn't appear on your keyboard but is part of the ISO Latin-1 character set implemented and supported by most browsers.

4.10.2 Inserting Special Characters

To include a special character in your HTML document, you enclose either its standard entity name or a hash mark (#) and its numeric position in the Latin-1 standard character set[*] inside a leading ampersand and an ending semicolon, without any spaces in between. Whew. That's a long explanation for what is really a simple thing to do, as the following example illustrates. It shows how to include a greater-than sign in a snippet of code by using the character's entity name. It also demonstrates how to include a greater-than sign in your HTML text by referencing its Latin-1 numeric value:

---

[*] The very familiar ASCII character set is a subset of the more comprehensive Latin-1 character set. Composed by the well-respected International Organization for Standardization (ISO), the Latin-1 set is a list of all the letters, numbers, punctuation marks, and so on, commonly used by Western language writers, organized by number and encoded with special names. Appendix D contains the complete Latin-1 character set and encodings.

```
if a &gt; b, then t = 0
if a &#62; b, then t = 0
```

Both examples cause the text to be rendered as:

```
if a > b, then t = 0
```

The complete set of character entity values and names are in Appendix D. You could write an entire HTML document using character encoding, but that would be silly.

5

Rules, Images, and Multimedia

While the body of most HTML documents is text, an appropriate seasoning of horizontal rules, images, and other multimedia elements make for a much more inviting and attractive document. These features of HTML are not simply gratuitous geegaws that make your documents look pretty, mind you. Multimedia elements bring HTML documents alive, providing a dimension of valuable information often unavailable in other media, such as print. In this chapter, we detail how you can insert special multimedia elements into your documents, when their use is appropriate and how to avoid overdoing it.

5.1 Using Horizontal Rules

Horizontal rules give you a way to visually separate sections of your document. That way, you give readers a clean, consistent, visual indication that one portion of your document has ended and another portion is beginning. Horizontal rules effectively set off small sections of text, delimit document headers and footers, and provide extra visual punch to headings within your document.

5.1.1 The <hr> Tag

The <hr> tag tells the browser to insert a horizontal rule across the display window. Like the <br> tag, <hr> forces a simple line break, although unlike <br>, <hr> causes the paragraph alignment to revert to the default (left-justified). The browser places the rule immediately below the current line, and content flow resumes below the rule. [
, 4.7.1]

\<hr\>

Function:
Break a text flow and insert a horizontal rule

Attributes:
ALIGN (extension)
NOSHADE (extension)
SIZE (extension)
WIDTH (extension)

End tag:
None

Contains:
Nothing

Used in:
body_content

The rendering of a horizontal rule is at the discretion of the browser. Typically, it extends across the entire document. Graphical browsers may render the rule with a chiseled or embossed effect; character-based browsers most likely use dashes or underscores to create the rule.

There is no additional space above or below a horizontal rule. If you wish to set it off from the surrounding text, explicitly place the rule in a new paragraph, followed by another paragraph containing the subsequent text. For example, note the spacing around the horizontal rules in the following source and in Figure 5-1:

```
This text is directly above the rule.
<hr>
And this text is immediately below.
<p>
Whereas this text will have space before the rule.
<p>
<hr>
<p>
And this text has space after the rule.
```

A paragraph tag following the rule tag is necessary if you want the content beneath the rule line aligned other than the default left.

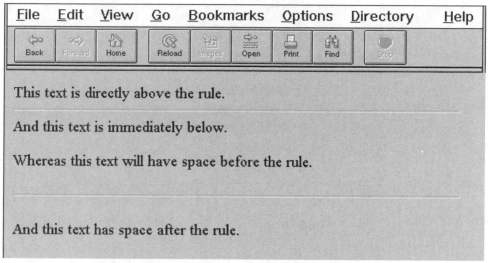

Figure 5–1: Paragraph tags give your text extra elbow room

5.1.1.1 The size attribute

Normally, Netscape Navigator and Internet Explorer render horizontal rules three pixels[*] thick with a chiseled, 3D appearance, making the rule look incised into the page. You may thicken the rules with the `size` attribute. The required value is the thickness, in pixels. You can see the effects of this attribute in Figure 5-2 as constructed from the following source:

```
<p>
This is conventional document text,
followed by a normal, 3-pixel tall rule line.
<hr>
The next three rule lines are 12, 36, and 72 pixels tall.
<hr size=12>
<hr size=36>
<hr size=72>
```

5.1.1.2 The noshade attribute

You may not want Netscape's 3D rule line, preferring a flat, 2D rule—the default for other graphical browsers. Just add the `noshade` attribute (no value required) to the `<hr>` tag to eliminate the effect.

---

[*] A pixel is one of the many tiny dots that make up the display on your computer. While display sizes vary, a good rule of thumb is that one pixel equals one point on a common 75 dot-per-inch display monitor. A point is a unit of measure used in printing and is roughly equal to 1/72 of an inch (there are 72.72 points in an inch, to be exact). Typical typefaces used by various browsers are usually 12 points tall, yielding six lines of text per inch.

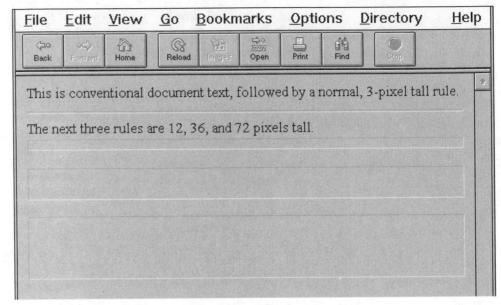

Figure 5–2: Netscape lets you vary the horizontal rule size

See the difference in appearance of a "normal" 3D Netscape rule versus the noshade 2D one in Figure 5-3? (We've also exaggerated the rule's thickness for obvious effect, as evident in the source HTML fragment.)

```
<hr size=32>
<hr size=32 noshade>
```

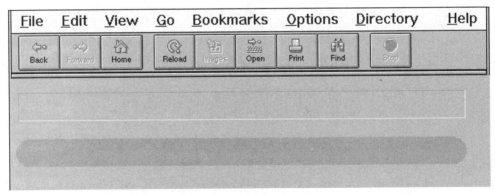

Figure 5–3: Netscape's 3D rule versus the noshade 2D option

5.1.1.3 The width attribute

Most browsers extend rule lines the full width of the view window. You can shorten or lengthen Netscape Navigator and Internet Explorer rules with the `width` attribute, creating rule lines that are either an absolute number of pixels wide or extend across a certain percentage of the page. The extended browsers automatically center partial-width rules; see the `align` attribute (below) to left- or right-justify horizontal rules.

Here are some examples of `width`-specified horizontal rules (Figure 5-4):

```
The following rules are 40 and 320 pixels wide
no matter the actual width of the browser window
<hr width=40>
<hr width=320>
Whereas these next two rules will always extend across
10 and 75 percent of the window, regardless of its width:
<hr width="10%">
<hr width="50%">
```

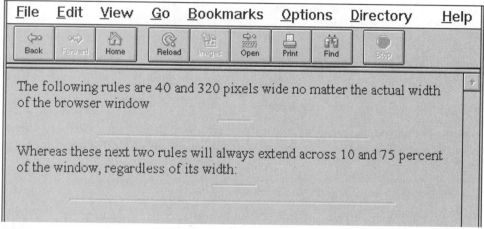

Figure 5-4: Absolute versus relative rule widths

Notice, too, that the relative (percentage) value for the `width` attribute is enclosed in quotes; the absolute (integer) pixel value is not. In fact, the quotes aren't absolutely necessary, but since the percent symbol (%) normally means that an encoded character follows, failure to enclose the percent width value in quotes may confuse other browsers and trash a portion of your rendered document.

In general, it isn't a good idea to specify the width of a rule as an exact number of pixels. Browser windows vary greatly in their width, and what might be a small rule on one browser might be annoyingly large on another. For instance, Netscape

Navigator's default window is tall and thin; Internet Explorer's is short and squat. For this reason, we recommend specifying rule width as a percentage of the window width. That way, when the width of the browser window changes, the rules retain their same relative size.

5.1.1.4 The align attribute

The `align` attribute for a horizontal rule in Netscape or Internet Explorer can have one of three values: `left`, `center`, or `right`. For those rules whose width is less than the current text flow, the rule will be positioned relative to the window margins accordingly. The default alignment is `center`.

A varied rule alignment makes for nice section dividers. For example, the source shown below alternates a 35 percent-wide rule from right to center to the left margin (Figure 5-5).

```
<hr width="35%" align=right>
<h3>Fruit Packing Advice</h3>
...
<hr width="35%" align=center>
<h3>Shipping Kumquats</h3>
...
<hr width="35%" align=left>
<h3>Juice Processing</h3>
...
```

5.1.1.5 Combining rule attributes

You may combine the various rule attribute extensions and their order isn't important. To create big squares, for example, combine the `size` and `width` attributes (Figure 5-6):

```
<hr size=32 width="50%" align=center>
```

In fact, some combinations of rule attributes are necessary—`align` and `width`, for example. `Align` alone appears to do nothing because the default rule width stretches all the way across the display window.

5.1.2 Using Rules to Divide Your Document

Horizontal rules provide a handy visual navigation device for your readers. To use `<hr>` effectively as a section divider, first determine how many levels of headings your document has and how long you expect each section of the document to be. Then decide which of your headings warrant being set apart by a rule.

A horizontal rule can also delimit the front matter of a document, separating the table of contents from the document body, for example. Use a rule also to separate the document body from a trailing index, bibliography, or list of figures.

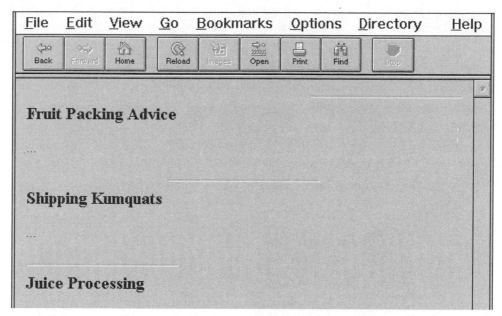

Figure 5–5: Varying horizontal rule alignment makes for subtle section dividers

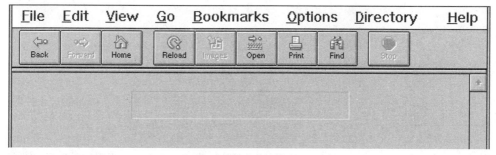

Figure 5–6: Combining rule attributes for special effects

Experienced HTML authors also use horizontal rules to mark the beginning and end of a form. This is especially handy for long forms that make users scroll up and down the page to view all the fields. By consistently marking the beginning and end of a form with a rule, you help users stay within the form, better ensuring they won't inadvertently miss a portion when filling out its contents.

5.1.3 *Using Rules in Headers and Footers*

A fundamental style approach to HTML document families is to have a consistent look and feel, including a standard header and footer for each document.

Typically, the header contains navigational tools that help users easily jump to internal sections as well as related documents in the family, while the footer contains author and document information as well as feedback mechanisms like an email link to the webmaster.

To ensure these headers and footers don't infringe on the main document contents, consider using rules directly below the header and above the footer. For example (also see Figure 5-7):

```
<body>
Kumquat Growers Handbook - Growing Season Guidelines
<hr>
<h1>Growing Season Guidelines</h1>
Growing season for the noble fruit varies throughout the
United States, as shown in the following map:
<p>
<img src="pics/growing-season.gif">
<p>
<hr>
<i>Provided as a public service by the
<a href="feedback.html">Kumquat Lovers of America</a></i>
```

By consistently setting apart your headers and footers using rules, you help users locate and focus upon the main body of your document.

5.2 Inserting Images in Your Documents

One of the most compelling features of HTML is its ability to include images with your document text, either as an intrinsic component of the document (inline images), as separate documents specially selected for download via hyperlinks, or, with Netscape and Internet Explorer, as background for your document. When judiciously added to the body content, images—static icons, pictures, illustrations, drawings, and so on—can make your documents more attractive, inviting, and professional looking, as well as informative and easier to browse. You may also specially enable an image so that it becomes a visual map of hyperlinks. When used to excess, however, images make your document cluttered, confusing, and inaccessible, as well as unnecessarily lengthen the time it takes for users to download and view your pages.

5.2.1 Understanding Image Formats

The HTML standard does not prescribe an official format for images. However, the popular browsers specifically accommodate only certain image formats; GIF and JPEG, in particular. Most other multimedia formats require special accessory applications that each browser owner must obtain, install, and successfully operate to

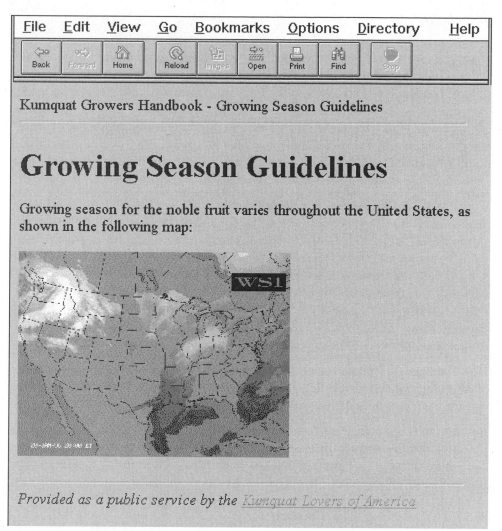

Figure 5–7: Clearly delineate headers and footers with horizontal rules

view the special files. So it's not too surprising that GIF and JPEG are the de facto image standards on the Web.

Both image formats were already in widespread use before the Web came into being, so there's lots of supporting software out there to help you prepare your graphics for either format. However, each has its own advantages and drawbacks, including features that some browsers exploit for special display effects.

5.2.1.1 GIF

The Graphics Interchange Format (GIF) was first developed for image transfer among users of the CompuServe online service. The format serves two purposes: its encoding is cross-platform, so that with appropriate GIF decoding software, graphics created and converted to GIF on a Macintosh, for example, can be loaded into a Windows-based PC, decoded, and viewed without a lot of fuss. The second main feature is that the GIF format uses special compression technology that can significantly reduce the size of the image file for faster transfer over a network. GIF compression is "lossless," too; none of an image's original data is altered or deleted, so the uncompressed and decoded image exactly matches its original.

Even though GIF image files invariably have the *.gif* (or *.GIF*) filename suffix, there actually are two GIF versions: the original GIF87 and an expanded GIF89a, which supports several new features including transparent backgrounds popular with HTML authors (see 5.2.1.2, below). The popular browsers support both GIF versions, which use the same encoding scheme that maps 8-bit pixel values to a color table, for a maximum of 256 colors per image. Most GIF images have even fewer colors and there are special tools to simplify the colors in more elaborate graphics. By simplifying the GIF images, you create a smaller color map and enhance pixel redundancy for better file compression and consequent faster downloading.

However, because of the limited number of colors, a GIF-encoded image is not always appropriate, particularly for photorealistic pictures (see JPEG discussion below). Rather, GIFs make excellent icons, reduced color images, and drawings.

Because most graphical browsers explicitly support the GIF format, it is currently the most widely accepted image-encoding format on the Web. It is acceptable for both inline images and externally linked ones. When in doubt as to which image format to use, choose GIF. It will work in almost any situation.

5.2.1.2 *Interlacing and transparency*

GIF images can be made to perform two special tricks: interlacing and transparency. With interlacing, a GIF image seemingly materializes on the display, rather than progressively flow onto it from top to bottom. Normally, a GIF encoded image is a sequence of pixel data, in order row-by-row, from top to bottom of the image. While the common GIF image renders onscreen like pulling down a window shade, interlaced GIFs open like a venetian blind. That's because interlacing sequences every fourth row of the image. That way, users get to see a full image—top to bottom, albeit fuzzy—in a quarter of the time it takes to download and display the remainder of the image. The resulting quarter-done image usually is clear enough so that users with slow network connections can evaluate whether or not to take the time to download the remainder of the image file.

Not all graphical browsers, although able to display an interlaced GIF, are actually able to display the materializing effects of interlacing. With those that do, users still can defeat the effect by choosing to delay image display until after download and decoding. NCSA Mosaic, on the other hand, always downloads and decodes images before display, so it doesn't support the effect at all.

The other popular effect available with GIF images—GIF89a formatted images actually—is the ability to make a portion of them transparent so that what's underneath—usually the browser window's background—shows through. The transparent GIF image has one color in its color map designated as the background color. The browser simply ignores any pixel in the image that uses that background color, thereby letting the display window's background show through. By carefully cropping its dimensions and by using a solid, contiguous background color, a transparent image can be made to seamlessly meld into a page's surrounding content or float above it.

Transparent GIF images are great for any graphic you want to meld into the document and not stand out as a rectangular block. Transparent GIF logos are very popular, as are transparent icons and dingbats—any graphic that should appear to have an arbitrary, natural shape. You may also insert a transparent image inline with conventional text to act as a special character glyph within conventional text.

The downside to transparency is that the GIF image will look lousy if you don't remove its border when included in a hyperlink anchor (<a> tag), or is otherwise specially framed. And, too, content flow happens around the image's rectangular dimensions, not adjacent to its apparent shape. That can lead to unnecessarily isolated images or odd-looking sections in your HTML pages.

Either and both GIF tricks—interlacing and transparency—don't just happen; you need special software to prepare the GIF file. Many picture tools now save your creations or acquired images in GIF format, although few are able to make interlaced files and fewer let you designate and enable transparency. Fortunately, there are a slew of shareware and freeware programs specialized for either task. Look into your favorite Internet software archives for GIF graphics and conversion tools and also see Chapter 12, *Tips, Tricks, and Hacks*, for details on creating transparent images.

5.2.1.3 JPEG

The Joint Photographic Experts Group is a standards body that developed what is now known as the JPEG image-encoding format. Like GIFs, JPEG images are platform independent and specially compressed for high-speed transfer via digital communication technologies. Unlike GIF, JPEG supports tens of thousands of colors for more detailed, photorealistic digital images. And JPEG uses special algorithms that yield much higher data-compression ratios. It is not uncommon, for example, for a 200-kilobyte GIF image (which uses lossless compression) to be reduced to a 30-kilobyte JPEG image. To achieve that amazing compression, JPEG does lose some image data. However, you can adjust the degree of "lossiness" with special JPEG tools, so that although the uncompressed image may not exactly match the original, it will be close enough that most people cannot tell the difference.

The JPEG format is nearly universally understood by today's graphical browsers. Some, most notably Netscape, have a built-in JPEG decoder. Others, like Mosaic, invoke an external viewing tool (helper application) for decoding and displaying JPEG files, which invariably are stored with a *.jpg* (or *.JPG*) filename suffix.

5.2.1.4 XBM

The X BitMap image format is an ASCII representation of a monochrome image. It is designed to capture small, black-and-white icons in a form that can be directly included in C and C++ programs. XBM format offers no compression features or support for color images.

XBM format images are typically supported by browsers that run under the X Window System, usually running on a UNIX platform. XBM format is useful for capturing small icons that might be used as bullets or dingbats within a document. It makes little sense to use XBM for any other type of image; the resulting XBM file would be far larger than the equivalent GIF version of the same image.

5.2.2 When to Use Images

Most pictures are worth a thousand words. But don't forget that no one pays attention to a blabbermouth. First and foremost, think of your HTML document images as visual tools, not gratuitous trappings. They should support your text content and help readers navigate your documents. Use images to clarify, illustrate, or exemplify the contents. Content supporting photographs, charts, graphs, maps, and drawings are all natural candidates for appropriate HTML images. Product photographs are essential components in online catalogs and shopping guides, for example. And link-enabled icons and dingbats can be effective visual guides to internal and external resources. If an image doesn't do any of these valuable services for your document, throw it out, already!

One of the most important considerations when adding images to a document is the additional delay they add to the retrieval time for a document over the network, particularly for modem connections. While a simple text document might run, at most, 10 or 15 thousand bytes, images can easily extend to hundreds of thousands of bytes each. And the total retrieval time for a document is not only equal to the sum of all its component parts, but also to compounded networking overhead delays since each image requires a separate connection and download request between the client browser and the Web server. Depending on the speed of the connection (*bandwidth*, usually expressed as bits or bytes per second) as well as network congestion that can delay connections, a single document containing one 100-kilobyte image may take anywhere from around 30 seconds through a 28.8 kilobit-per-second modem connection in the wee hours of the morning when most everyone else is asleep, to well over *ten minutes* with a 9600 bit-per-second modem at noontime. You get the picture?

5.2.3 *When to Use Text*

Text hasn't gone out of style. For some users, it is the only portion of your document they can access. We argue that, in most circumstances, your documents should be usable by readers who cannot view images or have disabled their automatic download in their browser to improve their low-speed connection. While the urge to add images to all of your documents may be strong, there are times when pure text documents make more sense.

Documents being converted to the Web from other formats rarely have embedded images. Reference materials and other serious content often is completely usable in a text-only form.

You should create text-only documents when access speed is critical and potentially slow. If you know that many users will have only low-speed connections to your pages, you should accommodate them by avoiding the use of images within your documents. Better yet, provide a home (leading) page that lets readers decide between duplicate collections of your work: one containing the images, and another stripped of them. (The popular graphics browsers include special picture icons as place holders for yet-to-be downloaded images, which can trash and muddle your document's layout into an unreadable mess.)

Text is most appropriate—supporting images only, without frills or nonessential graphics—if your documents are to be readily searchable by any of the many Web indexing services. Images are almost always ignored by these search engines. If the major content of your pages is provided with images, very little information about your documents will find its way into the online Web directories.

5.2.4 Speeding Image Downloads

There are several ways to ameliorate the overhead and delays inherent with images besides being very choosy about which to include in your documents.

Keep it simple

A full-screen, 24-bit color graphic, even when reduced in size by digital compression with one of the standard formats like JPEG or GIF, is still going to be a network bandwidth hog. Acquire and use the various image management software to optimize image dimensions and number of colors into the fewest number of pixels. Simplify your drawings. Stay away from panoramic photographs. Avoid large empty backgrounds in your images, as well as gratuitous borders and other space-consuming elements. Also avoid dithering (blending two colors among adjacent pixels to achieve a third color); the technique can significantly reduce the compressibility of your images. Strive for large areas of uniform colors, which compress readily in both GIF and JPEG format.

Reuse images

This is particularly true for icons. The popular browsers cache incoming document components in local storage for the very purpose of quick, network connection-less retrieval of data.

Divide up large documents

This is a general rule that includes images. Many small document segments, organized through hyperlinks (of course!) and effective tables of contents tend to be better accepted by users than a few large documents. In general, people would rather "flip" several pages than dawdle waiting for a large one to download. (It's related to the TV channel-surfing syndrome.) One accepted rule of thumb is to keep your documents under 50 kilobytes each, so even the slowest connections won't overly frustrate your readers.

Isolate necessarily large graphics

Provide a special link, perhaps one that includes a thumbnail of the graphic, thereby letting readers decide if and when they want to spend the time downloading the full image. And since the downloaded image isn't mixed with other document components like inline images, it's much easier for the reader to identify and save the image on their system's local storage for later study. (For details on non-inline image downloads, see 5.7).

Specify image dimensions

Finally, another way to improve performance is by including the image's rectangular height and width information in its tag. By supplying those dimensions, you eliminate the extra steps the extended browsers must take to download, examine, and calculate an image's space in the document. There is a downside to this approach, however, that we explore in 5.2.6.11.

5.2.5 JPEG or GIF?

You may choose to use only GIF or JPEG images in your HTML documents if your sources for images or your software toolset prefers one over the other format. Both are nearly universally supported by today's browsers, so there shouldn't be any user-viewing problems.

Nevertheless, we recommend that you acquire the facilities to create and convert to both formats, to take advantage of their unique capabilities. For instance, use GIF's transparency feature for icons and dingbats. Alternatively, use JPEG for large and colorful images for faster downloading.

5.2.6 The <img> Tag

The <img> tag lets you reference and insert a graphic image into the current text flow of your HTML document. There is no implied line or paragraph break before or after the <img> tag, so images can be truly "inline" with text and other content.

The format of the image itself is not defined by the HTML standard, although the popular graphical browsers specially support GIF and JPEG images. The HTML standard doesn't specify or restrict the size or dimensions of the image, either. Images may have any number of colors, but how those colors are rendered is highly browser dependent.

Image presentation in general is very browser specific. Images may be ignored by nongraphical browsers. Browsers operating in a constrained environment may modify the image size or complexity. And users, particularly those with slow network connections, may choose to defer image loading altogether. Accordingly, you should make sure your documents make sense and are useful, even if the images are completely removed.

5.2.6.1 The src attribute

The src attribute for the <img> tag is required; its value is the image file's URL, either absolute or relative to the HTML document referencing the image. To unclutter their document storage, HTML authors typically collect image files into a separate folder they often name something like "pics" or "images." [URLs, 6.2]

For example, this HTML fragment places an image of a famous kumquat packing plant into the narrative text (see Figure 5-8):

<img>

Function:

Inserts an image into a document

Attributes:

ALIGN

ALT

BORDER (extension)

CONTROLS (Internet Explorer only)

DYNSRC (Internet Explorer only)

HEIGHT (extension)

HSPACE (extension)

ISMAP

LOOP (Internet Explorer only)

SRC

LOWSRC (Netscape only)

START (Internet Explorer only)

VSPACE (extension)

WIDTH (extension)

USEMAP (extension)

End tag:

None

Contains:

Nothing

Used in:

text

```
Here we are, on day 17 of the tour, in front of the kumquat
packing plant:
<p>
<img src="pics/packing_plant.gif">
<p>
What an exciting moment, to see the boxes of fruit moving
```

In the example, the paragraph (`<p>`) tags surrounding the `<img>` tag causes the browser to render the image by itself with some vertical space after the preceding and before the trailing text. Text may also abut the image, as we describe in 5.2.6.4.

5.2.6.2 The lowsrc attribute

To the benefit of users, particularly those with slow Internet connections, the browser innovators at Netscape Communications have introduced the `lowsrc` companion to the `src` attribute in the `<img>` tag as a way to speed up document rendering. The `lowsrc` attribute's value, like `src`, is the URL of an image file that

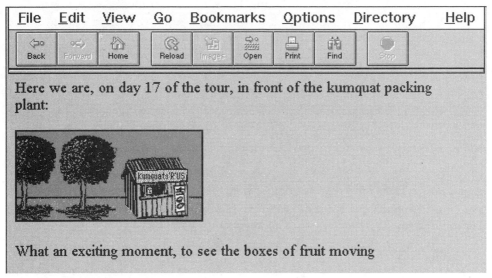

Figure 5-8: The mighty Kumquat

the browser loads and displays when it first encounters the `<img>` tag. Then, when the document has been completely loaded and can be read by the user, the Netscape browser goes back and retrieves the image specified by the `src` attribute.

Ostensibly, the `lowsrc` image is a low-resolution, abbreviated version of the final `src` image and which, therefore, loads faster by comparison to quickly give the reader an idea of its content until the final, higher-resolution image eventually replaces it onscreen. But the `lowsrc` attribute can also be used for some special effects.

For example, Netscape uses the `lowsrc` image's dimensions to reserve space in the document for both the `lowsrc` and `src` images, unless you explicitly allocate that space with the height and width attributes described below. Hence, if the dimensions of the image specified in the `src` attribute are different than those for the `lowsrc` image, the `src` image will be reduced, enlarged, stretched, and/or compressed to fit in the allotted space. Moreover, the `lowsrc` and `src` images needn't be identical, so you might take advantage of the delayed rendering of the `src` image for simple animation.

The `lowsrc` attribute is for Netscape version 2 only. Other browsers ignore it and only load the image specified by the `src` attribute. Netscape won't load either image if the user chooses not to auto-load images. In that case, both images will load in order when the user clicks the images button or clicks the image icon placeholder. No browser loads the `lowsrc` image only; you must include a `src` image, otherwise nothing will appear except the missing image icon.

5.2.6.3 The alt attribute

The `alt` attribute specifies alternative text the browser may show if image display is not possible or disabled by the user. It's an option, but one we highly recommend you exercise for every image in your document. This way, if the image is not available, the user still has some indication of what it is that's missing.

The value for the `alt` attribute is a text string of up to 1024 characters, enclosed in quotes if you include spaces or other punctuation. The alternative text may contain entity references to special characters, but it may not contain any other sort of markup; in particular, no style tags allowed.

Graphical browsers ignore the `alt` attribute if the image is available and downloading is enabled by the user. Otherwise, they insert the `alt` attribute's text as a label next to an image placeholder icon. Well-chosen `alt` labels thereby additionally support those users with a graphical browser who have disabled their automatic image download because of a slow connection to the Web.

Nongraphical, text-only browsers like Lynx put the `alt` text directly into the content flow just like any other text element. So, when used effectively, the `alt` tag sometimes can transparently substitute for missing images. (Your text-only browser users will appreciate not being constantly reminded of their second-class Web citizenship.) For example, consider using the asterisk (*) character as the `alt` attribute alternative to a special bullet icon:

```
<h3><img src="pics/fancy_bullet.gif" alt="*"></h3>
<h1>Introduction</h1>
```

A graphical browser displays the bullet image, while in a nongraphical browser the `alt` asterisk takes the place of the missing bullet. Similarly, use `alt` text to replace special image bullets for list items. For example, the following code:

```
<ul>
  <li> Kumquat recipes <img src="pics/new.gif" alt="(New!)">
  <li> Annual harvest dates
</ul>
```

displays the `new.gif` image with graphical browsers, and the text "(New!)" with text-only browsers.

The `alt` attribute lets you use even more complex text (see Figure 5-9):

```
Here we are, on day 17 of the tour, in front of the kumquat
packing plant:
<p>
<img src=" pics/packing_plant.gif"
   alt="[Image of our tour group outside the main packing plant]">
<p>
What an exciting moment, to see the boxes of fruit moving
```

```
Here we are, on day 17 of the tour, in front of the kumquat packing
plant:

[Image of our tour group outside the main packing plant]

What an exciting moment, to see the boxes of fruit moving




Commands: Use arrow keys to move, '?' for help, 'q' to quit, '<-' to go back
```

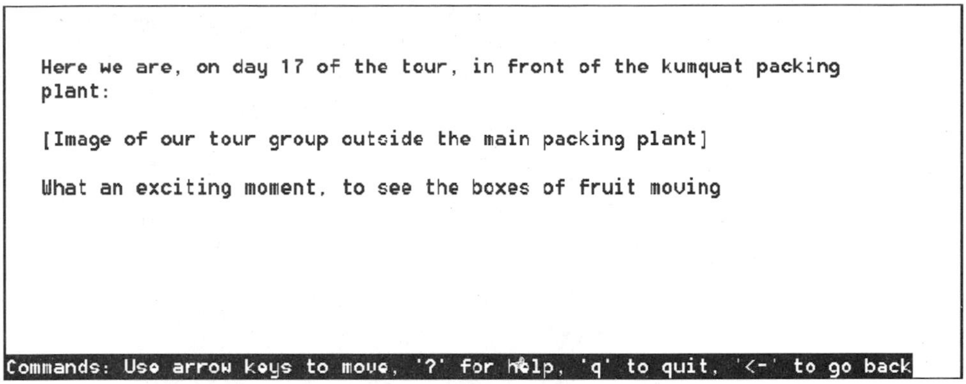

Figure 5-9: Text-only browsers like Lynx display an image's alt attribute text

5.2.6.4 *The align attribute*

The HTML standard does not define a default alignment for images with respect to other text and images in the same line of content, so you cannot absolutely predict how the mixture of text and images will look.[*] HTML images normally appear in line with a single line of text. Our common media like magazines typically wrap text around images, with several lines next to and abutting the image, not just a single line.

Fortunately, HTML document designers can extert some control over the alignment of images with body-content text through the `align` attribute for the `<img>` tag. The HTML standard specifies three image-alignment attribute values: `top`, `middle`, and `bottom`. The developers of Netscape Navigator have added four more alignment attributes to that list: `texttop`, `absmiddle`, `baseline`, and `absbottom`. These are Netscape-only; other browsers ignore them. Two other special, nonstandard image alignments—`left` and `right`—are supported by all the extended browsers, including Netscape, Internet Explorer, and Mosaic. They let you embed images into the flow of text so that not just one but several lines of words will wrap around one and even fill the gap between two images.

---

[*] Most of the popular graphical browsers normally insert an image so that its base aligns with the baseline of the text—the same alignment as that specified by the attribute value of `bottom`. Nonetheless, HTML document designers should assume that alignment varies between browsers and always include the desired type of image alignment.

The list below contains descriptions for the inline HTML image alignments. See Figure 5-10 for examples.

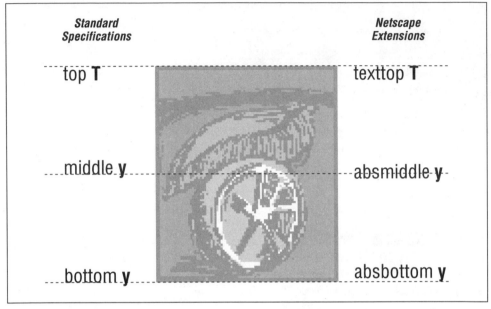

Figure 5-10: HTML standard and Netscape-extended inline image alignments with text

top

> The top of the image is aligned with the top edge of the tallest item in the current line of text. If there are no other images in the current line, the top of the image is aligned with the top of the text.

texttop (Netscape only)

> The `align=texttop` attribute and value tells Netscape to align the top of the image with the top of the tallest text item in the current line. This is slightly different from the standard HTML `top` option, which aligns the top of the image with the top of the tallest item, image or text, in the current line. If the line contains no other images that extend above the top of the text, `texttop` and `top` have the same effect.

middle

> The middle of the image is aligned with the baseline of the text in the current line. Note that the baseline of the text is not anywhere near the middle of the text, so that it is not possible to align the middle of the image with the true middle of the text.

`absmiddle` (Netscape only)

   If you set the `align` attribute of the `<img>` tag to `absmiddle`, Netscape will
   fit the absolute middle of the image to the absolute middle of the current line.
   This is different from the common `middle` option, which aligns the middle of
   the image with the baseline—the bottom of the characters—of the current
   line of text. With `absmiddle`, the center of the image aligns exactly with the
   center of the text.

`bottom`

   The bottom of the image is aligned with the baseline of the text in the current
   line. It is not possible to align the bottom of the image with the actual bottom
   of the current line. This type of alignment is most useful when inserting custom symbols and dingbats into a line of text.

`baseline` (Netscape only)

   The `baseline` value for the `align` attribute has exactly the same effect as
   the standard `bottom` option: it tells Netscape to align the bottom of the image
   with the baseline of the text line. Netscape's authors included this option simply because its name is more indicative of its effect on image alignment.

`absbottom` (Netscape only)

   The `align=absbottom` attribute has Netscape align the bottom of the image
   with the true bottom of the current line of text: the bottom of the tail on a "y,"
   for example, rather than at the baseline of the text, which is the bottom of the
   "v" in the "y" character.

Use the top or middle alignment values for best integration of icons, dingbats, or
other special inline effects with the text content. Otherwise, `align=bottom` usually gives the best appearance. When aligning one or more images on a single
line, select the alignment that gives the best overall appearance to your document.

5.2.6.5 Wrapping text around images

The `left` and `right` image alignment values tell the extended browsers to align
an image against the left or right margin, respectively, of the current text flow. The
browser then renders subsequent document content in the remaining portion of
the flow adjacent to the image. The net result is that the document content following the image is wrapped around the image.

Figure 5-11 shows text flow around a left-aligned image:

```
<img src="pics/kumquat.gif" align=left>
The kumquat is the smallest of the citrus fruits, similar
in appearance to a tiny orange. The similarity ends with its
appearance, however. While oranges are generally sweet,
kumquats are extremely bitter. Theirs is an acquired taste,
to be sure.
```

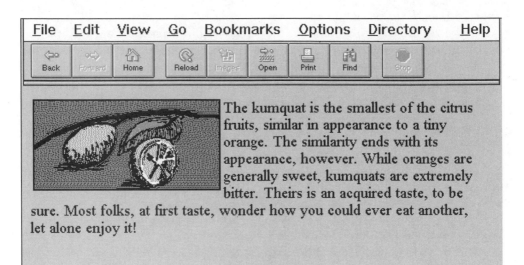

Figure 5–11: Text flow around a left-aligned image

You can place images against both margins simultaneously (Figure 5-12) and the text will run down the middle of the page between them:

```
<img src="pics/kumquat.gif" align=left>
<img src="pics/tree.gif" align=right>
The kumquat is the smallest of the citrus fruits, similar
in appearance to a tiny orange. The similarity ends with its
appearance, however. While oranges are generally sweet,
kumquats are extremely bitter. Theirs is an acquired taste,
to be sure.
```

While text is flowing around an image, the left (or right) margin of the page is temporarily redefined to be adjacent to the image as opposed to the edge of the page. This means that subsequent images with the same alignment will stack up against each other. The following source fragment achieves that staggered image effect, shown in Figure 5-13:

```
<img src="pics/marcia.gif" align=left>
Marcia!
<img src="pics/jan.gif" align=left>
Jan!
<img src="pics/cindy.gif" align=left>
Cindy!
```

When the text flows beyond the bottom of the image, the margin returns to its former position, typically at the edge of the browser window.

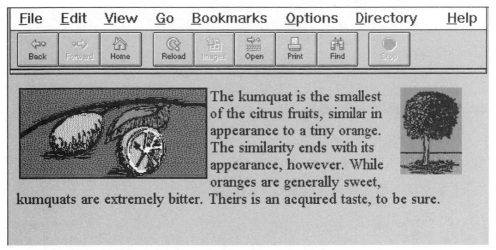

Figure 5–12: Running text between left- and right-aligned images

Figure 5–13: Three very lovely girls

5.2.6.6 Centering an image

Have you noticed that you can't vertically center an image in the browser window with the `align` attribute? The `middle` and `absmiddle` values center the image vertically with the current line, but the image is horizontally justified depending on what content comes before it in the current flow and the dimensions of the browser window.

You can vertically center an inline image in the browser window, but only if it's isolated from surrounding content, such as by paragraph or line break tags. Then, either use the `<center>` tag or the `align=center` attribute in the paragraph tag to center the image. For example:

```
Kumquats are tasty treats
<br>
<center>
<img src="pics/kumquat.gif">
</center>
that everyone should strive to eat!
```

Use the paragraph tag with its `align=center` attribute if want some extra space above and below the centered image:

```
Kumquats are tasty treats
<p align=center>
<img src="pics/kumquat.gif">
</p>
that everyone should strive to eat!
```

5.2.6.7 *The border attribute*

Browsers normally render images that also are hyperlinks (included in an `<a>` tag) with a two-pixel-wide colored border, indicating to the reader that the image can be selected to visit the associated document. Netscape and Internet Explorer let you change the thickness of that border with the `border` attribute to the `<img>` tag. The value of the `border` attribute is an integer equal to the border thickness in pixels.

Figure 5-14 shows you the thick and thin of image borders, as rendered from the following HTML source:

```
<a href="test.html">
 <img src="pics/kumquat.gif" border=1>
</a>
<a href="test.html">
  <img src="pics/kumquat.gif" border=2>
</a>
<a href="test.html">
  <img src="pics/kumquat.gif" border=4>
</a>
<a href="test.html">
  <img src="pics/kumquat.gif" border=8>
</a>
```

5.2.6.8 *Removing the image border*

You can eliminate the border around an image hyperlink altogether with the `border=0` attribute within the `<img>` tag. For some images, particularly image maps, the absence of a border can greatly improve the appearance of your pages. Images that are clearly link buttons to other pages may also look best without a border.

Be careful, though, that by removing the border, you don't diminish your page's usability. No border means you've removed a common visual indicator of a link,

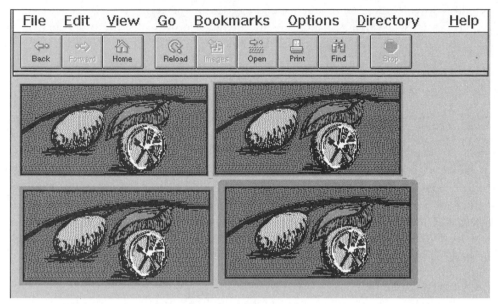

Figure 5–14: The thick and thin of image borders

making it less easy for your readers to find the links on the page. Browsers will change the mouse cursor as readers pass it over an image that is a hyperlink, but you should not assume they will, nor should you make readers test your border-less images to find hidden links.

We strongly recommend that you use some additional way with borderless images to let your readers know to click the images. Even including simple text instructions will go a long way to making your pages more accessible to readers.

5.2.6.9 The height and width attributes

Normally, a graphical browser determines the size of an image and, hence, the rectangular space to reserve for it in the display window, by retrieving the image file and extracting its embedded height and width specifications. This is not the most efficient way to render a document since the browser must sequentially examine each image file and calculate its screen space before rendering adjacent and subsequent document content. That can significantly increase the amount of time it takes to render the document and delay scanning by the user.

Netscape and Internet Explorer provide a more efficient way for HTML authors to specify an image's dimensions with `height` and `width` `<img>` attribute extensions. That way, the extended browser can calculate and reserve space before actually downloading an image, speeding document rendering. Both attributes require an integer value that indicates the image size in pixels; the order in which they appear in the <img> tag is not important.

5.2.6.10 Resized and flood-filling images

A hidden feature of the height and width <img> extension attributes is that you don't need to specify exact image dimensions; attribute values can be larger or smaller than the actual size of the image. The extended browsers automatically scale the image to fit the predefined space. This gives you a down-and-dirty way of creating thumbnail versions of large images and a way to enlarge very small pictures. Be careful, though: The browser still must download the entire file, no matter its final rendered size, and you will distort an image if you don't retain its original height versus width proportions. Moreover, the full-size image probably will ruin the appearance of the document altogether if displayed by a nonextended browser like Mosaic.

Another trick with the height and width image attributes provides an easy way to flood-fill areas of your page and can also improve document performance. Suppose you want to insert a colored bar across your document. Rather than create an image to the full dimensions, create one that is just one pixel high and wide and set it to the desired color. Then use the height and width <img> extensions to scale it to the larger size:

```
<img src="pics/one-pixel.gif" width=640 height=20>
```

The smaller image downloads much faster than a full-scale image, and the width and height attributes create the desired bar after the tiny image arrives at the browser (Figure 5-15). Nifty, no? No, if the reader uses Mosaic or another nonextended browser, all they'll see is a one-pixel dot. So, again, don't forget these are special image extensions, not universally available to readers.

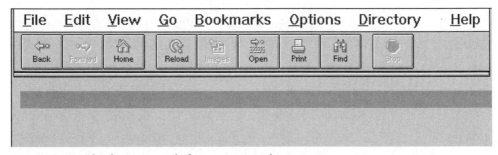

Figure 5–15: This bar was made from a one-pixel image

5.2.6.11   More problems with height and width

Although the `height` and `width` attributes for the `<img>` tag can improve performance and let you perform some neat tricks, there is a particularly knotty downside to using them. The extended browser sets aside the specified rectangle of space to the prescribed dimensions in the display window even if the user has turned off automatic download of images. What the user often is left with is a page full of semi-empty frames with a meaningless picture placeholder icon inside. The page looks terribly unfinished and is mostly useless. Without accompanying dimensions, on the other hand, the browser simply inserts a placeholder icon inline and usually sized to the surrounding text, so at least there's something there to read in the display.

We don't have an answer to this dilemma. We would, however, include extension attributes because we encourage any practice that improves network performance.

5.2.6.12   The hspace and vspace attributes

Graphical browsers usually don't give you much space between an image and the text around it. And unless you create a transparent image border that expands the space between them, the typical two-pixel buffer between an image and adjacent text is just too close for most designer's comfort. Add the image into a hyperlink, and the special colored border will negate any transparent buffer space you labored to create, as well as draw even more attention to how close the adjacent text butts up against the image.

The `<img>` extensions, `hspace` and `vspace`, supported by both Netscape and Internet Explorer, can give your images breathing room. With `hspace`, you specify the number of pixels of extra space to leave between the image and text on the left and right sides of the image; the `vspace` value is the number of pixels on the top and bottom. Figure 5-16 shows the difference between two wrapped images:

```
<img src="pics/kumquat.gif" align=left>
The kumquat is the smallest of the citrus fruits, similar
in appearance to a tiny orange. The similarity ends with its
appearance, however. While oranges are generally sweet,
kumquats are extremely bitter. Theirs is an acquired taste,
to be sure. Most folks, at first taste, wonder how you could
ever eat another, let alone enjoy it!
<p>
<img src="pics/kumquat.gif" align=left hspace=10 vspace=10>
The kumquat is the smallest of the citrus fruits, similar
in appearance to a tiny orange. The similarity ends with its
appearance, however. While oranges are generally sweet,
kumquats are extremely bitter. Theirs is an acquired taste,
to be sure. Most folks, at first taste, wonder how you could
ever eat another, let alone enjoy it!
```

 The kumquat is the smallest of the citrus fruits, similar in appearance to a tiny orange. The similarity ends with its appearance, however. While oranges are generally sweet, kumquats are extremely bitter. Theirs is an acquired taste, to be sure. Most folks, at first taste, wonder how you could ever eat another, let alone enjoy it!

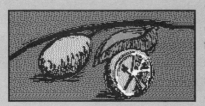 The kumquat is the smallest of the citrus fruits, similar in appearance to a tiny orange. The similarity ends with its appearance, however. While oranges are generally sweet, kumquats are extremely bitter. Theirs is an acquired taste, to be sure. Most folks, at first taste, wonder how you could ever eat another, let alone enjoy it!

Figure 5–16: Improve image/text interfaces with vspace *and* hspace *extensions*

We're sure you'll agree that the additional space around the image makes the text easier to read and the overall page more attractive.

5.2.6.13 The ismap and usemap attributes

The ismap and usemap attributes for the <img> tag tell the browser that the image is a special mouse-selectable visual map of one or more hyperlinks, commonly known as an *image map*. The ismap style of image maps is supported by all the graphical browsers. It may only be specified within an <a> tag hyperlink. [<a>, 6.3.1]

For example:

```
<a href="/cgi-bin/images/map2">
  <img src="pics/map2.gif" ismap>
</a>
```

The browser automatically sends the x,y position of the mouse (relative to the upper-left corner of the image) to the server when the user clicks somewhere on the `ismap` image. Special server software, the */cgi-bin/images/map2* program in the example, may then use those coordinates to determine a response.

The `usemap` attribute is supported by Netscape and Internet Explorer, version 2 or later. It's a client-side image map mechanism that effectively eliminates server-side processing of the mouse coordinates and its incumbant network delays and problems. Using special `<map>` and `<area>` extension tags, HTML authors provide a map of coordinates for the hyperlink-sensitive regions in the `usemap` image along with related hyperlink URLs. The value of the `usemap` attribute is a URL that points to that special `<map>` section. And the extended browser on the user's computer translates the coordinates of a click of the mouse on the image into some action, including loading and displaying another document. [`<map>` 6.5.3] [`<area>` 6.5.4]

For example, the following source specially encodes the 100-pixel wide by 100-pixel tall `map2.gif` image into four segments, each of which, if clicked by the user, links to a different document. Also notice we've included, validly, the `ismap` image map processing capability in the example `<img>` tag so that users of other, non-`usemap`-capable browsers have access to the alternative, server-side mechanism to process the image map:

```
<a href="/cgi-bin/images/map2">
  <img src="pics/map2.gif" ismap usemap="#map2">
</a>
...
<map name="map2">
  <area coords="0,0,49,49" href="link1.html">
  <area coords="50,0,99,49" href="link2.html">
  <area coords="0,50,49,99" href="link3.html">
  <area coords="50,50,99,99" href="link4.html">
</map>
```

Geographical maps make excellent `ismap` and `usemap` examples: Browsing a nationwide company's pages, for instance, the user might click their home town on a map to get the addresses and phone numbers for nearby retail outlets. The advantage of the `usemap` client-side image map processing is that it does not require a server or special server software and so, unlike the `ismap` mechanism, can be used in non-Web (networkless) environments, such as with local files or on CD-ROM.

Please read our more complete discussion of anchors and links, including image maps within links, in Chapter 6, *Links and Webs*.

5.2.6.14 Combining *<img>* attributes

You may combine any of the various standard and extension attributes for images where and when they make sense. The order for inclusion of multiple attributes in the `<img>` tag is not important, either. Just be careful not to use redundant attributes or you won't be able to predict the outcome.

5.2.7 Internet Explorer <img> Attributes for Video

Most of the extensions to HTML that Internet Explorer supports, including the various `<img>` tag attributes, were originally implemented and introduced to the Web by Netscape. However, the special `controls`, `dynsrc`, `loop`, and `start` attribute extensions for the `<img>` tag currently are unique to Internet Explorer. They let you embed an inline movie into the body content, just like an image.

It is a sorely needed innovation; movies otherwise require a separate helper application which the user must have installed and which displays the movie in a separate window (see 5.7). We, like many other Web aficionados, prefer integrated content.

However, the Internet Explorer movie extensions currently are very limited. They are not supported by any other browser and can only be used with Audio Video Interleave (AVI) formatted movie files, since that's the player format built into Internet Explorer and enabled through Windows 95. Moreover, recent innovations in browser technology, *applets* in particular, may make Internet Explorer's approach of extending the already overloaded `<img>` tag obsolete. See 5.6 for details.

5.2.7.1 The dynsrc attribute

You use the `dynsrc` attribute extension in the `<img>` tag to reference an AVI movie for inline display by Internet Explorer. Its required value is the URL of the movie file enclosed in quotes. For example, this is the tag and attribute for an AVI movie file entitled *intro.avi*:

```
<img dynsrc="movies/intro.avi">
```

The browser sets aside a video viewport in the HTML display window and plays the movie, with audio if included in the clip, similar to an inline image: in line with current body content and according to the dimension of the video frame. And, like common images, the `<dynsrc>` referenced movie file gets displayed immediately after download from the server. You may change those defaults and add some user controls with other attributes, as described below.

Because all other browsers currently ignore the special Internet Explorer attributes for movies, they may become confused by an `<img>` tag that does not contain the otherwise required `<src>` attribute and an image URL. We recommend that you include the `<src>` attribute and a valid image file URL in all `<img>` tags, including those that reference a movie for Internet Explorer users. The other browsers display the still image in place of the movie; Internet Explorer does the reverse and plays the movie, but does not display the image. Note that the order of attributes does not matter.

For example:

```
<img dynsrc="movies/intro.avi" src="pics/mvstill.gif">
```

Internet Explorer loads and plays the AVI movie *intro.avi*; all other graphical browsers will load and display the *mvstill.gif* image instead.

5.2.7.2 *The controls attribute*

Normally, Internet Explorer plays a movie inside a framed viewport once, without any user controls. To add controls the user may manipulate with the mouse, include the `controls` attribute, without a value, in the respective `<img>` tag. VCR-like play, fast-forward, reverse, stop, and pause controls are provided to the user; if the clip includes a sound track, an audio volume is provided as well.

For example:

```
<img dynsrc="movies/intro.avi" controls src="pics/mvstill.gif">
```

adds the various playback controls to the video window of the *intro.avi* movie clip, as shown in Figure 5-17.

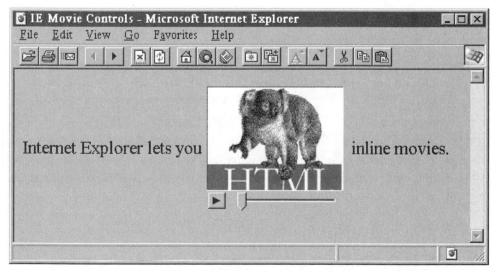

Figure 5–17: The controls attribute adds movie playback controls to the video playback frame

5.2.7.3 *The loop attribute*

Internet Explorer normally plays a movie clip from beginning to end once after download. The `loop` attribute for the movie `<img>` tag lets you have the clip play repeatedly an integer number of times set by the attribute's value, or forever if the value is `infinite`. Of course, the user can cut the loop short by pressing the stop button, if given controls (see above), or by moving on to another document.

The following *intro.avi* movie clip will play from beginning to end, then restart at the beginning and play through to the end nine more times:

```
<img dynsrc="movies/intro.avi" loop=10 src="pics/mvstill.gif">
```

Whereas the following movie will play over and over again, incessantly:

```
<img dynsrc="movies/intro.avi" loop=infinite src="pics/mvstill.gif">
```

Looping movies aren't necessarily meant to annoy. Some special effects animations, for instance, are a sequence of repeated frames or segments. Rather than string the redundant segments into one, long movie that extends its download time, simply loop the single, compact frame or segment.

5.2.7.4 *The start attribute*

Normally, an Internet Explorer movie clip starts playing as soon as it's downloaded. You can modify that behavior with the `start` attribute in the movie's `<img>` tag. By setting its value to `mouseover`, you delay playback until the user passes the mouse pointer over the movie viewport. The other valid `start` attribute value, `fileopen`, is the default: start playback just after download. It is included because both values may be combined in the `start` attribute to cause the movie to automatically playback once after download, and then whenever the user passes the mouse over its viewport. Add a value-separating comma, with no intervening spaces, or else enclose them in quotes, when combining the `start` attribute values.

For example, our by-now-infamous *intro.avi* movie will play once when its host HTML document is loaded by the user, and whenever he or she passes the mouse over the movie's viewport:

```
<img dynsrc="movies/intro.avi" start="fileopen,mouseover"
    src="pics/mvstill.gif">
```

5.2.7.5 *Combining movie <img> attributes*

Treat Internet Explorer inline movies as you would any image, mixing and matching the various movie-specific, as well as the standard and extended `<img>` tag attributes and values supported by the browser. For example, you might align the movie (or its image alternate, if displayed by another browser) to the right of the browser window:

```
<img dynsrc="movies/intro.avi" src="pics/mvstill.gif" align=right>
```

Combining attributes to achieve a special effect is good. We also recommend you combine attributes to give control to the user, when appropriate. For instance, if you set up a movie to loop incessantly, you should also include the `controls` attribute so the user can stop the movie without having to leave the HTML document.

As we stated in 5.2.7.4, by combining attributes you can also delay playback until the user passes the mouse over its viewport. Magically, the movie comes alive and plays continuously:

```
<img dynsrc="movies/magic.avi" start=mouseover
    loop=infinite src="pics/magic.gif">
```

5.3 Document Colors and Background Images

The HTML 2.0 standard makes no provision for controlling text color and background appearance for documents, instead allowing the local browser to determine the appearance of the documents. In order to give local users more control, browsers let them select text and background colors, as well as a background image to display behind each document. The user selections are applied to each document viewed.

In an egalitarian move, the browsers also extended HTML with various tags and attributes that let the document author control the document background and colors. These tags and attributes provide the maximum control to the author, letting colors and backgrounds be different for each document and allowing color changes for individual passages of text. [<font>, 4.6.3]

The local browser reigns supreme, however. User-selected color and background preferences can be made to override those contained in a document, undoing all the careful work of the document author.

5.3.1 Extensions to the <body> Tag

All extended attributes that control the document background, text color, and document margins are used with the **<body>** tag. [<body>, 3.7.1]

5.3.1.1 The bgcolor attribute

For Netscape and Internet Explorer users, you can change the default background color in the browser window to another hue with the `bgcolor` attribute for the `<body>` tag. Like the `color` attribute for the `<font>` and various heading tags, the required value of the `bgcolor` attribute may be expressed in either of two ways: as the red, green, and blue (RGB) components of the desired color or as a standard color name. Appendix E, *Color Names and Values*, provides a complete discussion of RGB color encoding along with a table of acceptable color names you can use with the `bgcolor` attribute.

Setting the background color is easy. To get a pure red background using RGB encoding, try:

```
<body bgcolor="#FF0000">
```

For a more subtle background, try:

```
<body bgcolor=peach>
```

5.3.1.2 The background attribute

If a splash of color isn't enough, you may also place an image into the background of a Netscape Navigator or Internet Explorer document display with the `background` attribute in its `<body>` tag.

The required value of the `background` attribute is the URL of an image. The browser automatically repeats (tiles) the image both horizontally and vertically to fill the entire window.

You normally should choose a small, somewhat dim image to create an interesting, but unobtrusive background pattern. Besides, a small, simple image traverses the network much faster than an intricate, full-screen image.

Figure 5-18 shows you how the extended browsers repeatedly render a single brick to create a wall of bricks for the document background:

```
<body background="pics/onebrick.gif">
```

Background images of various dimensions and sizes create interesting vertical and horizontal effects on the page. For instance, a tall skinny image might set off your document heading:

```
<body background="pics/vertical_fountain.gif">
<h3>Kumquat Lore</h3>
For centuries, many myths and legends have arisen around the kumquat.
```

If the *vertical_fountain.gif* is a narrow, tall image whose color grows lighter towards its base and whose length exceeds the length of the document body, the resulting document might look like the one shown in Figure 5-19.

Figure 5–18: One brick becomes many in a Netscape background

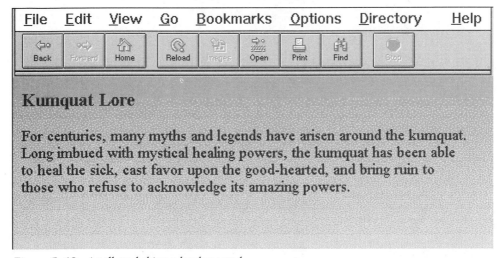

Figure 5–19: A tall and skinny background

You can achieve a similar effect horizontally with an image that is much wider than it is long (Figure 5-20).

5.3.1.3 *The bgproperties attribute*

The `bgproperties` attribute extension for the `<body>` tag is exclusive to Internet Explorer and only works in conjunction with the `background` attribute extension. The `bgproperties` attribute has a single value, `fixed`. It freezes the background image to the browser window, so it does not scroll with the other window contents. Hence, the example *H2Omark.gif* background image servers as a watermark for the document:

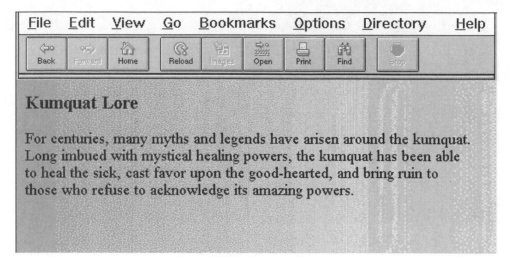

Figure 5-20: A long and skinny background

```
<body background="pics/H2Omark.gif" bgproperties="fixed">
```

5.3.1.4 The text attribute

Once you alter a document's background color or add a background image, you also might need to adjust the text color to ensure that users can read the text. The `text` attribute for the `<body>` tag does just that: it sets the color of all nonanchor text in the entire document.

Give the `text` attribute a color value in the same format as you use to specify a background color (see `bgcolor` above)—an RGB triplet or color name, as described in Appendix E. For example, to produce a document with blue text on a pale yellow background, use:

```
<body bgcolor="#777700" text="blue">
```

Of course, it's best to select a text color that contrasts well with your background color or image.

5.3.1.5 The link, vlink, and alink attributes

The `link`, `vlink`, and `alink` attributes of the `<body>` tag control the color of hypertext (`<a>` tag) in your documents. All three accept values that specify a color as an RGB triplet or color name, just like the `text` and `bgcolor` attributes.

The `link` attribute determines the color of all hyperlinks the user has not yet followed. The `vlink` attribute sets the color of all links the extended browser user had followed at one time or another. The `alink` attribute defines a color for active link text—one that is currently selected by the user and is under the mouse cursor with the mouse button depressed.

Interestingly, Netscape is the only browser that actually defines a separate color for `alink` text, so it's the only browser for which the `alink` attribute to the `<body>` tag applies; the others, including Internet Explorer, ignore it.

Like text color, you should be careful to select link colors that can be read against the document background. Moreover, the link colors should be different from the regular text as well as from each other.

5.3.1.6 The leftmargin attribute

Peculiar to Internet Explorer, the `leftmargin` attribute extension for the `<body>` tag lets you indent the left margin relative to the left edge of the browser's window, much like a margin on a sheet of paper. Other browsers ignore this attribute and normally left-justified body content abuts the left edge of the document window.

The value of the `leftmargin` attribute is the integer number of pixels for that left-margin indent; a value of 0 is the default. The margin is filled with the background color or image.

For example, Internet Explorer renders the following text justified against a margin 50 pixels away from the left edge of the browser window (Figure 5-21):

```
<body leftmargin=50>
Internet Explorer lets you indent the<br>
&lt;--left margin<br>
away from the left edge of the window.
</body>
```

5.3.1.7 The topmargin attribute

Like `leftmargin`, the `topmargin` attribute extension currently is exclusive to Internet Explorer. It may be included in the `<body>` tag to set a margin of space at the top of the document. The margin space is filled with the document's background color or image.

Body content begins flowing below the integer number of pixels you specify as the value for `topmargin`; a value of 0 is the default.

For example, Internet Explorer renders the following text at least 50 pixels down from the top edge of the browser window (Figure 5-22):

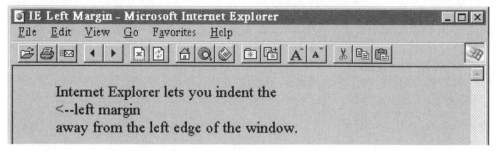

Figure 5–21: Internet Explorer's leftmargin attribute for indenting body content

```
<body topmargin=50>
<center>
^^^^^^^^^^^^^^^^^^^^^^^^^^^^^^^^^^^^^^^^^^^^^^^^^^
</center>
Internet Explorer can give your documents
a little extra headroom.
</body>
```

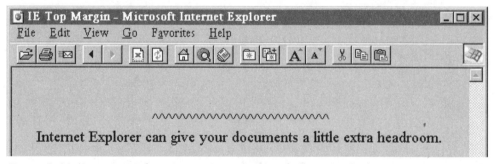

Figure 5–22: Internet Explorer's topmargin attribute for lowering body content

5.3.1.8 Mixing and matching body attributes

Although `background` and `bgcolor` attributes can appear in the same `<body>` tag, a background image will effectively hide the selected background color unless the image contains substantial portions of transparent color, as we described earlier in this chapter. But even if the image does hide the background color, go ahead and include the `bgcolor` attribute and some appropriate color value. That's because users can turn off image downloading, which includes background images, and so they may find your page otherwise left naked and unappealing. Moreover, without a `bgcolor` attribute or a downloaded (for whatever reason) background image, the extended browsers merrily ignore your text and link color attributes, too, reverting instead to its own default values, or the ones chosen by the user.

5.3.2 Extending a Warning

The various color and image extensions work wonderfully, particularly the colorful ones, assuming that all users have a 256-color display, lots of available memory, unlimited network bandwidth, and good visual acuity. In reality, many users have monochrome or limited color displays, limited memory for caching images, extremely restricted network bandwidth, and poor vision.

Because of these limitations, you should seriously consider not using any of these extensions in your documents. Much like early users of the Macintosh felt compelled to create documents using ransom-note typography ("I've got 40 fonts on this thing, and I'm going to use them all!"), many authors of Netscape- or Internet Explorer-specific documents cannot avoid adding some sort of textured background to every document they create ("I've got 13 wood grains and 22 kinds of marbling, and I'm going to use them all!").

In reality, except for the very clever ones, texture-mapped backgrounds add no information to your documents. The value of your document ultimately lies in its text and imagery, not the cheesy blue swirly pattern in the background. No matter how cool it looks, your readers are not benefiting and could be losing readability.

We advise you not to use the color extensions except for comparatively frivolous endeavors or unless the extension really adds to the document's value, such as for business advertising and marketing pages.

5.3.2.1 Problems with background images

Here are some of the things that can go wrong with background images:

- The time to load the document is increased by the amount of time needed to load the image. Until the background image is completely downloaded, no further document rendering is possible.

- The background image takes up room in the browser's local cache, displacing other images that might actually contain useful information. This makes other documents, which might not even have backgrounds, take that much longer to load.

- The colors in the image may not be available on the user's display, forcing the browser to dither the image. This replaces large areas of a single color with repeating patterns of several other closer, but not cleaner, colors and can make the text more difficult to read.

- Because the browser must actually display an image in the background, as opposed to filling an area with a single color, scrolling through the document can take much longer.

- Even if it's clear onscreen, text printed on top of an image invariably is more difficult if not impossible to read.

- Fonts vary widely between machines; the ones you use with your browser that work fine with a background pattern often end up jagged and difficult to read on another machine.

5.3.2.2 Problems with background, text, and link colors

There also are a slew of problems you will encounter if you play with background colors, including:

- The color you choose, while just lovely in your eyes, may look terrible to the user. Why annoy them by changing what users most likely have already set as their own default background color?

- While you may be a member of the "light text on a dark background" school of document design, many people also favor the "dark text on a light background" style that has been consistently popular for over three thousand years. Instead of bucking the trend, assume that the user has already set their browser to a comfortable color scheme.

- Some users are color-blind. What may be a nifty-looking combination of colors to you, may be completely unreadable to others. One combination in particular to avoid is green for unvisited links and red for visited links. Millions of men are afflicted with red/green color blindness.

- Your brilliant hue may not be available on the user's display, and the browser may be forced to choose one that's close instead. For displays with very few colors (like those of several million 16-color VGA Windows-based machines currently in use) the close colors for the text and the background might be the same color!

- For the same reasons above, active, unvisited, and visited links may all wind up the same color on limited-color displays.

- By changing text colors, particularly those for visited and unvisited links, you may completely confuse the user. By changing those colors, you effectively force them to experiment with your page, clicking a few links here and there to learn your color scheme.

- Most page designers have no formal training in either cognitive psychology, fine arts, graphic arts, or industrial design, yet feel fully capable of selecting appropriate colors for their documents. If you must fiddle with the colors, ask a professional to pick them for you.

5.3.2.3 And, then again

There is no denying the fact that these extensions result in some very stunning HTML documents. And they are fun to explore and play with. So, rather than leave this chapter on a sour note of caution, we encourage you to go ahead and play: just play carefully.

5.4 Background Audio

There is one other form of inline multimedia generally available to Web surfers—audio. Most browsers treat audio multimedia as separate documents, downloaded and displayed by special helper applications or applets. Internet Explorer, on the other hand, contains a built-in sound decoder and supports a special HTML tag that lets you integrate an audio file with your document that plays in the background as a soundtrack for your page.

We applaud the developers of Internet Explorer for providing a mechanism for more cleanly integrating audio into HTML documents. And the possibilites with audio are very enticing. But at the same time, we caution authors that the special tags and attributes for audio don't work with other browsers, and whether or not this is the method that the majority of browsers will eventually support is not at all assured. So, beware.[*]

5.4.1 The <bgsound> Tag

Use the <bgsound> tag to play a soundtrack in the background. This tag is for Internet Explorer documents only. All other browsers ignore the tag. It downloads and plays an audio file when the host HTML document is first downloaded by the user and displayed in their browser. The background sound file also will replay whenever the user refreshes the browser display.

5.4.1.1 The src attribute

The src attribute is required for the <bgsound> tag. Its value references the URL for the related sound file. For example, when the Internet Explorer user first downloads an HTML document containing the tag:

---

[*] There is an alternative way of providing background audio for Netscape, which we describe in Chapter 11, *Netscape Dynamic Documents.*

<bgsound> (Internet Explorer only)

Function:
    Plays a soundtrack in the document backgound

Attributes:
    LOOP (Internet Explorer only)
    SRC (Internet Explorer only)

End tag:
    None

Contains:
    Nothing

Used in:
    body_content

```
<bgsound src="audio/welcome.wav">
```

they will hear the *welcome.wav* audio file—perhaps an inviting message—play once through their computer's sound system.

Currently, Internet Explorer can handle three different sound formats files: `wav`, the native format for PCs; `au`, the native format for most UNIX workstations; and MIDI, a universal music-encoding scheme (also see Table 5-1, which appears in 5.7.1).

5.4.1.2 The loop attribute

Like Internet inline movies, the `loop` attribute for the browser's `<bgsound>` tag lets you replay a background soundtrack for a certain number of times, or over and over again forever—at least until the user moves on to another page or quits the browser.

The value of the `loop` attribute is the integer number of times to replay the audio file, or `infinite`, which makes the soundtrack repeat endlessly.

For example:

```
<bgsound src="audio/tadum.wav" loop=10>
```

repeats the ta-dum soundtrack ten times, whereas:

```
<bgsound src="audio/noise.wav" loop=infinite>
```

continuously plays the noise soundtrack.

5.5 Animated Text

In what appears to be an effort to woo advertisers, Internet Explorer has added a form of animated text to HTML. The animation is simple—text scrolling horizontally across the display—but effective for moving banners and other elements that readily and easily animate an otherwise static document. On the other hand, like the `<blink>` tag, animated text can easily become intrusive and abusive for the reader. Use with caution, please, if at all.

5.5.1 The *<marquee>* Tag

The `<marquee>` tag defines the text that scrolls across the Internet Explorer user's display.

<marquee> (Internet Explorer only)

Function:
Create a scrolling text marquee

Attributes:
ALIGN
BEHAVIOR
BGCOLOR
DIRECTION
HEIGHT
HSPACE
LOOP
SCROLLAMOUNT
SCROLLDELAY
VSPACE
WIDTH

End tag:
</marquee>; never omitted

Contains:
plain_text

Used in:
body_content

The `<marquee>` tag is for Internet Explorer only. The text contained between the `<marquee>` tag and its required `</marquee>` end tag scrolls horizontally across the display. The various tag attributes control the size of the display area, its appearance, its alignment with the surrounding text, and the scrolling speed.

The <marquee> tag and attributes are ignored by other browsers, but its contents are not. They are displayed as static text, sans any alignment or special treatments afforded by the <marquee> tag attributes.

5.5.1.1 *The align attribute*

Internet Explorer places <marquee> text into the surrounding body content just as if it were an embedded image. As a result, you can align the marquee within the surrounding text.

The align attribute accepts a value of top, middle, or bottom, meaning that the specified point of the marquee will be aligned with the corresponding point in the surrounding text. Thus:

```
<marquee align=top>
```

aligns the top of the marquee area with the top of the surrounding text. Also see the height and width, hspace and vspace attributes below that control the dimensions of the marquee.

5.5.1.2 *The behavior, direction, and loop attributes*

Together, these three attributes control the style, direction, and duration of the scrolling in your marquee.

The behavior attribute accepts three values:

scroll (default)
> The value of scroll causes the marquee to act like the grand marquee in Times Square: The marquee area initially is empty, the text then scrolls in from one side (controlled by the direction attribute), continues across until it reaches the other side of the marquee, and then scrolls off until the marquee is once again empty.

slide
> This value causes the marquee to start empty. Text then scrolls in from one side (controlled by the direction attribute), stops when it reaches the other side, and the text remains onscreen.

alternate
> Specifying alternate as the value for the behavior attribute causes the marquee to start with the text fully visible at one end of the marquee area. The text then scrolls until it reaches the other end, whereupon it reverses direction and scrolls back to its starting point.

If you do not specify a marquee behavior, the default behavior is scroll.

The `direction` attribute sets the direction for marquee text scrolling. Acceptable values are either `left` (the default) or `right`. Note that the starting end for the scrolling is opposite to the direction: `left` means that the text starts at the right of the marquee and scrolls to the left. Remember also that rightward-scrolling text is counter-intuitive to anyone who reads left to right.

The `loop` attribute determines how many times the marquee text scrolls. If an integer value is provided, the scrolling action is repeated that many times. If the value is `infinite`, the scrolling repeats until the user moves on to another document within the browser.

Putting some of these attributes together:

```
<marquee align=center loop=infinite>
  Kumquats aren't filling
  ..........      Taste great, too!
</marquee>
```

the example message starts at the right side of the display window (default direction), scrolls leftward all the way across and off the Internet Explorer display, and then starts over again until the user moves on to another page. Notice the intervening periods and spaces for the "trailer"; you cannot append one marquee to another.

Also, the `slide`-style of scrolling looks jerky when repeated and should only be scrolled once. Other scrolling behaviors work well with repeated scrolling.

5.5.1.3 The bgcolor attribute

The `bgcolor` attribute lets you change the background color of the marquee area. It accepts either an RGB color value or one of the standard color names. See Appendix E for a full discussion of both color-specification methods.

To create a marquee area whose color is yellow, you would write:

```
<marquee bgcolor=yellow>
```

5.5.1.4 The height and width attributes

The `height` and `width` attributes determine the size of the marquee area. If not specified, the marquee area extends all the way across the Internet Explorer display and will be just high enough to enclose the marquee text.

Both attributes accept either a numeric value, indicating an absolute size in pixels, or a percentage, indicating the size as a percentage of the browser window height and width.

For example, to create a marquee that is 50 pixels tall and occupies one-third of the display window, use:

```
<marquee height=50 width="33%">
```

While it is generally a good idea to ensure the `height` attribute is large enough to contain the enclosed text, it is not uncommon to specify a width that is smaller than the enclosed text. In this case, the text scrolls the smaller marquee area, resulting in a kind of "viewport" marquee familiar to most people.

5.5.1.5 *The hspace and vspace attributes*

The `hspace` and `vspace` attributes let you create some space between the marquee and the surrounding text. This usually makes the marquee stand out from the text around it.

Both attributes require an integer value specifying the space needed in pixels. The `hspace` attribute creates space to the left and right of the marquee; the `vspace` attribute creates space above and below the marquee. To create 10 pixels of space all the way around your marquee, for example, use:

```
<marquee vspace=10 hspace=10>
```

5.5.1.6 *The scrollamount and scrolldelay attributes*

These attributes control the speed and smoothness of the scrolling marquee.

The `scrollamount` attribute value is the number of pixels needed to move text each successive movement during the scrolling process. Lower values mean smoother, but slower scrolling; higher numbers create faster, but jerkier text motion.

The `scrolldelay` attribute lets you set the number of milliseconds to wait between successive movements during the scrolling process. The smaller this value, the faster the scrolling.

You can use a low `scrolldelay` to mitigate the slowness of a small, smooth `scrollamount`. For example:

```
<marquee scrollamount=1 scrolldelay=1>
```

scrolls the text one pixel for each movement, but does so as fast as possible. In this case, the scrolling speed is limited by the capabilities of the browser's computer.

5.6 *Executable Applications*

One of the more exciting developments in Web technologies is the ability to deliver applications directly to the user's browser, where they are executed on the client machine. These applications are typically small tools, hence the term "applet," that enhance the HTML page being displayed.

Although currently supported only by Netscape Navigator version 2.0 and HotJava from Sun Microsystems,[*] applets, particularly those prepared with the Java language, will become a sizeable part of mainstream Web activity. Many other browser vendors have promised support for Java.

Applets, like client-side image maps, represent a shift in the basic model of Web communications. Until recently, all computational work on the Web was performed by the server, with the browser being nothing more than a glorified terminal. With applets and client-side image maps, some or all of the computational load is shifted to the client and browser.

They also represent a way of extending a browser's features without forcing users to purchase or otherwise acquire a new browser, as is the case when developers implement new tag and attribute extensions to HTML. Nor do users have to acquire and install any special application, as is required for helper or plugin applications. This means that once users have a browser that supports applets, you can deliver HTML display and multimedia innovations immediately.

5.6.1 The Applet Model

Applets are like other accessory parts of an HTML document. When the page is loaded by the browser, it may contain special tags that identify applets to be downloaded and executed by the browser. Like other Web resources, applets are identified by a URL and retrieved via the normal HTTP protocol.

Once downloaded, the browser provides a portion of the document for the applet to use as its display space. The author may control the size and position of this display area; the applet controls what is presented inside.

After arriving on the browser, the applet begins execution. It has access to a restricted environment within the user's computer. Several applets may be placed in a single document; they all execute in parallel and may communicate with each other.

Applets have access to the mouse and keyboard, and may receive input from the user. They can initiate network connections and retrieve data from other servers on the Internet. In sum, applets are full-fledged programs, complete with a variety of input and output mechanisms, along with a full suite of network services. While the browser may limit their access to its computer system, applets have complete control of their virtual environment within the browser.

---

[*] Sun released an alpha version of HotJava in 1995. That version is now obsolete, but a new version has not been released as of March 1996.

5.6.2 *The Applet Advantage*

There are several advantages of applets, not the least of which is providing more compelling user interfaces within a Web page. For instance, an applet might create a graphical user interface and present the user with menus, choices, text fields, and similar input tools. When the user clicks a button within the applet's region, the applet can respond by displaying results within the region, signalling another applet, or even by loading a completely new page into the browser.

Without applets, interactions between the user and the HTML document are more restricted and less responsive—such as with forms—principally because a server and its incumbent Internet connections are involved. By allowing the action to occur locally via an applet, responsiveness is greatly improved, thereby opening up a wealth of interactive opportunities.

We don't mean to imply that the only use of applets is to enhance the user interface. An applet is a full-fledged program that can perform any number of computational and display tasks on the client computer. An applet might implement a real-time video display, or perform circuit simulation, or engage the user in a game, for instance.

5.6.3 *Using Applets Correctly*

An applet is nothing more than another tool you may use to produce compelling and useful Web pages. Keep in mind that an applet uses computational resources on the client to run and therefore places a load on the user's computer. It can degrade system performance.

Similarly, if an applet uses a lot of network bandwidth to accomplish its task (a real-time video feed, for example), it may make other network communication unbearably slow. While such applications are fun, they do little more than annoy your target audience.

To use an applet correctly, balance the load between the browser and the server: For each page, decide which tasks are best left to the server (forms processing, index searches, and the like) and which tasks are better suited for local processing (user interface enhancements, real-time data presentation, small animations, and so on). Divide the processing accordingly. Remember that many users have slower network connections and computers than you do and design your applets to satisfy the majority of your audience.

Used the right way, applets seamlessly enhance your pages and provide a satisfying experience for your audience. Used improperly, applets are just another annoying bandwidth waster, alienating your users and hurting your pages.

5.6.4 *Writing Applets*

Creating applets is a programming task, not necessarily a job for the HTML author, and certainly way beyond the scope of this book. For details, we recommend you consult any of the many applet programming texts that have recently appeared on bookshelves everywhere, including *Java in a Nutshell* from O'Reilly & Associates.

Today, one language dominates the applet programming world: Java. Developed by Sun Microsystems, Java is a restricted form of C++ and supports an object-oriented programming style wherein classes of applets can be used and reused to build complex applications. JavaScript, from Netscape Communications, is a simpler and compatible form of Java that makes programming somewhat easier. And, surely, other Java-like applet development environments will emerge as the technology catches on.

By invention, applets built from the same language should run with any browser that supports them. So far, that is the case for Java applets. But the technology is so new it's hard to predict whether cross-platform integrity and universal support for all common browsers and computers will prove a reality or a pipe dream. If the confusion of browsers is any indication. ... Well, be forewarned.

5.6.5 *The <applet> Tag*

The `<applet>` tag extension currently is supported only in Netscape 2.0 and Hot-Java. Use it within your HTML document to name an application to be downloaded and executed with the current document and to define a region within the document display for the application's display area. You may also supply alternative content within the `<applet>` tag for display by browsers that do not support applets.

The `<applet>` tag defines an application that is downloaded and executed within the current document with its display in a discrete region in the document window. One required attribute identifies the class name of the applet program. Optional attributes let you control the alignment and dimensions of the applet display region and specify an alternative URL for the class' code.

The browser inserts the applet display region into the containing text flow exactly like an inline image—without line breaks, as a single large entity.

Most applets require one or more parameters to control their execution. These parameters are placed between the `<applet>` tag and its corresponding `</applet>` end tag using the `<param>` tag. The browser retrieves the applet program from the server when the HTML document is displayed by the user. It

---

<applet> (Netscape only)

Function:
    Insert an application into the current text flow

Attributes:
    ALIGN
    ALTCODE
    CODE
    BASE
    HEIGHT
    HSPACE
    NAME
    VSPACE
    WIDTH

End tag:
    </applet>; never omitted

Contains:
    applet_content

Used in:
    text

---

then executes the applet, feeding it parameters from inside the `<param>` tag. Execution continues until the code terminates itself or when the user stops viewing the page containing the applet.

5.6.5.1 *The align attribute*

Like an image, you may control the alignment of an applet's display region with respect to its surrounding text. In fact, the `<applet>` tag's `align` attribute honors all the alignment values used by Netscape's `<img>` tag, including `top`, `texttop`, `middle`, `absmiddle`, `baseline`, `bottom`, and `absbottom,` as well as `left` and `right` alignments for wrapping text. [image alignment, 5.2.6.4]

5.6.5.2 *The alt attribute*

The `alt` attribute gives you a way to gracefully tell users something is missing if, for some reason, the applet cannot or will not run. Its value is a quote-enclosed message string that, like the `alt` attribute for images, gets displayed in lieu of the applet itself.

The `alt` message is only for browsers that support applets and is there to let the user know that they've disabled applet execution, that the applet may not be accessible, or that the applet may have executed incorrectly. See 5.6.5.8 to find out how to inform users of other browsers why they can't view an applet.

5.6.5.3 The code attribute

The code attribute is the only required one and defines the class of <applet> program code to be executed. Its value may be either a simple class name or a fully qualified package. Use a conventional name to specify a class. Define packages using a hierarchy of package names separated by periods (.).

For example, to execute an instance of a class named Clock, you might use:

```
<applet code=Clock>
</applet>
```

Similarly, if the Clock class is part of a package, you might use that package's fully qualified name:

```
<applet code=time.clock.Clock>
</applet>
```

The browser will locate the code for the applet using the current document's base URL. The browser automatically appends the suffix ".class" to the class name. Hence, if the current document's URL is:

```
http://www.kumquat.com/harvest_time.html
```

the browser would retrieve the applet code for our Clock class example above as:

```
http://www.kumquat.com/Clock.class
```

Package names get handled slightly differently. Each element of the package name becomes a directory within the URL path. Hence, the browser will retrieve our *time.clock.Clock* package example as:

```
http://www.kumquat.com/time/clock/Clock.class
```

5.6.5.4 The codebase attribute

The code attribute value is not a URL. Use the codebase attribute to provide an alternative base URL from which the applet code is to be retrieved. The value of this attribute is a URL pointing to a directory containing the class defined by the code attribute. The codebase URL overrides, but does not permanently replace the document's base URL, which is the default if no codebase is used. [URLs, 6.2]

Continuing with our previous example, suppose the Clock class is kept in a separate directory named classes. You could retrieve the applet by specifying:

```
<applet code=Clock codebase="http://www.kumquat.com/classes/">
</applet>
```

which resolves to the URL:

```
http://www.kumquat.com/classes/Clock.class.
```

Although we used an absolute URL in this example, you also can use a relative URL. For instance, in most cases the applets are stored on the same server as the host HTML documents, so we'd usually be better off, for relocation sake, specifying a relative URL for the codebase, such as:

```
<applet code=Clock codebase="/classes/">
</applet>
```

5.6.5.5 The name attribute

The `name` attribute lets you supply a unique name for this instance of the code class. This attribute is not required unless you need to reference the applet instance elsewhere in your document via another applet.

For example, suppose you have two clock applets in your document, along with two applets used to set those clocks. You provide unique names for the clocks using the `name` attribute, then pass those names to the setting applets using the `<param>` tag, which we discuss below:

```
<applet code=Clock name=clock1>
</applet>
<applet code=Clock name=clock2>
</applet>
<applet code=Setter>
  <param name=clockToSet value=clock1>
</applet>
<applet code=Setter>
  <param name=clockToSet value=clock2>
</applet>
```

Since we have no need to distinguish between the Setter applets, we choose not to name their instances.

5.6.5.6 The height and width attributes

Identical to the counterparts for the `<img>` tag, the `height` and `width` attributes define the size of the applet's display region in the document. They both accept values indicating the size of the region in pixels. [<img> height and width, 5.2.6.9]

The display region's dimensions often must match some other applet requirement, so be careful to check these values with the applet programmer. Sometimes, the applet may scale its display output to match your specified region.

For example, suppose our example clock applet should grow or shrink to fit nearly any size display region. Hence, we might create a square clock 100 pixels wide by 100 pixels tall:

```
<applet code=Clock height=100 width=100>
</applet>
```

5.6.5.7 *The hspace and vspace attributes*

As with an image, surrounding text tightly abuts the applet display region. The `hspace` and `vspace` attributes let you interpose some empty space around the applet region to set it off from the text. Both attributes accept a value that indicates pixels of space, with the `hspace` attribute creating a space to the left and right of the region; the `vspace` attribute adding space above and below the region.

For example, to give our clock some breathing room on the page, we could place an additional five pixels of space around it:

```
<applet code=Clock height=100 width=100
  hspace=5 vspace=5>
</applet>
```

5.6.5.8 *Supporting incompatible browsers*

Since most of today's browsers do not support applets or the `<applet>` tag, you may sometimes need to tell readers what they are missing. You do this by including HTML body content between the `<applet>` and `</applet>` tags.

Browsers that support the `<applet>` tags ignore the HTML content inside. (Use the `alt` attribute to notify applet-enabled browser users when the applet doesn't display for some reason.) Of course, browsers that don't support applets don't recognize the `<applet>` tags. Being generally tolerant of apparent HTML mistakes, they will usually ignore the unrecognized tag and blithely go on to display whatever content may appear inside. It's as simple as that. The following fragment tells applet-incapable browser users they won't see our clock example:

```
<applet code=Clock>
  If your browser were capable of handling applets, you'd see
  a nifty clock right here!
</applet>
```

Remember that this contained text is different from the text supplied by the `alt` attribute of the `<applet>` tag. The `alt` text is displayed by browsers that support the `<applet>` tag but cannot execute or display the specified applet. The contained text is displayed by browsers that do not support the `<applet>` tag at all. In order to accomodate both classes of browsers, the considerate author supplies both for each `<applet>` tag:

```
<applet code=Clock height=100 width=100
  alt="[ Clock applet not available ]">
  <param name=style value=analog>
```

```
    If your browser were capable of handling applets, you'd see
    a nifty analog clock right here!
</applet>
```

5.6.6 The <param> Tag

The `<param>` tag supplies parameters for the containing `<applet>` tag.

<param> (Netscape only)

Function:
    Supply a parameter to an <applet>

Attributes:
    NAME
    VALUE

End tag:
    None

Contains:
    Nothing

Used in:
    applet_content

The `<param>` tag has no content and no end tag. It appears, perhaps with other `<param>` tags, only between an `<applet>` tag and its end tag. Use the `<param>` tag to pass parameters to the applet program as required for it to function correctly.

5.6.6.1 The name and value attributes

The `<param>` tag has two required attributes: `name` and `value`. Both attributes accept strings as their value and together define a name/value pair that is passed to the applet.

For instance, our Clock applet example might let you specify the time zone by which it sets its hour hand. To pass the parameter named "timezone" with the value "EST" to our example applet, you would specify the parameters as:

```
<applet code=Clock>
  <param name=timezone value=EST>
</applet>
```

Since both attributes had simple strings for values, we did not enclose the values in quotes. For values with embedded punctuation and spaces, be sure to delimit the strings accordingly.

The browser will pass the name/value pairs to the applet, but that is no guarantee that the applet is expecting the parameters, that the names and values are correct, or that the applet will even use the parameters. Correct parameter names, including capitalization, and acceptable values are determined by the applet author. The wise HTML document author will work closely with the applet author or have detailed documentation to ensure that the applet parameters are named correctly and assigned valid values.

5.7 Other Multimedia Content

The Web is completely open-minded about the types of content that can be exchanged by servers and browsers. In this section, we look at a different way to reference images, along with audio, video, and other document formats.

5.7.1 Embedded Versus Referenced Content

Images currently enjoy a special status among the various media that can be included within an HTML document and displayed in line with other content by all but a few browsers. Sometimes, however, as we discussed earlier in this chapter, you may also reference images externally, particularly large ones whose details are important, but not immediately necessary to the document content. Other multimedia elements, including digital audio and video, currently must be referenced as separate documents external to the current one. However, recent innovations in browser technology and extensions to HTML are lifting those barriers and allowing for more integration of multimedia in Web documents. Internet Explorer, for instance, has extensions for inline movies and background audio. Applets with Netscape or HotJava also enable multimedia display integrated with the HTML page. [video extensions, 5.2.7] [background audio, 5.4] [applets, 5.6.1]

You normally use the anchor tag (<a>) to link external multimedia elements to the current document. Just like other link elements selected by the user, the browser downloads the multimedia object and presents it with help from a helper application to the user. Referenced content is always a two-step process: present the document that links to the desired multimedia object, then present the object if the user selects the link. [<a>, 6.3.1]

In the case of images, you can choose how to present images to the user: inline and immediately available via the <img> tag, or referenced and subsequently available via the <a> tag. If your images are small and critical to the current document, you should provide them inline. If they are large or are only a secondary element of the current document, make them available as referenced content via the <a> tag.

If you choose to provide images via the <a> tag, it is sometimes a courtesy to your readers to indicate the size of the referenced image in the referencing document and perhaps provide a thumbnail sketch. Users can then determine whether it is worth their time and expense to retrieve it.

5.7.2 *Referencing Audio, Video, and Images*

You reference any external document, regardless of type or format, in an HTML document via a conventional anchor (<a>) link:

```
The <a href="sounds/anthem.au">Kumquat Grower's Anthem</a> is
a rousing tribute to the thousands of 'quat growers around
the world.
```

Just like any referenced document, the server delivers the desired multimedia object to the browser when the user selects the link. If the browser finds the document is not HTML, but some other format, it automatically invokes an appropriate rendering tool to display or otherwise convey the contents of the object to the user.

You can configure your browser with special helper applications that handle different document formats in different ways. Audio files, for example, might be passed to an audio-processing tool, while video files are given to a video-playing tool. If a browser has not been configured to handle a particular document format, the browser will inform you and offer to simply save the document to disk. You can later use an appropriate viewing tool to examine the document.

Browsers identify and specially handle multimedia files from one of two different hints: either from the file's Multipurpose Internet Mail Extension (MIME) type provided by the server or from a special suffix in the file's name. The browser prefers MIME because of its richer description of the file and its contents, but will infer the file's contents (type and format) of the object by the file suffix; *.gif* or *.jpg*, for GIF and JPEG encoded images, for example, or *.au* for a special sound file.

Since not all browsers look for a MIME type, nor will they all be correctly configured with helper applications by their users, you should always use the correct file suffix in the names of multimedia objects. See Table 5-1 for examples.

Table 5–1: Common Multimedia Formats and Respective Filename Extensions

Format	Type	Extension	Platform of Origin
GIF	Image	*gif*	Any
JPEG	Image	*jpg, jpeg, jpe*	Any
XBM	Image	*xbm*	UNIX

Table 5-1: Common Multimedia Formats and Respective Filename Extensions (continued)

Format	Type	Extension	Platform of Origin
TIFF	Image	*tif, tiff*	Any
PICT	Image	*pic, pict*	Any
Rasterfile	Image	*ras*	Sun
MPEG	Movie	*mpg, mpeg*	Any
AVI	Movie	*avi*	Microsoft
QuickTime	Movie	*qt, mov*	Apple
AU	Audio	*au, snd*	Sun
WAV	Audio	*wav*	Microsoft
AIFF	Audio	*aif, aiff*	Apple
MIDI	Audio	*midi, mid*	Any
PostScript	Document	*ps, eps, ai*	Any
Acrobat	Document	*pdf*	Any

5.7.3 Appropriate Linking Styles

Creating effective links to external multimedia documents is critical. Since the browser cannot play or display the object directly (except for some inline images), the user needs some indication of what the object is and perhaps the kind of application the linked object needs to execute. Moreover, most multimedia objects are quite large, so common courtesy tells us to provide users with some indication of the time and expense involved in downloading it.

In lieu of, or in addition to, the anchor and surrounding text, a small thumbnail of large images or a familiar icon that indicates the referenced object's format may be useful.

5.7.4 Embedding Other Document Types

The Web can deliver nearly any type of electronic document, not just graphics, sound, and video files. To display them, however, the client browser needs a helper application installed and referenced. Recent browsers also support *plugin* accessory software and, as described earlier in this chapter, *applets* which may extend the browser for some special function, including inline display of multimedia objects.

For example, consider a company whose extensive product documentation was prepared and stored in some popular layout application like FrameMaker, Quark XPress, or PageMaker. The Web offers an excellent way for distributing that documentation over a worldwide network, but converting to HTML would be too costly at this time.

The solution is to prepare a few HTML documents that catalog and link the alternative files and invoke the appropriate display applet. Or, make sure the users' browsers have the plugin software or are configured to invoke the appropriate helper application—FrameMaker, for example, if the document is in FrameMaker format. Then, if a link to a FrameMaker document is chosen, the tool is started and accordingly displays the document.

5.8 Beyond HTML

Ever since the publication of Vernor Vinge's groundbreaking science-fiction novelette *True Names* in 1978, many computer programmers and users have been fascinated by the ideas of "virtual reality" and "cyberspace"—computer interfaces using 3D surround graphics with which a user could interact in something like the way our physical bodies interact with the real world.

In 1994, two Silicon Valley programmers with backgrounds in computer graphics went public with the provocative idea that the distributed-hypertext model of HTML might be used as a foundation for building cyberspace. A working group began adapting and enhancing a graphics-description language previously developed at Silicon Graphics Inc. to be used with HTML and Web software.

The result was Virtual Reality Markup Language (VRML). VRML follows the HTML model in several important respects. Like HTML, VRML is a content-based, plain-ASCII markup language that describes its universe at a high level, and leaves it up to the browser or client program to make detailed presentation decisions. VRML technology has since evolved even more rapidly than the Web itself. As of January 1996, several first-cut VRML browsers are available, including an add-on for the popular Netscape browser for PCs.

VRML documents describe worlds populated with 3D shapes. Developers build objects from basic shapes, such as cubes, cones, and spheres, with a variety of surface effects, including texture maps and lighting, available for composing realistic objects. It's possible to associate URLs with objects in a VRML world in such a way that when a user touches the object, they are transported to another VRML world, an HTML document, or a CGI script (which itself may generate a VRML world).

Some intriguing demonstration interfaces to large databases have already been built and suggest the beginnings of true cyberspace architecture. So far, however, these demonstrations fall short of the strong virtual-reality experience depicted in science-fiction books and movies. Three related problems bar the way. The design problem is that VRML currently has no capacity to do animation. VRML worlds are static. While it's easy to move the user's viewpoint in a VRML world, the only way to actually move or alter a VRML object is to generate an entirely new document and render it. Proposals to support animation description are in the works, but none have yet been adopted as of January 1996. This may well have changed by the time you read this.

The second, practical problem is that reasonably priced desktop machines in 1996 simply don't have the capacity to do realistic animation of general scenes. The computational cost of point-plotting, hidden-line elimination, texture-mapping, and lighting calculations gets very large, very quickly. Companies that care about animation, like Industrial Light and Magic, use multimillion-dollar special-purpose supercomputers for this job because they have to. Current VRML browsers, for example, frequently have to drop back from full-surface rendering to wire-frame mode when moving the viewer's eyepoint. Even without animation, rendering of static images including texture-mapping, spheres and sculpted surfaces can take many seconds, which is unacceptably slow.

The third problem is that VRML worlds are not yet shared spaces. For virtual reality to begin to approach the interactive richness of the real world, it must be possible to interact in a VRML world not merely with objects but with the "avatar" or cyberspatial manifestations of other users. This is an area of very active interest to the VRML developers (many of whom have been directly inspired by the Black Sun environment depicted in Neil Stephenson's immensely popular science-fiction novel, *Snow Crash*), but no single solution has yet emerged.

(There are other, comparatively minor problems: VRML has no sound capability, for example. But it's easy to imagine a solution for this one within current technology.)

Thus, VRML is still currently more a promise and a technology direction than a complete answer to the virtual-reality question. But the trend-curves of desktop hardware performance and the amount of money being poured into better multimedia graphics accelerators make it one worth careful watching. With another few years' hardware evolution and a few foreseeable VRML language enhancements, a true distributed cyberspace, built around and using WWW servers, may well be within our reach.

6

Links and Webs

Until this point, we've dealt with HTML documents as standalone entities, concentrating on the language elements you use for structure and to format your work. The true power of HTML, however, lies in its ability to join collections of documents together into a full library of information, and to link documents with other collections around the world. Just as readers have considerable control over how the document looks onscreen, with hyperlinks they also have control over the order of presentation as they navigate through your information. It's the "HT" in HTML—hypertext—and it's the twist that spins the Web.

6.1 Hypertext Basics

A fundamental feature of hypertext is that you can hyperlink documents; you can point to another place inside the current document, inside another document in the local collection, or inside a document anywhere on the Internet. The documents thereby become an intricately woven web of information. Get the name analogy now? The target document is usually somehow related to and enriches the source; the linking element in the source should convey that relationship to the reader.

Hyperlinks can be used for all kinds of effect. They can be used inside tables of contents and lists of topics. With a click of the mouse on their browser screen, readers select and automatically jump to a topic of interest in the same document or to another document located in an entirely different collection somewhere around the world.

Hyperlinks also point readers to more information about a mentioned topic. "For more information, see 'Kumquats on Parade,'" for example. HTML authors use hyperlinks to reduce repetitive information. For instance, we recommend you sign your name to each of your documents. Rather than include full contact information in each document, a hyperlink connects your name to a single place that contains your address, phone number, and so forth.

A hyperlink, or *anchor* in HTML standard parlance, is marked by the <a> tag and comes in two flavors. As we detail below, one type of anchor creates a hot spot in the document that, when activated and selected (usually with a mouse) by the user, causes the browser to link. It automatically loads and displays another portion of the same or another document altogether, or triggers some Internet service-related action, such as sending email or downloading a special file. The other type of anchor creates a label,[*] a place in an HTML document that can be referenced as a hyperlink.

6.2 Referencing Documents: The URL

As we discussed earlier, every document on the World Wide Web has a unique address. (Imagine the chaos if they didn't.) The document's address is known as its Uniform Resource Locator (URL).[†]

Several HTML tags include a URL attribute value, including hyperlinks, inline images, and forms. All use the same URL syntax to specify the location of a Web resource, regardless of the type or content of that resource. That's why it's known as a *Uniform* Resource Locator.

Since they can be used to represent almost any resource on the Internet, URLs come in a variety of flavors. All URLs, however, have the same top-level syntax:

```
scheme: scheme_specific_part
```

The *scheme* describes the kind of object the URL references; the *scheme_specific_part* is, well, the part that is peculiar to the specific scheme. The

---

[*] Both types of HTML anchors use the same tag; perhaps that's why they have the same name. Nonetheless, we find it's easier if you differentiate them and think of the one type that provides the hotspot and address of a hyperlink as the "link," and the other type that marks the target portion of a document as the "anchor."

[†] "URL" usually is pronounced "you are ell," not "earl."

important thing to note is that the *scheme* is always separated from the *scheme_specific_part* by a colon (:) with no intervening spaces.

6.2.1 Writing a URL

URLs are written using the displayable characters in the US-ASCII character set. If you need to use a character in a URL that is not part of this character set, you must encode the character using a special notation. The encoding notation replaces the desired character with three characters: a percent sign and two hexadecimal digits whose value corresponds to the position of the character in the ASCII character set.

This is easier than it sounds. One of the most common encoded special characters is the space character, whose position in the character set is 20 hexadecimal. To encode a space in a URL, replace it with %20:

```
http://www.kumquat.com/new%20pricing.html
```

This URL actually retrieves a document named *new pricing.html* from the server.

6.2.1.1 Handling reserved and unsafe characters

In addition to the nonprinting characters, you'll need to encode reserved and unsafe characters in your URLs as well.

Reserved characters are those characters that have a specific meaning within the URL itself. For example, many URLs use the slash character (/) to separate elements of a pathname within the URL. If you need to include a slash in a URL that is not intended to be an element separator, you'll need to encode it as %2F:

```
http://www.calculator.com/compute?3%2f4
```

This URL actually references the resource named *compute* on the *www.calculator.com* server and passes the string 3/4 to it, as delineated by the question mark (?). Presumably, the resource is actually a server-side program that performs some arithmetic function on the passed value and returns a result.

Unsafe characters are those that have no special meaning within the URL, but may have a special meaning in the context in which the URL is written. For example, the double-quote character (") is used to delimit URLs in many HTML tags. If you were to include a double-quote directly in a URL, you would probably confuse the HTML browser. Instead, encode the double-quote as %22 to avoid any possible conflict.

Other reserved and unsafe characters that should always be encoded are shown in Table 6-1.

Table 6-1: Reserved and Unsafe Characters and Their URL Encodings

Character	Description	Usage	Encoding
;	Semicolon	Reserved	%3B
/	Slash	Reserved	%2F
?	Question mark	Reserved	%3F
:	Colon	Reserved	%3A
@	At sign	Reserved	%40
=	Equal sign	Reserved	%3D
&	Ampersand	Reserved	%26
<	Less than sign	Unsafe	%3C
>	Greater than sign	Unsafe	%3E
"	Double quote	Unsafe	%22
#	Hash symbol	Unsafe	%23
%	Percent	Unsafe	%25
{	Left curly brace	Unsafe	%7B
}	Right curly brace	Unsafe	%7D
		Vertical bar	Unsafe	%7C
\	Backslash	Unsafe	%5C
^	Caret	Unsafe	%5E
~	Tilde	Unsafe	%7E
[	Left square bracket	Unsafe	%5B
]	Right square bracket	Unsafe	%5D
`	Back single quote	Unsafe	%60

In general, you should always encode a character if there is some doubt as to whether it can be placed "as-is" in a URL. As a rule of thumb, any character other than a letter, number, or any of the characters `$-_.+!*'()`, should be encoded.

It is never an error to encode a character, unless that character has a specific meaning in the URL. For example, encoding the slashes in an http URL will cause them to be used as regular characters, not as pathname delimiters, breaking the URL.

6.2.2 The http URL

The http URL is, by far, the most common within the World Wide Web. It is used to access documents stored on an http server, and it has two formats:

```
http://server:port/path#fragment
http://server:port/path?search
```

Some of the parts are optional. In fact, the most common form of the http URL simply is:

```
http://server/path
```

designating the unique server and the directory path and name of a document.

6.2.2.1 The http server

The *server* is the unique Internet name or Internet Protocol (IP) numerical address of the computer system that stores the Web resource. Like us, we suspect you'll mostly use more easily remembered Internet names for the servers in your URLs.[*] The name consists of several parts, including the server's actual name and the successive names of its network domain, each part separated by a period. Typical Internet names look like *www.ora.com* or *hoohoo.ncsa.uiuc.edu.*[†]

It has become something of a convention that webmasters name their servers *www* for quick and easy identification on the Web. For instance, O'Reilly & Associates's Web server's name is *www*, which along with the publisher's acronym-based domain name, becomes the very easily remembered website *www.ora.com*. Similarly, Sun Microsystems's Web server is named *www.sun.com*; Apple Computer's is *www.apple.com* and even Microsoft makes their Web server easily memorable as *www.microsoft.com*. The naming convention has very obvious benefits which you, too, should take advantage of if you are called upon to create a Web server for your organization.

You may also specify the address of a server using its numerical IP address. The address is a sequence of four numbers, zero to 255, separated by periods. Valid IP addresses look like 137.237.1.87 or 192.249.1.33.

---

[*] Each Internet-connected computer has a unique address; a numeric (IP) address, of course, because computers deal only in numbers. Humans prefer names, so the Internet folks provide us with a collection of special servers and software (Domain Name Service or DNS) that automatically resolve Internet names into IP addresses. InterNIC, a nonprofit agency, registers domain names mostly on a first-come, first-serve basis, and distributes new names to DNS servers worldwide.

[†] In the United States and for some Canadian establishments, the three-letter suffix of the domain name identifies the type of organization or business that operates that portion of the Internet. For instance, "com" is a commercial enterprise; "edu" is an academic institution; and "gov" identifies a government-based domain. Outside the United States, a less-descriptive suffix is assigned; typically a two-lettter abbreviation of the country name: "jp" for Japan and "de" for Deutschland, for instance. That convention indicates the traditional distribution of the Internet and presumably will change dramatically as the network proliferates in the rest of the world.

It'd be a dull diversion to tell you now what the numbers mean or how to derive an IP address from a domain name, particularly since you'll rarely if ever use one in a URL. Rather, this is a good place to hyperlink: Pick up any good Internet networking treatise for rigorous detail on IP addressing, such as Ed Krol's *The Whole Internet User's Guide and Catalog*, published by O'Reilly & Associates.

6.2.2.2 The http port

The *port* is the number of the communication port to which the client browser connects to the server. It's a networking thing: servers do many things besides serve up Web documents and resources to client browsers: electronic mail, FTP document fetches, filesystem sharing, and so on. Although all that network activity may come into the server on a single wire, it's typically divided into software-managed "ports" for service-specific communications—something analogous to boxes at your local post office.

The default URL port for Web servers is 80. Special secure Web servers (SHTTP or SSL) run on port 443. Most Web servers today use port 80; you need only to include a port number along with an immediately preceding colon in your URL if the target server does *not* use port 80 for Web communication.

When the Web was in its infancy many months ago, pioneer webmasters ran their Wild Wild Web connections on all sorts of port numbers. For technical and security reasons, system-administrator privileges are required to install a server on port 80. Lacking such privileges, these webmasters chose other, more easily accessible, port numbers.

Now that Web servers have become acceptable and are under the care and feeding of responsible administrators, documents being served on some port other than 80 or 443 should make you wonder if that server is really on the up and up. Most likely, the maverick server is being run by a clever user unbeknownst to the server's bona fide system administrators.

6.2.2.3 The http path

The document *path* is the UNIX-style hierarchical location of the file in the server's storage system. The pathname consists of one or more names separated by forward slashes (/). All but the last name represent directories leading down to the document; the last name is usually that of the document itself.

It has become a convention that for easy identification, HTML document names end with the suffix *.html* (they're otherwise plain ASCII text files, remember?). You can easily identify a PC-based server: DOS's restrictions on filenames mean you can have only the three-letter *.htm* name suffix for HTML documents.

Although the server name in a URL is not case-sensitive, the document pathname may be. Since most Web servers are run on UNIX-based systems and UNIX file names are case sensitive, the document pathname will be case-sensitive, too. Web servers running on DOS machines are not case-sensitive, so the document path-name is not, but since it is impossible to know the operating system of the server you are accessing, always assume that the server has case-sensitive pathnames and take care to get the case correct when typing your URLs.

Certain conventions regarding the document pathname have arisen. If the last element of the document path is a directory, not a single document, the server usu-ally will send back either a listing of the directory contents or the HTML index document in that directory. You should end the document name for a directory with a trailing forward slash (/) character, but in practice, most servers will honor the request even if the character is omitted.

If the directory name is just a forward slash alone or sometimes nothing at all, you will retrieve the first (top-level) HTML document or so-called *home page* in the uppermost root directory of the server. Every well-designed http server should have an attractive, well-designed "home page"; it's a shorthand way for users to access your Web collection since they don't need to remember the document's actual filename, just your server's name. That's why, for example, you can type *http://www.ora.com* into Netscape's "Open" dialog and get O'Reilly's home page.

Another twist: if the first component of the document path starts with the tilde character (~), it means the rest of the pathname begins from the personal HTML directory in the home directory of the specified user on the server machine. For instance, the URL *http://www.kumquat.com/~chuck/* would retrieve the top-level page from Chuck's document collection.

Different servers have different ways of locating documents within a user's home directory. Many search for the documents in a directory named *public_html*. UNIX-based servers are fond of the name *index.html* for home pages.

6.2.2.4 The http document fragment

The *fragment* is a named identifier that points to some key section of a document. In URL specifications, it follows the server and pathname and is separated by the hash (#) symbol. A fragment identifier indicates to the browser that it should begin displaying the target document at the indicated fragment name. As we describe in more detail below, you insert fragment names into a document with the `<a>` tag and the `name` attribute. Like pathnames, a fragment name may be any sequence of characters.

The fragment name and the preceding hash symbol are optional; omit them when referencing a document without defined fragments.

Formally, the fragment element only applies to target files that are HTML documents. If the target of the URL is some other document type, the fragment name may be misinterpreted by the browser.

Fragments are useful for long documents. By identifying key sections of your document with a fragment name, you make it easy for readers to link directly to that portion of the document, avoiding the tedium of scrolling or searching through the document to get to the section that interests them.

As a rule of thumb, we recommend that every section header in your documents be accompanied by an equivalent fragment name. By consistently following this rule, you'll make it possible for readers to jump to any section in any of your documents. Fragments also make it easier to build tables of contents for your document families.

6.2.2.5 The http search parameter

The *search* component of the http URL, along with its preceding question mark, is optional. It indicates that the path is a searchable or executable resource on the server. The content of the search component is passed to the server as parameters that control the search or execution function.

The actual encoding of parameters in the search component is dependent upon the server and the resource being referenced. The parameters for searchable resources are covered later in this chapter, when we discuss searchable documents. Parameters for executable resources are discussed in Chapter 8, *Forms*.

6.2.2.6 Sample http URLs

Here are some sample http URLs:

```
http://www.ora.com/catalog.html
http://www.ora.com/
http://www.kumquat.com:8080/
http://www.kumquat.com/planting/guide.html#soil_prep
http://www.kumquat.com/find_a_quat?state=Florida
```

The first example is an explicit reference to a bona fide HTML document named *catalog.html* that is stored in the root directory of the *www.ora.com* server. The second references the top-level home page on that same server. That home page may or may not be *catalog.html*. Sample three, too, assumes there is a home page in the root directory of the *www.kumquat.com* server, and that the Web connection is to the nonstandard port 8080.

The fourth example is the URL for retrieving the Web document named *guide.html* from the *planting* directory on the *www.kumquat.com* server. Once retrieved, the browser should display the document beginning at the fragment named *soil_prep.*

The last example invokes an executable resource named *find_a_quat* with the parameter named *state* set to the value *Florida.* Presumably, this resource generates an HTML response that is subsequently displayed by the browser.

6.2.3 The ftp URL

The ftp URL is used to retrieve documents from an FTP (File Transfer Protocol)[*] server. It has the format:

```
ftp://user:password@server:port/path;type=typecode
```

6.2.3.1 The ftp user and password

FTP is an authenticated service, meaning that you must have a valid user name and password in order to retrieve documents from a server. However, most FTP servers also support restricted, nonauthenticated access known as *anonymous FTP.* In this mode, anyone can supply the username "anonymous" and be granted access to a limited portion of the server's documents. Most FTP servers also assume (but may not grant, of course) anonymous access if the user name and password are omitted.

If you are using an ftp URL to access a site that requires a user name and password, include the *user* and *password* components in the URL, along with the colon (:) and "at" sign (@). More commonly, you'll be accessing an anonymous FTP server, and the user and password components can be omitted.

If you keep the user component along with the "at" sign, but omit the password and the preceding colon, most browsers will prompt you for a password after connecting to the FTP server. This is the recommended way of accessing authenticated resources on an FTP server, since it prevents others from seeing your password.

We recommend you *never* place an ftp URL with a user name and password in any HTML document. The reasoning is simple: anyone can retrieve the document, extract the user name and password from the URL, log into the FTP server, and tamper with its documents.

----

[*] FTP is an ancient Internet protocol that dates back to the Dark Ages, around 1975 or so. It was designed as a simple way to move files between machines and remains popular and useful to this day. Some people who are unable to run a true Web server will place their documents on a server that speaks FTP instead.

6.2.3.2 *The ftp server and port*

The ftp *server* and *port* are bound by the same rules as the server and port in an http URL, as described above. The server must be a valid Internet domain name or IP address of an FTP server. The port specifies the port on which the server is listening for requests.

If the port and its preceding colon are omitted, the default port of 21 is used. It is necessary to specify the port only if the FTP server is running on some port other than 21.

6.2.3.3 *The ftp path and transfer type*

The *path* component represents a series of directories, separated by slashes (/) leading to the file to be retrieved. By default, the file is retrieved as a binary file; this can be changed by adding the *typecode* (and the preceding `;type=`) to the URL.

If the typecode is set to `d`, the path is assumed to be a directory. The browser will request a listing of the directory contents from the server and display this listing to the user. If the typecode is any other letter, it is used as a parameter to the FTP type command before retrieving the file referenced by the path. While some FTP servers may implement other codes, most servers accept `i` to initiate a binary transfer and `a` to treat the file as a stream of ASCII text.

6.2.3.4 *Sample ftp URLs*

Here are some sample ftp URLs:

```
ftp://www.kumquat.com/sales/pricing
ftp://bob@bobs-box.com/results;type=d
ftp://bob:secret@bobs-box.com/listing;type=a
```

The first example retrieves the file named *pricing* from the *sales* directory on the anonymous FTP server at *www.kumquat.com*. The second logs into the FTP server on *bobs-box.com* as user `bob`, prompting for a password before retrieving the contents of the directory named *results* and displaying them to the user. The last example logs into *bobs-box.com* as `bob` with the password `secret` and retrieves the file named *listing*, treating its contents as ASCII characters.

6.2.4 *The file URL*

The file URL specifies a file stored on a machine without indicating the protocol used to retrieve the file. As such, it has limited use in a networked environment. Its real benefit, however, is that it can reference a file on the user's machine, and is particularly useful for referencing personal HTML document collections, such as those "under construction" and not yet ready for general distribution, or HTML document collections on CD-ROM. It has the format:

```
file://server/path
```

6.2.4.1 The file server

The file *server*, like the http server described above, must be the Internet domain name or IP address of the machine containing the file to be retrieved. No assumptions are made as to how the browser might contact the machine to obtain the file; presumably the browser can make some connection, perhaps via a Network File System or FTP, to obtain the file.

If the server is omitted, or the special name `localhost` is used, the file is assumed to reside on the same machine upon which the browser is running. In this case, the browser simply accesses the file using the normal facilities of the local operating system. In fact, this is the most common usage of the file URL. By creating document families on a diskette or CD-ROM and referencing your hyperlinks using the *file://localhost/* URL, you create a distributable, standalone document collection that does not require a network connection to use.

6.2.4.2 The file path

This is the path of the file to be retrieved on the desired server. The syntax of the *path* may differ based upon the operating system of the server; be sure to encode any potentially dangerous characters in the path.

6.2.4.3 Sample file URLs

The file URL is easy:

```
file://localhost/home/chuck/document.html
file:///home/chuck/document.html
file://marketing.kumquat.com/monthly_sales.html
```

The first URL retrieves */home/chuck/document.html* from the user's local machine. The second is identical to the first, except we've omitted the *localhost* reference to the server; the server name defaults to the local server. Do notice, however, the extra forward slash is required for this alternate form.

The third example uses some protocol to retrieve *monthly_sales.html* from the *marketing.kumquat.com* server.

6.2.5 The news URL

The news URL accesses either a single message or an entire newsgroup within the Usenet news system. It has two forms:

```
news:newsgroup
news:message_id
```

An unfortunate limitation in news URLs is that they don't allow you to specify a server for the *newsgroup*. Rather, users specify their news-server resource in their browser preferences. At one time, not long ago, Internet newsgroups were nearly universally distributed; all news servers carried all the same newsgroups and their respective articles, so one news server was as good as any. Today, the sheer bulk of disk space needed to store the daily volume of newsgroup activity is often prohibitive for any single news server, and there's also local censorship of newsgroups. Hence, you cannot expect that all newsgroups, and certainly not all articles for a particular newsgroup, will be available on the user's news server.

Moreover, many users' browsers may not be correctly configured to read news. We recommend you avoid placing news URLs in your documents except in rare cases.

6.2.5.1 Accessing entire newsgroups

There are several thousand newsgroups devoted to nearly every conceivable topic under the sun and beyond. Each group has a unique name, composed of hierarchical elements separated by periods. For example,

```
comp.infosys.www.announce
```

is the World Wide Web announcements newsgroup. To access this group, use the URL:

```
news:comp.infosys.www.announce
```

6.2.5.2 Accessing single messages

Every message on a news server has a unique message identifier (ID) associated with it. This ID has the form

```
unique_string@server
```

The *unique_string* is a sequence of ASCII characters; the server is usually the name of the machine from which the message originated. The *unique_string* must be unique among all the messages that originated from the server. A sample URL to access a single message might be:

```
news:12A7789B@news.kumquat.com
```

In general, message IDs are cryptic sequences of characters not readily understood by humans. Moreover, the lifespan of a message on a server is usually measured in days, after which the message is deleted and the message ID is no longer valid. The bottom line: single message news URLs are difficult to create, become invalid quickly, and are generally not used.

6.2.6   The nntp URL

The nntp URL goes beyond the news URL to provide a complete mechanism for accessing articles in the Usenet news system. It has the form:

```
nntp://server:port/newsgroup/article
```

6.2.6.1 The nntp server and port

The nntp *server* and *port* are defined similarly to the http server and port, described above. The server must be the Internet domain name or IP address of a nntp server; the port is the port on which that server is listening for requests.

If the port and its preceding colon are omitted, the default port of 119 is used.

6.2.6.2 The nntp newsgroup and article

The *newsgroup* is the name of the group from which an article is to be retrieved, as defined in the description of the news URL, above.

The *article* is the numeric id of the desired article within that newsgroup. Although the article number is easier to determine than a message id, it falls prey to the same limitations of single message references using the news URL, above. Specifically, articles do not last long on most nntp servers, and nntp URLs quickly become invalid as a result.

6.2.6.3 Sample nntp URLs

A sample nntp URL might be

```
nntp://news.kumquat.com/alt.fan.kumquats/417
```

This URL retrieves article 417 from the *alt.fan.kumquats* newsgroup on *news.kumquat.com*. Keep in mind that the article will only be served to machines that are allowed to retrieve articles from this server. In general, most nntp servers restrict access to those machines on that same local area network.

6.2.7 *The mailto URL*

The `mailto` URL causes an electronic mail message to be transmitted to a named recipient. It has the format:

```
mailto:address
```

The *address* is any valid email address, usually of the form:

```
user@server
```

Thus, a typical `mailto` URL might look like:

```
mailto:cmusciano@aol.com
```

6.2.8 *The telnet URL*

The telnet URL opens a telnet session with a desired server, allowing the user to log in and use the machine. Often, the connection to the machine automatically starts a specific service for the user; in other cases, the user must know the commands to type to use the system. The telnet URL has the form:

```
telnet://user:password@server:port/
```

6.2.8.1 *The telnet user and password*

The telnet *user* and *password* are used exactly like the user and password components of the ftp URL, described above. In particular, the same caveats apply regarding protecting your password and never placing it within a URL.

Just like the ftp URL, if you omit the password from the URL, the browser should prompt you for a password just before contacting the telnet server.

If you omit both the user and password, the telnet occurs without supplying a user name. For some servers, telnet automatically connects to a default service when no user name is supplied. For others, the browser may prompt for a username and password when making the connection to the telnet server.

6.2.8.2 *The telnet server and port*

The telnet *server* and *port* are defined similarly to the http server and port, described above. The server must be the Internet domain name or IP address of a telnet server; the port is the port on which that server is listening for requests.

If the port and its preceding colon are omitted, the default port of 23 is used.

6.2.9 *The gopher URL*

Gopher is a Web-like document retrieval system that achieved some popularity on the Internet just before the World Wide Web took off, completely replacing Gopher. Some Gopher servers still exist, though, and the gopher URL lets you access Gopher documents. The gopher URL has the form:

```
gopher://server:port/path
```

6.2.9.1 *The gopher server and port*

The gopher *server* and *port* are defined similarly to the http server and port, described above. The server must be the Internet domain name or IP address of a gopher server; the port is the port on which that server is listening for requests.

If the port and its preceding colon are omitted, the default port of 70 is used.

6.2.9.2 *The gopher path*

The path can take one of three forms:

```
type/selector
type/selector%09search
type/selector%09search%09gopherplus
```

The *type* is a single character value denoting the type of the gopher resource. If the entire path is omitted from the gopher URL, the type defaults to 1.

The *selector* corresponds to the path of a resource on the gopher server. It may be omitted, in which case the top-level index of the gopher server is retrieved.

If the gopher resource is actually a gopher search engine, the *search* component provides the string for which to search. The search string must be preceded by an encoded horizontal tab (%09).

If the gopher server supports Gopher+ resources, the *gopherplus* component supplies the necessary information to locate that resource. The exact content of this component varies based upon the resources on the gopher server. This component is preceded by an encoded horizontal tab (%09). If you want to include the *gopherplus* component but omit the search component, you must still supply both encoded tabs within the URL.

6.2.10 *Absolute and Relative URLs*

URLs come in two flavors: absolute and relative. An absolute URL is the complete address of a resource and has everything your system needs to find a document and its server on the Web. At the very least, an absolute URL contains the scheme and all required elements of the *scheme_specific_part* of the URL. It may also contain any of the optional portions of the *scheme_specific_part*.

With a relative URL you provide an abbreviated document address that, when automatically combined with a "base address" by the system, becomes a complete address for the document. Within the relative URL, any component of the URL may be omitted. The browser automatically fills in the missing pieces of the relative URL using corresponding elements of a base URL. This base URL is usually the URL of the document containing the relative URL, but may be another document specified with the **<base>** tag. [<base>, 6.7.1]

6.2.10.1 Relative schemes and servers

A common form of a relative URL is missing the scheme and server name. Since many related documents are on the same server, it makes sense to omit the scheme and server name from the relative URL. For instance, assume the base document was last retrieved from the server *www.kumquat.com*. The relative URL, then:

```
another-doc.html
```

is equivalent to the absolute URL:

```
http://www.kumquat.com/another-doc.html
```

Table 6-2 shows how the base and relative URLs in the example are combined to form an absolute URL.

Table 6–2: Forming an Absolute URL

	Protocol	Server	Directory	File
Base URL	http	*www.kumquat.com*	/	
Relative URL	↓	↓	↓	*another-doc.html*
↓	↓	↓	↓	↓
Absolute URL	http	*www.kumquat.com*	/	*another-doc.html*

6.2.10.2 Relative document directories

Another common form of a relative URL omits the leading slash and one or more directory names from the beginning of the document pathname. The directory of the base URL is automatically assumed to replace these missing components. It's the most common abbreviation because most HTML authors place their collection of documents and subdirectories of support resources in the same directory path as the home page. For example, you might have a *special/* subdirectory containing FTP files referenced in your HTML document. Let's say that the absolute URL for that HTML document is:

```
http://www.kumquat.com/planting/guide.html
```

A relative URL for the file *README.txt* in the *special/* subdirectory, then, looks like this:

```
ftp:special/README.txt
```

You'll actually be retrieving:

```
ftp://www.kumquat.com/planting/special/README.txt
```

Visually, the operation looks like that in Table 6-3:

Table 6-3: Forming an Absolute FTP URL

	Protocol	Server	Directory	File
Base URL	http	*www.kumquat.com*	*/planting*	*guide.html*
Relative URL	ftp	↓	*special*	*README.txt*
↓	↓	↓	↓	↓
Absolute URL	ftp	*www.kumquat.com*	*/planting/special*	*README.txt*

6.2.10.3 Using relative URLs

Relative URLs are more than just a typing convenience. Because they are relative to the current server and directory, you can move the entire set of documents to another directory or even another server and never have to change a single relative link. Imagine the difficulties if you had to go into every source HTML document and change the URL for every link every time you move it. We'd loathe using hyperlinks! Use relative URLs wherever possible.

6.3 Creating Hyperlinks

Use the HTML <a> tag to create links to other documents and to name anchors for fragment indentifiers within documents.

6.3.1 The <a> Tag

HTML authors use the `<a>` tag most commonly with its `href` attribute to create a hypertext link, or *hyperlink*, for short, to another place in the same document or to another document. In these cases, the current document is the source[*] of the link; the value of the `href` attribute, a URL, is the target.

<a>

Function:
Define anchors within a text flow

Attributes:
HREF
METHODS
NAME
REL
REV
TITLE
TARGET (Netscape only)
URN

End Tag:
</a>, always present

Contains:
a_content

Used in:
text

The other way you can use the `<a>` tag is with the `name` attribute to mark a hyperlink target, or fragment identifier, in an HTML document.

It is possible to use both the `name` and `href` attributes within a single `<a>` tag, defining a link to another document and a fragment identifier within the current document. We recommend against this, since it overloads a single tag with multiple functions, and some browsers may not be able to handle it.

Instead, use two `<a>` tags when such a need arises. Your HTML source will be easier to understand and modify, and will work better across a wider range of browsers.

---

[*] You may run across the terms "head" and "tail," which reference the target and source of a hyperlink. This naming scheme assumes that the referenced document (the head) has many tails that are embedded in many referencing documents throughout the Web. We find this naming convention confusing and stick to the concept of source and target documents throughout this book.

6.3.1.1 Allowed content

Between the <a> tag and its required end tag, you may put only regular text, line breaks, images, and headings. The browser renders all of these elements normally, but with the addition of some special effects to indicate that it is a hyperlink to another document. For instance, the popular graphical browsers typically under-line and color the text and draw a colored border around images that are enclosed by <a> tags.

While the allowed content may seem restricted (the inability to place style markup within an <a> tag is a bit onerous, for instance), most browsers let you put just about anything within an <a> tag that makes sense. To be compliant with the HTML standard, place the <a> tag inside other markup tags, not the opposite. For example, while most browsers make sense of either variation on this anchor theme:

```
To subscribe to
<cite><a href="ko.html">Kumquat Online</a></cite>,

To subscribe to
<a href="ko.html"> <cite>Kumquat Online</cite></a>,
```

only the first example is technically correct.

6.3.1.2 The href attribute

Use the href attribute to specify the URL of the target of the link. Its value is any valid document URL, absolute or relative, including a fragment identifier. If the user selects the contents of the <a> tag, the browser will retrieve and display the document indicated by the URL specified by the href attribute. [URLs, 6.2]

A simple <a> tag that references another document might be:

```
The <a href="http:growing_season.html">growing
season</a> for kumquats in the Northeast.
```

which appears in the Netscape display as shown in Figure 6-1.

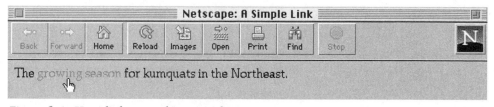

Figure 6–1: Hyperlink to another HTML document

Notice that the phrase "growing season" is specially rendered by the browser, let-ting the user know that it is a link to another document. Users also typically have the option to specially set the text color of the link and have the color change when a link is taken; blue initially and then red after it has been selected at least once, for instance.

More complex anchors might include images:

```
<ul>
  <li><a href="pruning_tips.html">
      <img src="pics/new.gif"> New pruning tips!</a>
  <li><a href="xhistory.html">
      <img src="pics/new2.gif">Kumquats throughout history</a>
</ul>
```

Mosaic, as do most graphical browsers, places a special border around images that are part of an anchor, as shown in Figure 6-2.

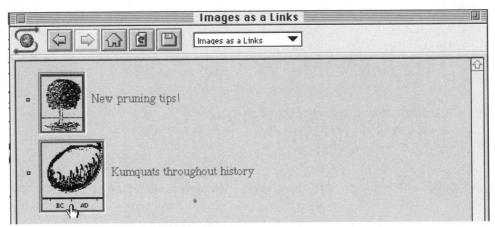

Figure 6–2: Mosaic puts a special border around an image that is inside an anchor

6.3.1.3 *The method attribute*

The `method` attribute tells the browser to specially process the document referenced by the `href` attribute. The value of the `method` is a space-separated list of names, each representing a particular document-processing method, usually an application name. The HTML standard does not define what these names might be; they are browser dependent.

For example, suppose you have a FrameMaker document called *harvesting.doc* that you want the browser to specially display. The link in the source document would be written:

```
<a href=" harvesting.doc" method="Frame">document</a>
```

telling the browser to expect and display a FrameMaker document when the user selects the link. The browser might augment the rendering of the anchor head, too, perhaps by adding a tiny FrameMaker icon, to tell the user what to expect when accessing that link.

In practice, the `method` attribute is rarely used. It is too dependent on the browser understanding how to deal with and be able to process the document according to the specified methods. Most often, authors include the `method` attribute in the `<a>` tag so that the browser might specially alter the appearance of the `<a>` tag's head content to indicate the particular method being used.

This `method` attribute only makes sense when used in conjunction with the `href` attribute; it is ignored when the `<a>` tag contains the `name` attribute.

6.3.1.4 The name attribute

Use the `name` attribute to place a fragment identifier within an HTML document. Once created, the fragment identifier becomes a potential target of a link.

An easy way to think of a fragment identifier is as the HTML analog of the `goto` statement label common in many programming languages. The `name` attribute within the `<a>` tag places a label within a document. When that label is used in a link to that document, it is the equivalent of telling the browser to `goto` that label.

The value of the `name` attribute is any character string, enclosed in quotes; for example:

```
<h2><a name="Pruning">Pruning Your Kumquat Tree</a></h2>
```

Notice that we set the anchor in a section header of presumably a large document. It's a practice we encourage you use for all major sections of your work for easier reference and future smart processing, such as automated extraction of topics.

The following link, when taken by the user:

```
<a href="growing_guide.html#Pruning">
```

jumps directly to the section of the document we named above.

The contents of the `<a>` tag are not displayed in any special way with the `name` attribute.

Technically, you do not have to put any document content within the `<a>` tag with the `name` attribute since it simply marks a location in the document. In practice, some browsers ignore the tag unless some document content—a word or phrase, even an image—is between the `<a>` and `</a>` tags. For this reason, it's probably a good idea to have at least one displayable element in the body of any `<a>` tag.

6.3.1.5 *The rel and rev attributes*

The `rel` and `rev` attributes express a formal relationship and direction between source and target documents. The `rel` attribute specifies the relationship from the source document to the target; the `rev` attribute specifies the relationship from the target to the source. Both attributes can be placed in a single `<a>` tag, and the browser may use them to specially alter the appearance of the anchor content or to automatically construct document navigation menus. Other tools also may use these attributes to build special link collections, tables of contents, and indexes.

The value of either the `rel` or `rev` attribute is a space-separated list of relationships. The actual relationship names and their meanings are up to you: they are not formally addressed by the HTML standard. For example, a document that is part of a sequence of documents might include its relationship in a link:

```
<a href="part-14.html" rel=next rev=prev>
```

The relationship from the source to the target is that of moving to the next document; the reverse relationship is that of moving to the previous document.

These document relationships are also used in the `<link>` tag in the document `<head>`. The `<link>` tag establishes the relationship without actually creating a link to the target document; the `<a>` tag creates the link and imbues it with the relationship attributes. [`<link>`, 6.7.2]

Commonly used document relationships appear in the list below.

next
    Links to the next document in a collection

prev
    Links to the previous document in a collection

head
    Links to the top-level document in a collection

toc
    Links to a collection's table of contents

parent
    Links to the document above the source

child
    Links to a document below the source

`index`

Links to the index for this document

`glossary`

Links to the glossary for this document

In general, few browsers take advantage of these attributes to modify the link appearance. However, these attributes are a great way to document links you create, and we recommend you take the time to insert them whenever possible.

6.3.1.6 The target attribute (Netscape only)

The latest version of Netscape Navigator (2.0) supports a special HTML document type known as a *frame*. A frame document may display several HTML documents simultaneously. The `target` attribute for the `<a>` tag lets you redirect the contents of a hyperlink document to load and display in a different frame or window from that which contains the hyperlink. For more information, see 10.6.1.

6.3.1.7 The title attribute

The `title` attribute lets you specify a title for the document to which you are linking. The value of the attribute is any string, enclosed in quotes. The browser might use it when displaying the link, perhaps flashing the title when the mouse passes over the link. The browser might also use the `title` attribute when adding this link to a user's hotlist.

The `title` attribute is especially useful for referencing an otherwise unlabeled resource, such as an image or a non-HTML document. For example, the browser might include the following title on this otherwise wordless image display page:

```
<a href="pics/kumquat.gif"
   title="A photograph of the Noble Fruit">
```

Ideally, the value specified should match the title of the referenced document, but it's not required.

6.3.1.8 The urn attribute

The `urn` attribute defines the more general Universal Resource Name (URN) for a referenced document. The value of this attribute is a string enclosed in quotes. The actual syntax and semantics of the URN have not yet been defined, making this attribute little more than a place keeper for future versions of HTML.

6.3.2 Linking to Other Documents

You make a hyperlink to another document with the `<a>` tag and its `href` attribute, which defines the URL of the target document. The contents of the `<a>` tag are presented to the user in some distinctive manner to indicate the link is available.

When creating a link to another document, you should consider adding the `title`, `rel`, and `rev` attributes to the `<a>` tag. They help document the link you are creating and allow the browser to further embellish the display anchor contents.

6.3.3 Linking Within a Document

Creating a link within the same HTML document or to a specific fragment of another document is a two-step process. The first step is to make the target fragment; the second is to create the link to the fragment.

Use the `<a>` tag with its `name` attribute to identify a fragment. The value of the `name` attribute is used in hyperlinks that point to the fragment. Here's a sample fragment identifier:

```
<h3><a name="Section_7">Section 7</a></h3>
```

A hyperlink to the fragment is an `<a>` tag with the `href` attribute, in which the attribute's value—the target URL—ends with the fragment's name, preceded by the hash character (#). A reference to the previous example's fragment identifier, then, might look like:

```
See <a href="index.html#Section_7">Section 7</a>
for further details.
```

By far, the most common use of fragment identifiers is in creating a table of contents for a lengthy document. Begin by dividing your document into several logical sections, using appropriate headers and consistent formatting. At the start of each section, add a fragment identifier for that section, typically as part of the section title as a header. Finally, make a list of links to those fragment identifiers at the beginning of your document.

Our sample document extolling the life and wonders of the mighty kumquat, for example, is quite long and involved, including many sections and subsections of interest. It is a document to be read and read again. To make it easy for kumquat lovers everywhere to quickly find their section of interest, we've included fragment identifiers for each major section, and placed an ordered list of links—a hotlinked table of contents, as it were—at the beginning of each of the Kumquat Lover's documents, a sample of which appears below along with sample fragment identifiers that appear in the same document. The ellipsis symbol (...) means there are intervening segments of content, of course.

```
...
<h3>Table of Contents</h3>
<ol>
  <li><a href="#soil_prep">Soil Preparation</a>
  <li><a href="#dig_hole">Digging The Hole</a>
  <li><a href="#planting">Planting the Tree</a>
</ol>
...
<h3><a name=soil_prep>Soil Preparation</a></h3>
...
<h3><a name=dig_hole>Digging the Hole</a></h3>
...
<h3><a name=planting>Planting the Tree</a></h3>
...
```

The kumquat lover can thereby click the desired link in the Table of Contents and jump directly to the section of interest, without lots of tedious scrolling.

Notice also that this example uses relative URLs—a good idea if you ever intend to move or rename the document without breaking all the hyperlinks.

6.4 Creating Effective Links

A document becomes hypertext by tossing in a few links in the same way that water becomes soup when you throw in a few vegetables. Technically, you've met the goal, but the outcome may not be very palatable.

Inserting anchors into your documents is something of an art, requiring good writing skills, HTML prowess, and an architectural sense of your documents and their relationships to others on the Web. Effective links flow seamlessly into a document, quietly supplying additional browsing opportunities to the reader without disturbing the current document. Poorly designed links scream out, interrupt the flow of the source document, and generally annoy the reader.

While there are as many linking styles as there are authors, here are a few of the more popular ways to link your documents. All do two things: they give the reader quick access to related information, and they tell the reader how the link is related to the current contents.

6.4.1 Lists of Links

Perhaps the most common way to present hyperlinks in HTML documents is in ordered or unordered lists in the style of a table of contents or list of resources.

Two schools of style exist: One puts the entire list item into the source anchor; the other abbreviates the item and puts a shorthand phrase in the source anchor. In the former, make sure you keep the anchor content short and sweet; in the latter, use a direct writing style that makes it easy to embed the link.

If your list of links becomes overly long, consider organizing it into several sublists grouped by topic. Readers can then scan the topics (set off, perhaps, as <h3> headers) for the appropriate list and then scan that list for the desired document.

The alternative list style is much more descriptive, but also more wordy, so you have to be careful it doesn't end up cluttered:

```
<p>
Kumquat-related documents include:
<ul>
   <li>A concise guide to <a href="kumquat_farming.html">
       profitable kumquat farming</a>,
       including a variety of business plans, lists of fruit
       packing companies, and farming supply companies.
   <li>101 different ways to <a href="kumquat_uses">
       use a kumquat</a>, including stewed kumquats and kumquat pie!
   <li>The kumquat is a hardy tree, but even the greenest of
       thumbs can use a few <a href="news:alt.kumquat_growers">
       growing tips</a> to increase
       their yield.
   <li>The business of kumquats is an expanding one, as
       shown by this 10 year overview of the
       <a href="http://www.ora.com/kumquat_report/">
       kumquat industry</a>.
</ul>
```

It sometimes gets hard to read a source HTML document. Imagine the clutter if we'd used anchors with fragment identifiers for each of the subtopics in the list item explanations. Nonetheless, it all looks pristine and easily navigable when displayed by the browser, such as with Mosaic as shown in Figure 6-3.

This more descriptive style of presenting a link list tries hard to draw readers into the linked document by giving a fuller taste of what they can expect to find. Because each list element is longer and requires more scanning by the reader, you should use this style sparingly and dramatically limit the number of links.

In general, use the brief list style when presenting large numbers of links to a well-informed audience. The second, more descriptive style is better suited to a smaller number of links for which your readership is less well-versed in the topic at hand.

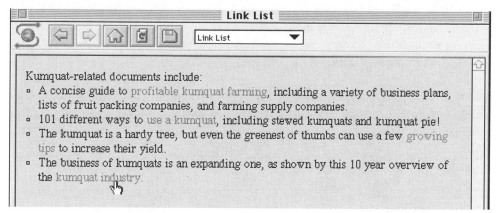

Figure 6–3: Wordy but effectively descriptive link list

6.4.2 *Inline References*

If you aren't collecting links into lists, you're probably sprinkling them throughout your document. So-called inline links are more in keeping with the true spirit of hypertext since they enable the reader to mark their current place in the document, visit the related topic in more depth or find a better explanation, and then come back to the original and continue reading. That's very personalized information processing.

The biggest mistake made by novice HTML authors, however, is to overload their documents with links and treat them as if they are panic buttons demanding to be pressed. You may have seen this style of linking; HTML pages with the word "here" all over the place, like the panic-ridden example in Figure 6-4 (we can't bring ourselves to show you the source HTML for this travesty).

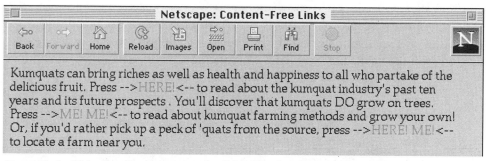

Figure 6–4: Links should not wave and yell like first-graders, "Here! Me! Me!"

As links, phrases like "click here" and "also available" are content-free and annoying. They make the person who is scanning the page for an important link read all the surrounding text to actually find the reference.

The better, more refined style for an inline link is to make every one contain a noun or noun/verb phrase relating to the topic at hand. Compare how kumquat farming and industry news references are treated in the Figure 6-5 to the "Here! Me! Me!" example in Figure 6-4.

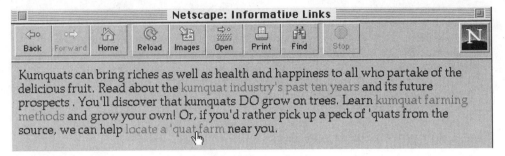

Figure 6–5: Kinder, gentler inline links work best

A quick scan of Figure 6-5 immediately yields useful links to "kumquat farming" and "industry's past ten years." There is no need to read the surrounding text to understand where the link will take you. Indeed, the immediately surrounding content in our example, as for most inline links, serves only as syntactic sugar in support of the embedded links.

Embedding links into the general discourse of a document takes more effort to create than link lists. You've got to actually understand the content of the current as well as the target documents, be able to express that relationship in just a few words, and then intelligently incorporate that link at some key place in the source document. Hopefully this key place is where you might expect the user is ready to interrupt their reading and ask a question or request more information. To make matters even more difficult, particularly for the traditional tech writer, this form of author-reader conversation is most effective when presented in active voice (he, she, or it does something to an object versus the object having something done to it). The effort expended is worthwhile, though, resulting in more informative, easily read documents. Remember, you'll write the document once, but it will be read thousands, if not millions, of times. Please your readers, please.

6.4.3 Linking Do's and Don'ts

Here are some hints for creating links:

• Keep the link content as concise as possible. Long links or huge inline graphic icons for links are visually disruptive and potentially confusing.

- Never place two links immediately adjacent to one another. Most browsers make it difficult to tell where one link stops and the next link starts. Separate them with regular text or line breaks.

- Be consistent. If you are using inline references, make all of your links inline references. If you choose to use lists of links, stick to either the short or long form; don't mix styles in a single document.

- Try reading your document with all the nonanchor text removed. If some links suddenly make no sense, rewrite them so that they stand on their own. (Many people scan documents looking only for links; the surrounding text becomes little more than a gray background to the more visually compelling links.)

6.4.4 *Using Images and Links*

It has become fashionable to use images and icons instead of words for link contents. For instance, instead of the word "next," some HTML authors might use an icon of a little pointing hand. A link to the home page is not complete without a picture of a little house. Links to searching tools must now contain a picture of a magnifying glass, question mark, or binoculars.

Resist falling prey to the "Mount Everest syndrome" of inserting images simply because you can. Again, it's a matter of context. If you or your document's readers can't tell at a glance what relationship a link has with the current document, you've failed. Use cute images for links sparingly, consistently, and only in ways that help readers scan your document for important information and leads. Also be ever mindful that your pages may be read by someone from nearly anywhere on Earth (perhaps beyond, even), and that images do not translate consistently across cultural boundaries. (Ever hear what the "okay" hand sign common in the United States means to a Japanese person?)

Creating consistent iconography for a collection of pages is a daunting task, one that really should be done with the assistance of someone formally schooled in visual design. Trust us, the kind of mind that produces nifty code and does good HTML is rarely suited to creating beautiful, compelling imagery. Find a good visual designer; your pages and readers will benefit immeasurably.

6.5 *Mouse-Sensitive Images*

Normally, an image placed within an anchor simply becomes part of the anchor content. The browser may alter the image in some special way (usually with a special border) to clue the reader that it is a link, but the user clicks the image in the same way they click a textual link.

The HTML standard provides a feature that lets you embed many different links inside the same image. Clicking different areas of the image causes the browser to link to different target documents. Such mouse-sensitive images, known as *image maps*, open up a variety of creative linking styles.

The traditional HTML mechanism, enabled by the `ismap` attribute for the `<img>` tag, requires access to a server and related image map processing applications. Netscape 2.0 and Internet Explorer support the `ismap` server-side image map, as well as a client-side image map option that is enabled via a special `usemap` extension for the `<img>` tag, along with special `<map>` and `<area>` tags. Since translation of the mouse position in the image to a link to another document happens on the user's machine, `usemap` image maps don't require a special server connection, and even can be implemented in non-Web environments, such as on a local hard drive or on a CD-ROM-based document collection. [<map>, 6.5.3] [<area>, 6.5.4]

6.5.1 The ismap <img> attribute

You add an image to an anchor simply by placing an `<img>` tag within the body of the `<a>` tag. Make that embedded image into a mouse-sensitive one by adding the `ismap` attribute to the `<img>` tag. This special `<img>` attribute tells the browser that the image is a special map containing more than one link. (The `ismap` attribute is ignored by the browser if the `<img>` tag is not within an `<a>` tag.) [<img>, 5.2.6]

When the user clicks some place within the image, the browser passes the coordinates of the mouse pointer along with the URL specified in the `<a>` tag to the document server. The server uses the mouse pointer coordinates to determine which document to deliver back to the browser.

When `ismap` is used, the `href` attribute of the containing `<a>` tag must contain the URL of a server application or, for some HTTP servers, a related map file that contains the coordinate and linking information. If the URL is simply that of a conventional document, errors may result and the desired document will most likely not be retrieved.

The coordinates of the mouse position are screen pixels counted from the upper-left corner of the image beginning with (0,0). The coordinates are added to the end of the URL, preceded by a question mark (?).

For example, if a user clicks 15 pixels down and 43 pixels over from the upper-left corner of the image displayed from the following link:

```
<a href="/cgi-bin/imagemap/toolbar.map">
<img ismap src="pics/toolbar.gif">
</a>
```

the browser sends the following search parameters to the HTTP server:

```
/cgi-bin/imagemap/toolbar.map?43,15
```

In the example, *toolbar.map* is a special image map file inside the *cgi-bin/imagemap* directory and containing coordinates and links. A special image map process uses that file to match the passed coordinates (43,15 in the example) and return with the selected hyperlink document.

6.5.1.1 Server-side <ismap> considerations

With mouse-sensitive <ismap>-enabled image maps, the browser is only required to pass along the URL and mouse coordinates to the server. Converting these coordinates into a specific document is handled by the document server. The conversion process differs between servers and is not defined by the HTML standard.

You need to consult with your Web server administrators and perhaps even read your server's documentation to determine how to create and program an image map. Most servers come with some software utility, typically located in a *cgi-bin/imagemap* directory, to handle image maps. And most of these use a text file containing the image map regions and related hyperlinks that is referenced by your image map URL to process the image map query.

Here's an example image map file that describes the sensitive regions in our example image:

```
# Imagemap file=toolbar.map

default                    dflt.html
circle 100,30,50           link1.html
rectangle 180,120,290,500  link2.html
polygon 80,80,90,72,160,90 link3.html
```

Each sensitive region of the image map is described by a geometric shape and defining coordinates in pixels, such as the circle with its center point and radius, the rectangle's upper-left and lower-right edge coordinates, and the loci of a polygon. All coordinates are relative to the upper-left corner of the image (0,0). Each shape has a related URL.

An image map processing application typically tests each shape in the order it appears in the image file and returns the document specified by the corresponding URL to the browser if the user's mouse x,y coordinates fall within the boundaries of that shape. That means it's okay to overlap shapes; just be aware which takes precedence. Also, the entire image need not be covered with sensitive regions: if the passed coordinates don't fall within a specified shape, the default document gets sent back to the browser.

This is just one example for how an image map may be processed and the accessory files required for that process. Please huddle with your webmaster and server manuals to discover how to implement a server-side image map for your HTML documents and system.

6.5.2 The usemap <img> Attribute

The obvious downside to server-side `ismap`-enabled image maps is that they require a server. That means you need access to the required HTTP server or its */cgi-bin/* directory. That's not always the case. And, server-side image maps limit portability since not all image map processing applications are the same.

Server-side image maps also mean delays for the user while browsing since the browser must get the server's attention to process the image coordinates. That's even if there's no action to take, such as a section of the image that isn't hyperlinked and doesn't lead anywhere.

Netscape and Internet Explorer support what are known as *client-side* image maps that suffer from none of these difficulties. Enabled by the `usemap` attribute for the `<img>` tag, and defined by special `<map>` and `<area>` extension tags, client-side image maps let HTML authors include in their documents a map of coordinates and links that describe the sensitive regions of an image. The extended browser on the client computer translates the coordinates of the mouse position within the image into an action, such as loading and displaying another document.

Include the `usemap` attribute itself as part of the `<img>` tag. Its value is the URL of a `<map>` segment in an HTML document that contains the map coordinates and related link URLs. The document in the URL identifies the HTML document containing the map; the fragment identifier in the URL identifies the map to be used. Most often, the map is in the same document as the image itself, and the URL can be reduced to the fragment identifier: a hash (#) symbol followed by the map name.

For example, the following source fragment tells the Netscape or Internet Explorer browser that the *map.gif* image is a client-side image map and that its mouse-sensitive coordinates and related link URLs are found in the map section of the document named *map*:

```
<img src="pics/map.gif" usemap="#map">
```

6.5.3 The <map> Tag

For client-side image maps to work, you must include somewhere in the HTML document a set of coordinates and URLs that define the mouse-sensitive regions of a client-side image map and the hyperlink to take for each region that is clicked by the user. You include those coordinates and links as values of attributes in special <area> tags; the collection of <area> specifications are enclosed within the <map> tag and its end tag </map>.

<map> (extension)

Function:
    Encloses client-side image map (usemap) specifications

Attributes:
    NAME

End Tag:
    </map>, always present

Contains:
    map_content

Used in:
    body_content

The <map> segment may appear anywhere in the body of any HTML document. Currently, only Netscape 2.0 and Internet Explorer recognize client-side image maps, so all other browsers, including earlier versions of Netscape, ignore the contents of the <map> tag. The <map> contents never get displayed in the browser window.

The required **name** attribute and its quote-enclosed value in the <map> tag is the name used by the **usemap** attribute in an <img> tag to locate the image map specification. The name must be unique and not used by another <map> in the document, but more than one image map may reference the same <map> specifications. [usemap, 6.5.2]

6.5.4 The <area> Tag

The guts of a client-side image map are the <area> tags within the map segment. These <area> tags define each mouse-sensitive region and the action the browser should take if that region is selected by the user in an associated client-side image map.

<area> (extension)

Function:
Defines coordinates and links for a region on a client-side image map

Attributes:
COORDS
HREF
NOHREF
SHAPE

End Tag:
None

Contains:
Nothing

Used in:
map_content

When the user moves the mouse pointer over any region defined by an `<area>` tag in the image's `<map>`, the pointer icon changes into a hand and the browser displays the URL of the related hyperlink at the bottom of the browser window. Regions of the client-side image map not defined in at least one `<area>` tag are not mouse-sensitive.

6.5.4.1 The coords attribute

The required `coords` attribute of the `<area>` tag defines coordinates of a mouse-sensitive region in a client-side image map. The number of coordinates and their meaning depend upon the region's shape as determined by the `shape` attribute, below. Currently, Netscape 2.0 supports only rectangular-shaped regions, while Internet Explorer supports rectangles, circles, and polygons. The appropriate values for each shape are:

circle
`coords="x,y,r"` where `x` and `y` define the position of the center of the circle ("0,0" is the upper-left corner of the image) and `r` is its radius in pixels.

polygon
`coords="x1,y1,x2,y2,x3,y3,..."` where each pair of x,y coordinates define a vertex of the polygon, with "0,0" being the upper left corner of the image. At least three pairs of coordinates are required to define a triangle, higher order polygons require a larger number of vertices. The polygon is automatically closed, so it is not necessary to repeat the first coordinate at the end of the list to close the region.

rectangle

> coords="x1,y1,x2,y2" where the first coordinate pair is one corner of the rectangle and the other pair is the diagonally opposite corner, with "0,0" being the upper-left corner of the image. Note that a rectangle is just a shortened way of specifying a polygon with four vertices.

For example, the following fragment defines a single mouse-sensitive region in the lower-right quarter of a 100x100 image and another circular region smack in the middle:

```
<map name="map1">
  <area shape=rectangle coords="75,75,99,99">
  <area shape=circle coords="50,50,25">
</map>
```

If the coordinates in one `<area>` tag overlap with another region, the first `<area>` tag takes precedence. The browsers ignore coordinates that extend beyond the boundaries of the image.

6.5.4.2 The href attribute

Like the `href` attribute for hyperlinks, the `href` attribute for the `<area>` tag defines the URL of the desired link if its region in the associated image map is clicked. The value of the `href` attribute is any valid URL, relative or absolute.

For example, Netscape will load and display the *link4.html* document if the user clicks in the lower-left quarter of a 100x100-pixel image, as defined by the following example image map `<area>` tag:

```
<map name="map">
  <area coords="75,75,99,99" href="link4.html">
</map>
```

6.5.4.3 The nohref attribute

The `nohref` attribute for the `<area>` tag lets you define a mouse-sensitive region in a client-side image map for which no action is taken even though the user may select it. You must include either an `href` or a `nohref` attribute for each `<area>` tag.

6.5.4.4 The shape attribute

This attribute defines the shape of the mouse-sensitive region. Netscape supports only one shape, a rectangle, specified by the value `rect`. Internet Explorer also supports circles and polygons as well as shortened forms of the shape names. Thus, Internet Explorer supports the values `circ`, `circle`, `poly`, `polygon`, `rect`, and `rectangle`.

The value of this attribute affects how the value of the `coords` attribute, above, is interpreted by the browser.

6.5.5 A Client-Side Image Map Example

The following example fragment draws together the various components of a client-side image map. It includes the `<img>` tag with the image reference and `usemap` attribute with a `name` that points to a `<map>` that defines four mouse-sensitive regions and related links:

```
<body>
...
<img src="pics/map.gif" usemap="#map1">
...
<map name="map1">
  <area shape=rectangle coords="0,0,49,49" href="link1.html">
  <area shape=polygon coords="50,0,99,0,99,49,50,49"
      href="link2.html">
  <area shape=circle coords="50,50,25"
      href="link3.html">
  <area coords="50,50,99,99" href="link4.html">
</map>
```

6.5.6 Handling Other Browsers

Unlike its server-side `ismap` counterpart, the client-side image map tag (`<img usemap>`) doesn't need to be included in an `<a>` tag. But it may be, so that you can gracefully handle browsers that are unable to process client-side image maps.

For example, Mosaic or early versions of Netscape simply load a document named *main.html* if the user clicks the *map.gif* image referenced in the following source fragment. The extended browsers, on the other hand, will divide the image into mouse-sensitive regions, as defined in the associated `<map>`, and link to a particular name anchor within the same *main.html* document if the image map region is selected by the user:

```
<a href="main.html">
  <img src="pics/map.gif" ismap usemap="map1">
</a>
...
<map name="map1">
  <area coords="0,0,49,49" href="main.html#link1">
  <area coords="50,0,99,49" href="main.html#link2">
  <area coords="0,50,49,99" href="main.html#link3">
  <area coords="50,50,99,99" href="main.html#link4">
</map>
```

To make an image map fully backward-compatible with all image map-capable browsers, you may also include both client-side and server-side processing for the same image map. Netscape 2.0 and Internet Explorer will honor the faster client-side processing; all other browsers will ignore the `usemap` attribute in the `<img>` tag and rely upon the referenced server process to handle user selections in the traditional way. For example:

```
<a href="/cgi-bin/images/map.proc">
  <img src="pics/map2.gif" usemap="map2" ismap>
</a>
...
<map name="map2">
  <area coords="0,0,49,49" href="link1.html">
  <area coords="50,0,99,49" href="link2.html">
  <area coords="0,50,49,99" href="link3.html">
  <area coords="50,50,99,99" href="link4.html">
</map>
```

6.5.7 Effective Use of Mouse-Sensitive Images

Some of the most visually compelling pages we've seen on the Web have mouse-sensitive images: maps with regions that when clicked, for example, lead to more information about a country or town, or result in more detail about the location and who to contact at a regional branch of a business. We've even seen a mouse-sensitive image of a fashion model whose various clothing parts lead to their respective catalog entries, complete with detailed description and price tag for ordering.

The visual nature of mouse-sensitive images coupled with the need for an effective interface means that you should strongly consider having an artist, user-interface designer, and even a human-factors expert evaluate your mouse-sensitive imagery. At the very least, engage in a bit of user testing to make sure people know where to click to move to the desired document. Make sure the "mouseable" areas of the image indicate this to the user using a consistent visual mechanism. Consider using borders, drop shadows, or color changes to indicate those areas that can be selected by the user.

Finally, always remember that the decision to use mouse-sensitive images is an explicit decision to exclude text-based and image-restricted browsers from your pages. This includes the many millions of browsers connecting to the Internet via slow modem connections. For these people, downloading your beautiful images is simply too expensive. To keep from disenfranchising a growing population, make sure any page that has a mouse-sensitive image has a text-only equivalent easily accessible from a link on the image-enabled version. Some thoughtful webmasters even provide separate pages for users preferring full graphics versus mostly text.

6.6 *Creating Searchable Documents*

Another extensible form of an HTML link that does not use the <a> tag is one that causes the server to search a database for a document that contains a user-specified keyword or words. An HTML document that contains such a link is known as a *searchable* document.

6.6.1 *The <isindex> Element*

For a searchable document designated by the <isindex> tag, the browser provides a way for the user to enter one or more search terms and passes those key words along with a search-engine's URL to the server. The server matches the keywords against a database of terms to select the next document for display.

<isindex>

Function:
   Indicates that a document can be searched

Attributes:
   PROMPT (Netscape only)

End tag:
   None

Contains:
   Nothing

Used in:
   head_content

When a browser encounters the <isindex> tag, it adds a standard search interface to the document (rendered by Netscape in Figure 6-6).

```
<html>
<head>
<title>Kumquat Advice Database</title>
<base href="cgi-bin/quat-query">
<isindex>
</head>
<body>
<h3>Kumquat Advice Database</h3>
<p>
Search this database to learn more about kumquats!
</body>
</html>
```

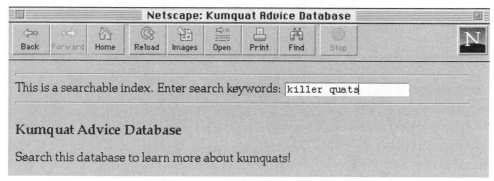

Figure 6–6: A searchable document

The user types a list of space-separated keywords into the field provided. When the user presses the return key, the browser automatically appends the query list to the end of a URL and passes the information along to the server for further processing.

While the HTML standard only allows the `<isindex>` tag to be placed in the document header, most browsers let the tag appear anywhere in the document and inserts the search field in the content flow where the `<isindex>` tag appears. This convenient extension lets you add instructions and other useful elements before presenting the user with the actual search field.

6.6.1.1 The prompt attribute (Netscape only)

The browser provides a leading prompt just above or to the left of the user-entry field. Netscape's default prompt, for example, is, "This is a searchable index. Enter search keywords:" (Figure 6-6). That default prompt is not the best for all occasions, so Netscape provides a way to change it with the `prompt` attribute extension.

When added to the `<isindex>` tag, the value of the `prompt` attribute is the string of text that precedes the keyword entry field placed in the document by Netscape.

For example, compare Figure 6-6 with Figure 6-7, in which we added the following prompt to the previous source example:

```
<isindex
    prompt="To learn more about kumquats, enter a keyword:">
```

Most other browsers ignore the `prompt` attribute, but there is little reason not to include a better prompt string for your Netscape-based readership.

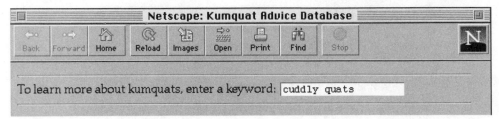

Figure 6–7: Netscape lets you put a custom prompt in a searchable document

6.6.1.2 *The query URL*

Besides the `<isindex>` tag in the header of a searchable document, the other important element of this special HTML tag is the query URL. By default, it is the URL of the source document itself—not good if your document can't handle the query. Rather, most authors use the `<base>` attribute to point to a different URL for the search. [`<base>`, 6.7.1]

The browser appends a question mark (?) to the query URL, followed by the specified search parameters. Nonprintable characters are appropriately encoded; multiple parameters are separated by a plus sign (+).

In the previous example, if a user types "insect control" in the search field, the browser would retrieve the URL:

```
cgi-bin/quat-query?insect+control
```

6.6.1.3 *Server dependencies*

Like image maps, searchable documents require support from the server to make things work. How the server interprets the query URL and its parameters is not defined by the HTML standard.

You should consult your server's documentation to determine how you can receive and use the search parameters to locate the desired document. Typically, the server breaks the parameters out of the query URL and passes them to a program designated by the URL. [server-side programming, 8.6.2]

6.7 *Establishing Document Relationships*

Very few HTML documents stand alone. Instead, a document is usually part of a collection of documents, each connected by the one or several of the hypertext strands we describe in this chapter. One document may be a part of several collections, linking to some documents and being linked to by others. Readers move between the document families as they follow the links that interest them.

You establish an explicit relationship between two documents when you link them. Conscientious authors use the `rel` attribute of the `<a>` tag to indicate the nature of the link. In addition, two other tags may be used within a document to further clarify the location and relationship of a document within a document family. These tags, `<base>` and `<link>`, are placed within the body of the `<head>` tag. [`<head>`, 3.6.1]

6.7.1   The `<base>` Header Element

As we previously explained, URLs within a document can be either absolute—with every element of the URL explicitly provided by the author—or relative, with certain elements of the URL omitted and supplied by the browser. Normally, the browser fills in the blanks of a relative URL by drawing the missing pieces from the URL of the current document. You can change that with the `<base>` tag.

\<base\>

Function:
  Define the base URL for other anchors in the document
Attributes:
  HREF
  TARGET (Netscape only)
End tag:
  None
Contains:
  Nothing
Used in:
  head_content

The `<base>` tag must appear only in the document header, not its body contents. The browser thereafter uses the specified base URL, not the current document's URL, to resolve all relative URLs, including those found in `<a>`, `<img>`, `<link>`, and `<form>` tags. It also defines the URL that will be used to resolve queries in searchable documents containing the `<isindex>` tag. [URLs, 6.2]

6.7.1.1   The *href* attribute

The `<base>` tag has only one required attribute: `href`. It must have a valid URL as its value. For example, the `<base>` tag in this document head,

```
<html>
<head>
<base href="http://www.kumquat.com/">
</head>
  . . .
```

tells the browser that any relative URLs within this document are relative to the top-level document directory on *www.kumquat.com*, regardless of the address and directory of the machine from which the user had retrieved the current document.

Notice in the example that, contrary to what you may have expected, we made the base URL relative, not absolute. The browser actually forms an absolute base URL out of this relative URL by filling in the missing pieces with the URL of the document itself. This property can be used to good advantage. For instance, in this next example,

```
<html>
<head>
<base href="/info/">
</head>
  . . .
```

the browser will make the <base> URL into one that is relative to the server's */info/* directory, which probably is not the same directory of the current document. Imagine if you had to re-address every link in your document with that common directory. Not only does the <base> tag help you shorten those URLs in your document that have a common root, it also lets you constrain the directory from which relative references are retrieved without binding the document to a specific server.

6.7.1.2 *The target attribute*

As mentioned earlier in this chapter while describing the `target` <a> tag attribute, the latest version of Netscape (2.0) includes a special HTML document type known as a frame. A frame document may display several HTML documents simultaneously. Similar to the `href` attribute, the `target` attribute for the <base> tag lets you establish the default name of one of the frames or windows in which Netscape is to display redirected hyperlinked documents. [frames, 10.1]

6.7.1.3 *Using <base>*

The most important reason for using <base> is to ensure that any relative URLs within the document will resolve into a correct document address, even if the document itself is moved or renamed. This is particularly important when creating a document collection. By placing the correct <base> tag in each document, you can move the entire collection between directories and even servers without breaking all of the links within the documents.

You also need to use the `<base>` tag for a searchable document (`<isindex>`) if you want user queries posed to a URL different from the host document.

Note that a document that contains both the `<isindex>` tag and other relative URLs may have problems if the relative URLs are not relative to the desired index processing URL. Since this is usually the case, do not use relative URLs in searchable documents that use the `<base>` tag to specify the query URL for the document.

6.7.2 The <link> Header Element

Use the `<link>` tag to define the relationship between the current document and another in a Web collection.

<link>

Function:
   Define a relationship between this document and another document

Attributes:
   HREF
   METHODS
   REL
   REV
   TITLE
   URN

End tag:
   None

Contains:
   Nothing

Used in:
   head_content

The `<link>` tags belongs in the `<head>` content, nowhere else. The attributes of the `<link>` tag are identical to that of the `<a>` tag, but their effects serve only to document the relationship between documents. The `<link>` tag has no content and no closing `</link>` element.

6.7.2.1 The href attribute

As with its other tag applications, the `href` attribute specifies the URL of the target `<link>` tag. It is a required attribute, too, and its value is any valid document URL. The specified document is assumed to have a relationship to the current document.

6.7.2.2 *The methods attribute*

The `methods` attribute tells the browser which methods process the document referenced by the `href` attribute. The value of the attribute is a space-separated list of names, each representing a particular method. The browser may then use the‚specified methods when retrieving and displaying the target document.

In practice, the `methods` attribute is hardly ever used. It is too browser-dependent, requiring that the browser understand the methods specified and be able to process the document accordingly.

6.7.2.3 *The rel and rev attributes*

The `rel` and `rev` attributes express the relationship between the source and target documents. The `rel` attribute specifies the relationship from the source document to the target; the `rev` attribute specifies the relationship from the target document to the source document. Both attributes can be included in a single `<link>` tag.

The value of either attribute is a space-separated list of relationships. The actual relationship names are not specified by the HTML standard, although some have come into common usage as listed in 6.3.1.5. For example, a document that is part of a sequence of documents might use:

```
<link href="part-14.html" rel=next rev=prev>
```

when referencing the next document in the series. The relationship from the source to the target is that of moving to the next document; the reverse relationship is that of moving to the previous document.

6.7.2.4 *The title attribute*

The `title` attribute lets you specify the title of the document to which you are linking. This attribute is useful when referencing a resource that does not have a title, such as an image or a non-HTML document. In this case, the browser might use the `<link>` title when displaying the referenced document. For example,

```
<link href="pics/kumquat.gif"
   title="A photograph of the Noble Fruit">
```

tells the browser to use the indicated title when displaying the referenced image.

The value of the attribute is an arbitrary character string, enclosed in quotes.

6.7.2.5 *The urn attribute*

The `urn` attribute defines the more general Universal Resource Name for the referenced document. The value of this attribute is a string, the actual syntax and semantics of which have not yet been defined, making this attribute little more than a place keeper for future versions of HTML that can better exploit the document URN.

6.7.2.6 How browsers might use <link>

Although the HTML standard does not require browsers to do anything with the information provided by the <link> tag, it's not hard to envision how this information might be used to enhance the presentation of a document.

As a simple example, suppose you consistently provide <link> tags for each of your documents that define next, prev, and parent links. A browser could use this information to place a standard toolbar at the top or bottom of each document containing buttons that would jump to the appropriate related document. By relegating the task of providing simple navigational links to the browser, you are free to concentrate on the more important content of your document.

As a more complex example, suppose a browser expects to find a <link> tag defining a glossary for the current document, and that this glossary document is itself a searchable document. Whenever a reader clicked on a word or phrase in the document, the browser could automatically search the glossary for the definition of the selected phrase, presenting the result in a small pop-up window.

As the Web and HTML evolve, expect to see more and more uses of the <link> tag to explicitly define document relationships on the Web.

6.8 Supporting Document Automation

There are two additional header tags whose primary function is to support document automation, interacting with the Web server itself and document-generation tools.

6.8.1 The <meta> Header Element

Given the rich set of HTML header tags for defining a document and its relationship with others that go unused by most HTML authors, you'd think we'd all be satisfied.

But, no. There's always someone with special needs. They want to be able to give even more information about their precious document, information that might be used by browsers, readers of the HTML source, or by document-indexing tools. The <meta> tag is for you who need to go beyond the beyond.

<meta>

Function:
   Supply additional information about a document

Attributes:
   CONTENT
   HTTP_EQUIV
   NAME

End tag:
   None

Contains:
   Nothing

Used in:
   head_content

The `<meta>` tag belongs in the document header and has no content. Instead, attributes of the tag define name-and-value pairs that associate the document. In certain cases, these values are used by the Web server serving the document to further define the document content type to the browser.

6.8.1.1 The name attribute

The `name` attribute supplies the name of the name/value pair defined by the `<meta>` tag. The HTML standard does not define any predefined `<meta>` names. In general, you are free to use any name that makes sense to you and other readers of your HTML source.

If the `name` attribute is not provided, the name of the name/value pair is taken from the `http-equiv` attribute.

6.8.1.2 The content attribute

The `content` attribute provides the value of the name/value pair. It can be any valid string, enclosed in quotes, if necessary. It should always be specified in conjunction with either a `name` or `http-equiv` attribute.

As an example, you might place the author's name in a document with

```
<meta name="Authors" content="Chuck Musciano & Bill Kennedy">
```

You could also include a list of keywords related to the document, such as

```
<meta name="Keywords"
  content="kumquats, cooking, peeling, eating">
```

6.8.1.3 *The http-equiv attribute*

The `http-equiv` attribute supplies a name for the name/value pair and instructs the server to include the name/value pair in the MIME document header that is passed to the browser before sending the actual document.

When a server sends a document to a browser, it first sends a number of name/value pairs. While some servers might send a number of these pairs, all servers send at least one:

```
content-type: text/html
```

This tells the browser to expect to receive an HTML document.

When you use the `<meta>` tag with the `http-equiv` attribute, the server will add your name/value pairs to the content header it sends to the browser. For example, adding:

```
<meta http-equiv="keywords"
  content="kumquats, cooking, peeling, eating">
<meta http-equiv="expires" content="31 Dec 99">
```

causes the header sent to the browser to contain

```
content-type: text/html
keywords: kumquats, cooking, peeling, eating
expires: 31 Dec 99
```

Of course, adding these additional header fields makes sense only if your browser accepts the fields and uses them in some appropriate manner.

6.8.2 *The <nextid> Header Element*

This tag appears in the HTML standard for historical reasons and should not be used.

The idea behind the `<nextid>` tag is to provide some way of automatically indexing fragment identifiers.

<nextid>

Function:
Define the next valid document entity identifier

Attributes:
n

End tag:
None

Contains:
Nothing

Used in:
head_content

6.8.2.1 The n attribute

The n attribute specifies the name of the next generated fragment identifier. Although the HTML standard does not define the format of this name, it is typically an alphabetic string followed by a two-digit number. A typical `<nextid>` tag might look like this:

```
<html>
<head>
<nextid n=DOC54>
</head>
...
```

An automatic-document generator might use the `nextid` information, then, to successively name fragment identifiers DOC54, DOC55, and so forth within this document.

7

Formatted Lists

Making information more accessible is the single most important quality of HTML. The language's excellent collection of text style and formatting tools helps you organize your information into documents readers quickly understand, scan, and extract, possibly with automated browser agents.

Beyond embellishing your text with specialized text tags, HTML also provides a rich set of tools that help you organize content into formatted lists. There's nothing magical or mysterious about HTML lists. In fact, the beauty of HTML lists is their simplicity. They're based on common list paradigms we encounter every day, such as an unordered laundry list, ordered instruction lists, and dictionary-like definition lists. All are familiar, comfortable ways of organizing content. All provide powerful means for quickly understanding, scanning, and extracting pertinent information from your HTML documents.

7.1 Unordered Lists

Like a laundry or shopping list, an unordered list in HTML is a collection of related items that have no special order or sequence. The most common unordered list you'll find on the Web is a collection of hyperlinks to other documents. Some topic, however vague like "Related Kumquat Lovers' Sites," allies the items in an unordered list, but they have no order among themselves.

7.1.1 The <ul> Tag

The <ul> tag signals the browser that the following content, ending with the </ul> tag, is an unordered list of items. Inside, each item in the unordered list is identified by a leading <li> tag. Otherwise, nearly anything HTML-wise goes, including other lists, text, and multimedia elements. [<li>, 7.3]

<ul>

Function:
    Define an unordered list
Attributes:
    COMPACT
    TYPE (Netscape only)
End tag:
    </ul>, never omitted
Contains:
    list_content
Used in:
    block

Typically, the browser adds a leading bullet character and formats each item on a new line, indented somewhat from the left margin of the document. The actual rendering of unordered lists, however, varies widely between browsers, so you shouldn't get bent out of shape trying to attain exact positioning of the elements. For instance, some browsers treat the start of an unordered list as a new paragraph and like the <p> tag leave a blank line above the list. Other browsers simply start the list item after a simple line break. Browsers vary, too, in how much space they use between list items. For example, the following source:

```
Popular Kumquat recipes:
<ul>
  <li>Pickled Kumquats
  <li>'Quats and 'Kraut (a holiday favorite!)
  <li>'Quatshakes
</ul>
There are so many more to please every palate!
```

appears to the Mosaic user as shown in the Figure 7-1.

Tricky HTML authors sometimes use nested unordered lists, with and without <li> tagged items, to take advantage of the automatic, successive indenting. You can produce some fairly slick text segments that way. Just don't depend on it for all browsers, including future ones.

The character used for the bullet at the beginning of each <li> tagged item in the list is not defined by the HTML standard, so browsers are free to use nearly any sort of bullet. Tradition does prevail. Most graphical browsers use either a round or square bullet; the Lynx character-based browser uses an asterisk to denote the start of each list element. You can also create custom bullets for your lists using definition lists, as we explain below.

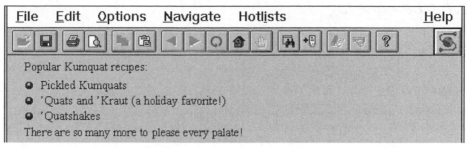

Figure 7–1: A simple unordered list

7.1.1.1 Compact unordered lists

If you like wide open spaces, you'll hate the optional `compact` attribute for the `<ul>` tag. It tells the browser to squeeze the unordered list into an even smaller, more compact text block. Typically, the browser reduces the line spacing between list items. And it may reduce the indentation between list items, if it does anything at all (usually it doesn't).

Some browsers ignore the `compact` attribute, so you should not overly depend on its formatting attributes.

7.1.1.2 Changing item bullets in unordered lists

The graphical browsers automatically bullet each item in an unordered list. Netscape uses a solid disc, for example; Mosaic precedes unordered list items with a hollow square (on the Mac) or a round ball (PC and UNIX). With Netscape you can use the `type` attribute to specify which bullet symbol you'd rather have precede items in an unordered list. The `type` attribute is Netscape-only; it is ignored by other browsers. It may have a value of either `disc`, `circle`, or `square`. All the items within that list will thereafter use the specified bullet symbol, unless an individual item overrides the list bullet type, as described below.

7.2 Ordered Lists

Ordered lists are used when the sequence of the list items is important. A list of instructions is a good example, as are tables of content and lists of document footnotes or endnotes.

7.2.1 The <ol> Tag

The typical browser formats the contents of an ordered list just like an unordered list, except that the items are numbered instead of bulleted. The numbering starts at 1 and is incremented by one for each successive ordered list element tagged with <li>. [<li>, 7.7.3]

<ol>

Function:
   Define an ordered list

Attributes:
   COMPACT
   START (extension)
   TYPE (extension)

End tag:
   </ol>, never omitted

Contains:
   list_content

Used in:
   block

In standard HTML 2.0 you can't start numbering at some value other than one, increment by a value other than one, or number the items with anything but whole Arabic numerals. Netscape and Internet Explorer, on the other hand, offer extensions that let you do all those things.

A sample ordered list might be:

```
<h3>Pickled Kumquats</h3>
Here's an easy way to make a delicious batch of pickled 'quats:
<ol>
  <li>Rinse 50 pounds of fresh kumquats
  <li>Bring eight gallons white vinegar to rolling boil
  <li>Add kumquats gradually, keeping vinegar boiling
  <li>Boil for one hour, or until kumquats are tender
  <li>Place in sealed jars and enjoy!
</ol>
```

This is rendered by Netscape as shown in Figure 7-2.

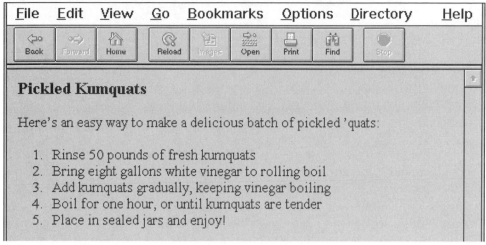

Figure 7–2: An ordered list

7.2.1.1 Compact ordered lists

Like the unordered list, the ordered list in HTML has an optional `compact` attribute. When instructed to compact the ordered list, the browser may reduce the indentation, reduce the amount of space between the sequence numbers and the list items, or both. Some browsers cannot compact and so do nothing.

7.2.1.2 The start attribute

Normally, browsers automatically number ordered list items beginning with the Arabic numeral 1. The `start` attribute is used by Netscape and Internet Explorer with the `<ol>` tag to let you change that beginning value. To start numbering a list at 5, for example:

```
<ol start=5>
  <li> This is item number 5.
  <li> This is number six!
  <li> And so forth...
</ol>
```

7.2.1.3 Changing the numbering style in ordered lists

By default, browsers number ordered list items with a sequence of Arabic numerals. Besides being able to start the sequence at some number other than 1, Netscape and Internet Explorer also let you use a `type` attribute with the `<ol>` tag to change the numbering style itself. With the `<ol>` tag, the `type` attribute may have a value of "`A`" for numbering with capital letters, "`a`" for numbering with lowercase letters, "`I`" for capital Roman numerals, "`i`" for lowercase Roman numerals, or "`1`" for common Arabic numerals. (See Table 7-1).

Table 7–1: Netscape and Internet Explorer Type Values for Numbering Ordered Lists

Type Value	Generated Style	Sample Sequence
A	Capital letters	A, B, C, D
a	Lowercase letters	a, b, c, d
I	Capital Roman numerals	I, II, III, IV
i	Lowercase Roman numerals	i, ii, iii, iv
1	Arabic numerals	1, 2, 3, 4

The `start` and `type` attribute extensions work in tandem. The `start` attribute sets the starting value of the item integer counter at the beginning of an ordered list. The `type` attribute sets the actual numbering style. For example, the following ordered list starts numbering items at 8, but because the style of numbering is set to i, the first number is the lowercase Roman numeral, "viii." Subsequent items are numbered with the same style, each value incremented by 1 as shown in (Figure 7-3):

```
<ol start=8 type="i">
  <li> This is the Roman number 8.
  <li> The numerals increment by 1.
  <li> And so forth...
</ol>
```

Figure 7–3: The Netscape start and type attributes work in tandem

The type and value of individual items in a list can be different from the list as a whole, as described in the next section.

7.3 The <li> Tag

It should be quite obvious to you by now that the `<li>` tag defines an item in a list. It's the universal tag for HTML list items in ordered (`<ol>`) and unordered (`<ul>`) lists, as we discuss above, and for directories (`<dir>`) and menus (`<menu>`), which we discuss in detail below.

<li>

Function:
Define an item within an ordered, unordered, directory, or menu list

Attributes:
TYPE (extension)
VALUE (extension)

End tag:
</li>, usually omitted

Contains:
flow

Used in:
list_content

Because the end of a list element can always be inferred by the surrounding document structure, most authors omit the ending </li> tags for their list elements. That makes sense because it becomes easier to add, delete, and move elements around within a list, so we recommend not using the </li> end tag.

Although universal in meaning, there are some differences and restrictions to the use of the <li> tag for each HTML list type. In unordered and ordered lists, what follows the <li> tag may be nearly anything, including other lists and multiple paragraphs. Typically, if it handles indentation at all, the browser successively indents nested list items, and the content in those items is justified to the innermost indented margin.

Directory and menu lists are another matter. They are lists of short items like a single word or simple text blurb and nothing else. Consequently, <li> items within <dir> and <menu> tags may not contain other lists or other block elements, including paragraphs, preformatted blocks, or forms.

Clean documents, fully compliant with the HTML standard, should not contain any text or other document item inside the unordered, ordered, directory, or menu lists that is not contained within an <li> tag. Most browsers are tolerant of violations to this rule, but then you can't hold the browser responsible for compliant rendering for exceptional cases, either.

7.3.1 Changing the Style and Sequence of Individual List Items

Just as Netscape and Internet Explorer let you can change the bullet or numbering style for all of the items in an unordered or ordered list, they also let you change the style for individual items within those lists. With ordered lists, you can also change the value of the item number. As you'll see, the combinations of changing style and numbering can lead to a variety of useful list structures, particularly when included with nested lists.

7.3.1.1 The type attribute

Acceptable values for the `type` attribute in the `<li>` tag are the same as the values for the appropriate list type: items within unordered lists may have their type set to `circle`, `square`, or `disc`, while items in an ordered list may have their type set to any of the values shown previously in Table 7-1. The change affects the current item and any subsequent items in the list.

There is no way to revert back to the list's default type once you have changed the type for a single item; you'll need to explicitly reset the type on the next item. Thus, to make a single item in a list different from the rest, you'll need to change two items: the actual item you want changed, and the next item, which must be changed back to the general list format.

Figure 7-4 shows the effect that changing the `type` for an individual item in an ordered list has on subsequent items, as rendered by Netscape from the following source:

```
<ol>
  <li type=A>Changing the numbering style
  <li type=a>Doesn't alter the order!
  <li> &lt;-- See? It's a "c"!
  <li type=I>Uppercase Roman numerals!
  <li type=i>Lowercase Roman numerals!
  <li type=1>Plain ol'numbers!
</ol>
```

Notice how the `type` attribute changes the display style of the number, but not the value of the number itself.

7.3.1.2 The value attribute

The `value` attribute extension in Netscape and Internet Explorer lets you change the number of a specific list item and the ones that follow it. Since the ordered list is the only HTML list with sequentially numbered items, the `value` attribute is only valid when used within an `<li>` tag inside an ordered list.

File
Edit
View
Go
Bookmarks
Options
Directory
Help
Back
Forward
Home
Reload
Images
Open
Print
Find
Stop
A. Changing the numbering style
b. Doesn't alter the order!
c. <-- See? It's a "c"!
IV. Uppercase Roman numerals!
v. Lowercase Roman numerals!
6. Plain ol'numbers!

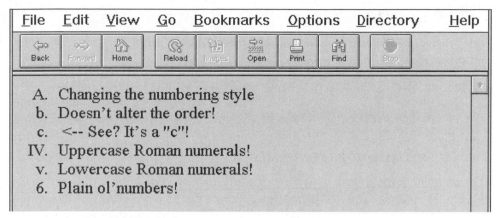

Figure 7-4: Changing the numbering style for each item in an ordered list

To change the current and subsequent numbers attached to each item in an ordered list, simply set the `value` attribute to any integer. For example, the following source uses the `value` attribute to jump the numbering on items in an ordered list, as shown rendered by Netscape in Figure 7-5:

```
<ol>
  <li>Item number 1
  <li>And thc second
  <li value=9> Jump to number 9
  <li>And continue with 10...
</ol>
```

File
Edit
View
Go
Bookmarks
Options
Directory
Help
Back
Forward
Home
Reload
Images
Open
Print
Find
Stop
1. Item number 1
2. And the second
9. Jump to number 9
10. And continue with 10...

Figure 7-5: The value attribute lets you change individual item numbers in an ordered list

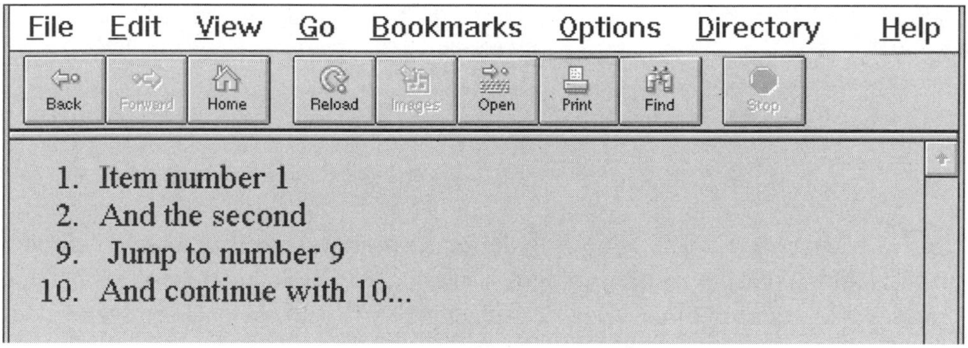

7.4 Nesting Lists

Except inside directories or menus, lists nested inside other lists are fine. Menu and directory lists can be embedded within other lists.

Indents for each nested list are cumulative, so take care not to nest lists too much; the list contents could quickly turn into a thin ribbon of text flush against the right edge of the browser document window.

7.4.1 Nested Unordered Lists

The items in each nested unordered list may be preceded by a different bullet character at the discretion of the browser. For example, Mosaic uses an alternating series of hollow and solid circular, square, and triangular bullets for the various nests in the following source HTML text as shown in Figure 7-6:

```
<ul>
   <li>Morning Kumquat Delicacies
   <ul>
     <li>Hot Dishes
     <ul>
       <li>Kumquat omelet
       <li>Kumquat waffles
       <ul>
         <li>Country style
         <li>Belgian
       </ul>
       <li>Kumquats and toast
     </ul>
     <li>Cold Dishes
     <ul>
       <li>Kumquats and cornflakes
       <li>Pickled Kumquats
       <li>Diced Kumquats
     </ul>
   </ul>
</ul>
```

Netscape lets you change the bullet style for each unordered list and even individual list items (see the `type` attribute discussion earlier in this chapter), but the browser's repertoire of bullets is limited. Figure 7-7 shows what Netscape does with the nested unordered list example above.

7.4.2 Nested Ordered Lists

HTML 2.0 standard browsers number the items in ordered lists beginning with the Arabic numeral 1, nested or not. It would be great if the HTML standard numbered

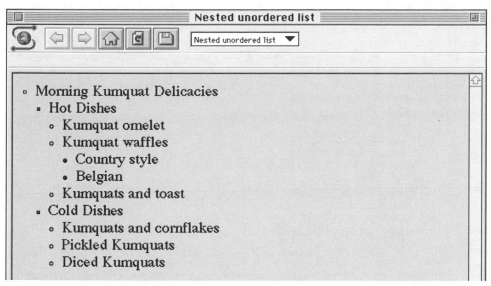

Figure 7–6: Bullets change for each nested unordered list item

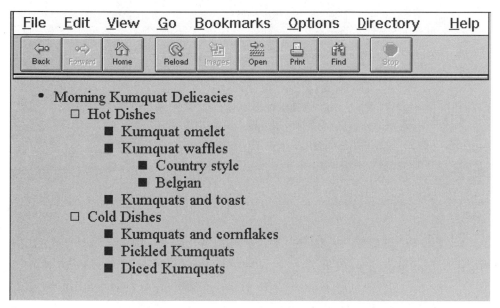

Figure 7–7: Netscape rendering of nested unordered lists

nested ordered lists in some rational, consecutive manner. For example, the items in the second nest of the third main ordered list might be successively numbered "3.2.1," "3.2.2," "3.2.3," and so on. Even the extended browsers don't do that.

With the extended browsers, however, you do have a lot more latitude in how you create nested ordered lists than the HTML 2.0 standard currently provides. An excellent example is the traditional style for outlining, which uses the many different ways of numbering items offered by the `type` attribute (Figure 7-8):

```
<ol type=A>
  <li>A History of Kumquats
  <ol type=1>
    <li>Early History
    <ol type=a>
      <li>The Fossil Record
      <li>Kumquats: The Missing Link?
    </ol>
    <li>Mayan Use of Kumquats
    <li>Kumquats in the New World
  </ol>
  <li>Future Use of Kumquats
</ol>
```

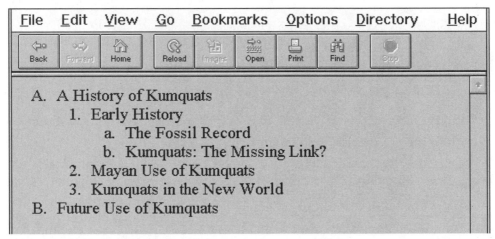

Figure 7–8: Netscape's type attribute lets you do traditional outlining with ordered lists

7.5 Directory Lists

The directory list is a specialized form of the unordered list. [`<ul>`, 7.1.1]

7.5.1 The *<dir>* Tag

The designers of HTML originally dedicated the `<dir>` tag for displaying lists of files. As such, the browser, if it treats `<dir>` and `<ul>` differently at all (most don't), expects the various list elements to be quite short, possibly no longer than 20 characters or so. Some browsers display the elements in a multicolumn format and may not use a leading bullet.

<dir>

Function:
    Define a directory list

Attributes:
    COMPACT
    TYPE (Netscape only)

End tag:
    </dir>, never omitted

Contains:
    list_content

Used in:
    block

Like the unordered list, directory list items are defined with the `<li>` tag. When used within a directory list, however, the `<li>` tag may not contain any block element, including paragraphs, other lists, preformatted text, or forms.

The following example puts the directory tag to its traditional task of presenting a list of filenames:

```
The distribution tape has the following files on it:
<dir>
   <li><code>README</code>
   <li><code>Makefile</code>
   <li><code>main.c</code>
   <li><code>config.h</code>
   <li><code>util.c</code>
</dir>
```

Notice we use the `<code>` tag to ensure that the filenames would be rendered in an appropriate manner (see Figure 7-9).

Like the other formatting tags we've seen so far, the `<dir>` tag has an optional `compact` attribute for producing an even more reduced list display, even though virtually none of the browsers is either willing or capable of compacting directory lists.

You can change the style Netscape uses to bullet the `<dir>` list items with the `type` attribute extension and the values `circle`, `square`, or `disc`. This behavior is identical to the usage of the `type` attribute in an unordered list.

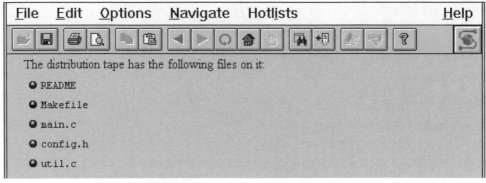

Figure 7–9: An example <dir> list

7.6 *Menu Lists*

The HTML menu list is yet another specialized form of the unordered list.

7.6.1 *The <menu> Tag*

The <menu> tag displays a list of short choices to the reader, such as a menu of links to other documents. The browser may use a special (typically more compact) representation of items in a menu list compared with the general unordered list, or even use some sort of graphical pulldown menu to implement the menu list. If the list items are short enough, the browser may even display them in a multicolumn format, and may not append a leading bullet with each list item.

<menu>

Function:
    Define a menu list

Attributes:
    COMPACT
    TYPE (Netscape only)

End tag:
    </menu>, never omitted

Contains:
    list_content

Used in:
    block

Like an unordered list, the menu list items are defined with the `<li>` tag. When used within a menu list, however, the `<li>` tag may not contain any block element, including paragraphs, other lists, preformatted text, or forms.

Compare the source text below and the Mosaic display (Figure 7-10) with the directory (Figure 7-9) and unordered (Figure 7-1) list displays we presented earlier in this chapter.

```
<p>
Some popular kumquat recipes include:
<menu>
   <li>Pickled Kumquats
   <li>'Quats and 'Kraut (a holiday favorite!)
   <li>'Quatshakes
</menu>
There are many more to please every palate!
```

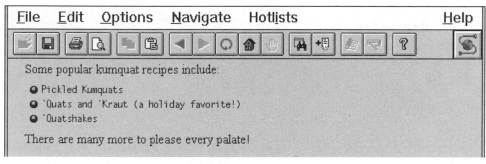

Figure 7–10: Sample <menu> list

The `<menu>` tag also has the `compact` attribute to produce an even more reduced list presentation, although in practice, few browsers are willing or able to implement the compacted menu list display. Netscape, in fact, doesn't distinguish between a menu and an unordered list.

You can change the style Netscape uses to bullet the `<menu>` list items with the `type` attribute extension and the values `circle`, `square`, or `disc`. This behavior is identical to that of the `type` attribute in an unordered list.

7.7 *Definition Lists*

HTML also supports a list style entirely different from the ordered, unordered, menu, and directory lists we've discussed so far: definition lists. Like the entries you find in a dictionary or encyclopedia, complete with text, pictures, and other multimedia elements, the definition list is the ideal way to present a glossary, list of terms, or other name-value lists in HTML.

7.7.1 The *<dl>* Tag

The definition list is enclosed by the `<dl>` and `</dl>` tags. Within those tags, each item in a definition list is composed of two parts: a term followed by its definition or explanation. Instead of `<li>`, each item name in a `<dl>` list is marked with the `<dt>` tag, followed by the item's definition or explanation as marked by the `<dd>` tag.

<dl>

Function:
    Define a definition list

Attributes:
    COMPACT

End tag:
    </dl>, never omitted

Contains:
    dl_content

Used in:
    block

Browsers typically render the item or term name at the left margin and render the definition or explanation below it and indented. If the definition terms are very short (typically less than three characters), the browser may choose to place the first portion of the definition on the same line as the term. See how the source HTML definition list below gets displayed by Netscape in Figure 7-11.

```
<h3>Common Kumquat Parasites</h3>
<dl>
  <dt>Leaf mites
  <dd>The leaf mite will ravage the Kumquat tree, stripping it
      of any and all vegetation.
  <dt>Trunk dropsy
  <dd>This microscopic larvae of the common opossum
      chigger will consume the structural elements of the
      tree trunk, causing it to collapse inward.
</dl>
```

Like other list types, you can add more space between the list items by inserting paragraph `<p>` tags between them.

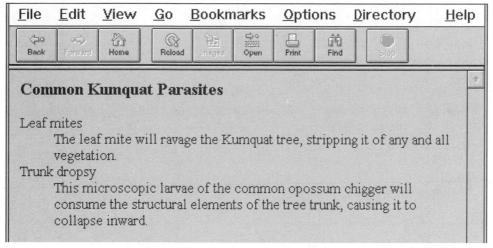

Figure 7–11: A definition list as presented by Netscape

7.7.1.1 *More compact definition lists*

The <dl> tag also has the compact attribute, advising the browser to make the list presentation as small as possible. The browser may choose to reduce the inter-item spacing, shift the definition to the left margin instead of indenting, or reduce the size of the type used to present the list. Whether or not a browser actually does any of these things is up to its manufacturer. Few do.

7.7.2 *The <dt> Tag*

This <dt> tag defines the term component of a definition list. It is only valid when used within a definition <dl> list preceding the term or item, before the <dd> tag and the term's definition or explanation.

Traditionally, the definition term that follows the <dt> tag is short and sweet—a word or few. Technically, it can be any length. If long, the browser may exercise the option of extending the item beyond the display window, or wrap it onto the next line where the definition begins.

Since the end of the <dt> tag immediately precedes the start of the matching <dd> tag, it is unambiguous and so not required.

<dt>

Function:
Define a definition list term

Attributes:
None

End tag:
</dt>, always omitted

Contains:
text

Used in:
dl_content

7.7.2.1 Formatting text with *<dt>*

In practice, browsers are either too lenient or too dumb to enforce the HTML rules, so some tricky HTML authors misuse the <dt> tag to shift the left margin right and left, respectively, for fancy text displays. (Remember, tab characters and leading spaces don't usually work with regular text.) We don't condone violating the HTML standard and caution you once again about tricked-up documents.

7.7.3 The *<dd>* Tag

The <dd> tag marks the start of the definition portion of an item in a definition list. According to the HTML standard, <dd> belongs only inside a definition <dl> list, immediately following the <dt> tag and term and preceding the definition or explanation.

The content that follows the <dd> tag may be any HTML construct, including other lists, block text, and multimedia elements. Although treating it otherwise identically as conventional content, browsers typically indent definition list <dd> definitions. And since the start of another term and definition (<dt>) or the required end tag of the definition (</dl>) unambiguously terminates the preceding definition, the </dd> tag is not needed and its absence makes your source text more readable.

<dd>

Function:
Define a definition list term

Attributes:
None

End tag:
</dd>, usually omitted

Contains:
flow

Used in:
dl_content

7.8 *Appropriate List Usage*

In general, use unordered lists for:

- Hotlists and other link collections

- Short, nonsequenced groups of text

- Emphasizing the high points of a presentation

In general, use ordered lists for:

- Tables of content

- Instruction sequences

- Sets of sequential sections of text

- Assigning numbers to short phrases that can be referenced elsewhere

In general, use definition lists for:

- Glossaries

- Custom bullets (make the item after the <dt> tag an icon-sized bullet image)

- Any list of name/value pairs

8

Forms

Forms, forms, forms, forms: we fill 'em out for nearly everything, from the moment we're born, 'til the moment we die. So what's to explain all the hoopla and excitement over HTML forms? Simply this: they make HTML truly interactive.

When you think about it, except for the limited input from users available through the `<isindex>` tag, HTML's interactivity is basically a lot of button pushing: click here, click there, go here, go there; there's no real user feedback, and it's certainly not personalized. Applets provide extensive user-interaction capability, but they can be difficult to write and are still not standardized for all browsers. Forms, on the other hand, are supported by almost every browser and make it possible to create documents that collect and process user input, and formulate personalized replies.

This powerful mechanism has far-reaching implications, particularly for electronic commerce. It finishes an online catalog by giving buyers a way to immediately order products and services. It gives nonprofit organizations a way to sign up new members. It gives market researchers a way to collect user data. It gives you an automated way to interact with your HTML document readers.

Mull over the ways you might want to interact with your readers while we take a look at both the client- and server-side details of creating forms.

8.1 Form Fundamentals

Unlike the `<isindex>` tag, you can put one or more forms in a single document. And unlike an `<isindex>` document, users can ignore the embedded forms, reading content and interacting with the document's links just as with a form-less document. [`<isindex>`, 6.6.1]

Forms are comprised of one or more text-input boxes, clickable (*radio*) buttons, multiple-choice checkboxes, and even pull-down menus and clickable images, all placed inside the `<form>` tag. Within a form, you may also put regular body content, including text and images. The text is particularly useful for providing instructions to the users on how to fill out the form and for form element labels and prompts.

Once a user fills out the various fields in the form, they click a special "Submit" button (or, sometimes, press the Return key) to submit the form to a server. The form-supporting browser packages up the user-supplied values and choices and sends them to a server.[*] The server then passes the information along to a supporting program or application that processes the information and creates a reply, usually in HTML. The reply may be simply a thank you or it might prompt the user how to fill out the form correctly or to supply missing fields. The server sends the reply to the browser client that presents it to the user.

The server-side data-processing aspects of forms are not part of the HTML standard; they are defined by the server's software. While a complete discussion of server-side forms programming is beyond the scope of this book, we'd be remiss if we did not include at least a simple example to get you started. To that end, we've included at the end of this chapter a few skeletal programs that illustrate the common styles of server-side forms programming.

8.1.1 The *<form>* Tag

You place a form anywhere inside the body of an HTML document with its elements enclosed by the `<form>` tag and its respective end tag `</form>`. You may, and we recommend you often do, include regular body content inside a form to specially label user-input fields and to provide directions, for example.

Browsers flow the special form elements into the containing paragraphs as if they were small images embedded into the text. There aren't any special layout rules for form elements, so you need to use other HTML elements, like the `<br>` and `<p>` tags, to control the placement of elements within the text flow. [`<p>`, 4.1.2] [`<br>`, 4.7.1]

All of the form elements within a `<form>` tag comprise a single form. The browser sends all of the values of these elements—blank, default, or user-modified—when the user submits the form to the server.

---

* Some browsers, Netscape in particular, may also encrypt the information, securing it from credit-card thieves, for example. However, the encryption facility must also be supported on the server-side as well: contact the browser manufacturer for details.

<form>

Function:
   Defines a form

Attributes:
   ACTION
   ENCTYPE
   METHOD

End tag:
   </form>; never omitted

Contains:
   form_content

Used in:
   block

You must define at least two special form attributes, which provide the name and address of the form's processing server and the method by which the parameters are to be sent to the server. A third, optional attribute lets you change how the parameters get encoded for secure transmission over the network.

8.1.1.1 The action attribute

The required `action` attribute for the `<form>` tag gives the URL of the application that is to receive and process the form's data.

Most webmasters keep their forms-processing applications in a special directory on their Web server, usually named *cgi-bin*, which stands for Common Gateway Interface[*] binaries. Keeping these special forms-processing programs and applications in one directory makes it easier to manage and secure the server.

A typical `<form>` tag with the `action` attribute looks like this:

```
<form action="http://www.kumquat.com/cgi-bin/update">
...
</form>
```

The example URL tells the browser to contact the server named *www.kumquat.com* and pass along the user's form values to the application named *update* located in the *cgi-bin* directory.

---

[*] The Common Gateway Interface (CGI) defines the protocol by which servers interact with programs that process form data.

In general, if you see a URL that references a document in a directory named *cgi-bin*, you can be pretty sure that the document is actually an application that creates the desired page dynamically each time it's invoked.

8.1.1.2 The enctype attribute

The browser specially encodes the form's data before it passes that data to the server so it does not become scrambled or corrupted during the transmission. It is up to the server to either decode the parameters or to pass them, still encoded, to the application.

The standard encoding format is the Internet Media Type named "application/x-www-form-urlencoded." You can change that encoding with the optional `enctype` attribute in the `<form>` tag. If you do elect to use an alternative encoding, the only other supported format is "multipart/form-data."

The reality is that you'll rarely if ever see the `enctype` attribute used. The only format common among the popular browsers and Web servers is the default application/x-www-form-urlencoded. Netscape is the only browser that currently supports the multipart/form-data alternative, which is required only for those forms that contain file-selection fields. Unless your forms need file-selection fields, you probably should ignore this attribute and simply rely upon the browser and your processing server to use the default encoding type. [file-selection fields, 8.2.2.3]

The standard encoding—application/x-www-form-urlencoded—converts any spaces in the form values to a plus sign (+), nonalphanumeric characters into a percent sign (%) followed by two hexadecimal digits that are the ASCII code of the character, and the line breaks in multiline form data into %0D%0A.

The standard encoding also includes a name for each field in the form. (A "field" is a discrete element in the form, whose value can be nearly anything, from a single number to several lines of text—the user's address, for example.) If there is more than one value in the field, the values are separated by ampersands ("&").

For example, here's what the browser sends to the server after the user fills out a form with two input fields labeled **name** and **address**; the former field has just one line of text, while the latter field has several lines of input:

```
name=O'Reilly+&+Associates&address=103+Morris+Street%0D%0A
Sebastopol,%0D%0ACA+95472
```

We've broken the value into two lines for clarity in this book, but in reality, the browser sends the data in an unbroken string. The **name** field is "O'Reilly & Associates" and the value of the **address** field, complete with embedded newline characters, is:

```
103 Morris Street
Sebastopol,
CA 95472
```

The multipart/form-data encoding encapsulates the fields in the form as several parts of a single MIME-compatible compound document. Each field has its own section in the resulting file, set off by a standard delimiter. Within each section, one or more header lines define the name of the field, followed by one or more lines containing the value of the field. Since the value part of each section can contain binary data or otherwise unprintable characters, no character conversion or encoding occurs within the transmitted data.

This encoding format is by nature more verbose and longer than the application/x-www-form-urlencoded format. As such, it can only be used when the `method` attribute of the `<form>` tag is set to `post`, as described below.

A simple example makes it easy to understand this format. Here's our previous example, when transmitted as multipart/form-data:

```
-----------------------------146931364513459
Content-Disposition: form-data; name="name"

O'Reilly & Associates
-----------------------------146931364513459
Content-Disposition: form-data; name="address"

103 Morris Street
Sebastopol,
CA 95472
-----------------------------146931364513459--
```

The first line of the transmission defines the delimiter that will appear before each section of the document. It always consists of thirty dashes and a long random number that distinguishes it from other text that might appear in actual field values.

The next lines contain the header fields for the first section. There will always be a Content-Disposition field indicating that this section contains form data and providing the name of the form element whose value is in this section. You may see other header fields; in particular, some file-selection fields include a Content-Type header field that indicates the type of data contained in the file being transmitted.

After the headers, there is a single blank line followed by the actual value of the field on one or more lines. The section concludes with a repeat of the delimiter line that started the transmission. Another section follows immediately, and the pattern repeats until all of the form parameters have been transmitted. The end of the transmission is indicated by an extra two dashes at the end of the last delimiter line.

As we pointed out earlier, use multipart/form-data encoding only when your form contains a file-selection field. Here's an example of how the transmission of a file-selection field might look:

```
----------------------------146931364513459
Content-Disposition: form-data; name="thefile"; filename="test"
Content-Type: text/plain

First line of the file
...
Last line of the file
----------------------------146931364513459
```

The only notable difference is that the Content-Disposition field contains an extra element, "filename," that defines the name of the file being transmitted. There might also be a Content-Type field to further describe the file's contents.

8.1.1.3 *The method attribute*

The other required attribute for the `<form>` tag sets the method by which the browser sends the form's data to the server for processing. There are two ways: the POST method and the GET method.

With the POST method, the browser sends the data in two steps: the browser first contacts the form-processing server specified in the `action` attribute, and once contact is made, sends the data to the server in a separate transmission.

On the server side, POST-style applications are expected to read the parameters from a standard location once they begin execution. Once read, the parameters must be decoded before the application can use the form values. Your particular server will define exactly how your POST-style applications can expect to receive their parameters.

The GET method, on the other hand, contacts the form-processing server and sends the form data in a single transmission step: the browser appends the data to the form's `action` URL, separated by the question mark (?) character.

The common browsers transmit the form information by either method; some servers receive the form data by only one or the other method. You indicate which of the two methods—POST or GET—your forms-processing server handles with the `method` attribute in the `<form>` tag. Here's the complete tag including the GET transmission `method` attribute for the previous form example:

```
<form method=GET
    action="http://www.kumquat.com/cgi-bin/update">
    ...
</form>
```

Which one to use if your form-processing server supports both the POST and GET methods? Here are some rules of thumb:

- For best form-transmission performance, send small forms with a few short fields via the GET method.

- Because some server operating systems limit the number and length of command-line arguments that can be passed to an application at once, use the POST method to send forms that have many fields, or ones that have long text fields.

- If you are inexperienced in writing server-side form-processing applications, choose GET. The extra steps involved in reading and decoding POST-style transmitted parameters, while not too difficult, may be more work than you are willing to tackle.

- If security is an issue, choose POST. GET places the form parameters directly in the application URL where they easily can be captured by network sniffers or extracted from a server log file. If the parameters contain sensitive information like credit card numbers, you may be compromising your users without their knowledge. While POST applications are not without their security holes, they can at least take advantage of encryption when transmitting the parameters as a separate transaction with the server.

If you want to invoke the server-side application outside the realm of a form, including passing it parameters, use GET because it lets you include form-like parameters as part of a URL. POST-style applications, on the other hand, expect an extra transmission from the browser after the URL, something you can't do as part of a conventional <a> tag.

8.1.1.4 *Passing parameters explicitly*

The foregoing bit of advice warrants some explanation. Suppose you had a simple form with two elements, named x and y. When the values of these elements are encoded, they look like this:

```
x=27&y=33
```

If the form uses `method=GET`, the URL used to reference the server-side application looks something like this:

```
http://www.kumquat.com/cgi-bin/update?x=27&y=33
```

There is nothing to keep you from creating a conventional <a> tag that invokes the form with any parameter value you desire, like so:

```
<a href="http://www.kumquat.com/cgi-bin/update?x=19&y=104">
```

The only hitch is that the ampersand that separates the parameters is also the character-entity insertion character. When placed within the `href` attribute of the `<a>` tag, the ampersand will cause the browser to replace the characters following it with a corresponding character entity.

To keep this from happening, you must replace the literal ampersand with its entity equivalent, either `&#38;` or `&amp;`. With this substitution, our example of the nonform reference to the server-side application looks like this:

```
<a href="http://www.kumquat.com/cgi-bin/update?x=19&amp;y=104">
```

Because of the potential confusion that arises from having to escape the ampersands in the URL, server implementors are encouraged to also accept the semicolon (;) as a parameter separater. You might want to check your server's documentation to see if they honor this convention. See Appendix D, *Character Entities*.

8.1.1.5 A simple example

In a moment we'll examine each element of a form in detail. Let's first take a quick look at a simple example to see how forms are put together.

This one (shown in Figure 8-1) gathers basic demographic information about a user:

```
<form method=POST action="http://www.kumquat.com/demo">
  Name:
    <input type=text name=name size=32 maxlength=80>
  <p>
  Sex:
    <input type=radio name=sex value="M"> Male
    <input type=radio name=sex value="F"> Female
  <p>
  Income:
    <select name=income size=1>
      <option>Under $25,000
      <option>$25,001 to $50,000
      <option>$50,001 and higher
    </select>
  <p>
  <input type=submit>
</form>
```

The first line of the example starts the form and indicates we'll be using the POST method for data transmission to the form-processing server. The form's user-input elements follow, each defined by an `<input>` tag and `type` attribute. There are three elements in the simple example, each contained within its own paragraph.

The first element is a conventional text-entry field, letting the user type in up to 80 characters, but displaying only 32 of them at a time. The next element is a

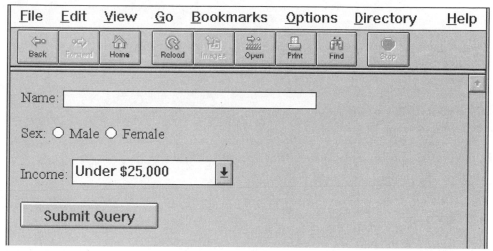

Figure 8-1: A simple form

multiple-choice option, which lets the user select only one of two radio buttons. This is followed by a pull-down menu for choosing one of three options. The final element is a simple submission button, which, when clicked by the user, sets the form's processing in motion.

8.2 Form Input Elements

You create most form elements with the `<input>` tag.

8.2.1 The *<input> Tag*

Use the `<input>` tag to define any one of a number of common form elements, including text fields, multiple-choice lists, clickable images, and submission buttons. Although there are many attributes for this tag, only the `type` and `name` attributes are required for each element (only `type` for a submission button; see below), and as we describe in detail below, each type of input element uses only a subset of the allowed attributes. Additional `<input>` attributes may be required based upon which type of form element you specify.

You select the type of element to include in the form with the `<input>` tag's required `type` attribute, and you name the field (used during the form-submission process to the server; see above) with the `name` attribute. Although, the value of the name attribute is technically an arbitrary string, we recommend you use a name without embedded spaces or punctuation. If you stick to just letters and

---

<input>

Function:
    Create an input element within a form

Attributes:
    ALIGN
    CHECKED
    MAXLENGTH
    NAME
    SIZE
    SRC
    TYPE
    VALUE

End tag:
    None

Contains:
    Nothing

Used in:
    form_content

---

numbers (but no leading digits) and represent spaces with the underscore (_) character, you'll have fewer problems. For example, "cost_in_dollars" and "overhead_percentage" are good choices for element names; "$cost" and "overhead %" might cause problems.

8.2.2 *Text Fields in Forms*

The HTML standard lets you include three types of text-entry fields in your forms: a conventional text entry field, a masked field for secure data entry, and a field that names a file to be transmitted as part of your form data. The first two are available with all browsers and accept `size`, `maxlength`, and `value` attributes. The file-selection field accepts only the `size` and `maxlength` attributes and is only supported by Netscape.

8.2.2.1 *Conventional text fields*

The most useful as well as the most common form-input element is the text-entry field. A text-entry field appears in the browser window as an empty box on one line and accepts a single line of user input that becomes the value of the element when the user submits the form to the server. To create a text entry field inside a form in your HTML document, set the `type` of the `<input>` form element to `text`. Include a `name` attribute as well; it's required.

What constitutes a line of text differs among the various browsers. Fortunately, HTML gives us a way, with `size` and `maxlength` attributes, to dictate the width, in characters, of the text-input display box, and how many total characters to accept from the user, respectively. The value for either attribute is an integer equal to the maximum number of characters you'll allow the user to see and type in the field. If `maxlength` exceeds `size`, then text scrolls back and forth within the text-entry box. If `maxlength` is smaller than `size`, there will be extra blank space in the text-entry box to make up the difference between the two attributes.

The default value for `size` is dependent upon the browser; the default value for `maxlength` is unlimited. We recommend you set them yourself. Adjust the `size` attribute so that the text-entry box does not extend beyond the right margin of a typical browser window (about 60 characters with a very short prompt). Set `maxlength` to a reasonable number of characters; for example, 2 for state abbreviations, 12 for phone numbers, and so on.

A text-entry field is usually blank at first until the user types something into it. You may, however, specify an initial default value for the field with the `value` attribute. The user may modify the default, of course. If the user presses a form's reset button, the value of the field is reset to this default value. [reset buttons, 8.2.5.2]

These are all valid text entry fields:

```
<input type=text name=comments>
<input type=text name=zipcode size=10 maxlength=10>
<input type=text name=address size=30 maxlength=256>
<input type=text name=rate size=3 maxlength=3 value="100">
```

The first example creates a text entry field set to the browser's default width and maximum length. As we argue above, this is not a good idea because defaults vary widely among browsers, and your form layout is sure to look bad with some of them. Rather, fix the width and maximum number of acceptable input characters as we do in the second example: It lets the user type in up to ten characters inside an input box ten characters wide. Its value will be sent to the server with the name "zipcode" when the user submits the form.

The third example field tells the browser to display a 30-character-wide text-input box into which the user may type up to 256 characters. The browser automatically scrolls text inside the input box to expose the extra characters.

The last text-input field is three characters wide, only lets the user type in three characters, and sets its initial value to 100.

Notice in the second and fourth example fields, it is implied that certain kinds of data are to be entered by the user—a postal code or a numeric rate, respectively. Except for limiting *how many*, HTML provides no way for you to dictate *what* characters may be typed into a text-input field. For instance, in the last example field, the user may type "ABC" even though you intend it to be a number less than 1,000. Your server-side application must trap erroneous or mistaken input, as well as check for incomplete forms, and send the appropriate error message to the user when things aren't right. That can be a tedious process, so we emphasize again, provide clear and precise instructions and prompts. Make sure your forms tell users what kinds of input you expect from them, thereby reducing the number of mistakes they may make when filling it out.

8.2.2.2 Masked text fields

Like the Lone Ranger, the mask is on the good guys in a masked text field. It behaves just like a conventional text field in a form, except that the user-typed characters don't appear onscreen. Rather, the browser obscures the characters in a masked text to keep such things as passwords and other sensitive codes from prying eyes.

To create a masked text field, set the value of the `type` attribute to `password`. All other attributes and semantics of the conventional text field apply to the masked field. Hence, you must provide a name, and you may (we recommend it) specify a `size` and `maxlength` for the field, as well as an initial `value`.

Don't be misled: A masked text field is not all that secure. The typed-in value only is obscured onscreen; the browser transmits it unencrypted when the form is submitted to the server. So, while prying eyes may not see them onscreen, devious bad guys may steal the information electronically.

8.2.2.3 File-selection fields

The file-selection form field currently is supported only by Netscape. As its name implies, the field lets users select a file stored on their computer and send it to the server when they submit the form.

Netscape presents the file-selection form field to the user like other text fields, but it's accompanied by a button labeled "Browse" to its right. Users either type the pathname directly as text into the field or, with the Browse option, select the name of a locally stored file from a system-specific dialog box.

Create a file-selection field in a form by setting the value of the `type` attribute to `file`. Like other text fields, the `size` and `maxlength` of a file-selection field should be set to appropriate values, with the browser creating a field 20 characters wide, if not otherwise directed. Since file and directory names differ widely among systems, it makes no sense to provide a default value for this field. As such, the value attribute is not used with this kind of text field.

The Browse button associated with the file-selection field opens a browser-specific file-selection dialog that allows users to select a value for the field. In this case, the entire pathname of the selected file is placed into the field, even if the length of that pathname exceeds the field's specified maxlength.

Unlike other form-input elements, the file-selection field only works correctly with a specific form data encoding and transmission method. If you include one or more file-selection fields in your form, you must set the `enctype` attribute of the `<form>` tag to `multipart/form-data` and the `<form>` tag's `method` attribute to `post`. Otherwise, the file-selection field behaves like a regular text field, transmitting its value (that is, the file's pathname) to the server instead of the contents of the file itself.

This is all easier than it may sound. For example, here is a form that collects a person's name and favorite file:

```
<form enctype="multipart/form-data" method=post
    action="cgi-bin/save_file">
Your name: <input type=text size=20 name=the_name>
<p>
Your favorite file: <input type=file size=20
name=fav_file>
</form>
```

The data transmitted from the browser to the server for this example form has two parts: The first contains the value for the name field, and the second contains the name and contents of the specified file:

```
----------------------------6099238414674
Content-Disposition: form-data; name="the_name"

One line of text field contents
----------------------------6099238414674
Content-Disposition: form-data; name="fav_file"; filename="abc"

First line of file
...
Last line of file
----------------------------6099238414674--
```

The current version of Netscape doesn't check that a valid file has been specified by the user. If no file is specified, the filename portion of the Content-Disposition header will be empty. If the file doesn't exist, its name appears in the filename subheader, but there will be no Content-Type header or subsequent lines of file content. Valid files may contain nonprintable or binary data; there is no way to restrict user-selectable file types. In light of these potential problems, the form-processing application on the server should be robust enough to handle missing files, erroneous files, extremely large files, and files with unusual or unexpected formats.

8.2.3 Checkboxes

The checkbox element gives users a way to quickly and easily select or deselect an item in your form. Checkboxes may also be grouped to create a set of choices, any of which may be selected or deselected by the user.

Create individual checkboxes by setting the `type` attribute for each `<input>` tag to `checkbox`. Include the required `name` and `value` attributes. If the item is selected, it will contribute a value when the form is submitted. If it is not selected, that element will not contribute a value. The optional `checked` attribute (no value) tells the browser to display a checked checkbox and include the value when submitting the form to the server unless the user specifically clicks the mouse to deselect (uncheck) the box.

The browsers includes the value of selected (checked) checkboxes with other form parameters when they are submitted to the server. The value of the checked checkbox is the text string you specify in the required `value` attribute.

By giving several checkboxes the same `name` attribute value, you create a group of checkbox elements. The browser automatically collects the values of a check-box group and submits their selected values as a comma-separated string to the server, significantly easing server-side form processing.

For example:

```
<form>
  What pets do you own?
  <p>
    <input type=checkbox name=pets value="dog"> Dog
  <br>
    <input type=checkbox checked name=pets value="cat"> Cat
  <br>
    <input type=checkbox name=pets value="bird"> Bird
  <br>
    <input type=checkbox name=pets value="fish"> Fish
</form>
```

creates a checkbox group as shown in Figure 8-2.

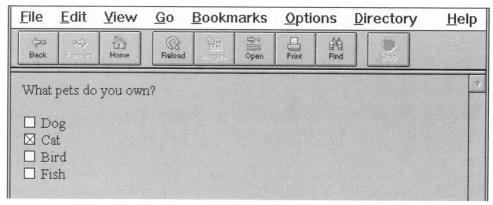

Figure 8–2: A checkbox group

Although part of the group, each checkbox element appears as a separate choice onscreen. Notice too, with all due respect to dog, bird, and fish lovers, that we've preselected the cat checkbox with the `checked` attribute in its tag. We've also provided text labels; the similar value attributes don't appear in the browser's window, but are the values included in the form's parameter list if the checkbox is selected and the form is submitted to the server by the user. Also, you need to use paragraph or line-break tags to control the layout of your checkbox group, as you do for other form elements.

In the example, if "Cat" and "Fish" are checked when the form is submitted, the value included in the parameter list sent to the server would be `pets=cat,fish`.

8.2.4 Radio Buttons

Radio-button[*] form elements are similar in behavior to checkboxes, except only one in the group may be selected by the user. Create a radio button by setting the `type` attribute of the `<input>` element to `radio`. Like checkbox elements, radio buttons each require a `name` and `value` attribute; buttons with the same name value are members of a group. One of them may be initially checked by including the `checked` attribute with that element. If no element in the group is `checked`, the browser automatically checks the first element in the group.

You should give each radio button element a different value, so the server can sort them out after submission of the form.

---

[*] Some of us are old enough, while not yet senile, to recall when automobile radios had mechanical pushbuttons for selecting a station. Pushing in one button popped out the previously depressed one, implementing a mechanical one-of-many choice mechanism.

Here's the previous example reworked so that now you get to choose only one animal as a favorite pet (see Figure 8-3):

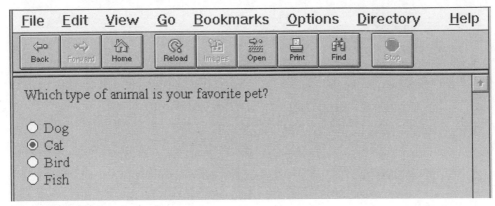

Figure 8–3: Radio buttons allow only one selection per group

```
<form>
   Which type of animal is your favorite pet?
   <p>
      <input type=radio name=favorite value="dog"> Dog
   <br>
      <input type=radio checked name=favorite value="cat"> Cat
   <br>
      <input type=radio name=favorite value="bird"> Bird
   <br>
      <input type=radio name=favorite value="fish"> Fish
</form>
```

Again, like the previous example with checkboxes, we've tipped our hat toward felines, making the "Cat" radio button the default choice. If you select an alternative—"Bird", for instance—the browser automatically deselects the cat. When the form is submitted to the server, the browser includes only one value with the name "favorite" in the list of form parameters; `favorite=bird,` if that was your choice.

Since one of the elements in a group of radio buttons is always selected, it makes no sense to create a single radio button; they should appear in your documents as pairs or more.

8.2.5 *Action Buttons*

Although the terminology potentially is confusing, there is another class of buttons for HTML forms. Unlike the radio buttons and checkboxes described above, these special types of `<input>` form elements act immediately, their effects cannot be reversed, and they affect the entire contents of the form, not just the value of a single field. These "action" buttons (for lack of a better term) include submit, reset, and clickable image buttons. When selected by the user, both the submit and image buttons cause the browser to submit all of the form's parameters to the form-processing server. The reset button acts locally to return a partially filled-out form to its original (default) state.

8.2.5.1 Submission buttons

The submit button (`<input type=submit>`) does what its name implies, setting in motion the form's submission to the server from the browser. You may have more than one submit button in a form. You may also include **name** and **value** attributes with the submit type of input form button.

With the simplest submit button (that without a **name** or **value** attribute), the browser displays a small rectangle or oval with the default label "Submit" (see Figure 8-1). Otherwise, the browser will label the button with the text you include with the tag's **value** attribute. If you provide a **name** attribute, the **value** attribute for the submit button will be added to the parameter list the browser sends along to the server. That's good, because it gives you a way to identify which button in a form was pressed, letting you process any one of several different forms with a single form-processing application.

The following are all valid submission buttons:

```
<input type=submit>
<input type=submit value="Order Kumquats">
<input type=submit value="Ship Overnight" name="ship_style">
```

The first one is also the simplest: the browser displays a button, labeled "Submit", which activates the form-processing sequence when clicked by the user. It does not add an element to the form's parameter list the browser passes to the form-processing server and application.

The second example button has the **value** attribute that makes the displayed button label "Order Kumquats," but like the first example, does not include the button's value in the form's parameter list.

The last example sets the button label and makes it part of the form's parameter list. When clicked by the user, that last example of the submission button will add the parameter `ship_style="Ship Overnight"` to the form's parameter list.

8.2.5.2 *Reset buttons*

The reset type of form `<input>` button is nearly self-explanatory: it lets the user reset—erase or set to some default value—all elements in the form. Unlike the other buttons, a reset button does not initiate form processing. Instead, the browser does the work of resetting the form elements. The server never knows, or cares for that matter, if or when the user might have pressed a reset button.

By default, the browser displays a reset button with the label "Reset." You can change that by specifying a `value` attribute with your own button label.

Here are two sample reset buttons:

```
<input type=reset>
<input type=reset value="Use Defaults">
```

The first one creates a reset button labeled "Reset"; the browser labels the second example reset button with "Use Defaults." They both initiate the same reset response in the browser.

8.2.5.3 *Custom buttons*

With the image type of `<input>` form element, you create a custom button, one that is a "clickable" image. It's a special button made out of your specified image that, when clicked by the user, tells the browser to submit the form to the server, and includes the x,y coordinates of the mouse pointer in the form's parameter list, much like the mouse-sensitive image maps we discussed in Chapter 6, *Links and Webs*. Image buttons require a `src` attribute with the URL of the image file, and you can include a `name` attribute. You may also include the `align` attribute to control image alignment within the current line of text, much like the `align` attribute for the `<img>` tag.

Here are a couple of valid image buttons:

```
<input type=image src="pics/map.gif" name=map>
<input type=image src="pics/xmap.gif" align=top name=map>
```

The browser displays the designated image within the form's content flow. The second button's image will be aligned with the top of the adjacent text, as specified by the `align` attribute. Some browsers, Netscape for instance, also add a border, as it does when an image is part of an anchor (`<a>` tag), to signal that the image is a form button.

When the user clicks the image, the browser sends the horizontal offset, in pixels, of the mouse from the left edge of the image and the vertical offset from the top edge of the image to the server. These values are assigned the name of the image as specified with the name attribute, followed by ".x" and ".y," respectively. Thus, if someone clicked the image specified above, the browser would send parameters named `map.x` and `map.y` to the server.

Image buttons behave much like mouse-sensitive image maps, and like the programs that process image maps, your form-processing application may use the x,y mouse-pointer parameters to choose a special course of action. You should use an image button when you need additional form information to process the user's request. If an image map of links is all you need, use a mouse-sensitive image map. Mouse-sensitive images also have the added benefit of providing server-side support for automatic detection of shape selection within the image, letting you deal with the image as a selectable collection of shapes. Buttons with images require you to write code that determines where the user clicked on the image and how this position can be translated to an appropriate action by the server.

8.2.5.4 Multiple buttons in a single form

You can have several buttons of the same or different types in a single form. Even simple forms have both reset and submit buttons, for example. To distinguish between them, make sure each has a different **value** attribute, which the browser uses for the button label. Depending on the way you program the form-processing application, you might also make the **name** of each button different, but it is usually easier to name all similarly acting buttons the same and let the button handling subroutine sort them out by value. For instance:

```
<input type=submit name=action value="Add">
<input type=submit name=action value="Delete">
<input type=submit name=action value="Change">
<input type=submit name=action value="Cancel">
```

When the user selects one of these example buttons, a form parameter named `action` will be sent to the server. The value of this parameter will be one of the button names. The server-side application gets the value and behaves accordingly.

Since an image button doesn't have a **value** attribute, the only way to distinguish between several image buttons on a single form is to ensure they all have different names.

8.2.6 Hidden Fields

The last type of form `<input>` element we describe in this chapter is hidden from view. No, we're not trying to conceal anything. It's a way to embed information into your forms that cannot be ignored or altered by the browser or user. Rather, the `<input type=hidden>` tag's required **name** and **value** attributes automatically get included in the submitted form's parameter list. These serve to "label" the form and can be invaluable when sorting out different forms or form versions from a collection of submitted and saved forms.

Another use for hidden fields is to manage user/server interactions. For instance, it helps the server to know that the current form has come from a person who made a similar request a few moments ago. Normally, the server does not retain this information and each transaction between the server and client is completely independent from all other transactions.

For example, the first form submitted by the user might have asked for some basic information, such as the user's name and where they live. Based on that initial contact, the server might create a second form asking more specific questions of the user. Since it is tedious for users to re-enter the same basic information from the first form, the server can be programmed to put those values in the second form in hidden fields. When the second form comes back, all the important information from both forms is there, and the second form can be matched to the first one, if necessary.

Hidden fields may also direct the server towards some specific action. For example, you might embed the hidden field:

```
<input type=hidden name=action value=change>
```

Therefore, if you have one server-side application that handles the processing of several forms, each form might contain a different action code to help that server application sort things out.

8.3 Multiline Text Areas

The conventional and hidden-text types for forms restrict user input to a single line of characters. The <textarea> form tag sets users free.

8.3.1 The <textarea> Tag

The <textarea> tag creates a multiline text-entry area in the user's browser display. In it, the user may type a nearly unlimited number of lines of text. Upon submission of the form, the browser collects all the lines of text, each separated by "%0D%0A" (carriage return/line feed), and sends them to the server as the value of this form element, using the name specified by the required **name** attribute.

You may include plain text inside the <textarea> tag and its end tag. That default text must be plain text—no tags or other special HTML elements. The contents may be modified by the user, and the browser uses that text as the default value if the user presses a reset button for the form. Hence, the text content is most often included for instructions and examples:

<textarea>

Function:
Create a multiline text input area

Attributes:
COLS
NAME
ROWS
WRAP (Extension)

End tag:
</textarea>; never omitted

Contains:
plain_text

Used in:
form_content

```
Tell us about yourself:
<textarea name=address cols=40 rows=4>
   Your Name Here
   1234 My Street
   Anytown, State Zipcode
</textarea>
```

8.3.1.1 The rows and cols attributes

A multiline text-input area stands alone onscreen: body content flows above and below, but not around it. You can control its dimensions, however, by defining the cols and rows attributes for the visible rectangular area set aside by the browser for multiline input. We suggest you do set these attributes. The common browsers have a habit of setting aside the smallest, least readable region possible for <textarea> input, and the user can't resize it. Both attributes require integer values for the respective dimension's size in characters. The browser automatically scrolls text that exceeds either dimension.

8.3.1.2 The wrap attribute

Normally, text typed in the text area by the user is transmitted to the server exactly as typed, with lines broken only where the user pressed the Enter key. Since this is often not the desired action by the user, you can enable word wrapping within the text area. When the user types a line that is longer than the width of the text area, the browser automatically moves the extra text down to the next line, breaking the line at the nearest point between words in the line.

With the `wrap` attribute set to `virtual`, the text is wrapped within the text area for presentation to the user, but the text is transmitted to the server as if no wrapping had occurred, except where the user pressed the Enter key.

With the `wrap` attribute set to `physical`, the text is wrapped within the text area and is transmitted to the server as if the user had actually typed it that way. This the most useful way to use word wrap, since the text is transmitted exactly as the user sees it in the text area.

To obtain the default action, set the `wrap` attribute to `off`.

As an example, consider the following sixty characters of text being typed into a 40-character-wide text area:

```
Word wrapping is a feature that makes life easier for users
```

With `wrap=off`, the text area will contain one line and the user will have to scroll to the right to see all of the text. One line of text will be transmitted to the server.

With `wrap=virtual`, the text area will contain two lines of text, broken after the word "makes." Only one line of text will be transmitted to the server: the entire line with no embedded newline characters.

With `wrap=physical`, the text area will contain two lines of text, broken after the word "makes." Two lines of text will be sent to the server, separated by a newline character after the word "makes."

8.4 Multiple Choice Elements

Checkboxes and radio buttons give you powerful means for creating multiple-choice questions and answers, but they can lead to long forms that are tedious to write and put a fair amount of clutter onscreen. The `<select>` tag gives you two, compact alternatives: pulldown menus and scrolling lists.

8.4.1 The <select> Tag

By placing a list of `<option>` tagged items inside the `<select>` tag of a form, you magically create a pull-down menu of choices.

As with other form tags, the `name` attribute is required and used by the browser when submitting the `<select>` choices to the server. Unlike radio buttons, however, no item is preselected, so if none is selected, no values are sent to the server when the form is submitted. Otherwise, the browser submits the selected item or collects multiple selections, each separated with commas, into a single parameter list and includes the `name` attribute when submitting `<select>` form data to the server.

<select>

Function:
  Create single- and multiple-choice menus
Attributes:
  MULTIPLE
  NAME
  SIZE
End tag:
  </select>; never omitted
Contains:
  select_content
Used in:
  form_content

8.4.1.1 The multiple attribute

To allow more than one option selection at a time, add the `multiple` attribute to the `<select>` tag. This causes the `<select>` to behave like an `<input type=checkbox>` element. If `multiple` is not specified, exactly one option can be selected at a time, just like a group of radio buttons.

8.4.1.2 The size attribute

The `size` attribute determines how many options are visible to the user at one time. The value of `size` should be a positive integer. If `size` is set to one and `multiple` is not specified, the `<select>` list is typically implemented as a pop-up menu, while values greater than one or specifying the `multiple` attribute cause the `<select>` to be displayed as a scrolling list.

In the following example, we've converted our previous checkbox example into a scrolling, multiple-choice menu. Notice also that the `size` attribute tells the browser to display three options at a time:

```
What pets do you own?
  <select name=pets size=3 multiple >
    <option>Dog
    <option>Cat
    <option>Bird
    <option>Fish
  </select>
```

The result is shown in Figure 8-4, along with the change in appearance when the `size` attribute is set to one and `multiple` is not specified.

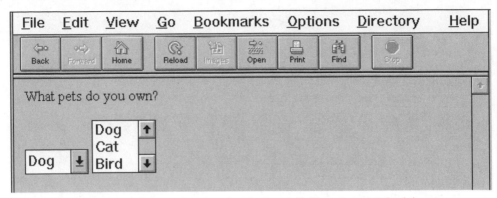

Figure 8–4: A <select> element, formatted with size=1 (left) and size=3 (right)

8.4.2 The <option> Tag

Use the <option> tag to define each item within a <select> form element.

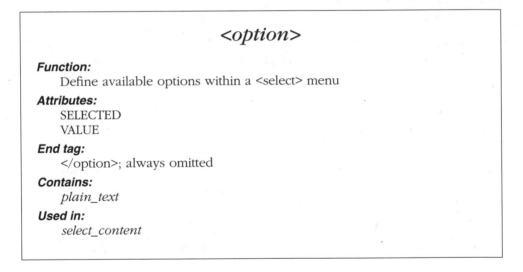

The browser displays the <option> tag's contents as an element within the <select> tag's menu or scrolling list, so the content must be plain text only, without any other sort of markup.

8.4.2.1 The value attribute

Use the value attribute to set a value for each option the browser sends to the server if that option is selected by the user. If the value attribute has not been specified, the value of the option is set to the content of the <option> tag.

As an example, consider these options:

```
<option value=Dog>Dog
<option>Dog
```

Both have the same value. The first is explicitly set within the `<option>` tag; the second defaults to the content of the `<option>` tag itself.

8.4.2.2 *The selected attribute*

By default, all options within a multiple-choice `<select>` tag are unselected. Include the `selected` attribute (no value) inside the `<option>` tag to preselect one or more options, which the user may then deselect. Single-choice `<select>` tags will preselect the first option if no option is explicitly preselected.

8.5 *Creating Effective Forms*

Properly done, a form can provide an effective user interface for your readers. With some server-side programming tricks, you can use forms to personalize the HTML documents you present to readers, and thereby significantly increase the value of your pages on the Web.

8.5.1 *Browser Constraints*

As with other HTML elements, browsers have varying abilities to display and manage forms.

8.5.1.1 *Browser limitations*

Unlike other graphical-user interfaces, browser displays are static. They have little or no capability for real-time data validation, for example, or to update the values in a form based upon user input, giving users help and guidance. Hence, poorly designed Web forms can be difficult to fill out.

Make sure your forms assist the user as much as possible in getting their input correct. Adjust the size of text-input fields to give clues on acceptable input; five- (or the new nine-) character-wide zipcode fields, for instance. Use checkboxes, radio buttons, and selection lists whenever possible to narrow the list of choices the user must make.

Make sure you also adequately document your forms. Explain how to fill them out, supplying examples for each field. Provide appropriate hyperlinks to documentation that describes each field, if necessary.

When the form is submitted, make sure the server-side application exhaustively validates the user's data. If an error is discovered, present the user with intelligent error messages and possible corrections. One of the most frustrating aspects of filling out forms is having to start over from scratch whenever the server discovers an error. To alleviate this ugly redundancy and burden on your readers, consider spending extra time and resources on the server side that returns the user's completed form with the erroneous fields flagged for changes.

While all of these suggestions require significant effort on your part, they will pay off many times over by making life easier for your users. Remember, you'll write the HTML for the form just once, but it may be used thousands or even millions of times by users.

8.5.1.2 Handling limited displays

The most common client on the Web is a PC running Windows on a 640x480 pixel display. The actual document-viewing window typically is around 600x400 pixels; roughly 75 readable characters wide and 30 to 50 lines tall. You should design your forms (and all your documents) so they are effective when viewed through a window of this size.

You should structure your form to naturally scroll into two or three logical sections. The user can fill out the first section, page down; fill out the second section, page down; and so forth.

You should also avoid wide input elements. It is difficult enough to deal with a scrolling-text field or text area without having to scroll the document itself horizontally to see additional portions of the input element.

8.5.2 User Interface Considerations

When you elect to create a form, you immediately assume another role: that of a user-interface designer. While a complete discussion of user interface design is beyond the scope of this book, it helps to understand a few basic design rules to create effective, attractive forms.

8.5.2.1 Basic user-interface design

Any user interface is perceived at several levels simultaneously. Forms are no different. At the lowest level, your brain recognizes shapes within the document, attempting to categorize the elements of the form. At a higher level, you are reading the text guides and prompts, trying to determine what input is required of you. At the highest level, you are seeking to accomplish a goal with the interface as your tool.

A good form accommodates all three of these perceptive needs. Input elements should be organized in logical groups so that your brain can process the form layout in chunks of related fields. Consistent, well-written prompts and supporting text assist and lead the user to enter the correct information. Text prompts also remind users of the task at hand and reinforce the form's goal.

8.5.2.2 Creating forms that flow

Users process forms in a predictable order, one element after another, seeking to find the next element as they finish the previous one. To accommodate this searching process, you should design your forms so that one field leads naturally to another, and that related fields are grouped together. Similarly, groups should lead naturally to one another and should be formatted in a consistent manner.

Simply stringing a number of fields together does not constitute an effective form. You must put yourself in the place of your users, who are using the form for the first time. Test your form on unsuspecting friends and colleagues before you release it on the general public. Is it easy to determine the purpose of the form? Where do you start filling things out? Can the user find a button to push to submit the form? Is there an opportunity to confirm decisions? Do readers understand what is expected of them for each field?

Your forms should lead the user naturally through the process of supplying the necessary data for the application. You wouldn't ask for a street address before asking for the user's name; other rules may dictate the ordering of other groups of input elements. To see if your form really works, make sure you view it on several browsers and have several people fill it out and comment on its effectiveness.

8.5.3 Good Form, Old Chap

At first glance, the basic rule of HTML—content, not style— seems in direct opposition to the basic rule of good interface design—precise, consistent layout. Even so, it is possible to use some HTML elements to greatly improve the layout and readability of most forms.

Traditional page layout uses a grid of columns to align common elements within a page. The resulting implied vertical and horizontal "edges" of adjacent elements give a sense of order and organization to the page, and makes it easy for the eye to scan and follow.

HTML makes it hard, but you can accomplish the same sort of layout for your forms. For example, you can group related elements and separate groups with empty paragraphs or horizontal rules.

Vertical alignment is more difficult but not impossible. In general, forms are easier
to use if you arrange the input elements vertically and aligned to a common margin. One popular form layout keeps the left edge of the input elements aligned,
with the element labels immediately to the left of the elements. This is done by
using preformatted text to insert a specific number of spaces in front of each element. For example, here is our previous form example, with the labels realigned
using the `<pre>` tag:

```
<form method=POST action="http://www.kumquat.com/demo">
  <pre>
      Name: <input type=text name=name size=32 maxlength=80>
       Sex: <input type=radio name=sex value="M"> Male
            <input type=radio name=sex value="F"> Female
    Income: <select name=income size=1>
              <option>Under $25,000
              <option>$25,001 to $50,000
              <option>$50,001 and higher
            </select>
  <input type=submit value="Submit Query">
  </pre>
</form>
```

Notice in the resulting rendered form shown in Figure 8-5 that the `<pre>` tag has
preserved extra spaces and blank lines, ensuring the elements will be properly
aligned. The only drawback to this technique is that the text of the labels is in a
monospace typeface.

You may find other consistent ways to lay out your forms. The key is to find a
useful layout style that works well across most browsers and stick with it. Even
though HTML has limited tools to control layout and positioning, take advantage of
what is available to make your forms more attractive and easier to use.

8.6 Forms Programming

If you create forms, sooner or later you'll need to create the server-side application
that processes your form. Don't panic. There is nothing magic about server-side
programming, nor is it overly difficult. With a little practice and some persever-
ance, you'll be cranking out forms applications.

The most important advice we can give about forms programming is easy to
remember: copy others' work. Writing a forms application from scratch is fairly
hard; copying a functioning forms application and modifying it to support your
form is far easier.

Fortunately, server vendors know this, and they usually supply sample forms
applications with their server. Rummage about for a directory named *cgi-src*, and
you'll discover a number of useful examples you can easily copy and reuse.

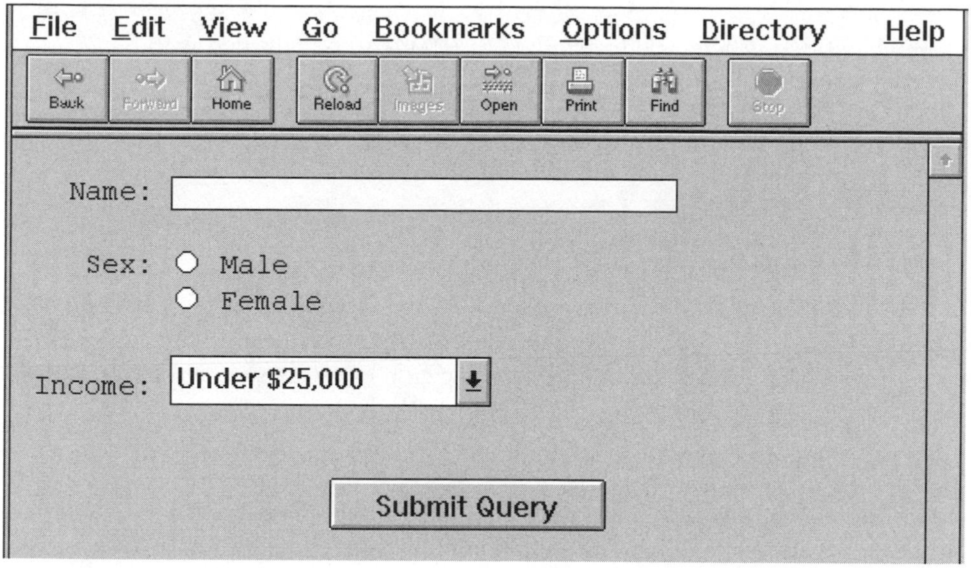

| File | Edit | View | Go | Bookmarks | Options | Directory | Help |

| Back | Forward | Home | Reload | Images | Open | Print | Find | Stop |

Name: [   ]

Sex: ○ Male
     ○ Female

Income: [Under $25,000   ▼]

[**Submit Query**]

Figure 8–5: Using a consistent vertical margin to align form elements

We can't hope to replicate all the useful stuff that came with your server, nor can we provide a complete treatise on forms programming. What we can do is offer a simple example of both GET and POST applications, giving you a feel for the work involved and hopefully getting you moving you in the right direction.

Before we begin, keep in mind that not all servers invoke these applications in the same manner. Our examples cover the broad class of servers derived from the original NCSA HTTP server. They also should work with the Netscape Communications family of server products and the public-domain Apache server. In all cases, consult your server documentation for complete details.

8.6.1 Returning Results

Before we begin, we need to discuss how server-side applications end. All server-side applications pass their results back to the server (and on to the user) by writing that result to the application's standard output as a MIME-encoded file. Hence, the first line of the application's output must be a MIME content-type descriptor. If your application returns an HTML document, the first line is:

```
Content-type: text/html
```

The second line must be completely empty. Your application can return some other content type, too—just include the correct MIME type. A GIF image, for example, is preceded with:

```
Content-type: image/gif
```

Generic text that is not to be interpreted as HTML can be returned with:

```
Content-type: text/plain
```

This is often useful for returning the output of other commands that generate plain text instead of HTML.

8.6.2 Handling GET Forms

One of two methods for passing form parameters from client to server is the GET method. In that way, parameters are passed as part of the URL that invokes the server-side forms application. A typical invocation of a GET-style application might use a URL like this:

```
http://www.kumquat.com/cgi-bin/dump_get?name=bob&phone=555-1212
```

When the server processes this URL, it invokes the application named *dump_get* stored in the directory named *cgi-bin*. Everything after the question mark is passed to the application as parameters.

Things diverge a bit at this point, due to the nature of the GET-style URL. While forms place name/value pairs in the URL, it is possible to invoke a GET-style application with only values in the URL. Thus,

```
http://www.kumquat.com/cgi-bin/dump_get?bob+555-1212
```

is a valid invocation as well, with parameters separated by a plus sign (+). This is a common invocation when the application is referenced by a searchable document with the `<isindex>` tag. The parameters typed by the user into the document's text-entry field are passed to the server-side application as unnamed parameters separated by plus signs.

If you invoke your GET application with named parameters, your server will pass those parameters to the application in one way; unnamed parameters are passed differently.

8.6.2.1 Using named parameters with GET applications

Named parameters are passed to GET applications by creating an environment variable named `QUERY_STRING` and setting its value to the entire portion of the URL following the question mark. Using our previous example, the value of `QUERY_STRING` would be set to:

```
name=bob&phone=555-1212
```

Your application must retrieve this variable and extract from it the parameter name/value pairs. Fortunately, most servers come with a set of utility routines that performs this task for you, so a simple C program that just dumps the parameters might look like:

```c
#include <stdio.h>
#include <stdlib.h>

#define MAX_ENTRIES 10000

typedef struct {char *name;
                char *val;
               }entry;

char *makeword(char *line, char stop);
char x2c(char *what);
void unescape_url(char *url);
void plustospace(char *str);

main(int argc, char *argv[])

{   entry entries[MAX_ENTRIES];
    int num_entries, i;
    char *query_string;

/* Get the value of the QUERY_STRING environment variable */
    query_string = getenv("QUERY_STRING");

/* Extract the parameters, building a table of entries */
    for (num_entries = 0; query_string[0]; num_entries++) {
        entries[num_entries].val = makeword(query_string, '&');

        plustospace(entries[num_entries].val);
        unescape_url(entries[num_entries].val);
        entries[num_entries].name =
            makeword(entries[num_entries].val, '=');
        }

/* Spit out the HTML boilerplate */
    printf("Content-type: text/html\n");
    printf("\n");

    printf("<html>");
    printf("<head>");
    printf("<title>Named Parameter Echo</title>\n");
    printf("</head>");
    printf("<body>");
    printf("You entered the following parameters:\n");
    printf("<ul>\n");

/* Echo the parameters back to the user */
    for(i = 0; i < num_entries; i++)
        printf("<li> %s = %s\n", entries[i].name,
                entries[i].val);

/* And close out with more boilerplate */
```

```
printf("</ul>\n");
printf("</body>\n");
printf("</html>\n");
```

The example program begins with a few declarations that define the utility routines that scan through a character string and extract the parameter names and values. The body of the program obtains the value of the QUERY_STRING environment variable using the *getenv()* system call, uses the utility routines to extract the parameters from that value, and then generates a simple HTML document that echoes back those values to the user.

For real applications, you'll want to insert your actual processing code after the parameter extraction and before the HTML generation. Of course, you'll also need to change the HTML generation to match your application's functionality.

8.6.2.2 Using unnamed parameters with GET applications

Unnamed parameters are passed to the application as command-line parameters. This makes writing the server-side application almost trivial. Here is a simple shell script that dumps the parameter values back to the user:

```
#!/bin/csh -f
#
# Dump unnamed GET parameters back to the user

echo "Content-type: text/html"
echo
echo '<html>'
echo '<head>'
echo '<title>Unnamed Parameter Echo</title>'
echo '</head>'
echo '<body>'
echo 'You entered the following parameters:'
echo '<ul>'

foreach i ($*)
   echo '<li>' $i
end

echo '</ul>'
echo '</body>'

exit 0
```

Again, we follow the same general style: output a generic document header, including the MIME content type, followed by the parameters and some closing boilerplate. To convert this to a real application, replace the *foreach* loop with commands that actually do something.

8.6.3 Handling POST Forms

Applications that use POST-style parameters expect to read encoded parameters from their standard input. Like GET-style application with named parameters, they can take advantage of the server's utility routines to parse these parameters.

Here is a program that echos the POST-style parameters back to the user:

```
#include <stdio.h>
#include <stdlib.h>

#define MAX_ENTRIES 10000

typedef struct {char *name;
                char *val;
               } entry;

char *makeword(char *line, char stop);
char *fmakeword(FILE *f, char stop, int *len);
char x2c(char *what);
void unescape_url(char *url);
void plustospace(char *str);

main(int argc, char *argv[])

{   entry entries[MAX_ENTRIES];
     int num_entries, i;

/* Parse parameters from stdin, building a table of entries */
    for (num_entries = 0; !feof(stdin); num_entries++) {
        entries[num_entries].val = fmakeword(stdin, '&', &cl);
        plustospace(entries[num_entries].val);
        unescape_url(entries[num_entries].val);
        entries[num_entries].name =
            makeword(entries[num_entries].val, '=');
        }

/* Spit out the HTML boilerplate */
    printf("Content-type: text/html\n");
    printf("\n");
    printf("<html>");
    printf("<head>");
    printf("<title>Named Parameter Echo</title>\n");
    printf("</head>");
    printf("<body>");
    printf("You entered the following parameters:\n");
    printf("<ul>\n");

/* Echo the parameters back to the user */
    for(i = 0; i < num_entries; i++)
        printf("<li> %s = %s\n", entries[i].name,
                entries[i].val);
```

```
/* And close out with more boilerplate */
    printf("</ul>\n");
    printf("</body>\n");
    printf("</html>\n");
}
```

Again, we follow the same general form. The program starts by declaring the various utility routines needed to parse the parameters, along with a data structure to hold the parameter list. The actual code begins by reading the parameter list from the standard input and building a list of parameter names and values in the array named `entries`. Once this is complete, a boilerplate document header is written to the standard output, followed by the parameters and some closing boilerplate.

Like the other examples, this program is handy for checking the parameters being passed to the server application while you are early in the forms and application debugging process. You can also use it as a skeleton for other applications by inserting appropriate processing code after the parameter list is built up and altering the output section to send back the appropriate results.

Tables

You may wonder, given HTML's deep roots in academia, why the language standard doesn't include any explicit support for data tables. None at all[*] for a community steeped in mountains of data. And, that's just the academic community. Tables are an age-old respected means for cross-comparing items of information for all types of endeavors.

Fortunately, the developers of the popular graphical browsers, including Netscape, Internet Explorer, and Mosaic, have stepped into the breach and come up with a fairly comprehensive set of HTML extensions for tables. In fact, they have eclipsed the Web standards organization devoted to HTML by including many of the table-handling features intended for inclusion in HTML version 3.2.

While it is relatively easy to swear off many of the other extensions to HTML, like frivolous background images or auto-scrolling text marquees, you simply will not be able to resist the siren call of the table extensions. They're just too useful to ignore.

9.1 The HTML Table Model

The model the extended browsers use for tables is fairly straightforward: tables are collections of numbers and words arranged and related in rows and columns of *cells*. Most cells contain the data values; others contain row and column headers that describe the data.

You define a table and include all of its elements between the `<table>` tag and its corresponding `</table>` end tag. Table elements, including data items, row and column headers, and captions, each have their own markup tag. Working

---

[*] The `<pre>` tag, although capable, is hardly "support" for tables.

from left to right and top to bottom, you define, in sequence, the header and data for each column cell across the table, and progress down row by row.

The latest browsers also support a collection of tag attributes that make your tables look good, including special alignment of the table values and headers, borders and table rule lines, and automatic sizing of the data cells to accommodate their content. Netscape and Internet Explorer each have a slightly richer set of attributes than Mosaic; we'll point out those variations as we go.

9.1.1 Table Contents

You may put nearly anything you might put within the body of an HTML document inside a table cell, including images, forms, rules, headings, and even another table. The browser treats each cell as a window unto itself, flowing the cell's content to fill the space, but with some special formatting provisions and extensions.

9.1.2 An Example Table

Here's a quick example that should satisfy your itching curiosity to see what an HTML table looks like in source code and when finally rendered as in Figure 9-1. More importantly, it shows you the basic structure of a table from which you can infer many of the elements, tag syntax and order, attributes, and so on, and to which you may refer back as you read the various detailed descriptions below:

```
<table border cellspacing=0 cellpadding=5>
  <caption align=bottom> Kumquat versus a poked
  eye, by gender</caption>
  <tr>
    <td colspan=2 rowspan=2></td>
    <th colspan=2 align=center>Preference</th>
  </tr>
  <tr>
    <th>Eating Kumquats</th>
    <th>Poke In The Eye</th>
  </tr>
  <tr align=center>
    <th rowspan=2>Gender</th>
    <th>Male</th>
    <td>73%</td>
    <td>27%</td>
  </tr>
  <tr align=center>
    <th>Female</th>
    <td>16%</td>
    <td>84%</td>
  </tr>
</table>
```

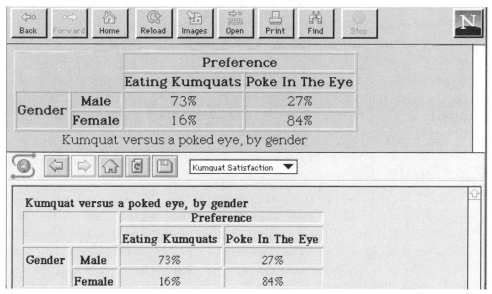

Figure 9–1: HTML table example rendered by Netscape (top) and by Mosaic (bottom)

9.1.3 Missing Features

HTML tables currently don't have all the features of a full-fledged table-generation tool you might find in a popular word processor. Rather than leave you in suspense, we'll list those things up front so you don't beat your head against the wall later trying to do something that just can't be done (at least, not yet):

- Most browsers, save for Internet Explorer and the latest version of Netscape Navigator (2.0), don't flow text around a table as they do for images. Rather, they isolate a table from the text content with line breaks. The table does inherit the alignment of the current text flow—normally left-justified as with regular text, or center-justified, if contained within the <center> tag. [<center>, 4.7.6]

- The general problem of text alignment in HTML carries over into tables. You may align values inside their individual cells, but you cannot align them between cells. For instance, you cannot vertically align the decimal points in a column of numbers, even though they all might have the same number of digits.

- Mosaic's table border and rule lines are all or nothing; either you include them or you don't. Netscape and Internet Explorer, on the other hand, give you the ability to set their thickness, but you get to use only one size line for the table's borders and rules, if you choose to include them at all. You can't have a thicker border separate the table headings from the table body, for example, or have a heavier border between rows at regular intervals. Nor can you have a different-sized outside border.

- HTML tables don't have running headers or footers. Of course, such things don't matter with an HTML browser where everything is on a single, infinitely long page. Running headers and footers are nice to have, though, when you print out a long table onto separate sheets of paper.

9.2 Table Tags

You create a wide variety of tables with only five tags: the `<table>` tag, which encapsulates a table and its elements in the HTML document's body content; the `<tr>` tag, which defines a table row; the `<th>` and `<td>` tags, which define the table's headers and data cells; and the `<caption>` tag, which defines a title or caption to the table. Each tag has one or more required and optional attributes, some of which affect not only the tag itself, but related tags. [`<tr>`, 9.2.2] [`<th>`, 9.2.3] [`<td>`, 9.2.3] [`<caption>`, 9.2.4]

9.2.1 The <table> Tag

The `<table>` tag and its `</table>` end tag define and encapsulate a table within the body of your HTML document. The browser stops the current text flow, breaks the line, inserts the table beginning on a new line, and then restarts the text flow on a new line below the table.

Unless overridden by the `align` attribute, the table's alignment in the browser window matches that of the containing text flow. Normally, this means that tables are aligned against the left margin of the current text flow. However, the table may be centered in the browser window if the preceding text is centered with the `<center>` tag or `<div align=center>`, or right-aligned by being in a right-aligned table cell (see the `align` attribute options below). [`<p>` 4.1.2] [`<th>`, 4.7.6]

The only content allowed within the `<table>` tag besides the optional `<caption>` tag is one or more `<tr>` tags, which define each row of table contents.

9.2.1.1 The align attribute

Like images, tables are rectangular objects that float in the browser display, aligned according to the current text flow: normally left-justified, abutting the left margin of the display window, or centered if under the influence of the `<center>` tag,

\<table\>

Function:
   Define a table

Attributes:
   ALIGN
   BGCOLOR (Internet Explorer only)
   BORDER
   BORDERCOLOR (Internet Explorer only)
   BORDERCOLORLIGHT (Internet Explorer only)
   BORDERCOLORDARK (Internet Explorer only)
   CELLPADDING (Netscape only)
   CELLSPACING (Netscape only)
   HSPACE (extension)
   VALIGN (Internet Explorer only)
   VSPACE (extension)
   WIDTH (extension)

End tag:
   \</table\>; never omitted

Contains:
   table_content

Used in:
   block

centered paragraph, or centered division. Unlike images, however, tables are normally not inline objects. Text content normally flows above and below a table, not beside it. You change that display behavior for Netscape or Internet Explorer with the `align` attribute for the `<table>` tag.

The `align` attribute accepts a value of either `left` or `right`, indicating that the table should be placed flush against the left or right margin of the text flow, with the text flowing around the table. This alignment style corresponds to the left and right alignment of images with text wrapping around the image.

You use the `align` attribute within the `<table>` tag differently than within the `<tr>`, `<td>`, and `<th>` tags. In those tags, the attribute controls text alignment within the table cells, not alignment of the table within the containing text flow.

This attribute is only supported by Internet Explorer and Netscape.

9.2.1.2 The bgcolor attribute

You may make the background of a table a different color than the document's background with the `bgcolor` attribute for the `<table>` tag. Honored only by Internet Explorer and ignored by all other browsers, the color value for the `bgcolor` attribute must be set to either an RGB color value or a standard color name. Both the syntax of color values and the acceptable color names are provided in Appendix E, *Color Names and Values.*

Internet Explorer gives every cell in the table this background color. Individual cell colors can be changed by providing the `bgcolor` attribute for those cells.

9.2.1.3 The bordercolor, bordercolorlight, and bordercolordark attributes

Supported by Internet Explorer only, these attributes set the color of the table borders, if displayed. Their values can be either an RGB hexadecimal color value or a standard color name, both of which are described fully in Appendix E.

Netscape and Internet Explorer normally draw a table border with three colors. Netscape uses black and shades of gray. Internet Explorer does, too, unless you set those colors with special attributes: The `bordercolorlight` and `border-colordark` colors shade the edges of the border to give it a 3D appearance, while `bordercolor` shades the central body of the border.

The effectiveness of the 3D effect is directly tied to the relationship of these three colors. In general, the light color should be about 25 percent brighter than the border color, and the dark color should be about 25 percent darker.

9.2.1.4 The border attribute

The optional `border` attribute for the `<table>` tag tells the browser to add a border around the table and the rows and cells within it, and enables the various other `<table>` attributes that affect the appearance and spacing of the border.

A border value is optional; alone, the attribute simply enables borders and a set of default characteristics. Mosaic ignores a border attribute value, if you include one; the browser provides only one style border line for tables (see Figure 9-1).

Netscape and Internet Explorer, on the other hand, let you supply an integer value for `border` equal to the pixel width of the chiseled-edge lines that make the table appear to be embossed onto the page. If you don't give it one, Netscape's and Internet Explorer's default border value is 1, and therefore draws the table borders with a chiseled edge that is one pixel wide. The border attribute value of 0 has the same effect as no border at all.

9.2.1.5 The cellspacing attribute

The `cellspacing` attribute is for Netscape only; Mosaic and Internet Explorer ignore it. This attribute controls the amount of space Netscape places between adjacent cells in a table and along the outer edges of cells along the edges of a table.

Netscape normally puts two pixels of space between cells and along the outer edges of the table. If you include a `border` attribute in the `<table>` tag, the cell spacing between interior cells grows by two more pixels (four total) to make space for the chiseled edge on the interior border. The outer edges of edge cells grow by the value of the `border` attribute.

By including the `cellspacing` attribute you can widen or reduce the interior cell borders. For instance, to make the thinnest possible interior cell borders, include the `border` and `cellspacing=0` attributes in the table's tag.

9.2.1.6 The cellpadding attribute

The `cellpadding` attribute is supported only by Netscape. It controls the amount of space between the edge of a cell and its contents, which by default is one pixel. You may make all the cell contents in a table touch their respective cell borders by including `cellpadding=0` in the table tag. You may also increase the cellpadding space by setting its value greater than 1.

9.2.1.7 Combining border, cellspacing, and cellpadding attributes

With Netscape, the interactions between the `border`, `cellpadding`, and `cellspacing` attributes of the `<table>` tag combine in ways that can be confusing. Figure 9-2 summarizes how these attributes interact to create interior and exterior borders of various widths.

While all sorts of combinations of the `border` and `cellspacing` attributes are possible, the most common are:

- `border=1` and `cellspacing=0` produces the narrowest possible interior and exterior borders: two pixels wide.

- `border=n` and `cellspacing=0` makes the narrowest possible interior borders (two pixels wide), with an external border that is n plus one pixels wide.

- `border=1` and `cellspacing=n` tables have equal-width exterior and interior borders, all with chiseled edges just one pixel wide. All borders will be n plus two pixels wide.

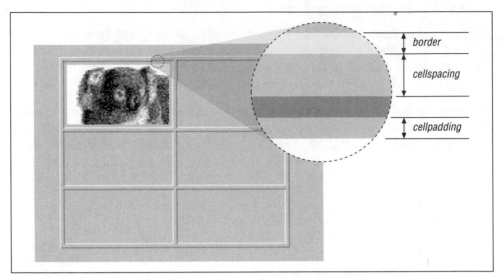

Figure 9–2: The border, cellspacing, and cellpadding attributes of a table

9.2.1.8 The <hspace> and <vspace> attributes

Just as with inline images, the `hspace` and `vspace` attributes tell Internet Explorer and Netscape to add some extra room on the left and right sides (for `hspace`) and the top and bottom (for `vspace`) of a table, thereby setting it off from the window edge and surrounding content. The attribute value is the integer number of pixels for that padding; a value of 0 is the default.

Figure 9-3 illustrates the effect of the `hspace` and `vspace` attribute spacing around a left-justified table with wraparound text.

9.2.1.9 The valign attribute

The `valign` attribute for the `<table>` tag currently is supported only by Internet Explorer. It sets the default vertical alignment of data in their cells for the entire table. You achieve similar effects in Netscape by including a `valign` attribute within the individual `<tr>`, `<td>`, and `<th>` tags.

Acceptable values for the `valign` attribute in `<table>` are `top` or `bottom`; the default vertical position is the center of the cell.

9.2.1.10 The width attribute

The extended browsers automatically make a table only as wide as needed to correctly display all of the cell contents. With Netscape and Internet Explorer, but not Mosaic, you can make a table wider with the `width` attribute.

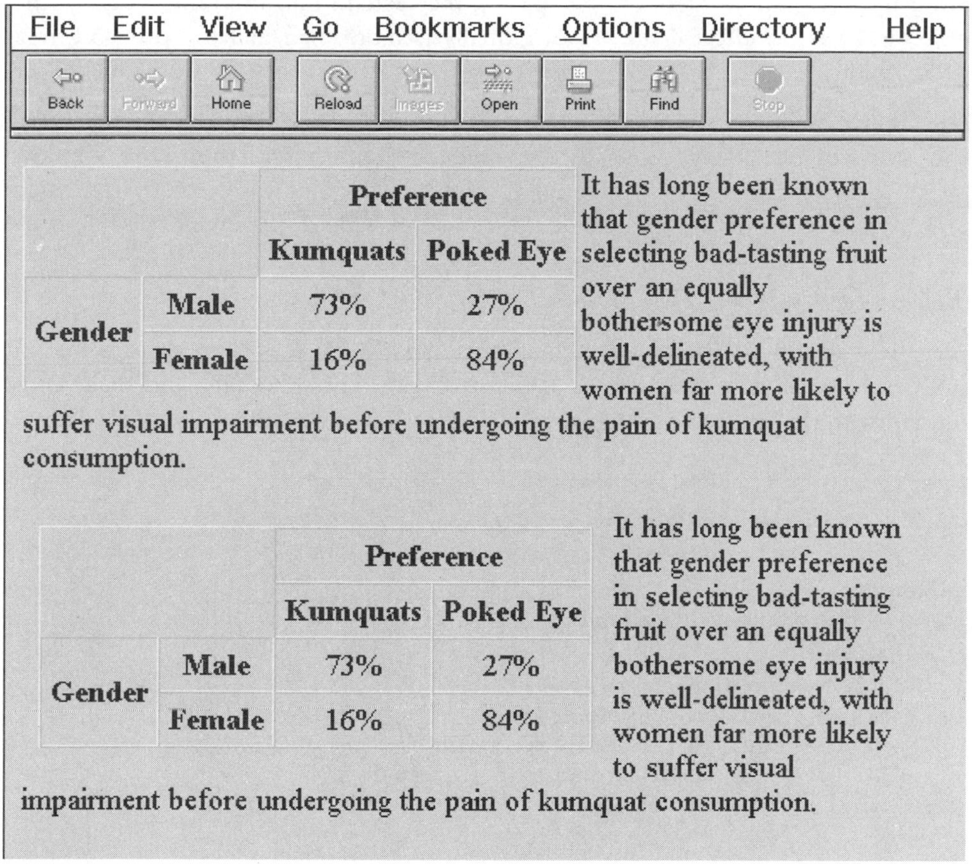

File	Edit	View	Go	Bookmarks	Options	Directory	Help

Back	Forward	Home	Reload	Images	Open	Print	Find	Stop

		Preference	
		Kumquats	Poked Eye
Gender	Male	73%	27%
	Female	16%	84%

It has long been known that gender preference in selecting bad-tasting fruit over an equally bothersome eye injury is well-delineated, with women far more likely to suffer visual impairment before undergoing the pain of kumquat consumption.

		Preference	
		Kumquats	Poked Eye
Gender	Male	73%	27%
	Female	16%	84%

It has long been known that gender preference in selecting bad-tasting fruit over an equally bothersome eye injury is well-delineated, with women far more likely to suffer visual impairment before undergoing the pain of kumquat consumption.

Figure 9–3: The hspace and vspace attributes give a table some breathing room

The value of the `width` attribute is either an integer number of pixels or a relative percentage of the screen width, including values greater than 100 percent. For example,

```
<table width=400>
```

tells the extended browser to make the table 400 pixels wide, including any borders and cell spacing that extend into the outer edge of the table. If the table is wider than 400 pixels, the browser ignores the attribute.

Alternatively,

```
<table width="50%">
```

tells the browser to make the table half as wide as the display window. Again, this width includes any borders or cell spacing that extend into the outer edge of the table, and has no effect if the table normally is more than half the user's current screen width.

Use relative widths for tables you want to automatically resize to the user's window; for instance, tables you always want to extend across the entire window (`<table width="100%">`). Use an absolute width value for carefully formatted tables whose contents will become hard to read in wide display windows.

9.2.2 The <tr> Tag

Every row in a table is created with a `<tr>` tag. Within the `<tr>` tag are one or more cells containing headers, each defined with the `<th>` tag, and data, each defined with the `<td>` tag (see below).

<h2 style="text-align:center"><tr></h2>

Function:
   Define a row within a table

Attributes:
   ALIGN (extension)
   BGCOLOR (Internet Explorer only)
   BORDERCOLOR (Internet Explorer only)
   BORDERCOLORLIGHT (Internet Explorer only)
   BORDERCOLORDARK (Internet Explorer only)
   VALIGN (extension)

End tag:
   </tr>; may be omitted

Contains:
   tr_content

Used in:
   table_content

Every row in a table has the same number of cells as the longest row; the browser automatically creates empty cells to pad rows with fewer defined cells.

9.2.2.1 The align attribute

The extended browsers automatically align cell contents inside their respective cells. The `align` attribute for the `<tr>` tag lets you change the default horizontal alignment of all the cells in a row. The attribute affects all the cells within the current row, but not subsequent rows.

An `align` attribute value of `left`, `right`, or `center` causes the extended browser to align the contents of each cell in the row against the left or right edge, or in the center of the cell, respectively. You also may change the alignment for individual cells within a row, overriding the value of the `align` attribute in the `<tr>` tag with the `align` attribute for the `<th>` and `<tr>` tags, as described below. Accordingly, use the `align` attribute in the `<tr>` tag to specify the most common cell content justification for the row (if not the default), and use a different `align` attribute for those individual cells that deviate from that common alignment.

Table 9-1 displays the horizontal (`align`) and vertical (`valign`) table cell-content attribute values and options. Values in parentheses are the defaults.

Table 9–1: Horizontal and Vertical Table Cell-Content Attribute Values and Options

Attribute	Netscape and Internet Explorer		Mosaic	
	Headers	Data	Headers	Data
align	Left	(Left)	(Left)	(Left)
	(Center)	Center	Center	Center
	Right	Right	Right	Right
valign[a]	Top	Top	(Top)	(Top)
	(Center)	(Center)	N/A[b]	N/A
	Bottom	Bottom	N/A	N/A
	Baseline	Baseline	N/A	N/A

[a] Internet Explorer also supports a universal `valign` attribute for the `<table>` tag
[b] Not available with Mosaic

9.2.2.2 The bgcolor attribute

Like its relative for the `<table>` tag, the `bgcolor` attribute for the `<tr>` tag is used by Internet Explorer only to set the background color of the entire row. Its value is either an RGB color value or a standard color name. Both the syntax of color values and the acceptable color names are provided in Appendix E.

Every cell in the row will be given this background color. Individual cell colors can be changed by providing the `bgcolor` attribute for those cells.

9.2.2.3 The bordercolor, bordercolorlight, and bordercolordark attributes

Like their brethren for the `<table>` tag, Internet Explorer lets you use these attributes to set the color of the borders within the current row.

Their values override any values set by the corresponding attribute in the containing `<table>` tag. See the corresponding description of these extensions in 9.2.1 for details. Color values can be either an RGB color value or a standard color name, both of which are described fully in Appendix E.

9.2.2.4 *The valign attribute*

With Netscape and Internet Explorer, you may change the default vertical alignment for the contents of data cells contained within a table row. Normally, the browsers render cell contents centered vertically. By including the `valign` attribute in the `<tr>` tag with a value of `top` or `bottom`, you tell the extended browsers to place the table row's contents flush against the top or bottom of their cells.

Besides `top`, `bottom`, and the default `center` values for `valign`, Netscape supports a fourth option, `baseline`, which specially aligns cell contents to the baseline of the top line of text in other cells in the row (Figure 9-4). The value `center`, although acceptable, has no real effect since it simply reiterates the default vertical alignment.

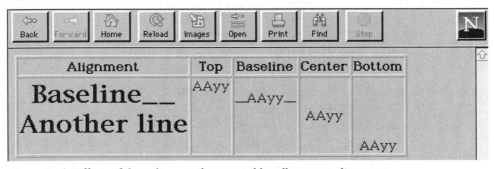

Figure 9–4: Effects of the valign attribute on table cell content alignment

```
<table border>
  <tr>
    <th>Alignment</th>
    <th>Top</th>
    <th>Baseline</th>
    <th>Center</th>
    <th>Bottom</th>
  </tr>
  <tr align=center>
    <th><h1>Baseline....<br>Line 2</h1></th>
    <td valign=top>AAyy</td>
    <td valign=baseline>AAyy</td>
    <td valign=center>AAyy</td>
    <td valign=bottom>AAyy</td>
  </tr>
</table>
```

9.2.3 The <td> and <th> Tags

The <th> and <td> tags go inside the <tr> tags of an HTML table to create the cells and contents within the row. The tags operate similarly; the only real differences are that Netscape and Mosaic render header text—meant to entitle or otherwise describe table data—in boldface font style and that the default alignment of their respective contents may be different (Table 9-1). Internet Explorer makes no special formatting for <th> and renders it identical to <td>.

<td> and <th>

Function:
  Define table data and header cells

Attributes:
  ALIGN
  BGCOLOR (Internet Explorer only)
  BORDERCOLOR (Internet Explorer only)
  BORDERCOLORLIGHT (Internet Explorer only)
  BORDERCOLORDARK (Internet Explorer only)
  COLSPAN
  NOWRAP
  ROWSPAN
  VALIGN (extension)
  WIDTH (extension)

End tag:
  </th> or </td>; may be omitted

Contains:
  body_content

Used in:
  tr_content

Like those available for the table row (<tr>) tag, the extended browsers provide a rich set of content-alignment attributes you may apply to a single data or header cell and override the default values for the current row. The browsers also support special attributes that control the number of columns or rows a cell may span in the table.

The contents of the <th> and <td> tags can be anything you might put in the body of an HTML document, including text, images, forms, and so on—even another table. And, as described earlier, the browser automatically creates a table large enough, both vertically and horizontally, to display all the contents of any and all the cells.

If a particular row has fewer header or data items than other rows, the browser adds empty cells at the end to fill the row. If you need to make an empty cell before the end of a row, for instance, to indicate a missing data point, create a header or data cell with no content.

Except with Mosaic, empty cells look different than those containing data or headers if the table has borders: the empty cell will not be seemingly embossed onto the window, but instead is simply left blank. If you want to create an empty cell that has incised borders like all the other cells in your table, be sure to place a minimal amount of content in the cell: a single `<br>` tag, for instance.

9.2.3.1 The align and valign attributes

The `align` and `valign` attributes are identical to those of the same name for the table row tag (`<tr>`; see above), except that when used with a `<th>` or `<td>` tag, they control the horizontal or vertical alignment of content in just the current cell. Their value overrides any alignment established by the respective `align` or `valign` attribute of the `<tr>` tag, but does not affect the alignment of subsequent cells. And, while `align` works with all the extended browsers, `valign` is not supported by NCSA Mosaic. See Table 9-1 for alignment details.

You may set the `align` attribute's value to `left`, `right`, or `center`, causing the browsers to align the cell contents against the left or right edge, or in the center of the cell, respectively. The `valign` attribute may have a value of `top`, `bottom`, `center`, or `baseline`, telling Netscape and Internet Explorer to align the cell's contents to the top or bottom edge, or in the center of the cell, or, with Netscape only, to the baseline of the first line of text in other cells in the row.

9.2.3.2 The width attribute

Like its twin in the `<table>` tag which lets you widen a table, the `width` attribute for Netscape's and Internet Explorer's (not Mosaic's) table cell tags lets you widen an individual cell and, hence, the entire column it occupies. You set the `width` to an integer number of pixels, or a percentage indicating the cell's width as a fraction of the table as a whole.

For example,

```
<th width=400>
```

sets the current header cell's width, and hence the entire column of cells, to 400 pixels wide. Alternatively,

```
<td width="40%">
```

creates a data cell whose column will occupy 40 percent of the entire table's width.

Since the extended browsers make all cells in a column the same width, you should place a `width` attribute in only one cell within a column, preferably the first instance of the cell in the first row for source readability's sake. If two or more cells in the same column happen to have `width` attributes, the widest one is honored. You can't make a column thinner than what the browser automatically determines is the minimum width needed to display all of any cell contents in the column. So, if the browser determines that the column of cells needs to be at least 150 pixels wide to accommodate all the cells' contents, it will completely ignore a width attribute in one of the column's cell tags that attempts to make the cell only 100 pixels wide.

9.2.3.3 *The colspan attribute*

It's common to have a table header that describes several columns beneath it, like the headers we use in Table 9-1. Use the `colspan` attribute in a table header or data tag to extend an HTML table cell across two or more columns in its row. Set the value of the `colspan` attribute to an integer value equal to the number of columns you want the header or data cell to span.

For example,

```
<td colspan=3>
```

tells the browser to make the cell occupy the same horizontal space as three cells in rows above or below it. The browser flows the contents of the cell to occupy the entire space.

What happens if there aren't enough extra cells on the right? The browser just extends the cell over as many columns as exist to the right; it doesn't add extra empty cells to each row to accommodate an over-extended `colspan` value. You may defeat that limitation by adding the needed extra, but content-less, cells to a single row. (Give them a single `<br>` tag as their contents if you want Netscape's embossed border around them.)

9.2.3.4 *The rowspan attribute*

Just as the `colspan` attribute layers a table cell across several columns, the `rowspan` attribute stretches a cell down two or more rows in the table.

You include the `rowspan` attribute in the `<th>` or `<td>` tag of the uppermost row of the table where you want the cell to begin and set its value equal to the number of rows you want it to span. The cell then occupies the same space as the current row and an appropriate number of cells below that row. The browser flows the contents of the cell to occupy the entire extended space.

For example,

```
<td rowspan=3>
```

creates a cell that occupies the current row plus two more rows below that.

Like the `colspan` attribute, the browser ignores over-extended `rowspan` attributes and will only extend the current cell down rows you've explicitly defined by other `<tr>` tags following the current row. The browsers will not add empty rows to a table to fill a rowspan below the last defined row in a table.

9.2.3.5 Combining colspan and rowspan

You may extend a single cell both across several columns and down several rows by including both the `colspan` and `rowspan` attributes in its table header or data tag. For example,

```
<th colspan=3 rowspan=4>
```

creates a header cell that, as you might expect, spans across three columns and down four rows, including the current cell and extending two more cells to the right and three more cells down. The browser flows the contents of the cell to occupy the entire space, aligned inside according to the current row's alignment specifications or to those you may explicitly include in the same tag, as described earlier.

9.2.3.6 The nowrap attribute

The extended browsers treat each table cell as though it's a browser window unto itself, flowing contents inside the cell as they would common body contents (although subject to special table-cell alignment properties). Accordingly, the browsers automatically wrap text lines to fill the allotted table cell space. The `nowrap` attribute, when included in a table header or data tag, stops that normal word wrapping. With `nowrap`, the browser assembles the contents of the cell onto a single line, unless you insert a `<br>` or `<p>` tag, which then forces a break so that the contents continue on a new line inside the table cell.

9.2.3.7 The bgcolor attribute

Yet again, Internet Explorer lets you change the background color—this time for an individual data cell. Its value is either an RGB hexadecimal color value or a standard color name. Both the syntax of color values and the acceptable color names are provided in Appendix E.

9.2.3.8 The bordercolor, bordercolorlight, and bordercolordark
attributes

Internet Explorer lets you alter the colors that make up an individual cell's border—if xtable borders are turned on with the `border` attribute, of course. See the respective attributes' descriptions under the `<table>` tag in 9.2.1 for details.

The values for these three attributes override any values set for the containing `<table>` or `<tr>` tag. Their values can be either an RGB color value or a standard color name, both of which are described fully in Appendix E.

9.2.4 The <caption> Tag

A table commonly needs a caption to explain its contents, so the extended browsers provide a table-caption tag. Authors typically place the `<caption>` tag and its contents immediately after the `<table>` tag, but it can be placed nearly anywhere inside the table and between the row tags. The caption may contain any body content, much like a cell within a table.

<caption>

Function:
    Define a table caption

Attributes:
    ALIGN (extension)
    VALIGN (Internet Explorer only)

End tag:
    </caption>; never omitted

Contains:
    body_content

Used in:
    table_content

Unfortunately for document authors, Netscape Navigator and NCSA Mosaic implement one method of caption alignment and positioning, while Internet Explorer provides a conflicting set of attributes for the same purpose. By default, the browsers center the caption, except Netscape and Internet Explorer center with respect to the table, including word wrapping when necessary. Mosaic centers the caption text within the browser window, not necessarily centered on its associated table. Mosaic does, however, specially embellish caption text with a boldfaced font style (Figure 9-1).

9.2.4.1 The align attribute

All the extended browsers let you put a caption above or below the table; they just can't agree on the details. All default to a caption on top. Netscape and Mosaic let you place it below the table with the `align` attribute set to the value `bottom` (the value `top`, of course, is equivalent to the default).

Internet Explorer, on the other hand, uses the `align` attribute to control the *horizontal* position of the caption and a special `valign` attribute to move it below the table. With Internet Explorer, you set the `align` attribute to `left`, `center` (the default), or `right`, which positions the caption to the respective locations relative to the table. The other browsers ignore Internet Explorer's different caption-xalign values, and vice versa.

9.2.4.2 The valign attribute

Internet Explorer alone recognizes a special `valign` attribute to control the vertical position of a caption. The `valign` attribute may be set to either `top` or `bottom`; if the attribute is not specified, `top` is assumed.

9.3 Beyond Ordinary Tables

On the face of it, HTML tables are ordinary: just a way for academics and other like-minded data crunchers to format items into columns and rows for easy comparison. Scratch below the surface, though, and you will see that tables are really extraordinary. Besides `<pre>`, the `<table>` tag and related attributes provide the only way for you to easily control the *layout* of your document in HTML. The content inside a `<pre>` tag, of course, is very limited. Tables, on the other hand, may contain nearly anything allowed in normal body content, including multimedia and forms. And the table structure lets you explicitly control where those elements appear in the users' browser window. With the right combinations of attributes, tables provide a way for you to create multicolumn text, and side and straddle heads in HTML. They also enable you to better set up your forms to make them easier to read, understand, and fill out. That's just for starters.

We don't know that we can recommend you get too caught up with page lay-out—tables or beyond. Remember, HTML is not about looks but about content. But. ...

It's easy to argue that at least tables of information benefit from some controlled layout, and that HTML forms follow a close second. And we expect that the HTML standards bearers will soon release their sanctioned version of HTML table tags that every browser manufacturer will scramble to incorporate with their software. So unlike some other browser-specific extensions to the language, you probably won't go wrong with the table extensions.

And now that we've whetted your appetite for page layout with tables, don't despair that we've let you down by ending this chapter without examples—we have several in 12.5.

10

Frames

Besides extending the capabilities of HTML documents, the innovators at Netscape Communications also recently introduced a device that extends the capability of the browser window itself. The newest versions of Netscape Navigator (2.0 and later) let you divide its main display window into independent window *frames*, each simultaneously displaying a different document—something like a wall of monitors in a TV control room.

10.1 An Overview of Frames

Figure 10-1 is a simple example of a Netscape frame display. It shows how the document window may be divided into columns and rows of individual frames separated by rules and scroll bars. Although it is not immediately apparent in the example, each frame in the window is displaying an independent document—HTML ones in this case—but the individual documents may be any valid content the browser is capable of displaying, including multimedia. If the frame's contents include a hypertext link the user selects, the new document's contents, even another frame document, may replace that same frame, another frame's content, or the entire browser window.

You enable Netscape frames with a special frame document. Its contents do not get displayed. Rather, the frame document contains extension HTML tags that tell the browser how to divide its main display window into discrete frames, and what documents go inside the frames.

The individual documents referenced and displayed in the frame document window act independently, to a degree; the frame document controls the entire window. So, for instance, the browser's "Back" and "Forward" buttons don't work for

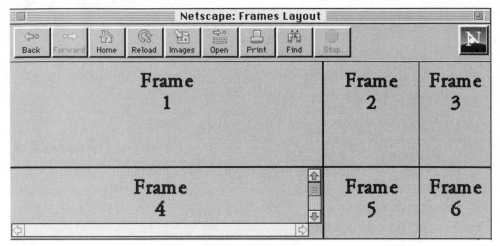

Figure 10–1: A simple six-panel frame layout for Netscape

an individual frame, but links the entire frame document with others you viewed previously.

You can, however, direct one frame's document to load new content into another frame. That's done by attaching a name to a frame and targeting the named frame with a special attribute for the hypertext link <a> tag.

10.2 Frame Tags

Netscape uses three new HTML tags to comprise the frame document: <frameset>, <frame>, and <noframes>.

A *frameset* is simply the collection of frames that make up the browser's window. Column- and row-definition attributes for the <frameset> tag let you define the number and initial sizes for the columns and rows of frames. The <frame> tag defines what document—HTML or otherwise—initially goes into the frames within those framesets, and is where you may give the frame a name to use for document hypertext links.

Here is the HTML source that generated Figure 10-1:

```
<html>
<head>
<title>Frames Layout</title>
</head>
<frameset rows="60%,*" cols="65%,20%,*">
  <frame src="frame1.html">
  <frame src="frame2.html">
  <frame src="frame3.html" name="fill_me">
  <frame scrolling=yes src="frame4.html">
```

```
<frame src="frame5.html">
<frame src="frame6.html">
<noframes>
  Sorry, this document can be viewed only with Netscape
  Navigator version 2.0 or later.
  <a href = "frame1.html">Take this link</a>
  to the first HTML document in the set.
</noframes>
</frameset>
</html>
```

Notice a few things in the simple frame example and its rendered image (Figure 10-1): First, the order in which Netscape fills the frames in a frameset goes across each row. Second, frame 4 sports a scrollbar because we told it to, even though the contents may otherwise fit without scrolling. (Scrollbars automatically appear if the contents overflow the frame's dimensions, unless explicitly disabled with a special attribute in the `<frame>` tag.)

Another item of interest is the `name` attribute in one of the frame tags. Once named, you can reference a particular frame as where to display a hypertext-linked document. To do that, you add a special `target` attribute to the anchor (`<a>`) tag of the source hypertext link. For instance, to link a document called "new.html" for display in our example window frame 3, which we've named "fill_me", the anchor looks like this:

```
<a href="new.html" target="fill_me">
```

If the Netscape browser user chooses the link, say in frame 1, the `new.html` document will replace the original `frame3.html` contents in frame three. [target for `<a>`, 10.6.1]

Finally, since Netscape is the only browser that supports frames, it is likely that some other browser users will try and view your frame documents. That's why each of your key frame documents should provide a backdoor to your HTML document collection with the `<noframes>` tag. Frame-compatible browsers display your frames; non-compatible browsers display the alternative `<noframes>` content.

10.2.1 *What's in a Frame?*

Anyone who has opened more than one window on their desktop display to compare contents or operate interrelated applications knows instinctively the power of frames.

One simple use for frames is to put content that is common in a collection, such as copyright notices, introductory material, and navigational aids, into one frame, with all other document content in an adjacent frame. As the user visits new pages, each loads into the scrolling frame, while the fixed-frame content persists.

A richer frame document-enabled environment provides navigational tools for your document collections. For instance, assign one frame to hold a table of contents and various searching tools for the collection. Have another frame hold the user-selected document contents. As users visit your pages in the content frame, they never lose sight of the navigational aids in the other frame.

Another beneficial use of Netscape's frame document is to compare a returned HTML form with its original for verification of the content by the submitting user. By placing the form in one frame and its submitted result in another, you let the user quickly verify that the result corresponds to the data entered in the form. If the results are incorrect, the form is readily available to be filled out again.

10.3 *Frame Layout*

Frame layout is similar to table layout. Using the `<frameset>` tag, you arrange frames into rows and columns while defining their relative or absolute sizes.

<frameset>

Function:
    Define a collection of frames

Attributes:
    COLS
    ROWS

End tag:
    </frameset>; never omitted

Contains:
    frameset_content

Used in:
    html_content

Use the `<frameset>` tag to define a collection of frames and other framesets. Framesets also may be nested, allowing for a richer set of layout capabilities.

Use the `<frameset>` tag in lieu of a `<body>` tag in the frame document. You may not include any other content except valid `<head>` and `<frameset>` content in a frame document, or the Netscape browser will ignore the frame HTML tags.

10.3.1 *The <rows> and <cols> attributes*

The `<frameset>` tag currently supports only two attributes. They let you define the size and number of columns (`cols`) and `rows` of either frames or nested framesets for the Netscape document window. Both attributes accept a quote-enclosed, comma-separated list of values that specify either the absolute or relative width (for columns) or height (for rows) for the frames. The number of attribute values determines how many rows or columns of frames Netscape will display in the document window.

You express each value in the `rows` or `cols` attribute in one of three ways: as an absolute number of pixels, a percentage of the total width or height of the frame-set, or as a portion of the space remaining after setting aside room for adjacent elements.

As with tables, Netscape will match the size specifications you give a frameset as closely as possible. The browser will not, however, extend the boundaries of the main document window to accommodate framesets that would otherwise exceed those boundaries or fill the window with empty space if the specified frames don't fill the window. Rather, Netscape allocates space to a particular frame relative to all other frames in the row and column and resolutely fills the entire document window. (Did you notice a frame document window does not have scroll bars?)

For example,

```
<frameset rows="150,300,150">
```

creates three rows of frames, each extending across the entire document window. The first and last frames are set to 150 pixels tall, the second to 300 pixels. In reality, unless the browser window is exactly 600 pixels tall, Netscape automatically and proportionately stretches or compresses the first and last frames so that each occupies one quarter of the window space. The center row occupies the remaining half of the window space.

Frame row and column size values expressed as a percentage of the window dimensions are more sensible. For instance, the following example is effectively identical to the previous one:

```
<frameset rows="25%,50%,25%">
```

Of course, if the percentages don't add up to 100 percent, the browser automatically and proportionally resizes each row to make up the difference.

If you are like us, making things add up is not a strength. Perhaps some of the Netscape designers suffer the same difficulty, which would explain why they included the very nifty asterisk (*) option for `<frameset>` `rows` and `cols` values. It tells the browser to size the respective column or row to whatever space is left over after putting adjacent frames into the frameset.

For example, when Netscape encounters the frame tag,

```
<frameset cols="100,*">
```

it makes a fixed-sized column 100 pixels wide, and then creates another frame column that occupies all of the remaining space in the frameset.

Here's a fancier layout example:

```
<frameset cols="10,*,10">
```

This one creates two very thin columns down the edges of the frameset and gives the remaining center portion to the middle column.

You may also use the asterisk for more than one row- or column-attribute value. In that case, the corresponding rows or columns equally divide the available space. For example,

```
<frameset rows="*,100,*">
```

creates a 100-pixel tall row in the middle of the frameset and equal-sized rows above and below it.

If you precede the asterisk with an integer value, the corresponding row or column gets proportionally more of the available space. For example,

```
<frameset cols="10%,3*,*,*">
```

creates four columns: the first column occupies 10 percent of the overall width of the frameset. Netscape then gives the second three-fifths of the remaining space, and the third and the fourth are each given one-fifth of the remaining space.

Using asterisks, especially with the numeric prefix, makes it easy to divide up the remaining space in a frameset.

Be aware, too, that unless you explicitly tell it not to, Netscape lets users manually resize the individual frame document's columns and rows, and hence change the relative proportions each frame occupies in their frames display. To prevent this, see the `noresize` attribute for the `<frame>` tag below.

10.3.2 Nesting *<frameset>* Tags

You can create some elaborate browser displays with a single `<frameset>`, but the frame layout is unimaginative. Rather, create staggered frames and other more complex layouts with multiple `<frameset>` tags nested within a top-level `<frameset>` in the frame document.

For example, create a layout of two columns, the first with two rows and the second with three rows (Figure 10-2), by nesting two `<frameset>` tags with row specifications within a top-level `<frameset>` that specifies the columns:

```
<frameset cols="50%,*">
  <frameset rows="50%,*">
    <frame src="frame1.html">
    <frame src="frame2.html">
  </frameset>
  <frameset rows ="33%,33%,*">
    <frame src="frame3.html">
    <frame src="frame4.html">
    <frame src="frame5.html">
  </frameset>
</frameset>
```

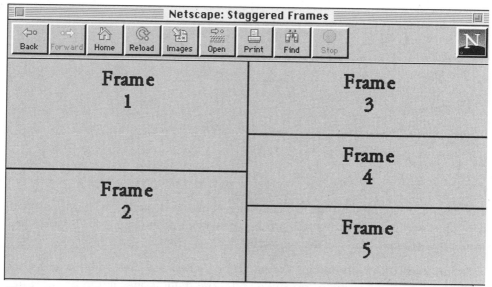

Figure 10-2: Staggered frame layouts use nested <frameset> tags

10.4 Frame Contents

A frame document contains no displayable content, except perhaps a message for nonframe enabled browsers (see `<noframes>` later in this chapter). Rather, `<frame>` tags inside the one or more `<frameset>` tags, which encapsulate the contents of a frame document, provide URL references to the individual documents that occupy each frame. [<noframes>, 10.5]

10.4.1 The <frame> Tag

The <frame> tag appears only within a <frameset>. Use it to set, via its associated src attribute, the URL of the document content that initially gets displayed inside the respective frame.

<frame>

Function:
    Define a single frame in a <frameset>

Attributes:
    MARGINHEIGHT
    MARGINWIDTH
    NAME
    NORESIZE
    SCROLLING
    SRC

End tag:
    </frame>; rarely included

Contains:
    Nothing

Used in:
    frameset_content

Frames are placed into a frameset column by column, from left to right, and then row by row, from top to bottom, so the sequence and number of <frame> tags inside the <frameset> tag are important.

Netscape displays empty frames for standalone <frame> tags without an associated src document attribute and value and those trailing ones in the frameset that do not have an associated <frame> tag. Such orphans, however, remain empty; you cannot put content into them later, even if they have a target "name" for display redirection (see the name attribute below).

10.4.1.1 The src attribute

The value of the src attribute for the <frame> tag is a URL of the document that is to be displayed in the frame. There is no other way to provide content for a frame. You shouldn't, for instance, include any <body> content within the frame document; Netscape will ignore the frame tags and display just the contents of a <body> tag if it comes first, or vice versa.

The document referenced by the `src` attribute may be any valid HTML document or displayable object, including images and multimedia. In particular, the referenced document may itself be composed of one or more frames. The frames are displayed within the referencing frame, providing yet another way of achieving complex layouts using nested frames.

Since the source may be a complete HTML document, all the features of HTML apply within a frame, including backgrounds and colors, tables, fonts, and the like. Unfortunately, this also means that multiple frames in a single browser window may conflict with each other. Specifically, if each nested frame document (not a regular HTML document) has a different `<title>` tag, the title of the overall browser window will be the title of the most recently loaded frame document. The easiest way to avoid this problem is to ensure that all related frame documents use the same title.

10.4.1.2 *The name attribute*

The optional `name` attribute for the `<frame>` tag labels that frame for later reference by Netscape's `target` attribute for the hypertext link anchor `<a>` tag. This way, you can alter the contents of a frame differently from the one that contains the link. Otherwise, like normal browser windows, hypertext-linked documents replace the contents of the source frame. We discuss names and targets in greater length later in this chapter. [target for <a>, 10.6.1]

The value of the `name` attribute is a text string enclosed in quotes.

10.4.1.3 *The noresize attribute*

Even though you may explicitly set their dimensions with attributes in the `<frameset>` tag, users can manually alter the size of a column or row of frames. To suppress this behavior, add the `noresize` attribute to the frame tags in the row or column whose relative dimensions you do not want users fiddling with. For a two-by-two frame document, a `noresize` attribute in any one of the four associated frame tags will effectively freeze the relative proportions of all the frames, for example.

The `noresize` attribute is especially useful for frames that contain fixed images serving as advertisements, a button bar, or a logo. By fixing the size of the frame to contain just the image and setting the `noresize` attribute, you guarantee that the image will be displayed in the intended manner and that the remainder of the browser window will always be given over to the other frames in the document.

10.4.1.4 *The scrolling attribute*

Netscape normally displays vertical and horizontal scrollbars with frames whose contents exceed the allotted window space. If there is sufficient room for the content, the scrollbars disappear. The scrolling attribute for the <frame> tag gives you explicit control over whether or not the scroll bars appear or disappear.

With scrolling="yes", Netscape adds scroll bars to the designated frame even if there is nothing to scroll. If you set the scrolling attribute value to "no," scrollbars will never be added to the frame, even if the frame contents are larger than the frame itself. The value auto works the same as if you didn't include the scrolling attribute in the tag; Netscape adds scrollbars as needed.

10.4.1.5 *The marginheight and marginwidth attributes*

Netscape normally places a small amount of space between the edge of a frame and its contents. You can change those margins with the marginheight and marginwidth attributes, each including a value for the exact number of pixels to place around the frame contents.

You cannot make a margin less than one pixel, or make it so large there is no room for the frame contents. That's because these attributes, like most other HTML ones, advise; they do not dictate to the browser. If your desired margin values cannot be accommodated, Netscape ignores them and renders the frame as it best sees fit.

10.5 *The <noframes> Tag*

A Netscape frame document has no <body>. In fact, it must not, since the browser will ignore any frame tags if it finds any <body> content before it encounters the first <frameset> tag. A frame document, therefore, is all but invisible to any non-frame capable browser. The <noframes> tag gives some relief to the frame disabled.

Use the <noframes> tag only within the outermost <frameset> tag of a frame document. The content inside the <noframes> tag and its required end tag (</noframes>) is not displayed by Netscape or other frame-capable browser, but is displayed in lieu of other contents in the frame document by browsers that do not handle frames. The contents of the <noframes> tag can be any normal HTML body content, including the <body> tag itself.

Although this tag is optional, experienced HTML authors typically include the <noframes> tag in their frame documents with content that warns a frame-

---

<noframes>

Function:
   Supply content for nonframe-compatible browsers

Attributes:
   None

End tag:
   </noframes>; sometimes omitted

Contains:
   body_content

Used in:
   frameset_content

---

incompatible browser user that they're missing the show. And smart authors will give those users a way out, if not direct access to the individual documents that make up the frame document contents. Remember our first frame example in this chapter? Figure 10-3 shows what happens when that frame document gets loaded into Mosaic:

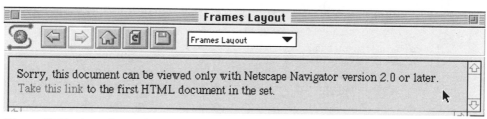

Figure 10-3: A <noframes> message in a nonframe-capable browser

```
<noframes>
   Sorry, this document can be viewed only with Netscape
   Navigator version 1.2 or later.
   <a href="frame1.html">Take this link</a>
   to the first HTML document in the set.
</noframes>
```

The reason <noframes> works is that most browsers are extremely tolerant of erroneous tags and incorrect documents. A nonframe browser simply ignores the frame tags. What's left, then, is the content of the <noframes> tag, which the browser dutifully displays.

If your browser strictly enforces some version of HTML that does not support frames, it may simply display an error message and refuse to display the document, even if it contains a <noframes> tag.

10.6 Named Frame or Window Targets

As we discuss above in the <frame> tag description section, you can label a frame by adding the name attribute to its <frame> tag. Once named, the frame may become the destination display window for a hypertext-linked document selected within a document displayed in some other frame. You accomplish this redirection by adding a special, Netscape-only (version 2.0 or later) target attribute to the anchor that references the document.

10.6.1 The target Attribute for the <a> Tag

If you include a target attribute within an <a> tag, Netscape will load and display the document named in the tag's href attribute in a frame or window whose name matches the target. If the named frame or window doesn't exist, Netscape will open a new window, give it the target's name, and load the new document into that window. Thereafter, hypertext-linked documents that target that name will load into the new window.

Targeted hypertext links makes it easy to create effective navigational tools. A simple table of contents document, for example, might redirect documents into a separate window:

```
<h3>Table of Contents</h3>
<ul>
  <li><a href="pref.html" target="view_window">Preface</a>
  <li><a href="chap1.html" target="view_window">Chapter 1</a>
  <li><a href="chap2.html" target="view_window">Chapter 2</a>
  <li><a href="chap3.html" target="view_window">Chapter 3</a>
</ul>
```

The first time the user clicks one of the table of contents hypertext links, Netscape will open a new window, name it "view_window," and display the desired document's contents inside it. If the user selects another link from the example table of contents and the "view_window" is still open, Netscape will again load the selected document into that window, replacing the previous document.

Throughout the whole process, the window containing the table of contents is accessible to the user. By clicking on a link in one window, the user causes the contents of the other window to change.

Similarly, you can place the table of contents into one frame of a two-frame document and use the adjacent frame for display of the selected documents:

```
<frameset cols="150,*">
  <frame src="toc.html">
  <frame src="pref.html" name="view_window">
</frameset>
```

When Netscape initially displays the two frames, the left frame contains the table of contents, and the right frame contains the preface (Figure 10-4).

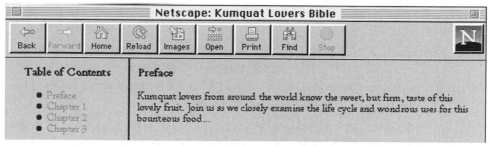

Figure 10–4: Table of contents frame controls content of adjacent frame

When a user selects a link from the table of contents in the left frame, Chapter 1 for example, Netscape loads and displays the associated document into the "view_window" frame on the right side (Figure 10-5). As other links are selected, the lower frame's contents change, while the upper frame continuously makes the table of contents available to the user.

Table of Contents	**Chapter 1: Introduction to Kumquats**
● Preface ● Chapter 1 ● Chapter 2 ● Chapter 3	The term "kumquat" comes from the Cantonese (Chinese) word "kam" (gold) and "kwat" (orange). Kumquat actually refers to any of several small citrus fruits from trees and bushes belonging to the rue family of the genus *Fortunella*. Kumquats, as the name implies, are golden orange-colored fruits with a spongy rind and juicy pulp. Unlike the orange, however, kumquat rinds are sweet and the pulp is

Figure 10–5: Chapter 1's contents get displayed in the adjacent frame

10.6.2 Special Targets

Netscape has reserved four target names for special document redirection actions. They are:

_blank

    Netscape always loads a `target="_blank"` linked document into a newly opened, unnamed window.

_self

    This target value is the default for all `<a>` tags that do not specify a target, causing the target document to be loaded and displayed in the same frame or window as source document. This target is redundant and unnecessary unless used in combination with the `target` attribute in Netscape's special `<base>` tag in a document's head (see below).

`_parent`

> The `_parent` target causes the document to be loaded into the parent window or frameset containing the frame containing the hypertext reference. If the reference is in a window or top-level frame, it is equivalent to the target `_self`.
>
> A brief example may help clarify how this link works. Consider a link in a frame that is part of a three-column frameset. This frameset, in turn, is a row in the top-level frameset being displayed in the browser window. This arrangement is shown in Figure 10-6.
>
> If no target were specified for the hypertext link, it would be loaded into the containing frame. If a target of `_parent` were specified, the document is loaded into the area occupied by the three-column frameset containing the frame containing the link.

`_top`

> This target causes the document to be loaded into the window containing the hypertext link, replacing any frames currently displayed in the window.
>
> Continuing with the frame hierarchy shown in Figure 10-6, using a target of `_top` would remove all the contained frames and load the document into the entire browser window.

All four of these names begin with the underscore (_) character. Any other window or target name beginning with an underscore is ignored by the browser. Don't use the underscore as the first character of the name of any frame you define in your documents.

10.6.3 The <base> Default Target

It can be tedious to specify a target for every hypertext link in your documents, especially when most are targeted at the same window or frame. To alleviate this problem, Netscape lets you add a `target` attribute to its `<base>` tag. [<base>, 6.7.1]

The `target` attribute in the `<base>` tag sets the default target for every hypertext link in the current document that does not contain an explicit `target` attribute. For example, in our example table of contents document, most every link causes the document to be displayed in another window named "view_window." Rather than include that target in each hypertext link, you should place the common target in the table of contents' `<base>` tag within its `<head>`:

```
<html>
<head>
<title>Table of Contents</title>
<base target="view_window">
```

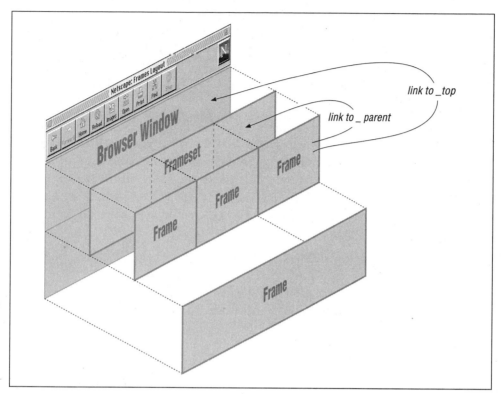

Figure 10–6: Using special hypertext targets in nested frames and framesets

```
</head>
<body>
<h3>Table of Contents</h3>
<ul>
   <li><a href="pref.html">Preface</a>
   <li><a href="chap1.html">Chapter 1</a>
   <li><a href="chap2.html" >Chapter 2</a>
   <li><a href="chap3.html">Chapter 3</a>
</ul>
</body>
</html>
```

Notice we don't include any other target references in the list of hyperlinks because Netscape will load and display all the respective documents in the base target "view_window."

10.6.3.1 Traditional link behavior

Before the onset of frames, each time you clicked on a hyperlink, the corresponding document replaced the contents of the browser window. With frames, this behavior is modified so that the corresponding document replaces the content of the referencing frame. This is often not the desired behavior and can be disconcerting to people browsing your documents.

For example, suppose you have arranged all of the documents on your site to present themselves in three frames: a navigational frame at the top of the browser window, a scrolling content frame in the middle, and a feedback form at the bottom. You named the content frame with the `name` attribute of the `<frame>` tag in the top-level document for your collection and used the `target` attribute of the `<base>` tag in every document on your site to ensure that all links will be loaded into the center content frame.

This arrangement works perfectly for all the documents on your site, but what happens when a user selects a link that takes them to a different site? The referenced document will still be loaded into the center content frame. Now the user is confronted by a document from some other site, surrounded by your navigation and feedback frames!

The solution is to make sure that every hypertext link that references a remote document has a `target` of `_top`. This way, when someone selects a link that takes them away from your site, the remote document will replace the contents of the entire browser window, including your navigation and feedback frames.

11

Netscape
Dynamic Documents

The standard HTML document model is a static one: once displayed on the browser, a document does not change unless the user initiates some activity like selecting a hyperlink with the mouse. The developers at Netscape Communications found that limitation unacceptable and built in some special features to the Netscape browser that lets you dynamically change HTML document content. In fact, they provide for two different mechanisms for dynamic documents, which we detail in this chapter.

We should mention at the outset that many people believe Netscape dynamic documents will be obsolete in a very short time, displaced by plug-in browser accessories and, in particular, applets. Nonetheless, Netscape continues to support dynamic documents, and we believe the technology has virtues you should be aware of, if not take advantage of, in your HTML documents. [applets, 5.6]

11.1 An Overview of Dynamic
Documents

If you remember from our discussion in Chapter 1, *HTML and the World Wide Web*, the client browser initiates data flow on the Web by contacting a server with a document request. The server honors the request by downloading the document. The client subsequently displays the document's contents to the user. For normal Web documents, a single transaction initiated from the client side is all that is needed to collect and display the document. Once displayed, however, it does not change.

Dynamic documents, on the other hand, are the result of multiple transactions initiated from either or both the server side and the client side. A *client-pull* document is one that initiates multiple transactions from the client side. When the server is the instigator, the dynamic document is known as a *server-push* document.

In a client-pull document, special HTML codes tell the client to periodically request and download another document from one or more servers on the network, dynamically updating the display.

Server-push documents also advance the way servers communicate with clients. Normally over the Web, the client stays connected with a server for only as long as it takes to retrieve a single document.[*] With server-push documents, the connection remains open and the server continues to periodically send data to the client, adding to or replacing the previous contents.

Netscape currently is the only browser able to handle dynamic HTML documents correctly. With other browsers, you'll see part of the dynamic document at best. At worst, the browser will completely reject the document. Unfortunately, because dynamic documents are client-server processes, they don't work without an HTTP server. That means you can't develop and test your dynamic HTML documents stored as local files, unless you have a server running locally, as well.

11.1.1 Another Word of Caution

As always, we tell you exactly how to use these exciting, but nonstandard features, and we admonish you not to use them unless you have a compelling and overriding reason to do so. We are particularly strident with that admonition for dynamic documents, not only because they aren't part of the HTML standard, but because dynamic documents can hog the network. They require larger, longer downloads than their static counterparts. And they require many more (in the case of client-pull) or longer-term (for server-push) client-server connections. Multiple connections on a single server are limited to a few of the vast millions of Web users at a time. We'd hate to see your readers miss out because you've created a jiggling image in a dynamic HTML document that would otherwise have been an effective and readily accessible static document more people could enjoy.

---

[*] One connection per document is true even for inline images browsers may automatically download from the server. If you don't believe us, just watch the status line at the bottom of your browser while you download an HTML document with several images. You should see many "Contacting the server" and "Reading the file..." or similar messages.

11.2 Client-Pull Documents

Client-pull documents are relatively easy to prepare. All you need do is embed a `<meta>` tag in the header of your HTML document. The special tag tells the client Netscape browser to display the current document for a specified period of time, and then load and display an entirely new one just as if the user had selected the new document from a hyperlink. (Note that currently there is no way to dynamically change just a portion of an HTML document using client-pull.) [`<meta>`, 6.8.1]

11.2.1 Uniquely Refreshing

Client-pull dynamic documents work with Netscape because the browser responds to a special HTTP header field called "Refresh."

You may recall from previous discussions that whenever an HTTP server sends a document to the client browser, it precedes the document's data with one or more header fields. One header field, for instance, contains a description of the document's content type, used by the browser to decide how to display the document's contents. For example, the server precedes HTML documents with the header "Content-type: text/html", whose meaning should be fairly obvious.

As we discussed at length in Chapter 6, *Links and Webs*, you may add your own special fields to an HTML document's HTTP header by inserting a `<meta>` tag into its `<head>`. [`<meta>`, 6.8.1]

The folks at Netscape have defined the HTTP Refresh field to implement client-pull dynamic HTML documents, enabled by the `<meta>` tag format:

```
<meta http-equiv="Refresh" content="field value">
```

The tag's `http-equiv` attribute tells the HTTP server to include the `Refresh` field, with a value specified by the `content` attribute (if any, carefully enclosed in quotes), in the string of headers it sends to the client browser just before it sends the rest of the document's content. Netscape, but no other browser, currently recognizes the Refresh header as the mark of a dynamic HTML document and responds accordingly, as we discuss below.

11.2.2 The Refresh Header Contents

The value of the `content` attribute in the special `<meta>` Refresh tag determines when and how Netscape updates the current document. Set it to an integer, and the browser will delay that many seconds before automatically loading another document. You may set the content field value to zero, meaning don't delay at all. In that case, Netscape loads the next document immediately after it finishes rendering the current one, by which you may achieve some very crude animation effects. [content, 6.8.1.2]

11.2.2.1 Refreshing the same document

If the Refresh field's content value is the number of seconds alone, Netscape reloads that same document over and over again, delaying the specified time between each cycle, until the user goes to another document or shuts down the browser.

For example, the browser will reload the following client-pull HTML document every 15 seconds:

```
<html>
<head>
<meta http-equiv="Refresh" content="15">
<title>Kumquat Market Prices</title>
</head>
<body>
<h3> Kumquat Market Prices</h3>
Kumquats are currently trading at $1.96 per pound.
</body>
</html>
```

The financial wizards among you may have noticed that with some special software tricks on the server side, you can update the price of kumquats in the HTML document so it acts like a ticker-tape machine: the latest kumquat commodity price updated every 15 seconds.

11.2.2.2 Refreshing with a different document

Rather than reload the same document repeatedly, you can tell Netscape to dynamically load a different document. You do so by adding that document's absolute URL after the delay time and an intevening semicolon (;) in the `<meta>` tag's `content` attribute. For example,

```
<meta http-equiv="Refresh"
  content="15; URL=http://www.kumquat.com/next.html">
```

would cause the browser to retrieve the `next.html` document from the *www.kumquat.com* Web server after having displayed the current document for 15 seconds.

The URL must be an absolute one, including server type and full pathname; relative URLs don't work.

11.2.2.3 Cycling among documents

Keep in mind that the effects of the Refresh `<meta>` tag only apply to Netscape and to the document in which it appears. Hence, to cycle among several documents, you must include a Refresh `<meta>` tag in each one. The `content` value for each document in the cycle must contain an absolute URL that points to the next document, with the last document pointing back to the first one to complete the cycle.

For example, the following are the `<meta>` tags for the headers of each in a three HTML-document cycle:

In the document *first.html*:

```
<meta http-equiv="Refresh"
 content="30; URL=http://www.kumquat.com/second.html">
```

The document *second.html* contains:

```
<meta http-equiv="Refresh"
 content="30; URL=http://www.kumquat.com/third.html">
```

And the *third.html* document has in its `<head>` (besides other crazy ideas):

```
<meta http-equiv="Refresh"
 content="30; URL=http://www.kumquat.com/first.html">
```

Left alone, the Netscape browser will endlessly loop among the three documents at 30-second intervals.

Cycling documents make excellent attractors, catching the attention of passers-by to a Web-driven kiosk, for example. Users may then navigate through the wider collection of kiosk documents by clicking hyperlinks in one of the kiosk's attractor pages and subsequent ones.[*]

To return to the cycling set of attractors, each document in the rest of the collection should have their own Refresh fields that eventually point back to the attractor. You should specify a fairly long delay period for the nonattractor pages—120 to 300 seconds or more—so that the kiosk doesn't automatically reset while a user is reading the current document. However, the delay period should be short enough so that the kiosk resets to the attractor mode in a reasonable period of time after the user finishes.

---

[*] This brings up a good point: the user may override the Refresh dynamic action at any time, for instance by clicking a hyperlink before the client-pull timeout expires. Netscape always ignores the Refresh action in lieu of user interaction.

11.2.3 Pulling Non-HTML Content

Netscape's client-pull feature is not restricted to HTML documents, although it is certainly easiest to create dynamic documents with HTML. With a bit of server-side programming, you can add a Refresh field to the HTTP header of any sort of document from audio files to images to video clips.

For example, create a real-time video feed by adding a Refresh header field in each of a sequence of images grabbed and digitized from a camera. Include a delay of zero with the URL that points to the next image, so that as quickly as Netscape displays one image, it retrieves the next. Assuming the network keeps up, the result is a crude (really crude) TV.

Since Netscape clears the window before presenting each subsequent image, the resulting flicker and flash make it almost impossible to present a coherent sequence of images. This technique is more effective when presenting a series of images designed to be viewed as a slide show, where the user expects some sort of display activity between each of the images.

Perhaps a better use of Netscape's client-pull feature is with long-playing multimedia documents for which Netscape uses special helper applications to display. On a multitasking computer, such as one running UNIX or Windows 95, Netscape downloads one document, while a helper application plays another. Combine Netscape's client-pull capabilities with that multitasking to improve multimedia document performance. Rather than wait for a single, large document like a movie or audio file to download before playing, break it into smaller segments, each automatically downloaded by the previous segment via the Refresh header. Netscape will play the first segment while downloading the second, then third, then fourth, and so on.

A good example that works even on a nonmultitasking machine is background music for your HTML document. Include an audio file in the HTML source that contains a Refresh field for a subsequent audio file, and so on. Since Netscape "displays" audio without disrupting the display of the current document, each musical segment or set of verbal instructions will play while the user views the document.

11.2.4 Combining Refresh with Other HTTP Header Fields

You can have your client-pull dynamic HTML documents perform some neat tricks by combining the effects of Netscape's Refresh with other HTTP header fields. One combination in particular, is most useful: Refresh with a "Redirect" field.

Every browser, not just Netscape, responds to the Redirect field from an HTTP server. The mechanism lets the server tell the browser to retrieve the requested document elsewhere at the field's accompanying URL value. The client browser automatically redirects its request to the new URL and gets the document from the new location, usually without telling the user. We retrieve redirected documents all the time and may never notice.

The most common cause for redirection is when someone moves their HTML document collection to a new directory or to a new server. As a courtesy, the webmaster programs the original host server to send an HTTP header field containing the Redirect field and new URL (without a document body) to any and all browsers that request the document from the original location. That way, the new document location is transparent to users, and they won't have to reset their browser bookmarks.

But sometimes you want the user to reset their bookmarks to the new location because the old one won't be redirecting browsers forever, perhaps because it's being taken out of service. One way to notify users of the new location is to have the redirection URL point to some HTML document other than the home page of the new collection that contains a message about the new location. Once noted, users then take a "Continue" hyperlink to the new home page location and set their bookmarks accordingly.

With Netscape, you can make that notification screen automatically move to the new home page with a combination of the Redirect and Refresh HTTP fields. If Netscape receives an HTTP header with both fields, it will honor both; it immediately fetches the redirected URL and displays it, and it sets the refresh timer and replacement URL, if specified. When the time expires, Netscape retrieves the next URL—your new home page location—automatically.

11.2.4.1 A random URL generator

Another application for the combination of Redirect and Refresh HTTP header fields with Netscape is a perpetual, random URL generator. You'll need some programming skills to create a server-side application that selects a random URL from a prepared list and outputs a Redirect field that references that URL along with a Refresh field that reinvokes the random-URL application after some delay.

When Netscape receives the complete header, it immediately loads and displays the randomly selected document specified in the Redirect field's URL. After the delay specified in the Refresh field, Netscape reruns the random-URL generator on the server (as specified in the Refresh URL), and the cycle starts over. The result is an endless cycle of random URLs displayed at regular intervals.

11.2.5 Performance Considerations

Client-pull documents consume extra network resources, especially when the refresh delay is small, since each refresh involves a completely new connection to a server. It may take Netscape several seconds to contact the server and begin retrieving the document. As a result, rapid updates generally are not feasible, especially over slow network connections.

Use client-pull dynamic documents for low-frequency updates of entire documents, or for cycling among documents without user intervention.

11.3 Server-Push Documents

Server-push dynamic documents are driven from the server side. The client-server connection remains open after an initial transfer of data, and the server periodically sends new data to the client, updating the document's display. Server-push is made possible by some special programming, not special HTML embedded tags, on the server side, and is enabled by the multipart mixed-media type feature of Multipurpose Internet Mail Extensions (MIME), the computer industry's standard for multimedia document transmission over the Internet.

11.3.1 The Multipart/Mixed-Media Type

As we mentioned earlier in this chapter in the discussion of client-pull dynamic documents, the HTTP server sends a two-part document to the client browser: a header describing the document followed by the document itself. The document's MIME type is part of the HTTP header field. Normally, the server includes `Content-type: text/html` in an HTML document's header before sending its actual contents. By changing that content type to multipart/mixed-media, you can send an HTML document or several documents in several pieces, rather than in a single chunk. Only Netscape, though, understands and responds to the multipart header field; the other browsers either ignore additional parts or refuse the document altogether.

The general form of the MIME multipart mixed-media content type header looks like this:

```
Content-type: multipart/mixed;boundary="SomeRandomString"
```

This HTTP header component tells the Netscape client to expect the document to follow in several parts and to look for `SomeRandomString`, which separates the parts. That boundary string should be unique and not appear anywhere in any of the individual parts. The content of the server-to-client transmission looks like this:

```
--SomeRandomString
Content-type: text/plain

Data for the first part
--SomeRandomString
Content-type: text/plain

Data for the second part

--SomeRandomString--
```

The above example has two document parts, both plain text. The server sends each part preceded by our `SomeRandomString` document-boundary delimiter preceded by two dashes, followed by the `Content-type` field, and then the data for each part. The last transmission from server to client is a single reference to the boundary string followed by two more dashes indicating that this was the last part of the document.

Upon receipt of each part, the Netscape browser automatically adds the incoming data to the current document display.

You've got to write a special HTTP server application to enable this type of server-push dynamic document; one that creates the special HTTP MIME multipart/mixed header and sends the various documents separated by the boundary delimiter.

11.3.2 *Multipart Mixed-Replace-Media Type*

Server-push dynamic document authors also may use an experimental variant of the MIME multipart mixed-media content known as *multipart mixed-replace-media*. The difference between this special content-type and its predecessor is that, rather than simply adding content to the current display, the "replace" version has each subsequent part replace the preceding one.

The format of the mixed-replace HTTP header is very similar to its multipart mixed counterpart; the only difference is in the `Content-type`:

```
multipart/x-mixed-replace;boundary=SomeRandomString
```

All other rules regarding the format of the multipart content are the same, including the boundary string used to separate the parts and the individual Content-type fields for each part of the content.

11.3.3 *Exploiting Multipart Documents*

It is easy to see how you can use the two special MIME multipart content types to create server-push dynamic documents. By delaying the time between parts, you might create an automatically scrolling message in the Netscape browser window. Or by replacing portions of the document through the x-mixed-replace MIME type, you might include a dynamic billboard in your document, perhaps even animation.

Note in particular, that server-push multipart documents need not apply only to HTML or other plain text documents. Images, too, are a MIME-encoded content type, so you can have the HTTP server transmit several images in sequence as parts of a multipart transmission. Since you may also have each new image replace the previous one, the result is crude animation. Done correctly over a network of sufficient bandwidth, the effect can be quite satisfying.

11.3.3.1 Efficiency considerations

Server-push documents keep a connection open between the client and server for the duration of the dynamic document's activity. For some servers, this may consume extra network resources and may also require that several processes remain active, servicing the open connection. Make sure the server-push process and, hence, the client-server connection expire upon completion or after some idle period. Otherwise, someone will inadvertently camp on an endlessly cycling server-push document and choke off other users' access to the server.

Before choosing to implement server-push documents, make sure your server can support the added processing and networking load. Keep in mind that many simultaneous server-push documents may be active, multiplying the impact on the server and seriously affecting overall server performance.

11.3.4 Creating a Server-Push Document

You create a special application that runs with the HTTP server to enable server-push dynamic documents. The application must create the special MIME Content-type header field that notifies the Netscape browser that the following document comes in several parts—added to or replacing a portion of the current document. The application must also create the appropriate boundary delimiter and send the Content-type header and data for each part, perhaps also delaying transmission of each part by some period of time. You will need to consult your server's documentation to learn how to create a server-side application that can be invoked by accessing a specific URL on the server. With some servers this may be as simple as placing the application in a certain directory on the server. With others, you may have to bend over backwards and howl at the moon on certain days.

11.3.4.1 Server-push example application for NCSA httpd

The NCSA *httpd* server runs on most UNIX systems. Administrators usually configure the server to run server-side applications stored in a directory named *cgi-bin*.

The following is a simple UNIX shell script that illustrates how to send a multipart
document to a Netscape client via NCSA *httpd:*[*]

```
#!/bin/sh
#
# Let the client know we are sending a multipart document
# with a boundary string of "NEXT"
#
echo "HTTP/1.0 200"
echo "Content-type: multipart/x-mixed-replace;boundary=NEXT"
echo ""
echo "--NEXT"
while true
do
#
# Send the next part, followed by a boundary string
# Then sleep five seconds before repeating
#
  echo "Content-type: text/html"
  echo ""
  echo "<html>"
  echo "<head>"
  echo "<title>Processes On This Server</title>"
  echo "</head>"
  echo "<body>"
  echo "<h3> Processes On This Server</h3>"
  echo "Date:"
  date
  echo "<p>"
  echo "<pre>"
  ps -el
  echo "</pre>"
  echo "</body>"
  echo "</html>"
  echo "--NEXT"
  sleep 5
done
```

In a nutshell, this example script updates a list of the processes running on the
server machine every five seconds. The update continues until the browser breaks
the connection by moving on to another document, or after completing 60 cycles
(about five minutes).

---

[*] It is an idiosyncrasy of NCSA *httpd* that no spaces are allowed in the Content-type field
that precedes your multipart document. Some authors like to place a space after the semicolon and before the boundary keyword. Don't do this with NCSA *httpd*; run the whole
Content-type together without spaces to get the server to recognize the correct multipart
content type.

We offer this shell script example to illustrate the basic logic behind any server-push document generator. In reality, you should create your server-side applications using a more conventional programming language like Perl or C. The applications run more efficiently and can better detect when the client has severed the connection to the server.

12

Tips, Tricks, and Hacks

We've sprinkled a number of tips, tricks, and hacks throughout this book, along with style guidelines, examples, and instructions. So why have a special chapter on tips, tricks, and hacks of HTML? Because it's where most readers will leaf to when they pick up this book for the first time. HTML is the language, albeit constrained, that makes the World Wide Web on the Internet the exciting place that it is. And interested readers want to know, "How do I do the cool stuff?"

12.1 Top of the Tips

The most important tip for even veteran HTML authors, and one that bears repeating, is surf for yourself. We can show and explain a few neat tricks to get you started, but there are thousands of HTML authors out there combining and recombining HTML tags and juggling content to create compelling and useful documents.

Get a bona fide Internet account; get a copy of Mosaic, Netscape, Internet Explorer, whatever; get connected; and get cruising. Collect Web site URLs from friends, business associates, and the traditional media. Even local TV and radio stations have taken to announcing some of their sponsors' Web site URLs. And consult the many different Internet Web directories like Yahoo and Webcrawler for new and up-to-date addresses for the Web sites that suit your lifestyle or business niche.

Examine (don't steal) their pages for eye-catching and effective pages and use them to guide your own creations. Capture and examine the source HTML documents for the juicy bits. Get a feel of the more effective Web collections. How are their documents organized? How large is each document? And so on.

We all learn from experience, so go get it.

12.1.1 Design for Your Audience

We continuously argue throughout the book that, with HTML documents, content matters most, not look. That doesn't mean presentation doesn't matter.

Effective HTML documents match your target audience's expectations, giving them a familiar environment in which to explore and gather information. Serious academicians expect a treatise on the physiology of the kumquat to appear journal-like: long on meaningful words, figures, and diagrams; short on frivolous trappings like cute bullets and font abuse. Don't insult the reader's eye, except when exercising artistic license to jar or attack your reader's sensibilities.

By anticipating your audience and by designing your documents to appeal to their tastes, you also subtly deflect unwanted surfers from your pages. Undesirables, such as penniless college students surfing your commercial site, may hog your server's resources and prevent the buying audience you desire from ready access to your pages.

For instance, use subtle colors and muted text transitions between sections for a classical art museum's collection to mimic the hushed environment of a real classical art museum. The typical rock-n-roll crazed Web surfer maniac probably won't spend more than a glance at your site, but the millionaire arts patron might.

Also, use effective layout to gently guide your readers' eyes to areas of interest in your documents. Do that by adhering to the basic rules of document layout and design, such as placing figures and diagrams nearby if not inline with their content reference. Nothing's worse than having to scroll up and down the browser window in a desperate search for a picture that can explain everything.

We won't lie and suggest that we're design experts. We aren't, but they're not hard to find. So, another tip for the serious Web page author: Seek professional help. The best situation is to have design experience yourself. Next best is to have a pro looking over your shoulder, or at least somewhere within earshot.

Make a trip to your local library and do some reading on your own, too. Even better yet, browse the various online HTML guides. Check out *Designing for the Web* by O'Reilly & Associates. Your readers will be glad you did. [design tools, 1.6]

12.1.2 Boilerplate HTML Documents

The next best tip we can give you is reuse your documents. Don't start from scratch each time. Rather, develop a consistent framework, even to the point of a content outline into which you add the detail and character for each page.

Here's our contribution to help start your boilerplate HTML document collection. The following source contains what the HTML standard currently tells us is the minimum content that should appear in every HTML document (regardless of what the browsers might let you get away with) and then some added for document clarity. Use it as a skeleton for your own HTML documents:

```
<html>
<head>
<title>Required--replace this title with your own</title>
</head>
<body>
<h3>Reiterate the title here</h3>
...Insert your document's contents here...
<address>Include your name and contact information
usually at the end of the document</address>
</body>
</html>
```

12.2 Trivial or Abusive?

There is perhaps no more abused or abusive HTML document device than the <blink> tag extension for text content currently supported by, thank heaven, only the Netscape browser.[*] It works by alternating the color of the text enclosed between the <blink> tag and its end tag (</blink>)—incessantly! It's not only ugly (reminiscent of the very bad video-text displays on a hotel TV), but it's excruciatingly annoying. The reader can't turn it off except to scroll beyond that portion of the document or hyperlink out of the document altogether. [<blink>, 4.5.3]

Okay, so it grabs readers' attention to an important point. Just make sure it's a *very* important point. And here's a tip: Make it easy for the reader to get by the blinking segment in your document. Surround it with empty space or with pleasant, but vacuous content that we don't have to read.

12.3 Title Marquee

Here's a cute trick that is trivial, too, but effective. Better than <blink> and <marquee>, its effects don't persist, and it perks readers' attentions before they view your pages.

The HTML standard dictates that every document have a title in its head. The standard doesn't say, however, that you can't have more than one title. Most current browsers display the title contents in the titlebar of the document's display window. By including several title tags in the same document, you create a marquee

---

[*] Few Web surfers use Internet Explorer, so you rarely and thankfully won't find many HTML documents using the browser's equally tacky <marquee> feature.

effect, flashing or scrolling text across that title bar once before the body contents are displayed. It happens quickly, but it catches most readers' peripheral attentions and gives them something to ponder ("What was that?") while waiting for the browser to render the rest of the document.

The following source illustrates the marquee effect. When rendered, the message, "We love to eat kumquats!" expands, then contracts in the browser's title space before getting replaced by the real title "Kumquat Lovers Homepage", which persists. (Notice we do include the final title at the beginning, in case an automated reader comes looking for it. Automated readers tend to look for what's expected and not beyond.)

```
<html>
<head>
<title>Kumquat Lovers Homepage</title>
<title>W</title>
<title>We</title>
<title>We </title>
<title>We l</title>
<title>We lo</title>
<title>We lov</title>
<title>We love</title>
<title>We love </title>
<title>We love t</title>
<title>We love to</title>
<title>We love to </title>
<title>We love to e</title>
<title>We love to ea</title>
<title>We love to eat</title>
<title>We love to eat </title>
<title>We love to eat k</title>
<title>We love to eat ku</title>
<title>We love to eat kum</title>
<title>We love to eat kumq</title>
<title>We love to eat kumqu</title>
<title>We love to eat kumqua</title>
<title>We love to eat kumquat</title>
<title>We love to eat kumquats!</title>
<title>We love to eat kumquats!</title>
<title>e love to eat kumquats!</title>
<title> love to eat kumquats!</title>
<title>love to eat kumquats!</title>
<title>ove to eat kumquats!</title>
<title>ve to eat kumquats!</title>
<title>e to eat kumquats!</title>
<title> to eat kumquats!</title>
<title>to eat kumquats!</title>
<title>o eat kumquats!</title>
<title> eat kumquats!</title>
<title>eat kumquats!</title>
<title>at kumquats!</title>
<title>t kumquats!</title>
```

```
<title> kumquats!</title>
<title>kumquats!</title>
<title>umquats!</title>
<title>mquats!</title>
<title>quats!</title>
<title>uats!</title>
<title>ats!</title>
<title>ts!</title>
<title>s!</title>
<title>!</title>
<title>Kumquat Lovers Homepage</title>
</head>
```

12.4 Custom Bullets

One common use of the definition list has nothing to do with definitions, but instead deals with adding custom bullets to an otherwise unordered list. In this trick, leave the <dt> tag empty, and add an <img> tag that references the desired bullet image at the beginning of each <dd> tag. [<dl>, 7.7.1]

For example,

```
<dl>
  <dt><dd><img src="fancy_bullet.gif"> Pickled Kumquats
  <dt><dd><img src="fancy_bullet.gif"> 'Quats and 'Kraut
  <dt><dd><img src="fancy_bullet.gif"> 'Quatshakes
  <dt><dd><img src="fancy_bullet.gif"> Liver with Fried 'Quats
</dl>
```

The fancier list is shown in Figure 12-1.

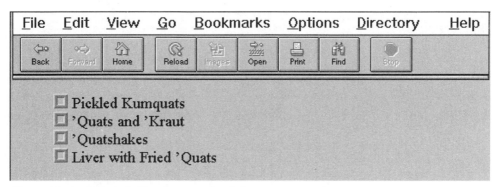

Figure 12–1: Custom bullets for unordered lists

Keep in mind that this trick only works well if your list items are short enough to not wrap within the browser window. If the item does wrap, the next line will start aligned with the left edge of the bullet, not the left edge of the text, as you might hope.

12.5 Tricks with Tables

Enough with the cheap tricks. On to some really good ones: tricks with the HTML `<table>` tag and attributes that add some attractive features to your documents.

By design, HTML tables let authors create appealing, accessible tables of information. But the HTML table tags also can be exploited to create innovative, attractive page designs that are otherwise unobtainable in standard HTML.

12.5.1 Multicolumn Pages

One popular page-layout element is completely missing from HTML: multiple columns of text. This is easily remedied by placing your document content inside a table of one row with two or more columns. Table-enabled browsers make the row as tall as the tallest column of text.

12.5.1.1 Basic multicolumn layout

The basic two-column layout has a single table row with three data cells: one each for the columns of text and an intervening empty cell to more attractively separate the two columns. (We've added a large `cellspacing` attribute value to create that intervening space between the columns, but that works only with Netscape.)

The following example table,

```
<table border=0 cellspacing=7>
  <tr>
    <td>Copy for column 1...
    <td><br>
    <td>Copy for column 2...
</table>
```

is an excellent template for a simple two-column text layout (see Figure 12-2)

The one thing the browsers won't do is automatically balance the text in the columns, resulting in adjacent columns of approximately the same length. You'll have to experiment with your document, manually shifting text from one column to another until you achieve a nicely balanced page.

Keep in mind, though, that users may resize their display windows and the columns' contents will shift accordingly. So, don't spend a lot of time getting the last sentences of each column to line up exactly; they're bound to be skewed in other browser window widths.

Of course, you can easily convert the example layout to three or more columns by dividing the text among more cells in the table. But keep in mind that pages with more than three columns may prove difficult to read on small displays where the actual column width might be quite small.

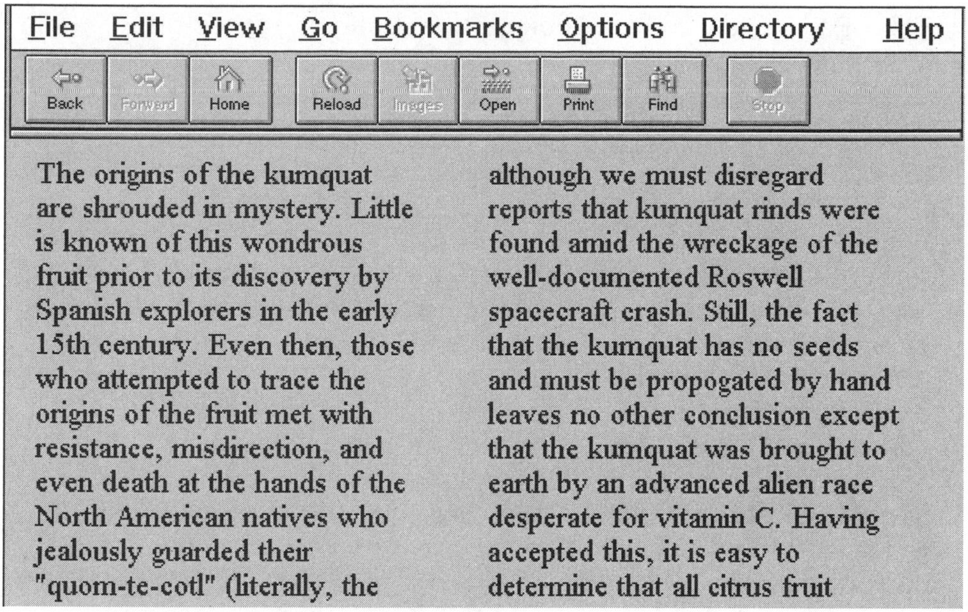

```
 File    Edit    View    Go    Bookmarks    Options    Directory    Help
```

```
 Back   Forward   Home      Reload   Images   Open    Print    Find    Stop
```

The origins of the kumquat
are shrouded in mystery. Little
is known of this wondrous
fruit prior to its discovery by
Spanish explorers in the early
15th century. Even then, those
who attempted to trace the
origins of the fruit met with
resistance, misdirection, and
even death at the hands of the
North American natives who
jealously guarded their
"quom-te-cotl" (literally, the

although we must disregard
reports that kumquat rinds were
found amid the wreckage of the
well-documented Roswell
spacecraft crash. Still, the fact
that the kumquat has no seeds
and must be propogated by hand
leaves no other conclusion except
that the kumquat was brought to
earth by an advanced alien race
desperate for vitamin C. Having
accepted this, it is easy to
determine that all citrus fruit

Figure 12-2: A simple two-column layout

12.5.1.2 Straddle Heads

The basic multicolumn format is just the start. By adding cells that span across the columns, you create headlines. Similarly, you can make figures span across more than one column: simply add the `colspan` attribute to the cell containing the headline or figure. Figure 12-3 shows an attractive three-column layout with straddle heads and a spanning figure, created from the following HTML source with table tags:

```
<table border=0 cellspacing=7>
  <tr>
    <th colspan=5><h2>The History of the Kumquat</h2>
  <tr valign=top>
    <td rowspan=2>Copy for column 1...
    <td rowspan=2 width=24><br>
    <td >Copy for column 2...
    <td width=24><br>
    <td >Copy for column 3...
  <tr>
    <td colspan=3 align=center><img src="pics/fruit.gif">
    <p>
    <i>The Noble Fruit</i>
</table>
```

To achieve this nice layout, we used the `colspan` attribute on the cell in the first row to span all five table columns (three with copy and the two intercolumn

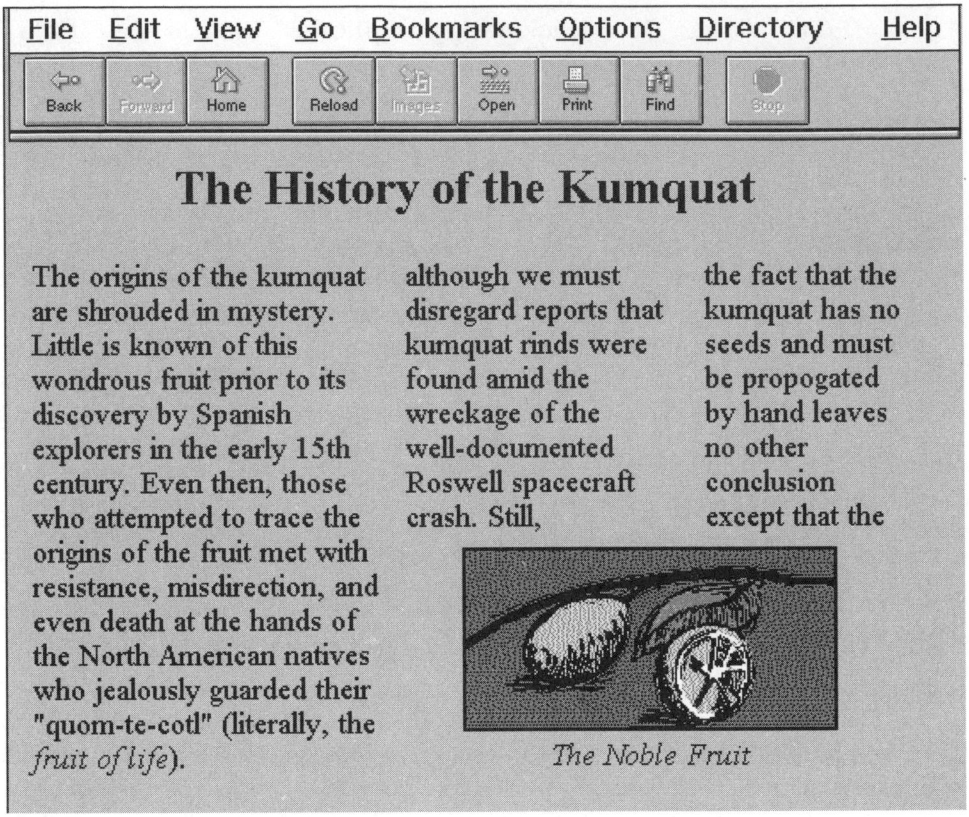

<u>F</u>ile	<u>E</u>dit	<u>V</u>iew	<u>G</u>o	<u>B</u>ookmarks	<u>O</u>ptions	<u>D</u>irectory	<u>H</u>elp

Back Forward Home   Reload Images Open Print Find   Stop

The History of the Kumquat

The origins of the kumquat are shrouded in mystery. Little is known of this wondrous fruit prior to its discovery by Spanish explorers in the early 15th century. Even then, those who attempted to trace the origins of the fruit met with resistance, misdirection, and even death at the hands of the North American natives who jealously guarded their "quom-te-cotl" (literally, the *fruit of life*).

although we must disregard reports that kumquat rinds were found amid the wreckage of the well-documented Roswell spacecraft crash. Still,

the fact that the kumquat has no seeds and must be propogated by hand leaves no other conclusion except that the

The Noble Fruit

Figure 12–3: *Fancy straddle heads and spanning figures with HTML table tags*

spaces). We use the `rowspan` attribute on the first column and its adjacent column spacer to extend the columns down beside the figure. The figure's cell has a `colspan` attribute so that the contents span the other two columns and intervening spaces.

12.5.2 Side Heads

The only text-heading features available in HTML are the `<h1>` through `<h6>` tags. These tags are always embedded in the text flow, separating adjacent paragraphs of text. Through multiple columns, you can achieve an alternative style that places headings into a separate side column, running vertically alongside the document text.

These so-called side heads are a bit more difficult to achieve with Mosaic than with Netscape or Internet Explorer because you can't control cell widths in Mosaic. Consequently, although you can make side heads with Mosaic, they aren't as attractive or as controllable as with Netscape or Internet Explorer.

Figure 12-4 shows you a fairly fancy pair of side heads, the result of the following bit of source HTML table code:

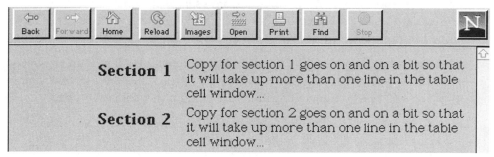

Figure 12–4: Table tags created these side heads

```
<table>
  <tr>
  <th width="30%" align=right>
    <h3>Section 1</h3>
  <td>
  <td>
    Copy for section 1 goes on and on a bit
    so that it will take up more than one line in the
    table cell window...
  <tr>
  <th align=right>
    <h3>Section 2</h3>
  <td>
  <td>
    Copy for section 2 goes on and on a bit
    so that it will take up more than one line in the
    table cell window...
</table>
```

Notice how we create reasonably attractive side heads set off from the left margin of the Netscape browser window by adjusting the first header cell's width and right-justifying the cell contents. Mosaic ignores the width attribute, so you'll find it renders the example with a much thinner first column, but otherwise the side heads are intact.

Just as in our multicolumn layout, the example side-head layout uses an empty column to create a space between the narrow left column containing the heading and the wider right column containing the text associated with that heading. For Netscape and Internet Explorer, you may tune the width of the heading column. It's best to specify the width as a percentage of the table width, rather than explicitly in numbers of pixels to make sure that the heading column scales to fit both wide and narrow display windows.

12.5.2.1 When tables aren't implemented

One of the dangers of being overly dependent on tables is that your documents are usually unreadable when viewed with browsers that don't support tables. In the case of side heads, though, your document will come out just fine on a "table-challenged" browser.

Most browsers follow one of the Internet's basic tenets: be liberal in what you accept and strict in what you create. This usually means the browser will ignore tags that don't make sense, including all of the markup that creates a table.

In the case of our side-head layout, the browsers that can't do tables ignore the table tags and only see this part of the document:

```
<h3>Section 1</h3>
  Copy for section 1 goes on and on a bit
  so that it will take up more than one line in the
  table cell window...
<h3>Section 2</h3>
  Copy for section 2 goes on and on a bit
  so that it will take up more than one line in the
  table cell window...
```

Of course, this is a perfectly valid sequence of HTML that generates a conventional document with sections divided by `<h3>` headers. Your document will look fine, regardless of the browser, table-capable or not.

12.5.3 Better Forms Layout

Of all the features in HTML, it's forms that cry out for better layout control. Unlike other structured elements in HTML, forms look best when rendered in a fixed layout with precise margins and vertical alignment of elements. However, except for carefully planned `<pre>` formatted form segments, the common language just doesn't give us any special tools to better control forms layout.

12.5.3.1 Basic form layout

Your forms will almost always look better and be easier for your readers to follow if you use a table to structure and align the form's elements. For example, you might use a vertical alignment to your forms, with field labels to the left and their respective form elements aligned to an adjacent vertical margin on the right. Don't try that with just standard HTML.

Rather, prepare a form that contains a two-column table. The following HTML source does just that, and it works with both Netscape (Figure 12-5) and Mosaic to nicely format the enclosed form:

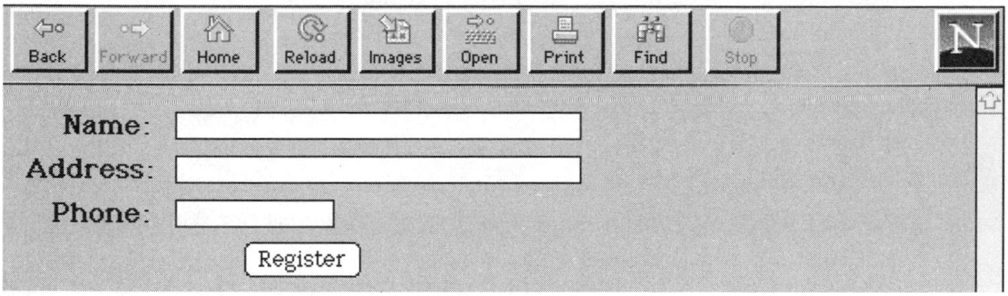

Figure 12–5: Nicely align your forms with tables

```
<form method=post action="http:/cgi-bin/process">
  <table>
    <tr>
      <th align=right>Name:
      <td><input type=text size=32>
    <tr>
      <th align=right>Address:
      <td><input type=text size=32>
    <tr>
      <th align=right>Phone:
      <td><input type=text size=12>
    <tr>
      <td colspan=2 align=center>
      <input type=submit value="Register">
  </table>
</form>
```

Of course, more complex form layouts can be managed with tables. We recommend you first sketch the form layout on paper and then plan how various combinations of table elements, including row- and column-straddled table cells might be used to effect the layout.

12.5.3.2 Building forms with nested tables

As we mentioned earlier, you may place a table inside the cell of another table. While this alone can lead to some elaborate table designs, nested tables also are useful for managing a subset of form elements within the larger table containing the entire form. The best application for using a nested table in a form is for laying out checkboxes and radio buttons.

For example, insert the following row containing a table into the form table in the previous example. It creates a checkbox with four choices:

```
<tr>
  <th align=right valign=top>Preferences:
  <td>
  <table>
    <tr>
```

```
      <td><input type=checkbox name=pref>Lemons
      <td><input type=checkbox name=pref>Limes
      <tr>
      <td><input type=checkbox name=pref>Oranges
      <td><input type=checkbox name=pref>Kumquats
   </table>
```

Figure 12-6 shows you how this nested table attractively formats the checkboxes, which browsers would otherwise render on a single line and not well aligned.

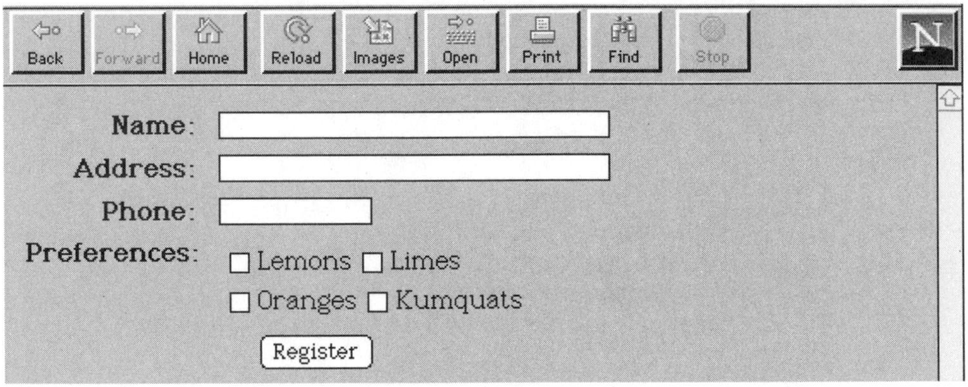

Figure 12–6: Nesting tables to format elements of a form

12.6 Transparent Images

One of the most popular tricks you'll find on everyone's HTML pages is the transparent image. They let the background show through, giving the remainder of the image the appearance of floating on the page. The effect is clever and is the only way to put nonrectangular images in your HTML document displays. [image formats, 5.2.1]

Creating a transparent image is easy, once you understand how the process works and which images are candidates for transparency.

12.6.1 Colors, Maps, and Indices

Images represent their colors in one of two ways: directly, or through a *colormap*.

In the direct method, each pixel in the image contains the actual RGB values that define the color of that pixel. Such images are often called *true color* images, since the number of distinct colors in the image is generally quite large. It is often the case that very few pixels in a true color image share the same color, with many pixels having subtly different variations of the same color. The most popular image format using this representation method is the JPEG format.

Colormap-based images keep all the different colors used in the image in a table known as the colormap. Each pixel in the image contains an index into the table of that pixel's color. In general, the table is fairly small, usually less than 256 colors. This means that many pixels share the same color, and that whole groups of pixels can have their color changed by simply altering the appropriate entry in the colormap. The most common image format using colormaps is the GIF format.

Image transparency is only possible with images containing a colormap, and is currently only defined for images using the GIF89a format. In this format, one entry in the colormap is tagged as the transparent color. All pixels containing the index of that entry will be made transparent when the image is displayed.

For example, consider an image containing eight colors. The colormap is eight entries long, with indices numbered zero through seven. Each pixel in the image contains a value from zero to seven, corresponding to its color in the colormap. If you indicate that the second entry in the color map, whose index is one, will be transparent, all pixels with the value one will be made transparent when the image is rendered.

12.6.2 *Creating a Potentially Transparent Image*

The cookbook way to create a transparent image is easy: take a conventional image; determine the color to be made transparent; and convert the image to GIF89a format, marking that color as transparent.

The most difficult part for most people is finding a conventional image that is suitable for conversion. To make the background of an image transparent, the *entire* background must be one color. Unfortunately, many images do not meet this simple criteria. Scanned images, for example, usually have backgrounds that are a mix of several slightly different shades of one color. Since only one color can be made transparent, the result is a mottled background, part transparent and part opaque.

Many image-editing tools use a process known as *dithering* to create certain colors in an image. Dithered colors are not pure, but are a mix of several other colors. This mixture is not amenable to transparency. You'll often find dithering being used on systems with small colormaps, like conventional 16-color VGA displays on some PCs.

Finally, some images have a pure background color, but that color is also used in parts of the image you want to keep opaque. Since every pixel having the appropriate colormap index is made transparent, these portions of the image become transparent as well.

In all cases, the problem can be solved by loading the image into an image editor, turning off dithering, and painting the background areas, usually by hand, to be a single color not used anywhere else in the image. Make sure you save the result as a GIF image, so that the colormap and pixel indexes will be retained.

12.6.3 Converting the Image

Once you have an acceptable image, and you've determined the color you wish to make transparent, you'll need to convert the image to GIF89a format.

For PC and UNIX users, a public-domain utility called *giftrans* does the job nicely. To convert an image, use this command:

```
giftrans -t index original.gif > new.gif
```

Replace *index* with the numeric index of the color to be made transparent. *Original.gif* and *new.gif* are the original nontransparent image and the resulting transparent image.

Apple Macintosh users have the advantage, though: they can use a single tool named *Transparency* to accomplish the conversion. It was written by Aaron Giles at Cornell University, who generously makes it available for free over the Internet. Check Yahoo or your favorite Archie resource to locate it on a server near you.

These tools can do far more than simply convert transparent images. For a complete discussion of transparency and image conversion, including links to the actual tools, visit:

```
http://melmac.corp.harris.com/transparent_images.html
```

In This Appendix:
- *Grammatical Conventions*
- *The Grammar*

HTML Grammar

For the most part, the exact syntax of an HTML document is not rigidly enforced by a browser. This gives authors wide latitude in creating documents and gives rise to documents that work on most browsers, but are actually incompatible with the standard. Stick to the standards unless your documents are fly-by-night affairs.

The HTML standard explicitly defines the ordering and nesting of tags and document elements. This syntax is embedded within the HTML Document Type Definition and is not readily understood by those not versed in SGML (see Appendix C, *The HTML DTD*). Accordingly, we provide an alternate definition of the allowable HTML syntax, using a fairly common tool called a "grammar."

Grammar, whether it defines English sentences or HTML documents, is just a set of rules that indicate the order of language elements. These language elements can be divided into two sets: *terminal*—the actual words of the language—and *nonterminal*—all other grammatical rules. In HTML, the words correspond to the embedded markup tags and text in a document.

To use the grammar to create a valid HTML document, follow the order of the rules to see where the tags and text may be placed to create a valid HTML document.

A.1 Grammatical Conventions

We use a number of typographic and punctuation conventions to make our grammar easy to understand.

A.1.1 Typographic and Naming Conventions

For our HTML grammar, we denote the terminals with a bold, monospaced Courier typeface. The nonterminals appear in italicized text.

We also use a simple naming convention for the majority of our nonterminals: if one defines the syntax of a specific HTML tag, its name will be the tag name followed by "_tag." If a nonterminal defines the various language elements that may be nested within a certain tag, its name will be the tag name followed by "_content."

For example, if you are wondering exactly which elements are allowed within an <a> tag, you can look for the *a_content* rule within the grammar. Similarly, to determine the correct syntax of a definition list created with the <dl> tag, look for the *dl_tag* rule.

A.1.2 Punctuation Conventions

Each rule in the grammar starts with the rule's name, followed by the replacement symbol (::=) and the rule's value. We've intentionally kept the grammar simple, but we do use three punctuation elements to denote alternation, repetition, and optional elements in the grammar.

A.1.2.1 Alternation

Alternation indicates that a rule may actually have several different values, and you must choose exactly one of them. Vertical bars (|) separate the alternatives for the rule.

For example, the *heading* rule is equivalent to any one of six HTML heading tags, and so appears in the table as:

heading	::=	*h1_tag*
	|	*h2_tag*
	|	*h3_tag*
	|	*h4_tag*
	|	*h5_tag*
	|	*h6_tag*

The *heading* rule tells us that wherever the *heading* nonterminal appears in a rule, you can replace it with exactly one of the actual heading tags.

A.1.2.2 Repetition

Repetition indicates that an element within a rule may be repeated some number of times. Repeated elements are enclosed in curly braces ({...}). The closing brace has a subscripted number other than one if the element must be repeated a minimum number of times.

For example, the <ul> tag may only contain <li> tags, or it may actually be empty. The rule, therefore, is:

ul_tag   ::=   <ul>
                         ${li\_tag}_0$
                         </ul>

The rule says that the syntax of the <ul> tag requires the <ul> tag, zero or more <li> tags, followed by a closing </ul> tag.

We spread this rule across several lines and indented some of the elements to make it more readable only; it does not imply that your documents must actually be formatted this way.

A.1.2.3 Optional elements

Some elements may appear in a document, but are not required. Optional elements are enclosed in square brackets ([and]).

The <table> tag, for example, has an optional caption:

table_tag   ::=   <table>
                             [*caption_tag*]
                             ${tr\_tag}_0$
                             </table>

In addition, the rule says that a table begins with the <table> tag, followed by an optional caption, zero or more table-row tags, and ends with the </table> tag.

A.1.3 More Details

Our grammar stops at the tag level; it does not delve further to show the syntax of each tag, including tag attributes. For these details, refer to the HTML Quick Reference card included with this book.

A.1.4 Predefined Nonterminals

The HTML standard defines a few specific kinds of content that correspond to various types of text. We use these content types throughout the grammar. They are:

literal_text
> Text is interpreted exactly as specified; no character entities or style tags are recognized.

plain_text
> Regular characters in the document character encoding, along with character entities denoted by the ampersand character.

style_text
> Like *plain_text*, with physical- and content-based style tags allowed.

A.2 The Grammar

The grammar is a composite of the HTML 2.0 standard tags and special extensions to the language as enabled by the latest versions of NCSA Mosaic, Netscape Communication's Netscape Navigator, and Microsoft's Internet Explorer.

The rules are in alphabetical order. The starting rule for an entire document is named *html_document*.

a_tag	::=	`<a>`
		$\{a\_content\}_0$
		`</a>`
a_content[a]	::=	*heading*
	|	*text*
address_tag	::=	`<address>`
		$\{address\_content\}_0$
		`</address>`
address_content	::=	*p_tag*
	|	*text*
applet_content	::=	$\{$`<param>`$\}_0$
		body_content
applet_tag	::=	`<applet>`
		applet_content
		`</applet>`
b_tag	::=	`<b>` *text* `</b>`

[a] *a_content* may not contain *a_tags*; you may not nest `<a>` tags within other `<a>` tags.

basefont_tag	::=	`<basefont>`
		body_content
		`</basefont>`
big_tag	::=	`<big>`
		text
		`</big>`
block	::=	{*block_content*}$_0$
block_content	::=	`<isindex>`
	|	*basefont_tag*
	|	*blockquote_tag*
	|	*center_tag*
	|	*dir_tag*
	|	*div_tag*
	|	*dl_tag*
	|	*form_tag*
	|	*listing_tag*
	|	*menu_tag*
	|	*nobr_tag*
	|	*ol_tag*
	|	*p_tag*
	|	*pre_tag*
	|	*table_tag*
	|	*ul_tag*
	|	*xmp_tag*
blockquote_tag	::=	`<blockquote>`
		body_content
		`</blockquote>`
body_content	::=	`<bgsound>`
	|	`<hr>`
	|	*address_tag*
	|	*block*
	|	*heading*
	|	*map_tag*
	|	*marquee_tag*
	|	*text*
body_tag	::=	`<body>`
		{*body_content*}$_0$
		`</body>`
caption_tag	::=	`<caption>`
		body_content
		`</caption>`

center_tag	::=	`<center>`
		body_content
		`</center>`
cite_tag	::=	`<cite>` *text* `</cite>`
code_tag	::=	`<code>` *text* `</code>`
content_style	::=	*cite_tag*
	|	*code_tag*
	|	*dfn_tag*
	|	*em_tag*
	|	*kbd_tag*
	|	*strong_tag*
	|	*var_tag*
dd_tag	::=	`<dd>`
		flow
		`</dd>`
dir_tag[a]	::=	`<dir>`
		{ *li_tag* }
		`</dir>`
dfn_tag	::=	`<dfn>` *text* `</dfn>`
div_tag	::=	`<div>`
		body_content
		`</div>`
dl_content	::=	*dt_tag dd_tag*
dl_tag	::=	`<dl>`
		{*dl_content* }
		`</dl>`
dt_tag	::=	`<dt>`
		text
		`</dt>`
em_tag	::=	`<em>` *text* `</em>`
flow	::=	{*flow_content* }$_0$
flow_content	::=	*block*
	|	*text*
font_tag	::=	`<font>` *style_text* `</font>`
form_content[b]	::=	`<input>`
	|	*body_content*
	|	*select_tag*
	|	*textarea_tag*

[a] The *li_tag* within the *dir_tag* may not contain any element found in a *block*.

[b] *form_content* may not contain *form_tags*; you may not nest one `<form>` within another `<form>`.

form_tag	::=	`<form>`
		{*form_content* }$_0$
		`</form>`
frameset_content	::=	`<frame>`
	|	*noframes_tag*
frameset_tag	::=	`<frameset>`
		{*frameset_content* }$_0$
		`</frameset>`
h1_tag	::=	`<h1>` *text* `</h1>`
h2_tag	::=	`<h2>` *text* `</h2>`
h3_tag	::=	`<h3>` *text* `</h3>`
h4_tag	::=	`<h4>` *text* `</h4>`
h5_tag	::=	`<h5>` *text* `</h5>`
h6_tag	::=	`<h6>` *text* `</h6>`
head_content	::=	`<base>`
	|	`<isindex>`
	|	`<link>`
	|	`<meta>`
	|	`<nextid>`
	|	*title_tag*
head_tag	::=	`<head>`
		{*head_content* }$_0$
		`</head>`
heading	::=	*h1_tag*
	|	*h2_tag*
	|	*h3_tag*
	|	*h4_tag*
	|	*h5_tag*
	|	*h6_tag*
html_content	::=	*head_tag body_tag*
	|	*head_tag frameset_tag*
html_document	::=	*html_tag*
html_tag	::=	`<html>`
		html_content
		`</html>`
i_tag	::=	`<i>` *text* `</i>`
kbd_tag	::=	`<kbd>` *text* `</kbd>`
li_tag	::=	`<li>`
		flow
		`</li>`
listing_tag	::=	`<listing>`

		literal_text
		`</listing>`
map_content	::=	$\{$`<area>`$\}_0$
map_tag	::=	`<map>`
		map_content
		`</map>`
marquee_tag	::=	`<marquee>`
		style_text
		`</marquee>`
menu_tag[a]	::=	`<menu>`
		$\{$*li_tag*$\}$
		`</menu>`
nobr_tag	::=	`<nobr>` *text* `</nobr>`
noframes_tag	::=	`<noframes>`
		$\{$*body_content*$\}_0$
		`</noframes>`
ol_tag	::=	`<ol>`
		$\{$*li_tag*$\}_1$
		`</ol>`
option_tag	::=	`<option>`
		plain_text
		`</option>`
p_tag	::=	`<p>`
		text
		`</p>`
physical_style	::=	*b_tag*
	|	*big_tag*
	|	*i_tag*
	|	*font_tag*
	|	*small_tag*
	|	*s_tag*
	|	*strike_tag*
	|	*sub_tag*
	|	*sup_tag*
	|	*tt_tag*
	|	*u_tag*
pre_content	::=	` `
	|	`<hr>`
	|	*a_tag*

[a] The *li_tag* within the *menu_tag* may not contain any element found in a *block*.

		|	*style_text*
pre_tag	::=	`<pre>`	

            {*pre_content*}$_0$

            `</pre>`

s_tag	::=	`<s>` *text* `</s>`
strike_tag	::=	`<strike>` *text* `</strike>`
select_tag	::=	`<select>`

            {*option_tag*}

            `</select>`

small_tag	::=	`<small>` *text* `</small>`
strong_tag	::=	`<strong>` *text* `</strong>`
sub_tag	::=	`<sub>` *text* `</sub>`
sup_tag	::=	`<sup>` *text* `</sup>`
table_cell	::=	*td_tag*
	|	*th_tag*
table_tag	::=	`<table>`

            [*caption_tag*]

            {*tr_tag*}$_0$

            `</table>`

td_tag	::=	`<td>`

            body_content

            `</td>`

text	::=	{*text_content*}$_0$
text_content	::=	` `
	|	`<img>`
	|	`<wbr>`
	|	*a_tag*
	|	*applet_tag*
	|	*content_style*
	|	*plain_text*
	|	*physical_style*
textarea_tag	::=	`<textarea>` *plain_text* `</textarea>`
th_tag	::=	`<th>`

            body_content

            `</th>`

title_tag	::=	`<title>` *plain_text* `</title>`
tr_tag	::=	`<tr>`

            {*table_cell*}$_0$

            `</tr>`

tt_tag	::=	`<tt>` *text* `</tt>`
u_tag	::=	`<u>` *text* `</u>`

ul_tag	::=	`<ul>`
		{*li_tag*}
		`</ul>`
var_tag	::=	`<var>` *text* `</var>`
wbr_tag	::=	`<wbr>`
xmp_tag	::=	`<xmp>`
		literal_text
		`</xmp>`

B

HTML Tag Quick Reference

In the following table, we list in alphabetical order all the known and some undocumented HTML tags and attributes currently supported by one or more of today's browsers.

You will notice a minus sign (−) in the far right column of certain tags and attributes. These indicate tags *not* supported by Netscape.

We include each tag's possible attributes (some required) indented below their respective tags. In the description, we give possible attribute values as either a range of integer numbers or a definitive list of options, where possible.

Some tag and attribute names are abbreviated forms of longer names; the expansion of these names appear in square brackets in the tag or attribute description.

`<a> ... </a>`	[Anchor] Create a hyperlink (`href` attribute) or fragment identifier (`name` attribute)
`href=`*url*	[Hypertext Reference] Specify the URL of a hyperlink target (required if not a name anchor)
`methods=`*list*	Specify a comma-separated `list` of browser-dependent presentation methods
`name=`*string*	Specify the name of a fragment identifier (required if not a hypertext reference anchor)
`rel=`*relationship*	Indicate the `relationship` from this document to the target
`rev=`*relationship*	Indicate the [reverse] `relationship` of the target to this document
`target=`*name*	Define the name of the frame or window to receive the referenced document
`title=`*string*	Provide a title for the target document

urn=*urn*	Specify the location-independent [Universal Resource Name] for this hyperlink
`<address>` ... `</address>`	The enclosed text is an address
`<applet>` ... `</applet>`	Define an executable applet within a text flow
align=*position*	Align the `<applet>` region to either the top, middle, bottom (default), left, right, absmiddle, baseline, or absbottom of the text in the line
alt=*string*	Specify alternative text to replace the `<applet>` region within browsers that support the `<applet>` tag, but cannot execute the application
code=*class*	Specify the class name of the code to be executed (required)
codebase=*url*	URL from which the code is retrieved
height=*n*	Specify the height, in pixels, of the `<applet>` region
hspace=*n*	Specify additional space, in pixels, to allow to the left and right of the `<applet>` region
name=*string*	Specify the name of this particular instance of the `<applet>`
vspace=*n*	Specify additional space, in pixels, to allow above and below the `<applet>` region
width=*n*	Specify the width, in pixels, of the `<applet>` region
`<area>`	Define a mouse-sensitive area in a client-side image map
coords=*list*	Specify a comma-separated list of shape-dependent [coordinates] that define the edge of this area
href=*url*	[Hypertext Reference] Specify the URL of a hyperlink target associated with this area
nohref	Indicate that no document is associated with this area; clicking in the area has no effect
shape=*shape*	Define the region's shape to be either circ, circle, poly, polygon, rect, or rectangle
`<b>` ... `</b>`	Format the enclosed text using a [bold] typeface
`<base>`	Specify the base URL for all relative URLs in this document
href=*url*	[Hypertext Reference] Specify the base URL (required)
target=*name*	Define the default target of all `<a>` links in the document
`<basefont>`	Specify the font size for subsequent text
size=*value*	Set the basefont size of 1 to 7 (required; default is 3)

`<bgsound>`	Define background audio for the document (Internet Explorer only) —
`loop=value`	Set the number of times to play the audio; `value` may be an integer or the value `infinite` —
`src=url`	Provide the URL of the audio file to be played —
`<big>` ... `</big>`	Format the enclosed text using a bigger typeface
`<blockquote>` ... `</blockquote>`	The enclosed text is a block quotation
`<body>` ... `</body>`	Delimit the beginning and end of the document body
`alink=color`	Set the color of active hypertext links in the document
`background=url`	Specify the URL of an image to be tiled in the document background
`bgcolor=color`	Set the background color of the document
`bgproperties=value`	With `value` set to `fixed`, prevent the background image from scrolling with the document content —
`leftmargin=value`	Set the size, in pixels, of the document's left margin —
`link=color`	Set the color of unvisited hypertext links in the document
`text=color`	Set the color of regular text in the document
`topmargin=value`	Set the size, in pixels, of the document's top margin —
`vlink=color`	Set the color of visited links in the document
` `	[Break] the current text flow, resuming at the beginning of the next line
`clear=margin`	Break the flow and move downward until the desired `margin`, either `left`, `right`, or `all`, is clear
`<caption>` ... `</caption>`	Define a caption for a table
`align=position`	For Netscape, set the vertical position of the caption to either `top` or `bottom`. For Internet Explorer, set the horizontal alignment of the caption to either `left`, `center`, or `right`.
`valign=position`	For Internet Explorer, set the vertical position of the caption to either `top` or `bottom` —
`<center>` ... `</center>`	Center the enclosed text
`<cite>` ... `</cite>`	The enclosed text is a [Citation]
`<code>` ... `</code>`	The enclosed text is a code sample
`<comment>` ... `</comment>`	For Internet Explorer only, place a comment in the document. Comments will be visible in all other browsers. —

`<dd> ... </dd>`	[Definition Definition] Define the definition portion of an element in a definition list
`<dfn> ... </dfn>`	Format the enclosed text as a [definition]
`<div> ... </div>`	[Division] Create a division within a document
`align=`*type*	Align the text within the division to `left`, `center`, or `right`
`<dir> ... </dir>`	Create a [Directory] list containing `<li>` tags
`compact`	Make the list more compact if possible
`<dl> ... </dl>`	Create a [definition list] containing `<dt>` and `<dd>` tags
`compact`	Make the list more compact if possible
`<dt> ... </dt>`	Define the [definition term] portion of an element in a definition list
`<em> ... </em>`	Format the enclosed text with additional [emphasis]
`<font> ... </font>`	Set the size or color of the enclosed text
`color=`*color*	Set the color of the enclosed text to the desired `color`
`face=`*list*	Set the typeface of the enclosed text to the first available font in the comma-separated `list` of font names
`size=`*value*	Set the size to absolute size 1 to 7, or relative to the `<basefont>` size using `+n` or `-n` (required)
`<form> ... </form>`	Delimit a form
`action=`*url*	Specify the URL of the application that will process the form (required)
`enctype=`*encoding*	[Encoding Type] Specify how the form element values will be encoded
`method=`*style*	Specify the parameter-passing `style`, either `get` or `post` (required)
`<frame> ... </frame>`	Define a frame within a frameset
`marginheight=`*n*	Place *n* pixels of space above and below the frame contents
`marginwidth=`*n*	Place *n* pixels of space to the left and right of the frame contents
`name=`*string*	Define the name of the frame
`noresize`	Disable user resizing of the frame
`scrolling=`*type*	Always add scrollbars (`yes`), never add scrollbars (`no`), or add scrollbars when needed (`auto`)
`src=`*url*	Define the URL of the source document for this frame
`<frameset> ... </frameset>`	Define a collection of frames or other framesets
`cols=`*list*	Specify the number and width of frames within a frameset

rows=*list*	Specify the number and height of frames within a frameset
<h*n*> ... </h*n*>	The enclosed text is a level *n* [header]; for level *n* from 1 to 6
align=*type*	Specify the heading alignment as either left (default), center, or right
<head> ... </head>	Delimit the beginning and end of the document head
<hr>	Break the current text flow and insert a [horizontal rule]
align=*type*	Specify the rule alignment as either left, center (default), or right
noshade	Do not use 3D shading to render the rule
size=*pixels*	Set the thickness of the rule to an integer number of pixels
width=*value* or %	Set the width of the rule to either an integer number of pixels or a percentage of the page width
<html> ... </html>	Delimit the beginning and end of the entire [HyperText Markup Language] document
version=*string*	Indicate the HTML version used to create this document
<i> ... </i>	Format the enclosed text in an [*italic*] typeface
<img>	Insert an [image] into the current text flow
align=*type*	For Mosaic and Internet Explorer, align the image to either the top, middle, bottom (default), left, or right of the text in the line. For Netscape Navigator, additionally to the absmiddle, baseline, or absbottom of the text.
alt=*text*	Provide alternative text for non-image-capable browsers
border=*n*	Set the pixel thickness of the border around images contained within hyperlinks
controls	Internet Explorer only, add playback controls for embedded video clips
dynsrc=*url*	Specify the URL of a video clip to be displayed
height=*n*	Specify the height of the image in scan lines
hspace=*n*	Specify the space, in pixels, to be added to the left and right of the image
ismap	Indicate that the image is mouse-selectable when used within an <a> tag
loop=*value*	Set the number of times to play the video; value may be an integer or the value infinite
lowsrc=*url*	Specify a low-resolution image to be loaded by the browser first, followed by the image specified by the src attribute

src=*url*	Specify the [source] URL of the image to be displayed (required)
start=*start*	Specify when to play the video clip, either fileopen or mouseover
usemap=*url*	Specify the map of coordinates and links that define the hypertext links within this image
vspace=*n*	Specify the [vertical space], in pixels, added at the top and bottom of the image
width=*n*	Specify the width of the image in pixels
<input type=checkbox>	Create a checkbox input element within a <form>
checked	Mark the element as initially selected
name=*string*	Specify the name of the parameter to be passed to the form-processing application if the input element is selected (required)
value=*string*	Specify the value of the parameter sent to the form-processing application if this form element is selected (required)
<input type=file>	Create a file-selection element within a <form>
maxlength=*n*	Specify the maximum number of characters to accept for this element
name=*string*	Specify the name of the parameter that is passed to the form-processing application for this input element (required)
size=*n*	Specify the number of characters to display for this element
<input type=hidden>	Create a hidden element within a <form>
maxlength=*n*	Specify the maximum number of characters to accept for this element
name=*string*	Specify the name of the parameter that is passed to the form-processing application for this input element (required)
size=*n*	Specify the number of characters to display for this element
value=*string*	Specify the value of this element that is passed to the form-processing application
<input type=image>	Create an image input element within a <form>
align=*type*	Align the image to either the top, middle, or bottom of the form element's text
name=*string*	Specify the name of the parameter to be passed to the form-processing application for this input element (required)
src=*url*	Specify the [source] URL of the image (required)
<input type=password>	Create a content-protected text-input element within a <form>

`maxlength=`*n*	Specify the maximum number of characters to accept for this element
`name=`*string*	Specify the name of the parameter to be passed to the form-processing application for this input element (required)
`size=`*n*	Specify the number of characters to display for this element
`value=`*string*	Specify the initial value for this element
`<input type=radio>`	Create a radio-button input element within a `<form>`
`checked`	Mark the element as initially selected
`name=`*string*	Specify the name of the parameter that is passed to the form-processing application if this input element is selected (required)
`value=`*string*	Specify the value of the parameter that is passed to the form-processing application if this element is selected (required)
`<input type=reset>`	Create a reset button within a `<form>`
`value=`*string*	Specify an alternate label for the reset button (default is "Reset")
`<input type=submit>`	Create a submit button within a `<form>`
`name=`*string*	Specify the name of the parameter that is passed to the form-processing application for this input element (required)
`value=`*string*	Specify an alternate label for the submit button, as well as the value passed to the form-processing application for this parameter if this button is clicked
`<input type=text>`	Create a text input element within a `<form>`
`maxlength=`*n*	Specify the maximum number of characters to accept for this element
`name=`*string*	Specify the name of the parameter that is passed to the form-processing application for this input element (required)
`size=`*n*	Specify the number of characters to display for this element
`value=`*string*	Specify the initial value for this element
`<isindex>`	Create a "searchable" HTML document
`action=`*url*	For Internet Explorer only, provide the URL of the program that will perform the searching action
`prompt=`*string*	Provide an alternate prompt for the input field
`<kbd> ... </kbd>`	The enclosed text is [keyboard]-like input
`<li> ... </li>`	Delimit a [list item] in an ordered (`<ol>`) or unordered (`<ul>`) list

`type=`*format*	Set the type of this list element to the desired `format`. For `<li>` within `<ol>`: A (capital letters), a (lowercase letters), I (capital Roman numerals), i (lowercase Roman numerals), or 1 (Arabic numerals; default). For `<li>` within `<ul>`: `circle`, `disc` (default), or `square`.
`value=`*n*	Set the number for this list item to *n*
`<link>`	Define a link between this document and another document in the document `<head>`
`href=`*url*	Specify the [hypertext reference] URL of the target document
`methods=`*list*	Specify a browser-dependent `list` of comma-separated display methods for this link
`rel=`*relation*	Indicate the `relationship` from this document to the target
`rev=`*relation*	Indicate the [reverse] `relationship` from the target to this document
`title=`*string*	Provide a title for the target document
`urn=`*urn*	Provide the location-independent [Universal Resource Name] for the target document
`<listing> ... </listing>`	Same as `<pre width=132> ... </pre>`; deprecated: don't use
`<map> ... </map>`	Define a map containing hotspots in a client-side image map
`name=`*string*	Define the name of this map (required)
`<marquee> ... </marquee>`	Create a scrolling-text marquee (Internet Explorer only) —
`align=`*position*	Align the marquee to the `top`, `middle`, or `bottom` of the surrounding text —
`behavior=`*style*	Define marquee style to be `scroll`, `slide`, or `alternate` —
`bgcolor=`*color*	Set the background color of the marquee —
`direction=`*dir*	Define the direction, `left` or `right`, the text is to scroll —
`height=`*value*	Define the height, in pixels, of the marquee area —
`hspace=`*value*	Define the space, in pixels, to be inserted left and right of the marquee —
`loop=`*value*	Set the number of times to animate the marquee; value is an integer or `infinite` —
`scrollamount=`*value*	Set the number of pixels to move the text for each scroll movement —
`scrolldelay=`*value*	Specify the delay, in milliseconds, between successive movements of the marquee text —
`vspace=`*value*	Define the space, in pixels, to be inserted above and below of the marquee —
`width=`*value*	Define the width, in pixels, of the marquee area —

`<menu> ... </menu>`	Define a menu list containing `<li>` tags
`compact`	Make the list more compact
`<meta>`	Provides additional information about a document
`content=`*string*	Specify the value for the meta-information (required)
`http-equiv=`*string*	Specify the [HTTP equivalent] name for the meta-information and cause the server to include the name and content in the HTTP header for this document when it is transmitted to the client
`name=`*string*	Specify the name of the meta-information
`<nextid>`	Define the labeling start point for automatic document-generation tools
`n=`*n*	Indicate the starting label number (required)
`<nobr> ... </nobr>`	[No break]s allowed in the enclosed text
`<noframes> ... </noframes>`	Define content to be presented by browsers that do not support frames
`<ol> ... </ol>`	Define an [ordered list] containing numbered (ascending) `<li>` elements
`compact`	Present the list in a more compact manner
`start=`*n*	Start numbering the list at *n*, instead of 1
`type=`*format*	Set the numbering format for this list to either A (capital letters), a (lowercase letters), I (capital Roman numerals), i (lowercase Roman numerals), or 1 (Ararbic numerals; default)
`<option> ... </option>`	Define an option within a `<select>` item in a `<form>`
`selected`	Make this item initially selected
`value=`*string*	Return the specified value to the form-processing application instead of the `<option>` contents
`<p> ... </p>`	Start and end a [paragraph]
`align=`*type*	Align the text within the paragraph to `left`, `center`, or `right`
`<param> ... </param>`	Supply a parameter to a containing `<applet>`
`name=`*string*	Define the name of the parameter
`value=`*string*	Define the value of the parameter
`<plaintext>`	Render the remainder of the document as preformatted plain text
`<pre> ... </pre>`	Render the enclosed text in its original, [preformatted] style, honoring line breaks and spacing verbatim
`width=`*n*	Size the text, if possible, so that *n* characters fit across the display window
`<s> ... </s>`	The enclosed text is struck through with a horizontal line

`<samp>` ... `</samp>`	The enclosed text is a [sample]
`<select>` ... `</select>`	Define a multiple-choice menu or scrolling list within a `<form>`, containing one or more `<option>` tags
multiple	Allow user to select more than one `<option>` within the `<select>`
name=*string*	Define the name for the selected `<option>` values that, if selected, are passed to the form-processing application (required)
size=*n*	Display *n* items using a pulldown menu for `size=1` (without `multiple` specified) and a scrolling list of *n* items otherwise
`<small>` ... `</small>`	Format the enclosed text using a smaller typeface
`<strike>` ... `</strike>`	The enclosed text is struck through with a horizontal line
`<strong>` ... `</strong>`	Strongly emphasize the enclosed text
`<sub>` ... `</sub>`	Format the enclosed text as a [subscript]
`<sup>` ... `</sup>`	Format the enclosed text as a [superscript]
`<table>` ... `</table>`	Define a table
align=*position*	Align the table either `left` or `right` and flow the subsequent text around the table
bgcolor=*color*	Define the background color for the entire table —
border=*n*	Create a border *n* pixels wide
bordercolor=*color*	For Internet Explorer, define the border color for the entire table —
bordercolordark=*color*	For Internet Explorer, define the dark border-highlighting color for the entire table —
bordercolorlight=*color*	For Internet Explorer, define the light border-highlighting color for the entire table —
cellpadding=*n*	Place *n* pixels of padding around each cell's contents
cellspacing=*n*	Place *n* pixels of spacing between cells
hspace=*n*	Specify the [horizontal space], in pixels, added at the left and right of the table
valign=*position*	Align text in the table to either the `top`, `center`, or `right` and flow the subsequent text around the table —
vspace=*n*	Specify the [vertical space], in pixels, added at the top and bottom of the table
width=*n*	Set the width of the table to *n* pixels or a percentage of the window width
`<td>` ... `</td>`	Define a table data cell
align=*type*	Align the cell contents to the `left`, `center`, or `right`
bgcolor=*color*	Define the background color for the cell —

bordercolor=*color*	For Internet Explorer, define the border color for the cell	—
bordercolordark=*color*	For Internet Explorer, define the dark border highlighting color for the cell	—
bordercolorlight=*color*	For Internet Explorer, define the light border highlighting color for the cell	—
colspan=*n*	Have this cell straddle *n* adjacent columns	
nowrap	Do not automatically wrap and fill text in this cell	
rowspan=*n*	Have this cell straddle n adjacent rows	
valign=*type*	Vertically align this cell's contents to the top, center, bottom, or baseline of the cell	
width=*n*	Set the width of this cell to *n* pixels or a percentage of the table width	
<textarea> ... </textarea>	Define a multiline text input area within a <form>; content of the <textarea> tag is the initial, default value	
cols=*n*	Display *n* [columns] of text within the text area	
name=*string*	Define the name for the text-area value that is passed to the form-processing application (required)	
rows=*n*	Display *n* rows of text within the text area	
wrap=*style*	Set word wrapping within the text area to off, virtual (display wrap, but do not transmit to server), or physical (display and transmit wrap)	
<th> ... </th>	Define a table header cell	
align=*type*	Align the cell contents to the left, center, or right	
bgcolor=*color*	Define the background color for the cell	—
bordercolor=*color*	For Internet Explorer, define the border color for the cell	—
bordercolordark=*color*	For Internet Explorer, define the dark border-highlighting color for the cell	—
bordercolorlight=*color*	For Internet Explorer, define the light border-highlighting color for the cell	—
colspan=*n*	Have this cell straddle *n* adjacent columns	
nowrap	Do not automatically wrap and fill text in this cell	
rowspan=*n*	Have this cell straddle n adjacent rows	
valign=*type*	Vertically align this cell's contents to the top, center, bottom, or baseline of the cell	
width=*n*	Set the width of this cell to *n* pixels or a percentage of the table width	
<title> ... </title>	Define the HTML document's title	
<tr> ... </tr>	Define a row of cells within a table	

`align=`*type*	Align the cell contents in this row to the `left`, `center`, or `right`	
`bgcolor=`*color*	Define the background color for this row	—
`border=`*n*	Create a border *n* pixels wide	
`bordercolor=`*color*	For Internet Explorer, define the border color for this row	—
`bordercolordark=`*color*	For Internet Explorer, define the dark border-highlighting color for this row	—
`bordercolorlight=`*color*	For Internet Explorer, define the light border-highlighting color for this row	—
`valign=`*type*	Vertically align the cell contents in this row to the `top`, `center`, `bottom`, or `baseline` of the cell	
`<tt>` ... `</tt>`	Format the enclosed text in [teletype]-style (monospaced) font	
`<ul>` ... `</ul>`	Define an [unordered list] of bulleted `<li>` elements	
`compact`	Display the list in a more compact manner	
`type=`*bullet*	Set the bullet style for this list to either `circle`, `disc` (default), or `square`	
`<var>` ... `</var>`	The enclosed text is a [variable]'s name	
`<wbr>`	Indicate a potential [word break] point within a `<nobr>` section	
`<xmp>` ... `</xmp>`	Same as `<pre width=80>` ... `</pre>`; deprecated, do not use	

The HTML DTD

The HTML 2.0 standard is formally defined as an SGML Document Type Definition (DTD). It is from this DTD that the standard is documented, and upon which this book is based. Note that we have reprinted this DTD verbatim and have not attempted to add extensions to it. Where our description and the DTD deviate, assume the DTD is correct.

C.1 The HTML DTD

```
<!--    html.dtd

        Document Type Definition for the HyperText Markup Language
                (HTML DTD)

        $Id: html.dtd,v 1.30 1995/09/21 23:30:19 connolly Exp $

        Author: Daniel W. Connolly <connolly@w3.org>
        See Also: html.decl, html-1.dtd
          http://www.w3.org/hypertext/WWW/MarkUp/MarkUp.html
-->

<!ENTITY % HTML.Version
        "-//IETF//DTD HTML 2.0//EN"

        -- Typical usage:

            <!DOCTYPE HTML PUBLIC "-//IETF//DTD HTML//EN">
            <html>
            ...
            </html>
        --
        >

<!--============ Feature Test Entities ========================-->
```

```
<!ENTITY % HTML.Recommended "IGNORE"
        -- Certain features of the language are necessary for
           compatibility with widespread usage, but they may
           compromise the structural integrity of a document.
           This feature test entity enables a more prescriptive
           document type definition that eliminates
           those features.
        -->


<![ %HTML.Recommended [
        <!ENTITY % HTML.Deprecated "IGNORE">
]]>


<!ENTITY % HTML.Deprecated "INCLUDE"
        -- Certain features of the language are necessary for
           compatibility with earlier versions of the specification,
           but they tend to be used and implemented inconsistently,
           and their use is deprecated. This feature test entity
           enables a document type definition that eliminates
           these features.
        -->


<!ENTITY % HTML.Highlighting "INCLUDE"
        -- Use this feature test entity to validate that a
           document uses no highlighting tags, which may be
           ignored on minimal implementations.
        -->


<!ENTITY % HTML.Forms "INCLUDE"
        -- Use this feature test entity to validate that a document
           contains no forms, which may not be supported in minimal
           implementations
        -->


<!--============== Imported Names ================================-->


<!ENTITY % Content-Type "CDATA"
        -- meaning an internet media type
           (aka MIME content type, as per RFC1521)
        -->


<!ENTITY % HTTP-Method "GET | POST"
        -- as per HTTP specification, in progress
        -->


<!--========= DTD "Macros" =====================-->


<!ENTITY % heading "H1|H2|H3|H4|H5|H6">


<!ENTITY % list " UL | OL | DIR | MENU " >


<!--======= Character mnemonic entities ==================-->


<!ENTITY % ISOlat1 PUBLIC
```

```
        "ISO 8879-1986//ENTITIES Added Latin 1//EN//HTML">
%ISOlat1;

<!ENTITY amp CDATA "&"         -- ampersand         -->
<!ENTITY gt CDATA ">"          -- greater than      -->
<!ENTITY lt CDATA "<"          -- less than          -->
<!ENTITY quot CDATA """        -- double quote       -->


<!--========= SGML Document Access (SDA) Parameter Entities ======-->

<!-- HTML 2.0 contains SGML Document Access (SDA) fixed attributes
in support of easy transformation to the International Committee
for Accessible Document Design (ICADD) DTD
        "-//EC-USA-CDA/ICADD//DTD ICADD22//EN".
ICADD applications are designed to support usable access to
structured information by print-impaired individuals through
Braille, large print and voice synthesis. For more information on
SDA & ICADD:
        - ISO 12083:1993, Annex A.8, Facilities for Braille,
          large print and computer voice
        - ICADD ListServ
          <ICADD%ASUACAD.BITNET@ARIZVM1.ccit.arizona.edu>
        - Usenet news group bit.listserv.easi
        - Recording for the Blind, +1 800 221 4792
-->


<!ENTITY % SDAFORM  "SDAFORM  CDATA  #FIXED"
          -- one to one mapping        -->
<!ENTITY % SDARULE  "SDARULE  CDATA  #FIXED"
          -- context-sensitive mapping -->
<!ENTITY % SDAPREF  "SDAPREF  CDATA  #FIXED"
          -- generated text prefix      -->
<!ENTITY % SDASUFF  "SDASUFF  CDATA  #FIXED"
          -- generated text suffix      -->
<!ENTITY % SDASUSP  "SDASUSP  NAME   #FIXED"
          -- suspend transform process -->

<!--========= Text Markup =====================-->

<![ %HTML.Highlighting [

<!ENTITY % font " TT | B | I ">

<!ENTITY % phrase "EM | STRONG | CODE | SAMP | KBD | VAR | CITE ">

<!ENTITY % text "#PCDATA | A | IMG | BR | %phrase | %font">

<!ELEMENT (%font;|%phrase) - - (%text)*>
<!ATTLIST ( TT | CODE | SAMP | KBD | VAR )
        %SDAFORM; "Lit"
        >
<!ATTLIST ( B | STRONG )
        %SDAFORM; "B"
        >
```

```
<!ATTLIST ( I | EM | CITE )
        %SDAFORM; "It"
        >

<!-- <TT>        Typewriter text                    -->
<!-- <B>         Bold text                          -->
<!-- <I>         Italic text                        -->

<!-- <EM>        Emphasized phrase                  -->
<!-- <STRONG>    Strong emphasis                    -->
<!-- <CODE>      Source code phrase                 -->
<!-- <SAMP>      Sample text or characters          -->
<!-- <KBD>       Keyboard phrase, e.g. user input   -->
<!-- <VAR>       Variable phrase or substitutable   -->
<!-- <CITE>      Name or title of cited work        -->

<!ENTITY % pre.content "#PCDATA | A | HR | BR | %font | %phrase">


]]>


<!ENTITY % text "#PCDATA | A | IMG | BR">

<!ELEMENT BR     - O EMPTY>
<!ATTLIST BR
        %SDAPREF; "
"
        >

<!-- <BR>        Line break        -->

<!--========= Link Markup =======================-->

<!ENTITY % linkType "NAMES">

<!ENTITY % linkExtraAttributes
        "REL %linkType #IMPLIED
        REV %linkType #IMPLIED
        URN CDATA #IMPLIED
        TITLE CDATA #IMPLIED
        METHODS NAMES #IMPLIED
        ">

<![ %HTML.Recommended [
        <!ENTITY % A.content    "(%text)*"
        -- <H1><a name="xxx">Heading</a></H1>
                is preferred to
           <a name="xxx"><H1>Heading</H1></a>
        -->
]]>

<!ENTITY % A.content    "(%heading|%text)*">

<!ELEMENT A      - - %A.content -(A)>
<!ATTLIST A
```

```
                HREF CDATA #IMPLIED
                NAME CDATA #IMPLIED
                %linkExtraAttributes;
                %SDAPREF; "<Anchor: #AttList>"
                >
```

```
<!-- <A>                  Anchor; source/destination of link    -->
<!-- <A NAME="...">        Name of this anchor                   -->
<!-- <A HREF="...">        Address of link destination           -->
<!-- <A URN="...">         Permanent address of destination      -->
<!-- <A REL=...>           Relationship to destination           -->
<!-- <A REV=...>           Relationship of destination to this   -->
<!-- <A TITLE="...">       Title of destination (advisory)       -->
<!-- <A METHODS="...">     Operations on destination (advisory)  -->
```

```
<!--========= Images ===========================-->
```

```
<!ELEMENT IMG    - O EMPTY>
<!ATTLIST IMG
        SRC CDATA  #REQUIRED
        ALT CDATA #IMPLIED
        ALIGN (top|middle|bottom) #IMPLIED
        ISMAP (ISMAP) #IMPLIED
        %SDAPREF; "<Fig><?SDATrans Img: #AttList>#AttVal(Alt)</Fig>"
        >
```

```
<!-- <IMG>                Image; icon, glyph or illustration    -->
<!-- <IMG SRC="...">      Address of image object               -->
<!-- <IMG ALT="...">      Textual alternative                   -->
<!-- <IMG ALIGN=...>      Position relative to text             -->
<!-- <IMG ISMAP>          Each pixel can be a link              -->
```

```
<!--========= Paragraphs========================-->
```

```
<!ELEMENT P     - O (%text)*>
<!ATTLIST P
        %SDAFORM; "Para"
        >
```

```
<!-- <P>          Paragraph         -->
```

```
<!--========= Headings, Titles, Sections ================-->
```

```
<!ELEMENT HR    - O EMPTY>
<!ATTLIST HR
        %SDAPREF; "

"

        >
```

```
<!-- <HR>         Horizontal rule -->
```

```
<!ELEMENT ( %heading )   - -   (%text;)*>
<!ATTLIST H1
        %SDAFORM; "H1"
```

```
            >
<!ATTLIST H2
        %SDAFORM; "H2"
            >
<!ATTLIST H3
        %SDAFORM; "H3"
            >
<!ATTLIST H4
        %SDAFORM; "H4"
            >
<!ATTLIST H5
        %SDAFORM; "H5"
            >
<!ATTLIST H6
        %SDAFORM; "H6"
            >

<!-- <H1>        Heading, level 1 -->
<!-- <H2>        Heading, level 2 -->
<!-- <H3>        Heading, level 3 -->
<!-- <H4>        Heading, level 4 -->
<!-- <H5>        Heading, level 5 -->
<!-- <H6>        Heading, level 6 -->

<!--========== Text Flows ======================-->

<![ %HTML.Forms [
        <!ENTITY % block.forms "BLOCKQUOTE | FORM | ISINDEX">
]]>

<!ENTITY % block.forms "BLOCKQUOTE">

<![ %HTML.Deprecated [
        <!ENTITY % preformatted "PRE | XMP | LISTING">
]]>

<!ENTITY % preformatted "PRE">

<!ENTITY % block "P | %list | DL
        | %preformatted
        | %block.forms">

<!ENTITY % flow "(%text|%block)*">

<!ENTITY % pre.content "#PCDATA | A | HR | BR">
<!ELEMENT PRE - - (%pre.content)*>
<!ATTLIST PRE
        WIDTH NUMBER #implied
        %SDAFORM; "Lit"
            >

<!-- <PRE>               Preformatted text              -->
<!-- <PRE WIDTH=...>     Maximum characters per line    -->
```

```
<![ %HTML.Deprecated [

<!ENTITY % literal "CDATA"
         -- historical, non-conforming parsing mode where
            the only markup signal is the end tag
            in full
         -->

<!ELEMENT (XMP|LISTING) - -  %literal>
<!ATTLIST XMP
         %SDAFORM; "Lit"
         %SDAPREF; "Example:
"

         >
<!ATTLIST LISTING
         %SDAFORM; "Lit"
         %SDAPREF; "Listing:
"

         >

<!-- <XMP>                 Example section         -->
<!-- <LISTING>             Computer listing        -->

<!ELEMENT PLAINTEXT - O %literal>
<!-- <PLAINTEXT>           Plain text passage      -->

<!ATTLIST PLAINTEXT
         %SDAFORM; "Lit"
         >
]]>

<!--========= Lists ==================-->

<!ELEMENT DL     - -  (DT | DD)+>
<!ATTLIST DL
         COMPACT (COMPACT) #IMPLIED
         %SDAFORM; "List"
         %SDAPREF; "Definition List:"
         >

<!ELEMENT DT     - O (%text)*>
<!ATTLIST DT
         %SDAFORM; "Term"
         >

<!ELEMENT DD     - O %flow>
<!ATTLIST DD
         %SDAFORM; "LItem"
         >

<!-- <DL>                 Definition list, or glossary  -->
<!-- <DL COMPACT>         Compact style list      -->
<!-- <DT>                 Term in definition list  -->
<!-- <DD>                 Definition of term      -->
```

```
<!ELEMENT (OL|UL) - -  (LI)+>
<!ATTLIST OL
        COMPACT (COMPACT) #IMPLIED
        %SDAFORM; "List"
        >
<!ATTLIST UL
        COMPACT (COMPACT) #IMPLIED
        %SDAFORM; "List"
        >
<!-- <UL>             Unordered list              -->
<!-- <UL COMPACT>     Compact list style          -->
<!-- <OL>             Ordered, or numbered list   -->
<!-- <OL COMPACT>     Compact list style          -->

<!ELEMENT (DIR|MENU) - -  (LI)+ -(%block)>
<!ATTLIST DIR
        COMPACT (COMPACT) #IMPLIED
        %SDAFORM; "List"
        %SDAPREF; "<LHead>Directory</LHead>"
        >
<!ATTLIST MENU
        COMPACT (COMPACT) #IMPLIED
        %SDAFORM; "List"
        %SDAPREF; "<LHead>Menu</LHead>"
        >

<!-- <DIR>            Directory list              -->
<!-- <DIR COMPACT>    Compact list style          -->
<!-- <MENU>           Menu list                   -->
<!-- <MENU COMPACT>   Compact list style          -->

<!ELEMENT LI    - O %flow>
<!ATTLIST LI
        %SDAFORM; "LItem"
        >

<!-- <LI>             List item                   -->

<!--========= Document Body ====================-->

<![ %HTML.Recommended [
        <!ENTITY % body.content "(%heading|%block|HR|ADDRESS|IMG)*"
        -- <h1>Heading</h1>
           <p>Text ...
                is preferred to
           <h1>Heading</h1>
           Text ...
        -->
]]>

<!ENTITY % body.content "(%heading | %text | %block |
                           HR | ADDRESS)*">

<!ELEMENT BODY O O  %body.content>
```

```
<!-- <BODY>      Document body   -->

<!ELEMENT BLOCKQUOTE - - %body.content>
<!ATTLIST BLOCKQUOTE
        %SDAFORM; "BQ"
        >


<!-- <BLOCKQUOTE>      Quoted passage  -->

<!ELEMENT ADDRESS - - (%text|P)*>
<!ATTLIST  ADDRESS
        %SDAFORM; "Lit"
        %SDAPREF; "Address:
"
        >

<!-- <ADDRESS>  Address, signature, or byline   -->

<!--======= Forms ====================-->

<![ %HTML.Forms [

<!ELEMENT FORM - - %body.content -(FORM) +(INPUT|SELECT|TEXTAREA)>
<!ATTLIST FORM
        ACTION CDATA #IMPLIED
        METHOD (%HTTP-Method) GET
        ENCTYPE %Content-Type; "application/x-www-form-urlencoded"
        %SDAPREF; "<Para>Form:</Para>"
        %SDASUFF; "<Para>Form End.</Para>"
        >

<!-- <FORM>                   Fill-out or data-entry form   -->
<!-- <FORM ACTION="...">      Address for completed form    -->
<!-- <FORM METHOD=...>        Method of submitting form     -->
<!-- <FORM ENCTYPE="...">     Representation of form data   -->

<!ENTITY % InputType "(TEXT | PASSWORD | CHECKBOX |
                       RADIO | SUBMIT | RESET |
                       IMAGE | HIDDEN )">
<!ELEMENT INPUT - O EMPTY>
<!ATTLIST INPUT
        TYPE %InputType TEXT
        NAME CDATA #IMPLIED
        VALUE CDATA #IMPLIED
        SRC CDATA #IMPLIED
        CHECKED (CHECKED) #IMPLIED
        SIZE CDATA #IMPLIED
        MAXLENGTH NUMBER #IMPLIED
        ALIGN (top|middle|bottom) #IMPLIED
        %SDAPREF; "Input: "
        >

<!-- <INPUT>                  Form input datum        -->
<!-- <INPUT TYPE=...>         Type of input interaction  -->
```

```
<!-- <INPUT NAME=...>            Name of form datum              -->
<!-- <INPUT VALUE="...">         Default/initial/selected value  -->
<!-- <INPUT SRC="...">           Address of image                -->
<!-- <INPUT CHECKED>             Initial state is "on"           -->
<!-- <INPUT SIZE=...>            Field size hint                 -->
<!-- <INPUT MAXLENGTH=...>       Data length maximum             -->
<!-- <INPUT ALIGN=...>           Image alignment                 -->

<!ELEMENT SELECT - - (OPTION+) -(INPUT|SELECT|TEXTAREA)>
<!ATTLIST SELECT
        NAME CDATA #REQUIRED
        SIZE NUMBER #IMPLIED
        MULTIPLE (MULTIPLE) #IMPLIED
        %SDAFORM; "List"
        %SDAPREF;
        "<LHead>Select #AttVal(Multiple)</LHead>"
        >

<!-- <SELECT>                    Selection of option(s)          -->
<!-- <SELECT NAME=...>           Name of form datum              -->
<!-- <SELECT SIZE=...>           Options displayed at a time     -->
<!-- <SELECT MULTIPLE>           Multiple selections allowed     -->

<!ELEMENT OPTION - O (#PCDATA)*>
<!ATTLIST OPTION
        SELECTED (SELECTED) #IMPLIED
        VALUE CDATA #IMPLIED
        %SDAFORM; "LItem"
        %SDAPREF;
        "Option: #AttVal(Value) #AttVal(Selected)"
        >

<!-- <OPTION>                    A selection option              -->
<!-- <OPTION SELECTED>           Initial state                   -->
<!-- <OPTION VALUE="...">        Form datum value for this option-->

<!ELEMENT TEXTAREA - - (#PCDATA)* -(INPUT|SELECT|TEXTAREA)>
<!ATTLIST TEXTAREA
        NAME CDATA #REQUIRED
        ROWS NUMBER #REQUIRED
        COLS NUMBER #REQUIRED
        %SDAFORM; "Para"
        %SDAPREF; "Input Text -- #AttVal(Name): "
        >

<!-- <TEXTAREA>                  An area for text input          -->
<!-- <TEXTAREA NAME=...>         Name of form datum              -->
<!-- <TEXTAREA ROWS=...>         Height of area                  -->
<!-- <TEXTAREA COLS=...>         Width of area                   -->


]]>


<!--======= Document Head =======================-->
```

```
<![ %HTML.Recommended [
        <!ENTITY % head.extra "">
]]>
<!ENTITY % head.extra "& NEXTID?">

<!ENTITY % head.content "TITLE & ISINDEX? & BASE? %head.extra">

<!ELEMENT HEAD O O  (%head.content) +(META|LINK)>

<!-- <HEAD>      Document head    -->

<!ELEMENT TITLE - -  (#PCDATA)*  -(META|LINK)>
<!ATTLIST TITLE
        %SDAFORM; "Ti"    >

<!-- <TITLE>    Title of document -->

<!ELEMENT LINK - O EMPTY>
<!ATTLIST LINK
        HREF CDATA #REQUIRED
        %linkExtraAttributes;
        %SDAPREF; "Linked to : #AttVal (TITLE) (URN) (HREF)>"    >

<!-- <LINK>              Link from this document            -->
<!-- <LINK HREF="...">   Address of link destination       -->
<!-- <LINK URN="...">    Lasting name of destination       -->
<!-- <LINK REL=...>      Relationship to destination       -->
<!-- <LINK REV=...>      Relationship of destination to this -->
<!-- <LINK TITLE="..."> Title of destination (advisory)    -->
<!-- <LINK METHODS="..."> Operations allowed (advisory)    -->

<!ELEMENT ISINDEX - O EMPTY>
<!ATTLIST ISINDEX
        %SDAPREF;
   "<Para>[Document is indexed/searchable.]</Para>">

<!-- <ISINDEX>              Document is a searchable index  -->

<!ELEMENT BASE - O EMPTY>
<!ATTLIST BASE
        HREF CDATA #REQUIRED    >

<!-- <BASE>              Base context document             -->
<!-- <BASE HREF="..."> Address for this document           -->

<!ELEMENT NEXTID - O EMPTY>
<!ATTLIST NEXTID
        N CDATA #REQUIRED    >

<!-- <NEXTID>           Next ID to use for link name        -->
<!-- <NEXTID N=...>     Next ID to use for link name        -->

<!ELEMENT META - O EMPTY>
<!ATTLIST META
```

```
           HTTP-EQUIV   NAME    #IMPLIED
           NAME         NAME    #IMPLIED
           CONTENT      CDATA   #REQUIRED    >

<!-- <META>                         Generic Meta-information     -->
<!-- <META HTTP-EQUIV=...>          HTTP response header name    -->
<!-- <META NAME=...>                Meta-information name        -->
<!-- <META CONTENT="...">           Associated information       -->


<!--======= Document Structure ==================-->

<![ %HTML.Deprecated [
       <!ENTITY % html.content "HEAD, BODY, PLAINTEXT?">
]]>
<!ENTITY % html.content "HEAD, BODY">

<!ELEMENT HTML O O  (%html.content)>
<!ENTITY % version.attr "VERSION CDATA #FIXED '%HTML.Version;'">

<!ATTLIST HTML
       %version.attr;
       %SDAFORM; "Book"
       >


<!-- <HTML>                         HTML Document    -->
```

C.2 Strict HTML DTD

This document type declaration refers to the HTML DTD with the "HTML.Recommended" entity defined as "INCLUDE" rather than "IGNORE"; that is, it refers to the more structurally rigid definition of HTML.

```
<!--    html-s.dtd

        Document Type Definition for the HyperText Markup Language
        with strict validation (HTML Strict DTD).

        $Id: html-s.dtd,v 1.3 1995/06/02 18:55:46 connolly Exp $

        Author: Daniel W. Connolly <connolly@w3.org>
        See Also: http://www.w3.org/hypertext/WWW/MarkUp/MarkUp.html
-->

<!ENTITY % HTML.Version
        "-//IETF//DTD HTML 2.0 Strict//EN"

        -- Typical usage:

            <!DOCTYPE HTML PUBLIC
                "-//IETF//DTD HTML Strict//EN">
            <html>
            ...
            </html>
```

```
          --
          >

<!-- Feature Test Entities -->
<!ENTITY % HTML.Recommended "INCLUDE">

<!ENTITY % html PUBLIC "-//IETF//DTD HTML 2.0//EN">
%html;
```

C.3 Level 1 HTML DTD

This document type declaration refers to the HTML DTD with the "HTML.Forms" entity defined as "IGNORE" rather than "INCLUDE." Documents that contain <FORM> elements do not conform to this DTD, and must use the level 2 DTD.

```
<!--    html-1.dtd

        Document Type Definition for the HyperText Markup Language
        with Level 1 Extensions (HTML Level 1 DTD).

        $Id: html-1.dtd,v 1.2 1995/03/29 18:53:10 connolly Exp $

        Author: Daniel W. Connolly <connolly@w3.org>
        See Also: http://info.cern.ch/hypertext/WWW/MarkUp/MarkUp.html
-->

<!ENTITY % HTML.Version
        "-//IETF//DTD HTML 2.0 Level 1//EN"

        -- Typical usage:

            <!DOCTYPE HTML PUBLIC
                "-//IETF//DTD HTML Level 1//EN">
            <html>
            ...
            </html>
        --
        >

<!-- Feature Test Entities -->
<!ENTITY % HTML.Forms "IGNORE">

<!ENTITY % html PUBLIC "-//IETF//DTD HTML 2.0//EN">
%html;
```

C.4 Strict Level 1 HTML DTD

This document type declaration refers to the level 1 HTML DTD with the
"HTML.Recommended" entity defined as "INCLUDE" rather than "IGNORE;" that is, it
refers to the more structurally rigid definition of HTML.

```
<!--     html-1s.dtd

         Document Type Definition for the HyperText Markup Language
         Struct Level 1

         $Id: html-1s.dtd,v 1.3 1995/06/02 18:55:43 connolly Exp $

         Author: Daniel W. Connolly <connolly@w3.org>
         See Also: http://www.w3.org/hypertext/WWW/MarkUp/MarkUp.html
-->

<!ENTITY % HTML.Version
         "-//IETF//DTD HTML 2.0 Strict Level 1//EN"

         -- Typical usage:

             <!DOCTYPE HTML PUBLIC
                 "-//IETF//DTD HTML Strict Level 1//EN">
             <html>
             ...
             </html>
         --
         >

<!-- Feature Test Entities -->

<!ENTITY % HTML.Recommended "INCLUDE">

<!ENTITY % html-1 PUBLIC "-//IETF//DTD HTML 2.0 Level 1//EN">
%html-1;
```

D

Character Entities

The following table collects the defined standard, proposed, and several nonstandard, but generally supported, character entities for HTML.

Entity names, if defined, appear for their respective characters and can be used in the HTML character-entity sequence `&name;` to define any character for display by the browser. Otherwise, or alternatively for named characters, use the character's three-digit numeral value in the sequence `&#nnn;` to specially define an HTML character entity. Actual characters, however, may or may not be displayed by the browser depending on the computer platform and user-selected font for display.

Not all 256 characters in the ISO character set appear in the table. Missing ones are not recognized by the browser as either named or numeric entities.

To be sure that your documents are fully compliant with the HTML 2.0 standard, use only those named character entities whose conformance column is blank. Characters whose conformance column contains a "P" (Proposed) are generally supported by the current browsers, although not part of the HTML standard. Defy compliance by using the nonstandard (N) entities.

Numeric Entity	Named Entity	Symbol	Description	Conformance
`&#009;`			Horizontal tab	
`&#010;`			Line feed	
`&#013;`			Carriage return	
`&#032;`			Space	
`&#033;`		!	Exclamation point	
`&#034;`	`&quot;`	"	Quotation mark	
`&#035;`		#	Hash mark	

Numeric Entity	Named Entity	Symbol	Description	Conformance
&#036;		$	Dollar sign	
&#037;		%	Percent sign	
&#038;	&amp;	&	Ampersand	
&#039;		'	Apostrophe	
&#040;		(	Left parenthesis	
&#041;		)	Right parenthesis	
&#042;		*	Asterisk	
&#043;		+	Plus sign	
&#044;		,	Comma	
&#045;		-	Hyphen	
&#046;		.	Period	
&#047;		/	Slash	
0 – 9		0 - 9	Digits 0 – 9	
&#058;		:	Colon	
&#059;		;	Semicolon	
&#060;	&lt;	<	Less than	
&#061;		=	Equals sign	
&#062;	&gt;	>	Greater than	
&#063;		?	Question mark	
&#064;		@	Commercial at sign	
A – Z		A – Z	Letters A – Z	
&#091;		[	Left square bracket	
&#092;		\	Backslash	
&#093;		]	Right square bracket	
&#094;		^	Caret	
&#095;		_	Underscore	
&#096;		`	Grave accent	
a – z		a – z	Letters a – z	
&#123;		{	Left curly brace	
|		|	Vertical bar	
&#125;		}	Right curly brace	
&#126;		~	Tilde	
&#130;		,		N
&#131;		*f*	Florin	N
&#132;		"	Right double quote	N
&#133;		...	Ellipsis	N
&#134;		†	Dagger	N
&#135;		‡	Double dagger	N
&#136;		^	Circumflex	N

Numeric Entity	Named Entity	Symbol	Description	Conformance
&#137;		‰	Permil	N
&#138;		–		N
&#139;		<	Less than sign	N
&#140;		Œ	Capital OE ligature	N
&#145;		'	Left single quote	N
&#146;		'	Right single quote	N
&#147;		"	Left double quote	N
&#148;		"	Right double quote	N
&#149;		•	Bullet	N
&#150;		—	Em dash	N
&#151;		–	En dash	N
&#152;		~	Tilde	N
&#153;		™	Trademark	N
&#154;		–		N
&#155;		>	Greater than sign	N
&#156;		œ	Small oe ligature	N
&#159;		Ÿ	Capital Y, umlaut	N
			Nonbreaking space	P
&#161;	&iexcl;	¡	Inverted exclamation point	P
&#162;	&cent;	¢	Cent sign	P
&#163;	&pound;	£	Pound sign	P
&#164;	&curren;	¤	General currency sign	P
&#165;	&yen;	¥	Yen sign	P
&#166;	&brvbar;	¦	Broken vertical bar	P
&#167;	&sect;	§	Section sign	P
&#168;	&uml;	¨	Umlaut	P
&#169;	&copy;	©	Copyright	P
&#170;	&ordf;	ª	Feminine ordinal	P
&#171;	&laquo;	«	Left angle quote	P
&#172;	&not;	¬	Not sign	P
&#173;	&shy;	–	Soft hyphen	P
&#174;	&reg;	®	Registered trademark	P
&#175;	&macr;	¯	Macron accent	P
&#176;	&deg;	°	Degree sign	P
&#177;	&plusmn;	±	Plus or minus	P
&#178;	&sup2;	²	Superscript 2	P
&#179;	&sup3;	³	Superscript 3	P
&#180;	&acute;	´	Acute accent	P
&#181;	&micro;	µ	Micro sign (Greek mu)	P

Numeric Entity	Named Entity	Symbol	Description	Conformance
&#182;	&para;	¶	Paragraph sign	P
&#183;	&middot;	·	Middle dot	P
&#184;	&cedil;	¸	Cedilla	P
&#185;	&sup1;	¹	Superscript 1	P
&#186;	&ordm;	º	Masculine ordinal	P
&#187;	&raquo;	»	Right angle quote	P
&#188;	&frac14;	¼	Fraction one-fourth	P
&#189;	&frac12;	½	Fraction one-half	P
&#190;	&frac34;	¾	Fraction three-fourths	P
&#191;	&iquest;	¿	Inverted question mark	P
&#192;	&Agrave;	À	Capital A, grave accent	
&#193;	&Aacute;	Á	Capital A, acute accent	
&#194;	&Acirc;	Â	Capital A, circumflex accent	
&#195;	&Atilde;	Ã	Capital A, tilde	
&#196;	&Auml;	Ä	Capital A, umlaut	
&#197;	&Aring;	Å	Capital A, ring	
&#198;	&AElig;	Æ	Capital AE ligature	
&#199;	&Ccedil;	Ç	Capital C, cedilla	
&#200;	&Egrave;	È	Capital E, grave accent	
&#201;	&Eacute;	É	Capital E, acute accent	
&#202;	&Ecirc;	Ê	Capital E, circumflex accent	
&#203;	&Euml;	Ë	Capital E, umlaut	
&#204;	&Igrave;	Ì	Capital I, grave accent	
&#205;	&Iacute;	Í	Capital I, acute accent	
&#206;	&Icirc;	Î	Capital I, circumflex accent	
&#207;	&Iuml;	Ï	Capital I, umlaut	
&#208;	&ETH;	Ð	Capital eth, Icelandic	
&#209;	&Ntilde;	Ñ	Capital N, tilde	
&#210;	&Ograve;	Ò	Capital O, grave accent	
&#211;	&Oacute;	Ó	Capital O, acute accent	
&#212;	&Ocirc;	Ô	Capital O, circumflex accent	
&#213;	&Otilde;	Õ	Capital O, tilde	
&#214;	&Ouml;	Ö	Capital O, umlaut	
&#215;	&times;	×	Multiply sign	P
&#216;	&Oslash;	Ø	Capital O, slash	
&#217;	&Ugrave;	Ù	Capital U, grave accent	
&#218;	&Uacute;	Ú	Capital U, acute accent	
&#219;	&Ucirc;	Û	Capital U, circumflex accent	
&#220;	&Uuml;	Ü	Capital U, umlaut	

Numeric Entity	Named Entity	Symbol	Description	Conformance
&#221;	&Yacute;	Ý	Capital Y, acute accent	
&#222;	&THORN;	Þ	Capital thorn, Icelandic	
&#223;	&szlig;	ß	Small sz ligature, German	
&#224;	&agrave;	à	Small a, grave accent	
&#225;	&aacute;	á	Small a, acute accent	
&#226;	&acirc;	â	Small a, circumflex accent	
&#227;	&atilde;	ã	Small a, tilde	
&#228;	&auml;	ä	Small a, umlaut	
&#229;	&aring;	å	Small a, ring	
&#230;	&aelig;	æ	Small ae ligature	
&#231;	&ccedil;	ç	Small c, cedilla	
&#232;	&egrave;	è	Small e, grave accent	
&#233;	&eacute;	é	Small e, acute accent	
&#234;	&ecirc;	ê	Small e, circumflex accent	
&#235;	&euml;	ë	Small e, umlaut	
&#236;	&igrave;	ì	Small i, grave accent	
&#237;	&iacute;	í	Small i, acute accent	
&#238;	&icirc;	î	Small i, circumflex accent	
&#239;	&iuml;	ï	Small i, umlaut	
&#240;	&eth;	ð	Small eth, Icelandic	
&#241;	&ntilde;	ñ	Small n, tilde	
&#242;	&ograve;	ò	Small o, grave accent	
&#243;	&oacute;	ó	Small o, acute accent	
&#244;	&ocirc;	ô	Small o, circumflex accent	
&#245;	&otilde;	õ	Small o, tilde	
&#246;	&ouml;	ö	Small o, umlaut	
&#247;	&divide;	÷	Division sign	P
&#248;	&oslash;	ø	Small o, slash	
&#249;	&ugrave;	ù	Small u, grave accent	
&#250;	&uacute;	ú	Small u, acute accent	
&#251;	&ucirc;	û	Small u, circumflex accent	
&#252;	&uuml;	ü	Small u, umlaut	
&#253;	&yacute;	ý	Small y, acute accent	
&#254;	&thorn;	þ	Small thorn, Icelandic	
&#255;	&yuml;	ÿ	Small y, umlaut	

Color Names and Values

Within Netscape Navigator 2.0 and Internet Explorer, you can change the color of various elements of your document, including these elements (partial list; see main text for all occasions):

Element	Associated Tag and Attribute
Document background	`<body bgcolor=`*color*`>`
All document text	`<body text=`*color*`>`
Active hyperlinks	`<body alink=`*color*`>`
Visited hyperlinks	`<body vlink=`*color*`>`
Regular hyperlinks	`<body link=`*color*`>`
Small portion of text	`<font color=`*color*`>`

Table cells (Internet Explorer only)	`<table bgcolor=`*color*`>`
	`<tr bgcolor=`*color*`>`
	`<td bgcolor=`*color*`>`
	`<th bgcolor=`*color*`>`

E.1 Color Values

In all cases, you may specify the color value as a six-digit hexadecimal number that represents the red, green, and blue (RGB) components of the color. The first two digits correspond to the red component of the color, the next two the green component, and the last two are the blue component. A value of 00 corresponds to the component being completely off; a value of FF (255) corresponds to the component being completely on. Thus, bright red is FF0000, bright green is

00FF00, and bright blue is 0000FF. Other primary colors are mixtures of two components, such as yellow (FFFF00), magenta (FF00FF), and cyan (00FFFF). White (FFFFFF) and black (000000) are also easy to figure out.

You use these values in a tag by replacing the color with the RGB triple, preceded by a hash (#) symbol. Thus, to make all visited links display as magenta, use this body tag:

```
<body vlink="#FF00FF">
```

E.2 Color Names

Unfortunately, determining the hexadecimal value for more esoteric colors like "papaya whip" or "navajo white" is very difficult. You can go crazy trying to adjust the RGB triple for a color to get the shade just right, especially when each adjustment requires loading a document into your browser to view the result.

The folks at Microsoft and Netscape thought so, too, and gave their browsers the ability to use color names directly in any of the color tags. Simply use the color name for the color-attribute value enclosed in quotes. Single-word color names don't require enclosing quotes, but it's good practice to include them anyway. For example, you can make all visited links in the display magenta with the following attribute and value for the body tag:

```
<body vlink="magenta">
```

The standard color names currently supported by Internet Explorer are:

aqua	gray	navy	silver
black	green	olive	teal
blue	lime	purple	yellow
fuchsia	maroon	red	white

Not to be outdone, Netscape 2.0 and higher supports named colors as well; they just don't document the fact. Even better, Netscape supports the several hundred color names defined for use in the X Window System. Note that color names may contain no spaces; also, the word "gray" may also be spelled "grey" in any color name.

Those colors marked with an asterisk (*) actually represent a family of colors numbered one through four. Thus, there are actually four variants of blue, named "blue1," "blue2," "blue3," and "blue4," along with plain old "blue." Blue1 is the lightest of the four; blue4 the darkest. The unnumbered color name is the same color as the first; thus, blue and blue1 are identical.

Finally, if all that isn't enough, there are one hundred variants of gray (and grey) numbered 1 through 100. "Gray1" is the darkest, "gray100" is the lightest, and "gray" is very close to "gray75."

The Netscape-supported colors are:

aliceblue	darkturquoise	lightseagreen	palevioletred*
antiquewhite*	darkviolet	lightskyblue*	papayawhip
aquamarine*	deeppink*	lightslateblue	peachpuff*
azure*	deepskyblue*	lightslategray	peru
beige	dimgray	lightsteelblue*	pink*
bisque*	dodgerblue*	lightyellow*	plum*
black	firebrick*	limegreen	powderblue
blanchedalmond	floralwhite	linen	purple*
blue*	forestgreen	magenta*	red*
blueviolet	gainsboro	maroon*	rosybrown*
brown*	ghostwhite	mediumaquamarine	royalblue*
burlywood*	gold*	mediumblue	saddlebrown
cadetblue*	goldenrod*	mediummorchid*	salmon*
chartreuse*	gray	mediumpurple*	sandybrown
chocolate*	green*	mediumseagreen	seagreen*
coral*	greenyellow	mediumslateblue	seashell*
cornflowerblue	honeydew*	mediumspringgreen	sienna*
cornsilk*	hotpink*	mediumturquoise	skyblue*
cyan*	indianred*	mediumvioletred	slateblue*
darkblue	ivory*	midnightblue	slategray*
darkcyan	khaki*	mintcream	snow*
darkgoldenrod*	lavender	mistyrose*	springgreen*
darkgray	lavenderblush*	moccasin	steelblue*
darkgreen	lawngreen	navajowhite*	tan*
darkkhaki	lemonchiffon*	navy	thistle*
darkmagenta	lightblue*	navyblue	tomato*
darkolivegreen*	lightcoral	oldlace	turquoise*
darkorange*	lightcyan*	olivedrab*	violet
darkorchid*	lightgoldenrod*	orange*	violetred*
darkred	lightgoldenrodyellow	orangered*	wheat*
darksalmon	lightgray	orchid*	white
darkseagreen*	lightgreen	palegoldenrod	whitesmoke
darkslateblue	lightpink*	palegreen*	yellow*
darkslategray*	lightsalmon*	paleturquoise*	yellowgreen

Index

About the Authors

Chuck Musciano (*CMusciano@aol.com*) grew up on the East Coast, having spent time in Maryland, Georgia, and New Jersey before acquiring a B.S. in computer science from Georgia Tech in 1982. Since then, he has resided in Melbourne, Florida, in the employ of Harris Corporation. He began his career as a compiler writer and crafter of tools and went on to join Harris's Advanced Technology Group to help develop large-scale multiprocessors. This led to a prolonged interest in user-interface research and development, which finally gave way to his current position, Manager of UNIX Systems in Harris's Corporate Data Center. Along the way, he grew to know and love the Internet, having contributed a number of publicly available tools to the Net and started the still-running *Internet Movie Ratings Report*. The Web was a natural next step, and he has been running various Web sites within and without Harris for several years. Chuck has written on UNIX-related topics in the trade press for the past decade, most visibly as the "Webmaster" columnist for *Sunworld Online* (*http://www. sun.com/sunworldonline*). In his spare time he enjoys life in Florida with his wife Cindy, daughter Courtney, and son Cole.

Bill Kennedy (*bkennedy@activmedia.com*) is currently president and chief technology officer for *Activ*Media, Inc., a high-tech marketing and market-research firm based in cyberspace (*http://www.activmedia.com*). Among other ventures, he is actively involved in the development and sales of mobile robotics platforms used primarily in artificial intelligence and fuzzy logic research, and for training. In past lives, Bill acquired a Ph.D. and performed basic research for 12 years in the fields of biochemistry and biophysics; developed educational software with Kinemation; was editor-in-chief of *A+ Publishing*; and was a technical, then senior editor for *SunWorld/Advanced Systems* magazine.

Colophon

Our look is the result of reader comments, our own experimentation, and distribution channels. Distinctive covers complement our distinctive approach to technical topics, breathing personality and life into potentially dry subjects. UNIX and its attendant programs can be unruly beasts. Nutshell Handbooks help you tame them.

The animal featured on the cover of *HTML: The Definitive Guide* is a koala. The koala is an Australian marsupial, the only member of the Phascolarctidae family. This cuddly looking animal was the original model for teddy bears, although it actually is not related to bears.

Koalas use their extremely sharp claws for climbing eucalyptus trees. They subsist almost exclusively on eucalyptus leaves and bark. They are picky eaters, eating only about 20 of the approximately 350 species of eucalyptus in Australia. Since eucalyptus leaves contain the precursors to hydrocyanic acid, or cyanide, koalas also occasionally eat soil, which helps detoxify their food. Koalas in the wild rarely, if ever, drink water. Eucalyptus leaves contain approximately 67% water, and that is enough for the koala diet.

Koalas are tiny, approximately one half of a gram, when they are born. Twin births are very unusual, but a mother koala will adopt an abandoned baby if she finds one. The young koala stays in its mother's pouch for approximately seven months. Unlike most marsupials, the koala's pouch opens towards the rear, not towards the head. At the end of the seven month period, the mother begins to wean the baby off of a purely milk diet by introducing it to predigested eucalyptus leaves. After leaving the pouch, the young koala is carried on its mother's back until it is a year old. Koalas leave their mother's home range at 18 months. While trying to establish their own home range, koalas have a very high mortality rate.

Koalas were once plentiful in Australia, but as a result of epidemics in 1887–1889 and 1900–1903 and unrestrained hunting throughout the 20th century, koalas came close to extinction. They are a protected species and are rebuilding their population, but at present they survive only in eastern Australia.

Edie Freedman designed the cover of this book, using a 19th-century engraving from the Dover Pictorial Archive. The cover layout was produced with Quark XPress 3.3 using the ITC Garamond font.

The inside layout was designed Jennifer Niederst and Nancy Priest. Text was prepared in SGML using the DocBook 2.1 DTD. The print version of this book was created by translating the SGML source into a set of gtroff macros using a filter developed at ORA by Norman Walsh. Steve Talbott designed and wrote the underlying macro set on the basis of the GNU troff -gs macros; Lenny Muellner adapted them to SGML and implemented the book design. The GNU groff text formatter version 1.09 was used to generate PostScript output. The text and heading fonts are ITC Garamond Light and Garamond Book. The illustrations that appear in the book were created in Macromedia Freehand 5.0 by Chris Reilley. This colophon was written by Clairemarie Fisher O'Leary.

More Titles from O'REILLY™

Developing Web Content

Building Your Own WebSite

By Susan B. Peck & Stephen Arrants
1st Edition July 1996
514 pages, ISBN 1-56592-232-8

A hands-on reference for Windows® 95 and Windows NT™ desktop users who want to host their own site on the Web or on a corporate intranet. This step-by-step guide will have you creating live Web pages in minutes. You'll also learn how to connect your web to information in other Windows applications, such as word processing documents and databases. Packed with examples and tutorials on every aspect of Web management. Includes highly acclaimed WebSite™ 1.1—all the software you need for Web publishing.

Web Client Programming with Perl

By Clinton Wong
1st Edition Fall 1996
250 pages (est.), ISBN 1-56592-214-X

Web Client Programming with Perl teaches you how to extend scripting skills to the Web. This book teaches you the basics of how browsers communicate with servers and how to write your own customized Web clients to automate common tasks. It is intended for those who are motivated to develop software that offers a more flexible and dynamic response than a standard Web browser.

JavaScript: The Definitive Guide, Beta version

By David Flanagan
1st Edition August 1996
472 pages, ISBN 1-56592-193-3

Includes coverage of the frustrating bugs encountered in the beta version of JavaScript, the HTML extension that gives Web pages programming-language capabilities. With JavaScript you can control Web browser behavior, add dynamically created text to Web pages, interact with users through HTML forms, and even control and interact with Java applets and Navigator plugins. Available online (http://www.ora.com) and at your bookstore.

HTML: The Definitive Guide

By Chuck Musciano & Bill Kennedy
1st Edition April 1996
410 pages, ISBN 1-56592-175-5

A complete guide to creating documents on the World Wide Web. This book describes basic syntax and semantics and goes on to show you how to create beautiful, informative Web documents you'll be proud to display. The HTML 2.0 standard and Netscape extensions are fully explained.

Designing for the Web: Getting Started in a New Medium

By Jennifer Niederst with Edie Freedman
1st Edition April 1996
180 pages, ISBN 1-56592-165-8

Designing for the Web gives you the basics you need to hit the ground running. Although geared toward designers, it covers information and techniques useful to anyone who wants to put graphics online. It explains how to work with HTML documents from a designer's point of view, outlines special problems with presenting information online, and walks through incorporating images into Web pages, with emphasis on resolution and improving efficiency.

WebMaster in a Nutshell

By Stephen Spainhour & Valerie Quercia
1st Edition Fall 1996
150 pages (est.), ISBN 1-56592-229-8

Web content providers and administrators have many sources of information, both in print and online. *WebMaster in a Nutshell* pulls it all together into one slim volume— for easy desktop access. This quick-reference covers HTML, CGI, Perl, HTTP, server configuration, and tools for Web administration.

For information: **800-998-9938**, 707-829-0515; **info@ora.com; http://www.ora.com/**
To order: **800-889-8969** (credit card orders only); **order@ora.com**

World Wide Web Journal

World Wide Web Journal: Volume 1, Issue 1

A publication of O'Reilly & Associates and
the World Wide Web Consortium (W3C)
Winter 1995/1996
748 pages, ISBN 1-56592-169-0

The *World Wide Web Journal* provides timely, in-depth coverage of the W3C's technological developments, such as protocols for security, replication, and caching, HTML and SGML, and content labeling. It also explores the broader issues of the Web with Web luminaries and articles on controversial legal issues such as censorship and intellectual property rights. Whether you follow Web developments for strategic planning, application programming, or Web page authoring and designing, you'll find the in-depth information you need here.

The *World Wide Web Journal* is published quarterly. This issue contains 57 refereed technical papers presented at the Fourth International World Wide Web Conference, held December 1995 in Boston, Massachusetts. It also includes the two best papers from regional conferences.

World Wide Web Journal: Volume 1, Issue 2

A publication of O'Reilly & Associates and
the World Wide Web Consortium (W3C)
Spring 1996
356 pages, ISBN 1-56592-190-9

The key specifications that describe the architecture of the World Wide Web and how it works are maintained online at the World Wide Web Consortium. This issue of the *World Wide Web Journal* collects these key papers in a single volume as an important reference for the Webmaster, application programmer, or technical manager.

In this valuable reference, you'll find the definitive specifications for the core technologies in the Web: Hypertext Markup Language (HTML), Hypertext Transfer Protocol (HTTP), and Uniform Resource Locators (URLs); plus the emerging standards for portable graphics (PNG), content selection (PICS), and style sheets (CSS).

World Wide Web Journal: Volume 1, Issue 3

A publication of O'Reilly & Associates and
the World Wide Web Consortium (W3C)
Summer 1996
226 pages, ISBN 1-56592-210-7

As the World Wide Web continues exploding across the technology scene, it may seem impossible to keep track of myriad new protocols, standards, and applications. The World Wide Web Consortium is chartered to help members understand the forces behind these developments and to lead the way to further innovation— and the *World Wide Web Journal* is your direct connection to its work. Every quarter, the W3J provides timely, in-depth coverage of W3C's activities as well as independently refereed papers from around the world.

Issue 3 is a reflection on the web after five years: how millions of users later, today's Web is still trying to capture the small-scale, collaborative vision of its earliest incarnations while also posing unprecedented challenges as a commercial, mass medium. In an interview with Tim Berners-Lee, the inventor of the Web and Director of the W3C, we learn that the Web was built to be an interactive, intercreative, two-way medium from the beginning. At the opposite scale, as a mass medium, are urgent questions about the Web's size, character, and users. These issues are addressed in selections from the MIT/W3C Workshop on Web Demographics and Internet Survey Methodology, along with commerce-related papers selected from the Fifth International World Wide Web Conference, which took place from May 6-10 in Paris.

Other contributions include technical proposals from the W3C, lively debates on the size of the Web, the impact of advertising on caching, and ethical guidelines for using such data.

This issue also marks a reinauguration of the W3 Journal itself, with a new editor and an expanded structure. The first part contains a log of the wide-ranging activities of the Consortium, profiles of the researchers and developers behind the scenes, and interviews with experts in the field. The second section, "W3C Reports," includes the latest technical reports, standards, and papers from the W3 Consortium, including its Workshops and Working Groups. The third section, "Technical Papers," is an independent academic forum for the latest in Web-related research.

Perl

Programming Perl

By Larry Wall, Randal L. Schwartz & Tom Christiansen
2nd Edition Fall 1996
700 pages (est.), ISBN 1-56592-149-6

This heavily revised second edition of *Programming Perl* contains a full explanation of Perl version 5.002 features. It's the authoritative guide to Perl—the scripting utility now established as the World Wide Web programming tool of choice. The book is coauthored by Larry Wall, the creator of Perl.

"The Perl book is splendid. It is clearly written and very craftily draws the reader into wanting to learn more."—John Ward, Professor, Oxford College

Learning Perl

By Randal L. Schwartz, Foreword by Larry Wall
1st Edition November 1993
274 pages, ISBN 1-56592-042-2

Learning Perl is ideal for system administrators, programmers, and anyone else wanting a down-to-earth introduction to this useful language. Written by a Perl trainer, its aim is to make a competent, hands-on Perl programmer out of the reader as quickly as possible. The book takes a tutorial approach and includes hundreds of short code examples, along with some lengthy ones. The relatively inexperienced programmer will find *Learning Perl* easily accessible.

Each chapter of the book includes practical programming exercises. Solutions are presented for all exercises.

For a comprehensive and detailed guide to advanced programming with Perl, read O'Reilly's companion book, *Programming Perl.*

"Intended as 'a gentle introduction to Perl'—the Practical Extraction and Report Language of the Unix world, a powerful set of tools to manipulate text. If you're going to spend much time on a Unix operating system, chances are you will want to learn how to use Perl."—Book Review, *ISOC News*

CGI Programming on the World Wide Web

By Shishir Gundavaram
1st Edition March 1996
450 pages, ISBN 1-56592-168-2

The World Wide Web is more than a place to put up clever documents and pretty pictures. With a little study and practice, you can offer interactive queries and serve instant information from databases, worked up into colorful graphics. That is what the Common Gateway Interface (CGI) offers.

This book offers a comprehensive explanation of CGI and related techniques for people who hold on to the dream of providing their own information servers on the Web. Gundavaram starts at the beginning, explaining the value of CGI and how it works, then moves swiftly into the subtle details of programming. For most of the examples, the book uses the most common platform (UNIX) and the most popular language (Perl) used for CGI programming today. However, it also introduces the essentials of making CGI work with other platforms and languages.

Perl 5 Desktop Reference

By Johan Vromans
1st Edition February 1996
39 pages, ISBN 1-56592-187-9

This booklet gives you quick, well-organized access to the vast array of features in Perl, version 5. Perl is a language for easily manipulating text, files, and processes.

Having first established itself as the UNIX programming tool of choice, Perl is now becoming the World Wide Web programming tool of choice. This guide provides a complete overview of the language, from variables to input and output, from flow control to regular expressions, from functions to document formats—all packed into a convenient, carry-around booklet.

Perl 5 Desktop Reference is the perfect companion to *Learning Perl,* a carefully paced tutorial course by Randal L. Schwartz, and *Programming Perl,* the complete, authoritative reference work coauthored by Perl developer Larry Wall, Tom Christiansen, and Randal L. Schwartz.

Stay in touch with O'REILLY™

Visit Our Award-Winning World Wide Web Site

http://www.ora.com/

VOTED

> "Top 100 Sites on the Web" —*PC Magazine*
> "Top 5% Websites" —*Point Communications*
> "3-Star site" —*The McKinley Group*

Our Web site contains a library of comprehensive product information (including book excerpts and tables of contents), downloadable software, background articles, interviews with technology leaders, links to relevant sites, book cover art, and more. File us in your Bookmarks or Hotlist!

Join Our Two Email Mailing Lists

LIST #1 NEW PRODUCT RELEASES: To receive automatic email with brief descriptions of all new O'Reilly products as they are released, send email to: listproc@online.ora.com and put the following information in the first line of your message (NOT in the Subject: field, which is ignored): **subscribe ora-news "Your Name" of "Your Organization"** (for example: **subscribe ora-news Kris Webber of Fine Enterprises)**

List #2 O'REILLY EVENTS: If you'd also like us to send information about trade show events, special promotions, and other O'Reilly events, send email to: **listproc@online.ora.com** and put the following information in the first line of your message (NOT in the Subject: field, which is ignored): **subscribe ora-events "Your Name" of "Your Organization"**

Visit Our Gopher Site

- Connect your Gopher to **gopher.ora.com**, or
- Point your Web browser to **gopher://gopher.ora.com/**, or
- telnet to **gopher.ora.com** (login: **gopher**)

Get Example Files from Our Books Via FTP

There are two ways to access an archive of example files from our books:

REGULAR FTP — ftp to: **ftp.ora.com** (login: **anonymous**—use your email address as the password) or point your Web browser to: **ftp://ftp.ora.com/**

FTPMAIL — Send an email message to: **ftpmail@online.ora.com** (write "help" in the message body)

Contact Us Via Email

order@ora.com — To place a book or software order online. Good for North American and international customers.

subscriptions@ora.com — To place an order for any of our newsletters or periodicals.

software@ora.com — For general questions and product information about our software.
  • Check out O'Reilly Software Online at **http://software.ora.com/** for software and technical support information.
  • Registered O'Reilly software users send your questions to **website-support@ora.com**

books@ora.com — General questions about any of our books.

cs@ora.com — For answers to problems regarding your order or our products.

booktech@ora.com — For book content technical questions or corrections.

proposals@ora.com — To submit new book or software proposals to our editors and product managers.

international@ora.com — For information about our international distributors or translation queries.
  • For a list of our distributors outside of North America check out:
  http://www.ora.com/www/order/country.html

O'REILLY™

101 Morris Street, Sebastopol, CA 95472 USA
TEL 707-829-0515 or 800-998-9938 (6 A.M. to 5 P.M. PST)
FAX 707-829-0104

TO ORDER: **800-889-8969** (CREDIT CARD ORDERS ONLY); **order@ora.com; http://www.ora.com/**
OUR PRODUCTS ARE AVAILABLE AT A BOOKSTORE OR SOFTWARE STORE NEAR YOU.

Listing of Titles from O'REILLY™

INTERNET PROGRAMMING

CGI Programming on the
World Wide Web
Designing for the Web
Exploring Java
HTML: The Definitive Guide
Web Client Programming with Perl
Learning Perl
Programming Perl, 2nd.Edition
(Fall '96)
JavaScript: The Definitive Guide, Beta
Edition (Summer '96)
Webmaster in a Nutshell
The World Wide Web Journal

USING THE INTERNET

Smileys
The Whole Internet User's Guide
and Catalog
The Whole Internet for Windows 95
What You Need to Know:
Using Email Effectively
Marketing on the Internet (Fall 96)
What You Need to Know: Bandits on the
Information Superhighway

JAVA SERIES

Exploring Java
Java in a Nutshell
Java Language Reference
(Fall '96 est.)
Java Virtual Machine

WINDOWS

Inside the Windows '95 Registry

SOFTWARE

WebSite™ 1.1
WebSite Professional™
WebBoard™
PolyForm™

SONGLINE GUIDES

NetLearning
NetSuccess for Realtors
NetActivism (Fall '96)

SYSTEM ADMINISTRATION

Building Internet Firewalls
Computer Crime:
A Crimefighter's Handbook
Computer Security Basics
DNS and BIND
Essential System Administration,
2nd ed.
Getting Connected:
The Internet at 56K and Up
Linux Network Administrator's Guide
Managing Internet Information Services
Managing Usenet (Fall '96)
Managing NFS and NIS
Networking Personal Computers
with TCP/IP
Practical UNIX & Internet Security
PGP: Pretty Good Privacy
sendmail
System Performance Tuning
TCP/IP Network Administration
termcap & terminfo
Using & Managing UUCP (Fall '96)
Volume 8: X Window System
Administrator's Guide

UNIX

Exploring Expect
Learning GNU Emacs, 2nd Edition
(Fall '96 est.)
Learning the bash Shell
Learning the Korn Shell
Learning the UNIX Operating System
Learning the vi Editor
Linux in a Nutshell (Fall '96 est.)
Making TeX Work
Linux Multimedia Guide (Fall '96)
Running Linux, 2nd Edition
Running Linux Companion
CD-ROM, 2nd Edition
SCO UNIX in a Nutshell
sed & awk
Unix in a Nutshell: System V Edition
UNIX Power Tools
UNIX Systems Programming
Using csh and tsch
What You Need to Know:
When You Can't Find Your
UNIX System Administrator

PROGRAMMING

Applying RCS and SCCS
C++: The Core Language
Checking C Programs with lint
DCE Security Programming
Distributing Applications Across
DCE and Windows NT
Encyclopedia of Graphics File
Formats, 2nd ed.
Guide to Writing DCE Applications
lex & yacc
Managing Projects with make
ORACLE Performance Tuning
ORACLE PL/SQL Programming
Porting UNIX Software
POSIX Programmer's Guide
POSIX.4: Programming for
the Real World
Power Programming with RPC
Practical C Programming
Practical C++ Programming
Programming Python (Fall '96)
Programming with curses
Programming with GNU Software
(Fall '96 est.)
Pthreads Programming
(Fall '96)
Software Portability with imake
Understanding DCE
Understanding Japanese Information
Processing
UNIX Systems Programming for SVR4

BERKELEY 4.4 SOFTWARE DISTRIBUTION

4.4BSD System Manager's Manual
4.4BSD User's Reference Manual
4.4BSD User's Supplementary Docs.
4.4BSD Programmer's Reference Man.
4.4BSD Programmer's Supp. Docs.

X PROGRAMMING
THE X WINDOW SYSTEM

Volume 0: X Protocol Reference Manual
Volume 1: Xlib Programming Manual
Volume 2: Xlib Reference Manual
Volume. 3M: X Window System
User's Guide, Motif Ed.
Volume. 4: X Toolkit Intrinsics
Programming Manual
Volume 4M: X Toolkit Intrinsics
Programming Manual, Motif Ed.
Volume 5: X Toolkit Intrinsics
Reference Manual
Volume 6A: Motif Programming Man.
Volume 6B: Motif Reference Manual
Volume 6C: Motif Tools
Volume 8 : X Window System
Administrator's Guide
Programmer's Supplement for Release 6
X User Tools (with CD-ROM)
The X Window System in a Nutshell

HEALTH, CAREER, & BUSINESS

Building a Successful Software Business
The Computer User's Survival Guide
Dictionary of Computer Terms
The Future Does Not Compute
Love Your Job!
Publishing with CD-ROM

TRAVEL

Travelers' Tales: Brazil (Summer '96 est.)
Travelers' Tales: Food (Summer '96)
Travelers' Tales: France
Travelers' Tales: Hong Kong
Travelers' Tales: India
Travelers' Tales: Mexico
Travelers' Tales: San Francisco
Travelers' Tales: Spain
Travelers' Tales: Thailand
Travelers' Tales: A Woman's World

International Distributors

Customers outside North America can now order O'Reilly & Associates books through the following distributors. They offer our international customers faster order processing, more bookstores, increased representation at tradeshows worldwide, and the high-quality, responsive service our customers have come to expect.

EUROPE, MIDDLE EAST AND NORTHERN AFRICA (except Germany, Switzerland, and Austria)

INQUIRIES
International Thomson Publishing Europe
Berkshire House
168-173 High Holborn
London WC1V 7AA, United Kingdom
Telephone: 44-171-497-1422
Fax: 44-171-497-1426
Email: **itpint@itps.co.uk**

ORDERS
International Thomson Publishing Services, Ltd.
Cheriton House, North Way
Andover, Hampshire SP10 5BE,
United Kingdom
Telephone: 44-264-342-832 (UK orders)
Telephone: 44-264-342-806 (outside UK)
Fax: 44-264-364418 (UK orders)
Fax: 44-264-342761 (outside UK)
UK & Eire orders: **itpuk@itps.co.uk**
International orders: **itpint@itps.co.uk**

GERMANY, SWITZERLAND, AND AUSTRIA

International Thomson Publishing GmbH
O'Reilly International Thomson Verlag
Königswinterer Straße 418
53227 Bonn, Germany
Telephone: 49-228-97024 0
Fax: 49-228-441342
Email: **anfragen@arade.ora.de**

AUSTRALIA

WoodsLane Pty. Ltd.
7/5 Vuko Place, Warriewood NSW 2102
P.O. Box 935, Mona Vale NSW 2103
Australia
Telephone: 61-2-9970-5111
Fax: 61-2-9970-5002
Email: **info@woodslane.com.au**

NEW ZEALAND

WoodsLane New Zealand Ltd.
21 Cooks Street (P.O. Box 575)
Wanganui, New Zealand
Telephone: 64-6-347-6543
Fax: 64-6-345-4840
Email: **info@woodslane.com.au**

ASIA (except Japan & India)

INQUIRIES
International Thomson Publishing Asia
60 Albert Street #15-01
Albert Complex
Singapore 189969
Telephone: 65-336-6411
Fax: 65-336-7411

ORDERS
Telephone: 65-336-6411
Fax: 65-334-1617

JAPAN

O'Reilly Japan, Inc.
Kiyoshige Building 2F
12-Banchi, Sanei-cho
Shinjuku-ku
Tokyo 160 Japan
Telephone: 81-3-3356-5227
Fax: 81-3-3356-5261
Email: **kenji@ora.com**

INDIA

Computer Bookshop (India) PVT. LTD.
190 Dr. D.N. Road, Fort
Bombay 400 001
India
Telephone: 91-22-207-0989
Fax: 91-22-262-3551
Email: **cbsbom@giasbm01.vsnl.net.in**

THE AMERICAS

O'Reilly & Associates, Inc.
101 Morris Street
Sebastopol, CA 95472 U.S.A.
Telephone: 707-829-0515
Telephone: 800-998-9938 (U.S. & Canada)
Fax: 707-829-0104
Email: **order@ora.com**

SOUTHERN AFRICA

International Thomson Publishing Southern Africa
Building 18, Constantia Park
240 Old Pretoria Road
P.O. Box 2459
Halfway House, 1685 South Africa
Telephone: 27-11-805-4819
Fax: 27-11-805-3648

O'REILLY™

O'Reilly & Associates, Inc.
101 Morris Street
Sebastopol, CA 95472-9902
1-800-998-9938

Visit us online at:
http://www.ora.com/
orders@ora.com

O'REILLY WOULD LIKE TO HEAR FROM YOU

Which book did this card come from?

_____

Where did you buy this book?
- ❑ Bookstore
- ❑ Computer Store
- ❑ Direct from O'Reilly
- ❑ Class/seminar
- ❑ Bundled with hardware/software
- ❑ Other _____

What operating system do you use?
- ❑ UNIX
- ❑ Macintosh
- ❑ Windows NT
- ❑ PC(Windows/DOS)
- ❑ Other _____

What is your job description?
- ❑ System Administrator
- ❑ Programmer
- ❑ Network Administrator
- ❑ Educator/Teacher
- ❑ Web Developer
- ❑ Other _____

❑ Please send me O'Reilly's catalog, containing a complete listing of O'Reilly books and software.

Name _____ Company/Organization _____

Address _____

City _____ State _____ Zip/Postal Code _____ Country _____

Telephone _____ Internet or other email address (specify network) _____

Nineteenth century wood engraving
of a bear from the O'Reilly &
Associates Nutshell Handbook®
Using & Managing UUCP.

POST CARD

BUSINESS REPLY MAIL

FIRST CLASS MAIL   PERMIT NO. 80   SEBASTOPOL, CA

Postage will be paid by addressee

O'Reilly & Associates, Inc.
101 Morris Street
Sebastopol, CA 95472-9902